Advances in the House-Tree-Person Technique: Variations and Applications

Advances in the House-Tree-Person Technique: Variations and Applications

Edited by

John N. Buck
Chief Psychologist (Retired)
Lynchburg State Colony, Va.

and

Emanuel F. Hammer, Ph.D.
Faculty, Clinical Doctoral Program
New York University Graduate School
of Arts and Sciences

Published by

WESTERN PSYCHOLOGICAL SERVICES
PUBLISHERS AND DISTRIBUTORS
12031 WILSHIRE BOULEVARD
LOS ANGELES, CALIFORNIA 90025

A DIVISION OF MANSON WESTERN CORPORATION

Advances in the House-Tree-Person Technique:
Variations and Applications

Library of Congress Catalog Card Number: 66-29864

Standard Book Number: 87424-302-5

To FAN, BARB, and GURT

and

To ISADORE and BELLE

Contents

Foreword

Chronological Milestones in the Development of the H-T-P

John N. Buck

The author presents a "highlighted" synopsis of the birth and development of the H-T-P which has both historical value (in its providing the student and the practitioner with a rich background tapestry) and considerable human interest.

It is particularly interesting to note how the techniques beginning (as has been the case in many "discoveries") was the result of a happy combination of the serendipity factor and a creative mind which sensed and grasped the potentials imbedded in the chance clinical moment. EFH.

1937: At the Lynchburg State Colony, Colony, Virginia, in the fall of that year, the writer was attempting to persuade a nine year old girl to answer questions—any questions. She steadfastly refused. Finally, in sheer desperation, the writer asked her if she would be willing to draw something. She nodded assent. She was given paper and pencil, and she immediately produced a series of drawings in which sexual symbols predominated. While the child was drawing, the writer resumed his attempts at interrogation; to his astonishment, the child responded with a fluency that contrasted strikingly with her previous stony silence.

For the next few months, the writer attempted to capitalize on this "pencil-release" factor whenever he encountered a seriously withdrawn subject. It was soon obvious, however, that the S's drawings themselves would provide even more useful dynamic information than the S's replies to direct questioning while he was drawing.

1938: Early in that year, the writer had each S – regardless of his or her ability or willingness to verbalize – draw a House, a Tree, and a Person. These items were selected because it had been found that (1) they were the items most commonly drawn by Ss spontaneously; (2) they were ordinarily accepted without protest by Ss of most ages; and (3) they appeared to stimulate verbalization (spontaneous or induced) more than other items.

The previous wholly unstructured approach to item choice was abandoned because it had been discovered that it was highly profitable to compare a given S's drawings (1) with drawings of the same items which he had produced at other stages of his maladjustment or life span, and (2) with the drawings of the same items produced by other Ss.

At that time, emphasis was placed largely on the quantitative aspects of the drawings, and a simple system of quantitative scoring was devised.

1939: By the summer of the year, it was apparent that qualitative analysis and interpretation of the drawings of House, Tree, and Person could provide a wealth of information concerning the S's total personality. A ten category system of qualitative analysis was constructed.

1941: Issue No. 12, of Vol. 2 of the *Virginia Mental Hygiene Survey* contained the first published description of the JNB Drawing Test – as the H-T-P was then known.

The H-T-P at this time was serving as test No. 10 in a ten test scale of intelligence (five items verbal, five non-verbal) that the writer was attempting to standardize. Later, when the Wechsler Intelligence Scale was introduced, the writer abandoned his fledgling intelligence scale and began to concentrate on refining the H-T-P as a projective technique.

1943: A quantitative study of sets of drawings of House, Tree, and Person produced by 140 carefully selected, reasonably well adjusted white adults of seven predetermined intelligence levels was begun.

1944: Standardization of the quantitative scoring system for adults (with *adult* arbitrarily defined as "fifteen years of age or older") was completed.

The first formal attempt to make the H-T-P a verbal, as well as a graphic, procedure was begun; following up the suggestion made to the writer by Dr. Elizabeth Fehrer, then of Bryn Mawr College.

At the University of Virginia Hospital, Charlottesville, Virginia (with the gracious cooperation of Dr. David Wilson, Chief of the Psychiatric Staff and Mrs. Dorota Rymarkiewiczowa, Chief Psychologist) the writer began a qualitative study of sets of drawings of House, Tree, and Person produced by 150 white adults who were grossly categorized as either maladjusted, psychopathic, psychoneurotic, psychotic, or epileptic.

1945: The qualitative study was completed and a system of analysis and interpretation was devised.

At the University of Virginia Hospital, Mr. John T. Payne began to accumulate *crayon* drawings of House, Tree, and Person in an attempt to answer his question, "What effect does the introduction of color have on a subject's H-T-P productions?"

The first workshop ever given on the H-T-P was conducted by the writer in Charlottesville, Va.

1946: A rather elaborate system of Post-Drawing Interrogation was drawn up by the writer to provide the S with ample opportunity to describe, define, and interpret his drawings of House, Tree, and Person, and their respective symbolic environments, as well as to associate concerning them.

The H-T-P was formally introduced to the profession by papers presented by the writer to the Psychology Section of the Virginia Academy of Science at its meeting in Charlottesville, Virginia, and to the American Psychological Association at its meeting at the University of Pennsylvania in Philadelphia.

1947: A preliminary manual[1] for use with the H-T-P was prepared and mimeographed for distribution to psychologists and psychiatrists requesting information about the technique.

1948: Randolph Boring introduced his ingenious "incomplete" (partly structured) variation of the H-T-P and he and Dr. Robert Topper began extensive use of an extended variation of the H-T-P as a group screening device at the Veterans Administration Hospital in Tuscaloosa, Alabama.

A brief article by the writer describing the H-T-P and illustrating its use in a single case appeared in the April issue of the *Journal of Clinical Psychology.*

The first description of the H-T-P in a foreign language appeared in the article describing psychological tests used in the United States by Dr. Curt Bondy and Miss Anne Sullivan (of the University of Hamburg) in the July issue of *Die Sammlung.*

Dr. Fred Brown suggested that it might be well to ask the subject, after he had completed his drawings of House, Tree, and Person, to draw a Person of the sex opposite to that of the Person he had just completed.

Verlin Spencer, at San Quentin Penitentiary in California, began to work with his highly imaginative extension of the chromatic phase of the H-T-P by seeking water color as well as crayon drawings. He also began work with a 3-dimensional H-T-P using modelling clay as the medium of expression.

In October, the first formal manual for use with the technique was published as Monograph Supplement No. 5, of the *Journal of Clinical Psychology.*

1949: Early in that year it became standard procedure to seek chromatic as well as achromatic drawings. This expanded the scope of the technique greatly. Not only did it double the quantity of the graphic material and produce still more verbal material, but most importantly, it provided (1) a miniature longitudinal study of the S and (2) an invaluable series of checks upon the internal consistency of the S's behavior.

An abbreviated P-D-I was drawn up for use following the chromatic graphic phase when lack of time prohibited the employment of the full P-D-I.

1950: The Veterans Administration very kindly recorded and mimeographed the material which the writer had presented at a workshop which he had conducted at the Veterans Administration Hospital at Richmond, Virginia, that spring.

This compilation, which was known as *The Richmond Proceedings Material,* served as a Manual Supplement. It contained a detailed discussion of the theoretical postulates on which the H-T-P was based, described the now standard administration

---

[1] The critical comments of Miss Selma Landisberg, who was then the writer's first assistant, contributed greatly to its production.

procedure of (1) achromatic drawings, (2) full P-D-I, (3) chromatic drawings, and (4) abbreviated (if not full) P-D-I, and for the first time listed the qualitative scoring points segregated as to House, Tree and Person.

During that year the Post-Drawing Interrogation Folder and the Scoring Folder were revised.

1951: The qualitative implications of the quantitative scores and score patterns were identified and reported upon by the writer in an article entitled, "The Quality of the Quantity," which appeared in the October issue of the *Journal of Clinical Psychology.* This "quality of the quantity" increased still further the amount of diagnostic and prognostic material derivable from the drawings and provided additional checks upon the internal consistency of performance—all at no additional expenditure of time.

1952: Isaac Jolles' *Catalogue for the Qualitative Interpretation of the H-T-P* was published by Western Psychological Services.

Isaac Jolles reported (in the *Journal of Clinical Psychology*) upon the results of two studies of the validity of some hypotheses for the qualitative interpretation of the H-T-P for children of elementary school age.

The first comprehensive description of the H-T-P in a foreign language appeared in *Revista de Psicologia General y Aplicada* (Vol. 7, No. 2) of Madrid, Spain, under the title, "Una Descripcion Breve de la Technica C-A-P" (Casa-Arbol-Persona).

1953: Dr. Emanuel F. Hammer's discussion of the role of the H-T-P in the prognostic battery (Eastern Psychological Convention, April) advanced the use of the technique by one more important step.

1954: Dr. Hammer's "Guide for Qualitative Research with the H-T-P"[2] in which, for the first time, various signs suggestive of the same personality factor were grouped together, appeared in the *Journal of General Psychology.*

Dr. Solomon Diamond published two articles in the *Journal of Clinical Psychology* describing his *verbal* variation of the H-T-P.

1955: Dr. Hammer and Miss Selma Landisberg conducted a summer workshop on the H-T-P[3] in New York City.

Dr. Bernard C. Meyer, Dr. Fred Brown, and Mr. Abraham Levine reported (in the November-December issue of *Psychosomatic Medicine*) on their "Observations on the House-Tree-Person Drawing Test Before and After Surgery." This was the first published report on what has come to be the most widely used variation of the orthodox H-T-P: that is, the H-T-P-*P* in which the House, the Tree, and the Person are sought in customary fashion and the S is then asked to draw a Person of the sex opposite to the one which he has just drawn spontaneously.

Dr. Hammer published (in the *Journal of Genetic Psychology*) the first report on the use of the H-T-P with Negro subjects (in this instance children and adolescents).

Isaac Jolles began to use a 16-color set of crayons (Crayola #16) routinely after (as he wrote the writer) " . . . I became concerned about the need of a flesh

---

[2] This was later expanded and incorporated into Dr. Hammer's *H-T-P Clinical Research Manual* which was published by Western Psychological Services.

[3] They have conducted similar workshops every summer since.

color for the Person in order to be sure that, when yellow was used, it meant hostility. The #16 Crayolas not only provided a rose pink (close to flesh) but also a white crayon. Subjects using the white crayon were definitely revealing anti-social attitudes."

1956: Isaac Jolles' Children's Revision of the H-T-P Post-Drawing Interrogation Folder was published by Western Psychological Services.

1957: Western Psychological Services published an up-dated H-T-P Bibliography (listing publications by title, author, and journal or book) compiled by Dr. V. J. Bieliauskas.

1958: Dr. Hammer's monumental work, *The Clinical Application of Projective Drawings* – which has quite aptly been termed the projective drawing Bible – was published by Charles C. Thomas & Co. In this volume, which covers the entire field of projective drawings, the H-T-P was given a major place, and the chromatic phase was discussed extensively by Dr. Hammer.

1963: Dr. Bieliauskas compiled an extended H-T-P Bibliography in which, for the first time, a brief description and a critical comment were given for each item listed: this was published by Western Psychological Services as *The House-Tree-Person (H-T-P) Research Review.*

1964: Western Psychological Services published: (1) Jolles' revised and expanded edition of his *Catalogue for the Qualitative Interpretation of the H-T-P* and (2) the writer's revised and expanded edition of the former *Richmond Proceedings Material* now entitled, *The House-Tree-Person Manual Supplement.*

1965: A letter to the writer from Dr. B. Mohl-Hansen, Chief of the Educational Division of Lillemosegard, Denmark, indicated that a committee had been set up there to assist Mr. Borge Nielsen in translating the H-T-P into Danish.

Under date of October 19th, Dr. Mieczyslaw Choynowski, Head of the Psychometrical Laboratory of the Polish Academy of Sciences, Warsaw, Poland, wrote the writer in part, " . . . you can mention it at most in your book, saying that the objective validation of the H-T-P has been undertaken in the Psychometrical Laboratory . . . under my direction."

1966: Western Psychological Services published the writer's expanded, updated, more fully illustrated, and indexed revision of *The House-Tree-Person Technique: Revised Manual.*

The book, *The House-Tree-Person Technique: Variations and Applications,* was compiled by the writer and his one-time colleague and long-time friend, Emanuel F. Hammer,[*] with the aid of a number of distinguished collaborators, in order (1) to present the principal variations of the H-T-P that are being generally employed, and (2) to illustrate as many as possible of the varied uses to which the technique is being put.

As the reader will note, the H-T-P has been expanded and elaborated in many ways since it was first presented to the profession. The present work is a synthesis of the state of the technique to-day – twenty years later – not a full-dress, final presentation. It is hoped that the technique will continue to undergo further objectification and refinement in the years ahead as our field advances.

---

[*] Without whose invaluable collaboration this work would never have been undertaken. JNB

After completing his internship and simultaneous with his obtaining his Ph.D. in Clinical Psychology in 1951 from New York University, Emanuel F. Hammer came to the Lynchburg State Colony, Virginia, to work with John N. Buck and the H-T-P. Shortly thereafter, Dr. Hammer was appointed Director of Intern Training.

He later returned to New York as Senior Research Scientist at the New York State Psychiatric Institute. At the National Psychological Association for Psychoanalysis he then undertook analytic practice, is on the faculty and a training analyst at the Metropolitan Institute of Psychoanalytic Studies. He is head of the Psychiatric Clinic, Chief Psychological Consultant at the Lincoln Institute for Psychotherapy, and has recently been appointed to the faculty of the New York University Clinical Psychology doctoral program.

He has written approximately fifty papers and four books, among which are the well-known *The Clinical Application of Projective Drawings*, Springfield, Ill., Charles Thomas, 1958, and *Creativity*, New York, Random House, 1961. He is presently at work on a book, *Interpretation in Treatment: Its Place, Role, Scope, Depth, and Art*.

Honors and offices which he has held include: Fellow, American Psychological Association; Liaison Fellow, American Anthropological Association; Diplomate in Clinical Psychology, American Board of Examiners in Professional Psychology; Secretary, Society of Projective Techniques and Personality Assessment; President, New York Society of Clinical Psychologists.

Chapter 1

Hierarchal Organization of Personality and the H-T-P, Achromatic and Chromatic [1]

Emanuel F. Hammer, Ph.D.

Dr. Hammer illuminates the importance of establishing the relative levels of a subject's personality structure. He compares data derived from the H-T-P with that elicited by the other projective techniques generally employed in the examining battery. He then focuses upon the contribution of the chromatic phase as an extension of the H-T-P which has greatly enhanced the technique's value as a diagnostic and prognostic tool. In doing this, he first offers impressive clinical and secondly experimental-statistical evidence in support of his interrelated set of hypotheses.

The author concludes this stimulating survey by presenting (1) his concept of the relative depth of the personality tapped by the various projective techniques and (2) patterns of achromatic-chromatic H-T-P relationships which have been found to have prognostic significance.

Consideration of the concept of "levels" of personality structure, as they come through in the projective battery, has moved into the center of clinical concern as the use of projectives has gained in sophistication (Bellak, 1954;

---

[1]Thanks are appreciatively extended to the *Journal of Projective Techniques and Personality Assessment* and to Charles Thomas, Publisher, Springfield, Ill. for permission to use material, to the latter for material from Hammer, E. F., *The Clinical Application of Projective Drawings,* 1958, from which the present chapter is synthesized and expanded.

Eysenck, 1947; Hammer, 1953; Klopfer *et al,* 1954; Murray, 1938; Piotrowski, 1952; Rapaport, 1946; and Schafer, 1954). As both personality theory and the projectives have become more refined, the clinician has addressed himself to gaining a picture of not only the patient's conflicts and defenses, but more often of their hierarchal relationships.

For example, when an excess of both hostile and tender feelings come through, how can the clinician decide whether the hostile feelings are used to ward off people in an effort to avoid the danger of experiencing affection with others, or whether the tender feelings are exaggeratedly employed to deny the underlying hostility.

One might answer that, in everyday practice, projective protocols are not interpreted "blindly," and the behavioral picture tells us which of the opposing traits is on the surface. But in terms of understanding our projective tools, in terms of refining our theory around the projective techniques, it is important to clarify our thinking concerning the way in which the protocols reflect the imprint of surface versus underlying dimensions. Also, frequently we must differentiate between sub-surface and sub-sub-surface layers of feelings, and here the case history or clinical interview is not always helpful.

When a projective protocol reveals feelings of both deadness and also eruptive emotions, how do we decide when the deadening and dampening of affect is in the service of controlling volatile, eruptive potentials, or when a seeking of excitement and "kicks" is employed in an effort to get a sense of life, to taste affect?

To take another example, how do we decide from a protocol whether expansive, grandiose feelings are a compensation for feelings of insignificance and lack of worth, or whether feelings of humbleness, humility, and modesty are a form of leaning over backward to deny underlying arrogance?

Or, how do we distinguish, when both passivity and aggression flood a projective protocol between the two situations:

(A) passivity as a cloak for underlying aggression, and

(B) aggression as a disguise for inner passivity.

When two common denominators are apparent—helpless inadequacy, on the one hand, and ambitious need for status, on the other hand —what are the clues we go by to differentiate the status-striving which is a compensation for feelings of insufficiency, from the outer role of innocuousness and ineffectuality, which is a protective disguise for secret ambitiousness and forbidden competitiveness?

In the projective protocol of a child, we may frequently find marked ambivalence toward a parent. How do the records differ in the case of the child who employs hate and bristling antagonism in an effort to push off his mother because of unacceptable dependency on her, as opposed to a situation in which the dependency side of the coin is uppermost as a covering and screening for the forbidden feelings of hatred?

When we find a clash between anger and feelings of being easily exploited or controlled by others, when might we predict that the patient will fight off the therapist with antagonism in an effort to avoid his fear of being dominated, and when might we predict that the patient will be docile in accepting interpretations because he will perceive disagreement as a forbidden aggressive act?

The most frequent fault I find in reports written by the interns and psychologists I supervise is that while a patient's defenses are described, their *place* in the total picture is not delineated. If we find a patient relying to excess on the defensive mechanism of "denial," we want to know what he will resort to when this mechanism is blocked by the therapist confronting him with certain of his feelings. Which of his defenses will he give up first, because it is superimposed upon which other one? *What is the order in the series of buffer systems or layers of defense which guard the approach to that which is repressed?*

The point is to avoid chain-like interpretations in which each trend is simply juxtaposed to other trends, and no *hierarchy* of importance, push and restraint, is established.

Personality may be regarded as encompassing a number of organizational levels, "varying in the degree of accessibility to observation from the outside and to self-observation," (Hanfmann & Getzels, 1953). It is, after all, this concept of levels upon which our earliest psychoanalytic understanding is based. The existence of conscious, preconscious and unconscious areas, the phenomenon of repression which is rather central to all dynamic systems of personality theory, and the clinically observed mechanism of reaction-formation are all based upon a hierarchal view of personality structure.

The concept of layers is used, not in the form of stratified rock — immobile, sedentary, and with no fluidity of permeable membranes between — but rather in a form more like a river, with warm currents at the surface and colder currents beneath, which at times flow juxtaposed — and because of this contact, influence each other, reacting and interacting.

Comparison of Data from the H-T-P and from Other Projective Techniques: Prognostic Implications

The H-T-P serves as a canvas upon which the subject etches aspects of his inner world, his personality strengths and weaknesses, including the degree to which he can mobilize his inner resources to handle his psychodynamic conflicts. In this respect it is similar to other projective techniques. If the H-T-P device is to be given a recognized place in the battery, it must make a unique contribution to the clinical picture not completely overlapped by the other tests.

In attempting to harness projective drawings to prognostic usefulness, it has been found that deeper conflicts frequently press into view more readily on the drawing page than elsewhere. Wyatt (1949) explains that "in drawings, deeper, more primary, and less differentiated levels of experience are tapped." In addition to Wyatt, both Bellak (1953) and Symonds (1953) have pointed out that drawing techniques tap deeper layers of the personality than the verbal projective techniques such as the Rorschach and the TAT. I am in agreement with them in their view that drawings *per se*, on the other hand, do provide a grosser personality picture with less of the nuances filled in. The verbal phases (Post-drawing Interrogation) of the H-T-P, however, frequently provide pertinent data with which to round out the personality picture.

In explaining the deeper though more narrow tapping of the unconscious by projective drawings, Stern (1952) writes, "The technique used in (drawings) is on a level with primitive pictorial thought. It is on the same plane as the unconscious thought itself . . . It seems that the affect emanating from a picture reaches into the unconscious more deeply than does that of language, due to the fact that pictorial expression is more adequate to the developmental stage in which the trauma occurred; it has remained more within range of the concrete and physical than has the verbal expression."

To further compare projective drawings with the best known of all projective techniques, the Rorschach, it may be pointed out that drawings tap predominately effector (outgoing) processes whereas the Rorschach taps predominantly perceptual (incoming) processes. Zucker (1948) found that drawings are the first to show incipient psychopathology, and here their prognostic use is underscored, and the last to lose signs of illness after the patient remisses. Zucker concludes that drawings are more highly sensitive to psychopathological trends than are the other projective techniques. Hence, negative latent factors foreshadowing a gloomy prognosis are indicated by an H-T-P heavy with pathology in conjunction with a relatively clearer Rorschach.

Intra-Whole H-T-P Comparisons

Another advantage of using drawing techniques for the solution of prognostic problems lies in the tool's capacity for simultaneous tapping of body-images on different personality levels. It has been felt, for example, that whereas the drawing of a Person taps the patient's degree of adjustment on a psycho-social level, the drawing of the Tree appears to tap basic, more enduring and deeper intrapsychic feelings and self-attitudes. Therefore, the drawing of the Tree has held up as being less susceptible to change on re-testing than the drawing of the Person. Whereas psychotherapy of a non-intensive kind will frequently show improvement in the drawn Person, as a rule only deep psychoanalytic therapy, or highly significant alterations in the life situation, will produce any but minor changes in the Tree.

Also, since it is easier to attribute more conflictful or emotionally disturbing negative traits and attitudes to the drawn Tree than the drawn Person because the former is "less close to home" as a self-portrait as far as the subject is concerned, the deeper or more forbidden feelings can more readily be projected onto the Tree than onto the Person, with less fear of revealing oneself and less need for ego-defensive maneuvers.

A pre-schizophrenic recently conveyed his surface adjustment of stability by drawing a Person whose feet were planted widely and firmly on the ground, but his underlying potential for imminent loss of personality equilibrium gave itself away in his uprooted and toppling Tree.

In regard to the H-T-P's capacity for tapping different personality levels, the House appears to lie somewhere between the Person and the Tree on this particular continuum. Focus has been given to the Tree and Person because they represent extremes, prognostically most fruitful for comparison. As may be expected the prognosis is poorest when House, Tree and Person are all flooded with psychopathology indicators.

Since the drawing of the Tree taps more basic layers than the drawing of the Person, a positive prognosis is suggested by a Tree conveying a healthier picture of the personality than is conveyed by the drawn Person. In such cases latent positive resources are currently overshadowed by the effects of a reactive or situation-induced emotional upheaval. Conversely, a negative prognosis is indicated by the drawn Tree steeped in more psychopathology than the drawn Person, by the Tree conveying an impression of a "split tree", a Tree with broken branches or trunk, a Tree with a scarred trunk, a Tree depicted as toppling over, unconvincing life-like leaves joined to a dilapidated tree trunk, and so on.

Achromatic-Chromatic H-T-P Comparison

At this point, the writer presents a series of clinical observations, to the end that further study by investigators in various institutions can eventually more firmly establish, or refute, the deductions forced upon the writer, first in an atmosphere of skepticism and ultimately in an atmosphere of increasing empirically-based conviction.

The data, a liberal sample of which is presented, suggest the deduction that the achromatic (pencil) and chromatic (crayon) drawing phases of the H-T-P actually tap somewhat different *levels* of personality. The chromatic H-T-P cuts through the defenses to lay bare a deeper level of personality than does the achromatic set of drawings, and in this manner a crude hierarchy of the subject's conflicts and his defenses is established and a richer personality picture derived.

The chromatic series is designed to supplement the achromatic series, to take advantage of the fact that two samples of behavior are always better than one. But the chromatic series is more than a second H-T-P sample because the subject who produces it must, I believe, be in a somewhat more vulnerable state than he was when he produced his achromatic drawings. Even to the best adjusted subject, the achromatic H-T-P and the subsequent searching Post-Drawing-Interrogation is an emotional experience, for many memories, pleasant and unpleasant, are aroused, at the least.

Thus the chromatic series becomes a behavioral sample that is obtained with the subject at a level of frustration that is different from that which pertained when the achromatic series was sought. If the achromatic (as it frequently is for the well-adjusted subject) was a welcome catharsis, the subject may be far less tense than he was at the beginning. In the average clinical case seen for differential diagnosis, however, this will scarcely be the case – such a subject will almost inevitably be so emotionally aroused that his chromatic series will reveal still more about his basic needs, mechanisms of defense, etc., than the achromatic, and point up the disparity between his functioning and his potential pattern of behavior.

But I shall allow the data to speak for themselves; this they do rather eloquently, I think:

CASE ILLUSTRATIONS
A Brief Description of the Chromatic H-T-P Administration

After the achromatic set of H-T-P drawings has been completed, the examiner substitutes a fresh set of drawing blanks for the completed set, and a set of crayons for the pencil. The pencil is taken away so that the subject cannot do the outline of the drawing in pencil, and then color in the drawing as one might in a coloring book. A set of Crayola[2] crayons is employed; the set consists of eight crayons, colored respectively, red, green, yellow, blue, brown, black, purple and orange. The subject is asked to identify the crayons by color. If he cannot do this, it is imperative that the examiner test more formally for the presence of color blindness.

The initial instructions are, "Now, please draw as good a house as you can using any of the colors you wish," with parallel requests then following for the Tree and the Person. The subject is purposely not asked to draw *another* House, *another* Tree or *another* Person, for to most subjects the word "another" would imply that they must not duplicate their achromatic drawings. The intent is to provide the subject with the widest latitude of choice.

The subject is allowed to use any or all of the eight crayons, with all questions as to how he should proceed handled in a non-directive manner, thus maximizing the subject's self-structuring of the task.

In the achromatic series, the subject is afforded every opportunity to employ corrective measures: he may erase as much as he likes, and the pencil is a relatively refined drawing instrument. In the chromatic series, the only corrective measure available is concealment with heavy shading and the drawing instrument, the crayon, is relatively crude.

Thus, at the beginning, with the subject in as full possession of his defensive mechanisms as he will presumably be, he is given tools which permit expressive defensiveness; in the second phase, by which time the subject will be more likely to have lost at least part of his defensive control (if he is going to lose it at all), he is provided with a grosser instrument, and with an opportunity to express symbolically (through his choice and use of color) the emotions which have been aroused by the achromatic series and Post-Drawing-Interrogation.

Case A: A Pseudo-energetic Man

The subject, a thirty-one-year-old, married male, had had two and one-half years of college and was employed as a draftsman.

For his achromatic House he drew a slightly pretentious and showy House, suggesting a degree of status consciousness. His achromatic female Person is depicted as dancing, conveying bouyancy and activity. The achromatic male Person is likewise a picture of energy and action. The suspicion may arise in the clinician's mind as to whether or not the subject, in Shakespeare's words, "doth protest too much" by his so emphatic underscoring of the components of energy and activity in his projection.[3] On the other hand, it is still conceivable that this may actually be a man of outstanding vitality and bouyancy, and the clinician is uncertain as to whether to take the drawings at face value or to view them as a defensive personality blanket.

The introduction of the chromatic phase of the H-T-P resolves the issue as neatly as it does dramatically.

---

[2] A popular commercial brand put out by the American Crayon Company, Sandusky, Ohio, and easily obtained at any children's toy counter or stationary store.

[3] Particularly when we note the spindly shank protruding from the trouser cuff and the fact that the suit–the cloak of social behavior–fits very badly. The latter conveys the strong implications that his role is not an essentially satisfying one.

Fig. 1, Case A (above)

Fig. 2, Case A (below)

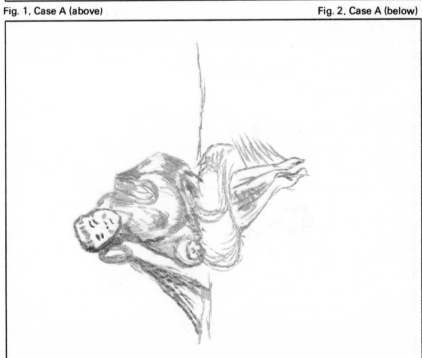

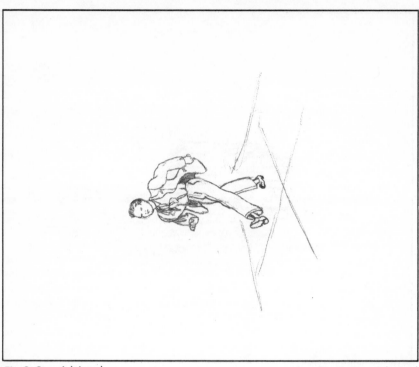

Fig. 3, Case A (above)　　　　　　　　　　　　　Fig. 4, Case A (below)

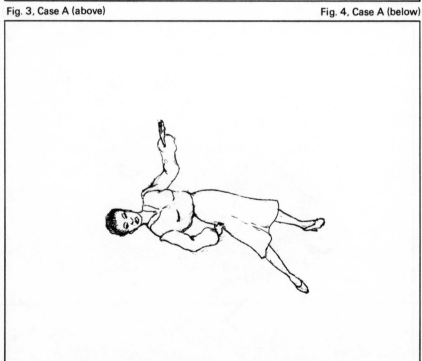

On the deeper chromatic level, a crude log cabin replaces the elaborate, over-adorned, and impressive achromatic House. The patient's pretentious front collapses into a portrayal of insufficiency and, by comparison, almost abject insignificance. The picture of wealth and "have" is replaced by poverty and "have not," comfort is replaced by bare essentials, ornateness by barrenness, and an expansive, many-roomed front, conveyed by the achromatic drawing, which compensates for his essential lack of worth (deserving no better than a crude log cabin as a home), was also supported by his flashy dress, conspicuous jewelry, and his use of pedantic vocabulary.

His chromatic female collapses into a sitting position, and even then has not the strength to keep her head erect, but must lean it against something. A sapping of energy and drive may thus be seen actually to exist beneath the patient's energetic front. By the time the patient comes to the task of drawing the chromatic male, his basic feelings of the futility of overstriving come to the fore and he depicts a Person who reclines still further to a horizontal position, and one who is described as "sixty years old," thus reflecting a mixture of feelings of impotency, decline and decrepitude along with his underlying passivity. On deeper symbolic levels, we note that he will lose his beard and possibly be in the hands of a razor-wielding adult.

The chromatic House and two Persons are devalued concepts which mirror the subject's depression and depreciated self-concept beneath his three achromatic projections.

Fig. 5, Case A

Fig. 6, Case A (above)

Fig. 7, Case B (below)

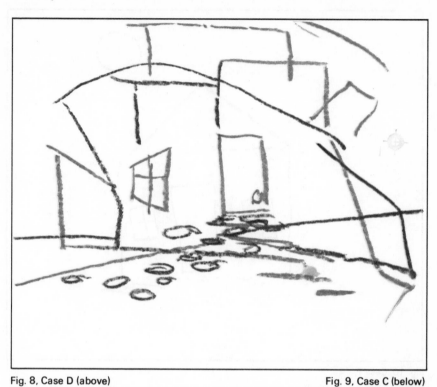

Fig. 8, Case D (above)   Fig. 9, Case C (below)

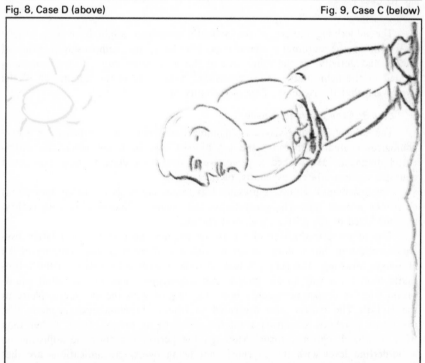

Fig. 10, Case B

The underlying picture of the patient's pathology might have been largely lost without the chromatic redrawings. Similarly, the compensatory front of energy and activity, as the other side of the personality coin, is clearly demonstrated in the achromatic, more superficial level. It is in the integration of the two levels, that the richness of the personality picture is derived.

Case B: A Pre-psychotic Female

The subject, a thirty-six-year-old unmarried female, was referred for a psychological evaluation because the psychiatrist was in doubt about the differential diagnosis. He wished a projective examination done to help evaluate a neurotic, against a latent psychotic, picture.

Her achromatic House is presented as insecurely anchored to an amorphous cloud-like ground line. The presentation thus suggests that contact with reality, as symbolized by the ground, is at best uncertain.

The achromatic drawing of the House implies the presence of a latent psychotic condition, but it does not do so with any of the dramatic certainty of the chromatic drawing. The subject's lack of firm contact with reality on the achromatic level gives way to an obvious and catastrophic loss of emotional equilibrium when a deeper personality level was tapped with the chromatic phase of the H-T-P. The House, now presented as frankly toppling over, suggests that the latent psychotic condition is of the incipient or pre-psychotic, rather than of a stabilized, chronic, form. Although the person may now be adjusting on a borderline level with the psychosis not being overt, the indications are that in the immediate future there will be a clear-cut loss of contact with reality.

The patient's subsequent confinement to an institution, four months after the administration of the psychological examination, provided empirical proof of the deeper, and prophesying, level of the chromatic drawings.

Case C: A Pre-psychotic Male

The subject, a twenty-three-year-old, single, male, was also referred for purposes of establishing a differential diagnosis.

This case also illustrated the thesis that personality clues hinted at in the achromatic drawings, often come through full-blown, in more clear-cut fashion, in the chromatic drawings. The tenuous contact with reality, as suggested by the choppy groundline and the drawn Person's spotty contact with it, in the achromatic drawings, gives way (as with the case of the previous pre-psychotic) to a more frank loss of personality balance under the impact of color. (Also noteworthy as pathology indicators are the absolute profile and the progressively less realistic proportion from massive head to tiny feet).

A large number of sets of drawings, which cases B and C illustrate, have served to convince the writer that *incipient or latent psychological conditions are most frequently presented by being hinted at in the achromatic drawings and then more vividly and dramatically overtly portrayed in the chromatic expression.*

Fig. 11, Case C

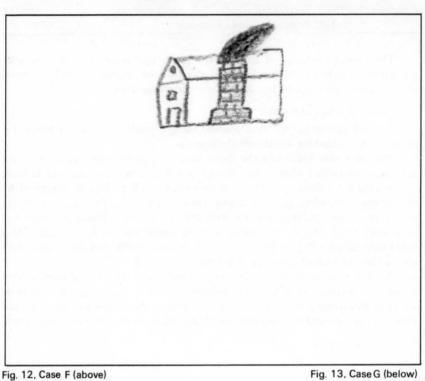

Fig. 12, Case F (above)   Fig. 13, Case G (below)

Fig. 14, Case D (above)

Fig. 15, Case E (below)

Case D: An Overtly Psychotic Patient

A comparison of the achromatic and chromatic sets of drawings produced by the patient, a twenty-eight-year-old male, confined to an institution, again illustrates the relatively stronger stimuli represented by the chromatic phase and its greater efficacy in cutting through the patient's defenses.

In spite of the psychotic process, strongly suggested by the gross distortion of reality apparent in the depiction of smoke blowing simultaneously in two directions and the window shades extended outside the window down the front of the building, a degree personality intactness is suggested by the over-all integration of the healthier quality. The only evidence of frank psychosis apparent in the achromatic Tree is the unusual similarity between root network and branch structure; psychotic patients occasionally offer a drawing such as this which just as appropriately represents the concept asked for if it is viewed upside down. The desperate clutching grip of the roots is suggestive of a fear of losing one's hold on reality. The personality picture which evolves from a consideration of the achromatic drawings only is one of severe maladjustment of probably psychotic proportions with certain delusional areas, but a degree of personality integration and some fair defensive resources upon which to fall back. There appears to be a degree of "give" to his personality structure, and the clinician may wonder whether when the patient is driven over the line into the borderlands of psychosis he will not be able to recover and return to reality once again.

The later introduction of the chromatic drawings into the clinical consideration, however, shatters the clinician's prognostic optimism by revealing the patient's defenses to be actually paper thin.

Under the emotional impact of color, the patient's defenses do not strengthen, but totally crumble. The House disintegrates entirely, the stones composing the pathway to the door appear to float up off the ground, and the patient himself may be presumed to fall apart on the spot. The patient projects this inner feeling verbally by commenting spontaneously that the branches of the chromatic tree are "falling off." Chaotic emotional impulses are clearly indicated by his inability to contain his coloring within the outline of the drawn Tree as well as by his choice of clashing red, green, orange and yellow heaped helter-skelter onto the page. The Tree itself topples. The wind is bizarrely discribed as blowing not from the left and not from the right, but straight down upon the Tree from above, reflecting the terrible feelings of pressure which beset the patient. Thus, the projection of himself clinging hard to reality, as conveyed by the overemphasized roots of the achromatic Tree clutching at the ground, is replaced by the self-portrait of total personality collapse and disintegration on the chromatic level.

Case E: A Mentally Defective Psychotic

Still another example of the chromatic drawing phase bringing forth into fuller relief that which generally comes through in less intense fashion in the achromatic drawings, is offered by a seventeen-year-old male psychotic functioning on an intellectual level of "imbecile" to "moron."

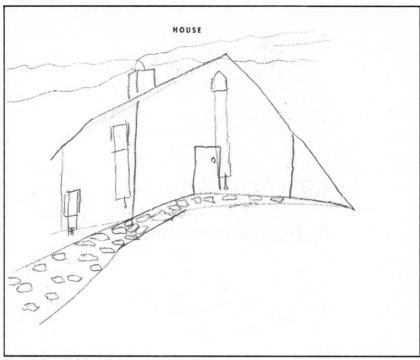

Fig. 16, Case D (above)

Fig. 17, Case D (below)

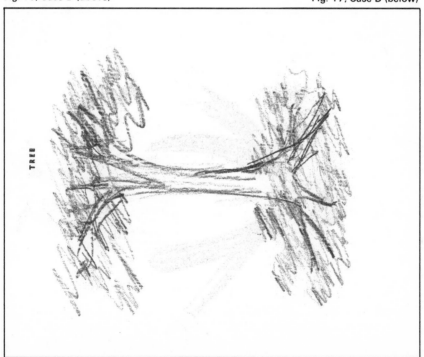

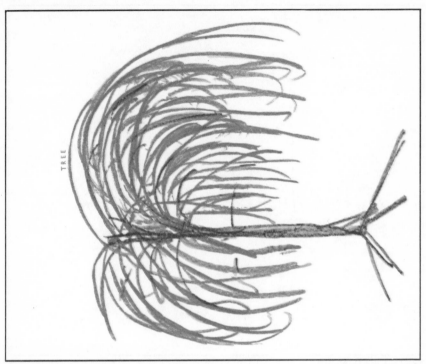

TREE

Fig. 18, Case J (above)   Fig. 19, Case J (below)

PERSON

Fig. 20, Case G (above)

Fig. 21, Case F (below)

HOUSE

Fig. 22, Case E

His face-like achromatic House reflects the anthropomorphism with which psychotics will frequently endow inanimate objects. The achromatic House (Figure 22) is doused so heavily in anthropomorphism that it seems to leave no latitude for any more human quality to come through on the chromatic level. But the crayons can, and do actually, stimulate a still more anthropomorphic House; two twin, ear-like chimneys, now complete the face.

Case F: An Exhibitionist

The subject, a forty-two-year-old, married male, had gotten into trouble with the law by exposing his penis to a group of twelve-year-old girls who were playing across the street from his window.

In the achromatic House, his need for drawing attention to protuberances is hinted at by the somewhat oversized chimney. In his drawing of the chromatic House, however, his exhibitionistic needs are thrown into fuller relief by the tremendous full-length chimney, with smoke pouring forth, presented as the focus of the drawing. His choice of colors follows the same pattern of spotlighting the phallic symbol. Black crayon is employed to devalue everything but the chimney, which he then colors in a bright, erotic, attention-getting red.

All of the above cases have been presented to support the thesis that the chromatic level brings forth the deeper personality picture, as a rather direct contrast to the achromatic level. The cases thus far have all been examples of deeper pathology surging beneath the relatively more calmly rippling surface.

Perhaps an even more important clinical yield occurs when the chromatic drawings uncover relatively greater health, rather than sickness, within. The next two cases are presented as illustrations of this type of clinical finding.

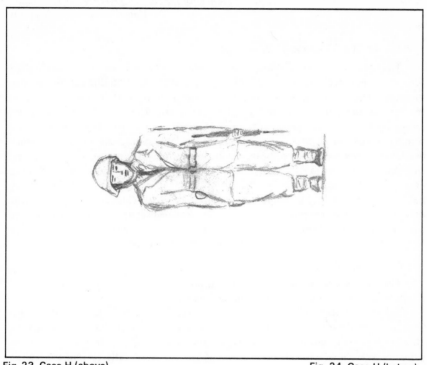

Fig. 23, Case H (above)

Fig. 24, Case H (below)

Case G: A Reactive Condition

The patient, a twenty-three-year-old male, was referred by a psychiatrist for personality evaluation because of recurring nightmares following an elevator accident. The accident, which occurred eight months earlier, had resulted in the loss of the patient's right leg. The achromatic House, reflecting the more recent and superficial personality picture, reflects the patient's feelings concerning precariously attached appendages by the placement of the chimney overhanging the roof in a position easily susceptible to toppling. On the deeper, chromatic level, he moves his chimney into a position of more secure footing away from the dangerous *edge* of the roof. Thus, it is suggested that the anxiety he is discharging in his nightmares is rooted in a relatively reactive, rather than earlier developmental situation. This was subsequently supported in the psychiatrist's later therapeutic collaboration with the patient, as well as the case history data indicating loss of the patient's limb during adulthood.

Case H: A "He-man" Character Disorder

The subject, a twenty-eight-year-old male, presents a set of drawings of a type not infrequently obtained from adolescent males.

Subjects of the adolescent age group frequently convey in their drawings, their need to demonstrate virility as compensation for their lack of full maturation and growth, and for their delayed attainment of status. In a subject of the patient's age, however, the persistence of such a need reflects immaturity, as well as the same compensatory character-armoring suggested by his various vocational choices which included truck driving, boxing, and during the war, volunteering for paratrooper duty.

The projective drawings were administered five years after the patient had been in service; hence his achromatic drawing of a soldier conveys his clinging to the self-concept of a warrior as a badge of virile manliness. His defensive masculine strivings then intensify and become still more frank in his chromatic drawing of a muscular weight-lifter exhibiting his prowess. Beneath the compensatory muscles of the drawn Person, however, exists a somewhat short and organically less adequate frame, a hint of the inner doubts beneath the patient's virility strivings.

Whereas the achromatic soldier suggests the twin possibilities of either virility strivings or aggressive impulses, the chromatic data throws the evidence on the side of the need to demonstrate manliness.

Whereas this subject's defenses deepen on the chromatic level (showing a consistency with the diagnosis of character disorder), the next case presented is one whose defenses, in neurotic fashion, give way rather than intensify as the subject proceeds from the achromatic to the chromatic levels.

Case I: A Child in the Cloak of a Warrior

The subject's drawings proceed from the achromatic surface of an Indian brave whose conspicuous headdress testifies to his being a leader among hunters and warriors, to the deeper chromatic level which eloquently conveys the core of his self-concept: a little boy masquerading in the garb of a virile adult (i.e., wearing a sailor suit). On the achromatic level, some hint at lassitude and pas-

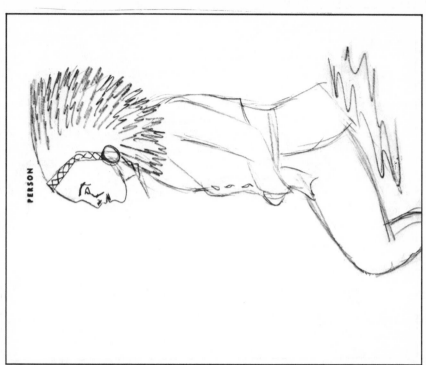

Fig. 25, Case I (above)   Fig. 26, Case I (below)

Fig. 27, Case J (above)

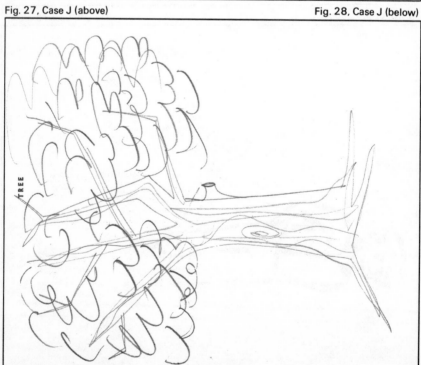

Fig. 28, Case J (below)

sivity beneath the virile front comes through in the position of the drawn Indian, who sinks into a sitting posture. But it is in the chromatic phase that the basic person–a child playing at being a man–is seen. The "shrinkage" in size of the figure is as striking as the change in content.

Case J: A Mild Case of Don Juanism

The patient, a 30-year-old, married male with two children, entered psychotherapeutic collaboration because of a heavy sense of guilt which pervaded a recent onset of extramarital activities.

The subject, for his achromatic male Person, drew a well-dressed person in a nonchalant pose, whom he then described as about his own age, or leaning a bit on the younger side (i.e., "twenty-six to thirty"), and as "sophisticated, dapper and self-assured." From merely the achromatic level, one would get little impression of the extent of the basic problem lying beneath the surface (and brought up by the impact of color). Beneath this surface impression of himself, the chromatic male which he later drew indicates that the patient is beginning inwardly to entertain grave doubts concerning his youth, vigor and virility. In the chromatic drawing, the male figure loses his confident and self-assured casualness of pose. The hands are held in a position of helpless ineffectuality, and the facial tone changes to a pathetically empty and depressed one. The achromatic Person's smile is replaced by a morose frown and his bright, alert facial expression gives way to a vacuous one. A premature fear of decline, impotence and decrepitude, associated with "old age," is dramatically conveyed in his description of the chromatic male: "This is the same man years later, his hair is gone, his money is gone, his waist is gone, and his poise is gone. (The drawing is complementary to the Rorschach response the subject gave on Card VI, of a "penis with a beard on it.")

The inner doubts generated by this self-concept appear as the motivational mainspring behind this attempt to recapture his earlier "sophisticated, dapper, self-assured" picture of himself through extramarital activities with his twenty-year-old secretary, his nineteen-year-old clerk, and another twenty-one-year-old woman.

In his achromatic and chromatic drawings of Trees, the two levels of his self-concept again are graphically and dramatically portrayed. Thus, his Tree drawings parallel his Person drawings. For his achromatic Tree he drew a sturdy oak which he then describes as "full-grown, stately and very solid." Beneath this surface impression of himself, he apparently inwardly harbors a self-concept actually possessed of just the opposite traits: for his chromatic Tree he draws a weeping willow (conveying his underlying depression) which he then describes as "weak-looking."

The patient is presently panicked by the cracks he is beginning to experience in his self-esteem. The conspicuous sawed-off limb protruding from his otherwise sturdy and intact achromatic Tree might suggest that he is beginning to experience his feelings of impairment, inadequacy and "castration" on increasingly closer-to-conscious levels.

Experimental Follow-up Study

On an empirical basis, the foregoing data are rather impressive; but can an experimental design yield equally demonstrative data in support of the central hypothesis—i.e. that the drawings produced in crayon tend to emanate from a relatively deeper region than those produced in pencil?

For the experimental phase of the study, sixty cases were accumulated over the years. These were individuals who had been initially referred for projective technique assessment, and had then been treated by a therapist, in the majority of cases by the psychiatrist who had referred the case for diagnostic evaluation.

The writer adminstered the H-T-P, made and ·recorded his H-T-P derived diagnosis on the basis of a comparison of the pencil and the crayon drawings, and only then proceeded to administer the remainder of the projective battery. The guideposts he employed for the diagnosis based on the achromatic-chromatic H-T-P comparison were those distilled, on an empirical basis, from the sort of cases presented in this chapter. The following rules of thumb, derived from the hypothesis that chromatic drawings tend to tap deeper personality "levels" than do achromatic drawings, were employed:

Neurotic conditions will be reflected in relatively opposite personality polarities elicited by the chromatic and the achromatic H-T-P, respectively (with the latter representing defenses and the former, what is defended against). See, for example, Cases A, I and J.

Character disorders will reflect themselves in the same defense (and drawing theme) appearing and deepening as the subject progresses from the achromatic to the chromatic rendition. See, as illustrations, Cases F and H.

Reactive conditions (latent psychotic, ambulatory or preschizophrenic conditions) will yield dramatically sicker chromatic than achromatic H-T-P's, with the achromatic almost "passing" as non-psychotic. See Cases B and C.

Schizophrenic reactions will produce evidence of frank pathology in both the achromatic and the chromatic drawings, with the chromatic H-T-P's being even more pathological than the achromatic. See Cases D and E.

Organicity: Confusion, perseveration and organic flavoring[*] will not become worse on the chromatic than on the achromatic drawings (as things, on the contrary, do get worse on the chromatic drawings of neurotic, pre-schizophrenic, and schizophrenic patients).

Relatively healthy or "essentially normal" people will reveal relative personality resiliency, stability or effectiveness which will not diminish on the chromatic drawings, and will be more or less integrated and undisrupted on both levels.

Because the psychotherapists required a report from the psychologist, almost invariably during the first five sessions, the psychotherapist's diagnosis of each case was not the original one formulated during the first phase of treatment, because it was felt that that diagnostic impression might well have been

---

[*]For a listing of such signs of organic flavoring on the H-T-P, see pages 11 and 12 of Hammer, E. F., *H-T-P Clinical Research Manual,* Los Angeles, California, Western Psychological Services, 1954.

influenced by the psychological report. Instead, the psychotherapist was con-
tacted six months later and asked for his final diagnosis in the case. The psychotherapist was asked to place patient into the category in which the patient
most essentially fit: Neurosis, Character Disorder, Reactive Condition, Latent
Condition, Schizophrenic Reaction, Organic, or Essentially Normal. By thus
obtaining the diagnosis six months after treatment had been inaugurated, the
writer hoped to minimize, if not almost eliminate, the influence of the original
psychological report on the diagnosis. Presumably, after a psychotherapist has
been working with a patient for a full half year, his clinical impression will
be founded on his observations and intimate knowledge of the patient himself
rather than on earlier diagnostic impressions of others. This, at least, is the assumption upon which the experimental section of this study is based.

The basic operational hypothesis, stated in null form, is that the diagnoses
based on a comparison of the achromatic-chromatic H-T-P will agree no better
than chance with the criteria of the psychotherapist's diagnosis on the same
patient after six months of treatment.

Of the sixty cases, we find, when the data is accumulated, that agreement
of the H-T-P derived with the later psychotherapists' diagnoses occurs in forty-
eight cases, or in 80% of the instances. In computing the statistics, the more parsimonious assumption was employed that by pure chance the diagnoses derived from each source had an even or fifty-fifty chance of agreeing with one
another. In actuality, pure chance would produce agreement in much less than
half the cases, since there are seven categories, rather than two from which each
diagnostician can choose. But on the other hand, it is not a case of chance allowing one chance out of seven either. The respective diagnosticians are not equally
prone to employ any one of the seven diagnostic alternatives, in that in general
practice the diagnosis of neurosis, as one example, occurs much more frequently
than does an organic or essentially healthy diagnosis. The situation thus becomes
more complicated.

However, even with the parsimonious base of pure chance yielding agreement in thirty of the sixty cases, the Chi square obtained is 21.60, statistically
significant at the .001 level of confidence. In addition to the Chi square results,
the face value of exact "correlation" over seven categories in forty-eight out of
sixty instances is confirming. Here we obtain encouraging experimental support
for the empirically-derived view that the addition of the chromatic H-T-P to
the achromatic H-T-P provides a diagnostically useful extension of the projective drawings, probing relatively deeper into the underlying personality regions.

As for the particular *subgroup* of a diagnostic entity, each is really so small
that it does not make sense to individually employ statistical treatment with
one or another separately. But *purely for descriptive purposes* we may turn to
Table I for a breakdown of the various diagnostic entities, as they were nu-
merically represented in the overall study. We find that with each one of the
diagnostic groups, the data is in the predicted directions. With the category of
Neurosis there is agreement in fourteen out of eighteen cases; with that of
Character Disorder in four of five cases; with the *Reactive Conditions* in three

of four cases; with the *Latent Conditions* in twelve of fifteen cases; with the *Schizophrenic Reactions* in nine of eleven cases; with *Organicity* in three of the three, and with the *Essentially Healthy* agreement occurs in three of the four cases. These four "Essentially Normal" cases, it later turned out, were two actors and two psychiatrists. Each of the actors had sought a psychoanalytic experience in the interest of deepening his awareness or of liberating greater richness or creativeness for his artistry, and the two psychiatrists were in analysis as a part of their psychoanalytic training.

TABLE I

Comparison of Psychiatric Diagnosis Made Six Months After Therapy Began and the Initial Projective Drawing Hypothesis

	CASES	
	Agreement	Disagreement
NEUROSIS: Opposite personality polarity comes out on chromatic H-T-P as opposed to achromatic (with the latter representing defenses and the former, what is defended against)	14	4
CHARACTER DISORDER: Same defense (and drawing theme) deepens from achromatic to chromatic	4	1
REACTIVE CONDITIONS: "Healthier-looking" chromatic than achromatic drawings	3	1
LATENT CONDITIONS: (Latent, ambulatory, and pre-schizophrenic conditions): Dramatically sicker chromatic than achromatic, with achromatic almost "passing" as non-psychotic	12	3
SCHIZOPHRENIC REACTIONS: Pathology frank on both levels, although even more overt on chromatic level	9	2
ORGANICITY: Confusion, perseveration and organic flavoring* do not become worse on the chromatic than on the achromatic drawings, (as things do get worse on the chromatic drawings of neurotic and schizophrenic patients)	3	0
HEALTH ("ESSENTIALLY NORMAL" DIAGNOSIS): Personality resilience, stability and effectiveness do not get worse on chromatic, and are relatively integrated and undisrupted on both levels.	3	1

Discussion

In its concern with the deciphering of the symbolic meaning of the different individual colors in various projective art techniques, psychodiagnostic psychology has by-passed an awareness of the perhaps richer clinical yield: the tapping of the generally deeper level of the personality by chromatic, as compared to the achromatic, projective drawings. The two levels can produce a more definitive picture of the stratification of the subject's personality structure.

The chromatic drawing phase strips away the closer-to-conscious personality layers; it more easily raises the deeper layers of the unconscious to eye-level.

Observation of subjects engaging in the achromatic and chromatic drawing task suggests a three-factor rationale to go along with the empirical data presented.

Firstly, the crayon drawing task tends to elicit reactions to, and tolerance for, emotional stimuli. In this manner it supplies an impact similar to the Rorschach chromatic cards in getting beneath the subject's defenses.

The second factor probably operative in the chromatic phase of projective drawings, which enables it to dig down deeper into the personality structure, is the associative value of the crayons which tends to elicit childhood adjustment levels in adult subjects. It seems almost as if crayons appeal in some degree to the residue of childish layers in the adult's personality, and cut through to tap this level.

The third factor which probably contributes to the efficacy of the chromatic phase, in descending deeper beneath the subject's defenses than the achromatic phase, is a temporal factor. As routinely administered, the chromatic H-T-P is asked for after the subject has produced an achromatic set of drawings and has been questioned at length concerning them. Thus, by the time he is asked to enter the chromatic phase, he may be psychologically in a more vulnerable position, with his conflicts stirred up, his emotions aroused and, as is the case with some subjects, his defenses ajar. It is through this chink in his armor that the chromatic phase penetrates.

Thus, a three-factor hypothesis is offered in explanation of the clinically-observed phenomenon that chromatic drawings reveal a deeper personality picture than achromatic drawings: (a) the emotional impact of colors; (b) the childhood associations to crayons, and (c) the repetition of the drawing task[*] (after a questioning period).

With colored pencils, crayons that leave a pencil line (achromatic), and a procedure in which the chromatic drawing phase precedes the achromatic one, the writer is presently following through a research design which attempts to separate the three factors and thus evaluate their relative contributions to the, as presently conceived, more potent chromatic clinical instrument.

Color Symbolism on the H-T-P

Earlier in this chapter, the chromatic drawings were discussed as if they were merely deeper-tapping pencil drawings. A consideration of the specific use of different colors now will be added to round out the total picture of the chromatic contribution.

Some subjects approach the crayons with the hesitant anxiety so characteristic of their customary everyday patterns of behavior. Their crayon lines are faint and uncertain with the color choices restricted to the safer black, brown, or blue. They reveal their personality constriction and interpersonal uncer-

---

[*]This last factor is the basis upon which the Eight-Card Redrawing Test is effective in providing successively deeper personality pictures.

tainties by not daring to open up with the bolder reds, oranges and yellows. This color usage reveals those subjects to be at the end of the personality continuum where over-cautiousness in exchanging pleasure or pain with others prevails.

Psychologically healthier subjects, by contrast, plunge more deeply into the chromatic task, confidently employ the warmer colors, utilize a firm, sure pressure on the crayon, and thus reflect their greater self-assurance in the emotional areas that colors represent.

On the other side of this healthier range in the continuum, are those subjects who employ an almost savage pressure (frequently bearing down so heavily that they snap the crayons) and a clash of inharmonious hot colors. Excessive lability, turbulent emotions and jarring inner needs, in a tension-laden setting, characterize the psychological state of the subjects in this group.

From a normative standpoint, the use of from three to five colors for the House represents the average range, as does two to three for the Tree, and three to five for the Person.

An inhibited use of color, below this average range, is exhibited by subjects unable to make warm, sharing personal relationships freely. The most "emotion-shy" subjects tend to use the crayon as if it were a pencil, employing no coloring-in whatsoever.

A more expansive use of color than the normative middle range, particularly if combined with an unconventional employment of colors, occurs most frequently in those manifesting an inability to exercise adequate control over their emotional impulses. One psychotic recently indicated his inadequate control, as well as his break with conventional reality, by drawing each of the eight windows in his House a different color.

Anastasi and Foley (1943) found that an extensive variety of color usage occurred almost exclusively among schizophrenic patients and manic-depressives in the manic phase. Both Lindberg (1938) and Eysenck (1947), among others, demonstrated a decrease of number of colors employed with increasing age in children, evidence in accord with the increase of emotional control with age. England (1952) differentiated problem children from normal children by the former's inappropriate use of color. Since the younger more uncontrolled child and the adult with lessened control (schizophrenics and manics) manifest a more expansive color usage, they supply support for the projective drawing hypothesis relating this type of color employment with inadequate control over emotionality.

John Payne (1948) offers an interesting and fruitful fourfold scheme for the classification of the color output on the H-T-P:

(a) "Empathetic intensity" is defined as color emphasis of a particular item, and is reported to occur in the drawings of normal, flexibly-adjusted subjects.

(b) "Tensional intensity" which refers to repeated reinforcement of a color by going back over it again and again, is found in the drawing productions of anxious subjects in the normal and neurotic ranges, particularly in anxiety states.

(c) "Clash intensity," an intensification of conventionally inharmonious color combinations, is evidence of a disturbance of a more profound degree, approaching and within the psychotic range. The schizophrenic patient, previously mentioned, who drew each of his eight windows a different color illustrates this classification. Manics also frequently exhibit "clash intensity."

(d) "Pressure intensity," refers to improperly modulated and excessively heavy pressure on the crayon. Payne finds this in the chromatic H-T-P's of mental defectives and organics. The present writer finds "pressure intensity" occurring also with two other groups of patients: aggressive "psychopaths" and paranoids.

In regard to the specific symbolic connotations of the individual colors, research in the area is in general agreement that the use of reds and yellows is a more spontaneous form of expression (Zimmerman and Garfinkel, 1942), than an emphasis on the blues or greens, which are more representative of controlled behavior (Alschuler and Hattwick 1943, 1947; Kadis, 1950).

Black and brown are more common to states of inhibition (Bieber and Herkimer, 1948), repression (Napoli, 1946), and possibly regression (Precker, 1950).

Brick (1944), in his study of 200 children between the ages of two and fifteen, found an overemphasis upon yellow to be significant as an expression of hostility and aggression. This finding may be related to the study of Griffiths (1935), in which yellow was found to be the preferred color at the earliest stage of a child's engaging in drawings. This may be viewed as consistent with Brick's finding, in that young childhood is the stage of the freest experience of rage and open release of hostility.

Buck (1948) has found purple to be the preferred color of paranoids and regards any considerable use of it as presumptive evidence of strong power-striving drives, usually paranoid-tinged. Whether the grandiose need of the paranoid taps the same associative stream which links purple with royalty is not presently known. The idea, even if highly speculative, is certainly engaging.

Summary

Empirical and experimental data have been presented which suggest that by the addition of the chromatic phase to the projective drawing task, the clinician is provided with an instrument which taps a deeper personality layer, and hence, when taken with the achromatic drawings, provides a richer and more accurate picture of the hierarchy of the patient's conflicts and defenses. A three-factor rationale, offered along with the empirical data, views the emotional impact of color, the childhood association with crayons, and the repetition of the drawing task as all working in the same direction to enable the chromatic drawings to penetrate deeper beneath the patient's defenses and bring the more basic personality levels to view.

There is a prevalent tendency to think of the "inner" man as the "real" man and the "outer" man as illusion or pretender. But the unconscious of a man represents a deeper domain, not a "truer" one. Though a man may not always be what he appears to be, what he appears to be is always a significant part of what he is. A man is the sum total of *all* his behavior.

Inhibited or expansive color usage has been related to the corresponding personality correlates. Overemphasis upon any of the eight colors has been discussed and the research correlating color preference with personality traits has been presented.

We might, then, conceptualize the relationship between the more popularly-used techniques in the projective battery as, among other things, *more or less tending* to tap relatively different "depths" or "levels" of personality with the MMPI at the top, the TAT extending below this, the Rorschach going farther down, and the House-Tree-Person (H-T-P) projective drawing descending still more deeply.

In drawings, deeper, more primary and less differentiated levels are tapped. Affect emanating from a picture someone is actively engaged in drawing reaches into him more deeply than does that shaped by language; and this because pictorial expression is more adequate to the earliest developmental stages. It tends, in a relative way, somewhat more to elicit expression from the child within the man.

Within the H-T-P, the Tree was found to tap deeper than the Person drawings by virtue of its representing a more elemental entity. Since it also is easier to attribute more conflictful or emotionally disturbing negative traits and attitudes to the drawn Tree than to the drawn Person—because the former is "less close to home" as a self-portrait—the deeper or more forbidden feelings can more readily be projected onto the Tree with less fear of revealing oneself and less need for ego-defensive maneuvers.

The bulk of this chapter addressed itself to demonstrating the recent innovation of a still deeper element of projective drawings: a chromatic phase in which a set of new drawings is then asked for from the patient, this time in crayon.

Figure 29 illustrates this conception, with the figure tapering as it goes from top to bottom to illustrate that while the graphic techniques tend to tap more deeply than do the verbal projective tools, they do not sample as broad a picture as do the Rorschach, TAT and MMPI. The wavy or peaked line between techniques is used to suggest their considerable overlap, particularly from patient to patient and as varyingly used in the hands of different clinicians. (The dotted line at the bottom of the figure is to indicate the space reserved for techniques and approaches yet to be devised.)

Empirical evidence accumulated thus far leads us to believe that on the H-T-P, a positive prognosis is suggested by either.

(A) The drawn Tree conveying a healthier impression than the drawn Person, or

(B) The crayon drawings indicating a better adjustment level than the pencil drawings, or

(C) The H-T-P representing a healtheir personality picture than the Rorschach.

Where such relationships occurred, a reactive maladjustment such as war neurosis, reactive depression, etc., in which latent positive resources were currently over-shadowed by the effects of an emotion upheaval, later proved to be the clinical diagnosis.

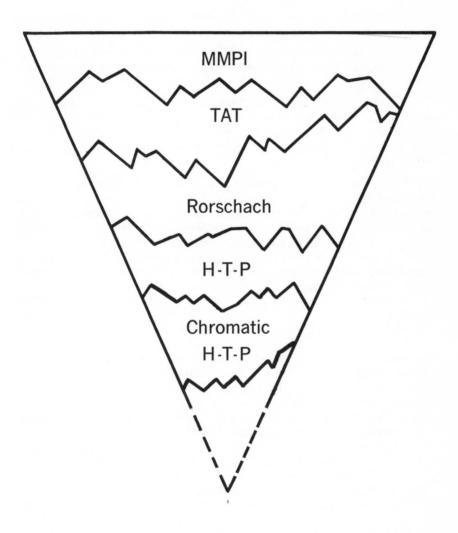

Figure 29

On the other hand, a negative prognosis is suggested by either:

(A) The chromatic set of drawings steeped in more psychopathology than the achromatic set, or

(B) The drawn Tree conveying a sicker impression than the drawn Person, or

(C) The H-T-P carrying negatively-toned feelings more prominently than the Rorschach.

Where such a relationship existed, later follow-up disclosed clinical diagnosis of incipient, latent, pre-, or pseudoneurotic schizophrenic or severe neurotic states.

Instances in which the House, Tree, and Person are all rife with psychopathology, or where achromatic and chromatic sets are both flavored with illness, or where H-T-P and Rorschach personality pictures are mutually flooded with pathology indicators have occurred only in cases carrying the gloomiest prognosis.

These relationships are hypothesized from empirical observations only. At the present time, the prognostic indicators have proven to possess a pragmatic usefulness. It is hoped that these clinical observations will stimulate research and the gathering of data by other psychologists, working in varied installations, in investigation of the presented empirically-derived prognostic hypothesis. A start is offered in the yield of the experimental following on the empirically-founded hypothesis and sub-hypothesis on the relationship between pencil and crayon drawings.

References

Alschuler, and Hattwick, W.: Easel painting as an index of personality in pre-school children. *Am. J. Orthopsychiat.,* 13:616-625.

—————————————— Painting and personality. Chicago, Univ. Chicago Press, I and II:590, 1947.

Anatasi, A., and Foley, J. P.: An analysis of spontaneous artistic productions by the abnormal. *J. Gen. Psychol.,* 28:297-313, 1943.

Bellak, L. Comments at Society of Projective Techniques Meeting, New York Psychiatric Institute, Jan. 15, 1953.

————— *The Thematic Apperception Test and the Children's Apperception Test in Clinical Use.* New York, Grune & Stratton, 1954.

Bieber, I., and Herkimer, J.: Art in psychotherapy. *Amer. J. Psychiat.,* 104:627-631,1948.

Brick, M.: The mental hygiene value of children's art work. *Amer. J. Ortho.,* 14:136-146, 1944.

Buck, J. N.: The H-T-P technique: A quantitative and qualitative scoring manual. *Clin. Psychol. Monogr.* 5:1-120, 1948.

————— Personal communication, Feb. 1953.

England, A. O.: Color preference and employment in children's drawings. *J. Child Psychiat.,* 2:343-349, 1952.

Eysenck, H. J.: *Dimensions of Personality*. London, Kegan Paul, 1947.

Griffiths, R.: *A Study of Imagination in Early Childhood*. London, Kegan Paul, Trench, Trubner & Co., 1935.

Hammer, E. F.: The role of the H-T-P in the prognostic battery. *J. Clin. Psychol.,* 9:371-374.

_____ Guide to qualitative research with the H-T-P. *J. Gen. Psychol.,* 1954, 51, 41-60.

Hanfmann, Eugenia, & Getzels, J. W.: Studies of the sentence completion test. *J. Proj. Tech.,* 1953, 17, 280-294.

Kadis, A.: Fingerpainting as a projective technique. In Abt, L., and Bellak, L.: *Projective Psychology*. New York, Knopf, 403-431, 1950.

Klopfer, B., Ainsworth, M. D., Klopfer, W. G., and Holt, R. R.: Developments in the Rorschach Technique. In Vol. I, *Technique and Theory*. New York, World Bk. Co., 1954.

Lindberg, B. J.: Experimental studies of colour and non-colour attitudes in school children and adults. *Acto. Psychiat. Neurol.,* 16:1938.

Murray, H. A.: *Explorations in Personality*. New York, Oxford Univ. Press, 1938.

Napoli, P.: Fingerpainting and personality diagnosis. *Genet. Psychol. Monogr.,* 34:129-231, 1946.

Payne, J. J.: Comments of the analysis of chromatic drawings. In Buck, J. N.: The H-T-P techniques: A quantitative and qualitative scoring manual. *Clin. Psychol. Monogr.,* 5:1-120, 1948.

Piotrowski, Z. A.: Sexual crime, alcohol, and the Rorschach test. *Psychiat. Quart. Supp.,* 56:248-260, 1952.

Precker, K.: Painting and drawing in personality assessment. *J. Proj. Rech., 14:262-286, 1950.*

Rapaport, D.: *Diagnostic Psychological Testing*. Chicago, Year Bk. Co., I and II: 1946.

Schafer, R.: *Psychoanalytic Interpretation in Rorschach Testing*. New York, Grune & Stratton, 1954.

Stern, M.: Free painting as an auxiliary technique in psychoanalysis. In G. Bychowski and J. Despert (Eds.) *Specialized Techniques in Psychotherapy*. New York: Basic Books, 1952, Pp. 65-83.

Symonds, P.: Comments at Society of Projective Techniques Meeting, New York, Psychiatric Institute, Jan. 15, 1953.

Wyatt, F.: In J. Bell (Ed.) The case of Gregor: Interpretation of test data. *J. Proj. Tech.,* 1949, 13, 155-205.

Zimmerman, J. and Garfinkel, L.: Preliminary study of the art productions of the adult psychotic. *Psychiat. Quart.,* 16:313-318, 1942.

Zucker, L.: A case of obesity: Projective techniques before and after treatments. *J. Proj. Tech.,* 1948, 12, 202-215.

Verlin Spencer received his Bachelor's Degree from Colorado State College and his Master's Degree from Stanford University, then completed further graduate work at the University of Southern California.

He became interested in progressive education and was the principal of a junior high school at the time of his crime.

After his confinement in San Quentin, California, Mr. Spencer worked for the Chief Psychiatrist who requested him to organize a psychology department. Mr. Spencer did so and functioned as an inmate psychologist for the following thirteen years. Many nationally known psychiatrists and psychologists became interested in Mr. Spencer's work and assisted him by personal visits or through correspondence.

Over the years, first in San Quentin, and later at Soledad and Vacaville, California, Mr. Spencer completed a number of research studies, some of which are listed below. (Until recently, prisoners in California were not permitted to submit professional articles for publication extra-murally).

"A Rorschach study of aggression in murderers and forgers" was a report to the psychiatric clinic at San Quentin Prison in 1952. "A study of the color reactions of normals and schizophrenics" was another report in 1952 to this psychiatric clinic. "A quest for the missing dimension in the psychopathic personality: as the psychopathic personality derives his I.Q. on the Wechsler-Bellevue Intelligence Scale, is the scatter pattern of his subtests more like the scatter pattern of the schizophrenic or the mental defective?" was another report in 1953. "Drug addiction can be cured" was reported to the annual district conference on alcoholism and drug addiction, Vacaville, the California Medical Facility, 1956. "Emotional help for the delinquent; what kind does he want? From whom does he want it? Why?" was reported to the correctional counseling services, Soledad, California Correctional Training Facility, 1962.

In collaboration with Dr. W.C. Keating and Dr. T.L. Clanon, Mr. Spencer had the following four articles published by the prison in pamphlet form: "A quick look at correctional counseling for the newly employed correctional officer." (Vacaville) 1964; "Anxiety, the most compelling force in our era: a neo-Freudian point of view," (Vacaville) 1965; "The gambler," (Vacaville); "Who goes to school in the California Medical Facility?" (Vacaville) 1965.

Chapter 2

The Use of Watercolors to Increase Chromatic H-T-P Productivity[1]

Verlin Spencer, M.A.

Mr. Spencer's ingenious extension of the graphic phase of the H-T-P should provide a welcome and fascinating addition to the armamentarium of techniques used by psychologists engaged in 1) group-testing in school settings, hospitals, clinics, criminal institutions, or industry; (2) projective technique research into deeper domains; (3) cross-cultural investigations; and (4) the clinical examination of subjects who cannot, or will not, verbalize.

Soon after John N. Buck devised the H-T-P he encouraged the writer to experiment with a variety of chromatic drawing H-T-P and a three-dimensional H-T-P using modeling clay. As the experimentation progressed, it seemed that a combination of the crayon H-T-P and the watercolor H-T-P produced more diagnostic and prognostic material than either one alone. A lack of time precluded pursuing the three-dimensional H-T-P to fruitful conclusions. However, the combination of crayon and watercolor H-T-P work continued with promising results. One study is reported here.

Buck (1948, 1964), Hammer (1958) and other H-T-P workers have established reasonably well that the chromatic H-T-P tends to cut through the defenses to reach the deeper levels of the personality. When it is used with the achro-

---

[1] The writer is especially indebted to William C. Keating, Jr., M.D., Superintendent, California Medical Facility, Vacaville, California, who made it possible for the writer, a life-term prisoner, to conduct the study on which this report is based. Preparing this report provided a much needed relief from institutional monotony and was a means of realizing a degree of fulfillment through genuine achievement.

matic H-T-P, much dynamic material (most of it symbolic) will be produced. From this material, the examiner can construct a crude hierarchy of the subject's personality strengths and weaknesses.

After considerable experimentation with crayons for a chromatic H-T-P, the writer felt that the use of crayons suffered from some of the limitations and restrictions previously thought to be peculiar to the achromatic lead pencil drawings. Long periods of training and practice have provided most people in our culture with a relatively high degree of control over the pencil and pencil-like objects. Consequently, this control can be a barrier to the expression of the personality's strivings and needs, particulary those of a lower amplitude. It follows then that a drawing medium around which learning, experience, and cultural impact had not erected inhibitory walls would be useful.

A good example of such a device is the brush-watercolor combination, since the average person in the American culture is not trained or experienced in the use of the brush and watercolors.[2] Also because of its flexibility and sensitivity, the brush-watercolor combination permits a greater variety of line, hue, and saturation to be used than the crayons do. These features qualify it for revealing some of the more subtle changes in personality adjustments. It is possible that, on the one hand, it identifies and magnifies obscure but important clues of underlying morbidity and, on the other hand, brings to view less obvious traces of potentials making for ego strength. In brief, the watercolor H-T-P in combination with the crayon H-T-P appears to have qualities which extend considerably the range of the achromatic H-T-P findings.

Hypothesis

The achromatic H-T-P combined with the crayon H-T-P and the water-color H-T-P, as the writer had been using it, seemed to be proving its usefulness in the clinical situation, but the writer felt that before he reported this formally, its efficacy should ˅be tested more objectively. The hypothesis is: "When both crayons and watercolors are used in series for the chromatic H-T-P, more diagnostic and prognostic material is obtained than when either is used alone." To test this hypothesis, the writer administered the achromatic H-T-P, the crayon H-T-P, and the watercolor H-T-P to a representative sample of prisoners under conditions and with materials that were standard for their prison.

Subjects

A random sample was obtained by selecting for testing the first man in each major crime category to enter the Vacaville Reception and Guidance Center each week. Each subject was interviewed before testing and asked to volunteer to make some pictures for the research department; he was told that making the pictures had nothing to do with determining his prison program or making recommendations about him to the parole board. His pictures would

---

[2] In China and other areas where people are trained to use a brush in much the same way that Americans use a pencil, a brush-watercolor combination might suffer from some of the limitations attributed to the pencil and pencil-like objects. Fortunately, this did not apply in the experimental situation under which this study was conducted.

be used only for research purposes. Fourteen men refused and 148 men consented. All subjects had been sent to the Reception and Guidance Center for processing and assignment to the different prisons in California.

No subject had used crayons or watercolors since his elementary school days. One had worked about 6 months with a commercial artist, and after imprisonment had painted with oils as a hobby (Case#5): and another had done some sign painting (Case #3). All the other subjects had had no formal training in art after leaving elementary school.

Nineteen of the subjects were transferred to the California Medical Facility for group psychotherapy and participated in such therapy while this study was in progress. The Reception and Guidance Center and the California Medical Facility are in different wings of the same prison. The crimes which the subjects had committed, their mean age, mean I.Q., educational attainment level, and ethnic group are presented in Tables II, III, IV.

TABLE II
Crimes Represented

Crime	Number	Percentage
Murder	22	14.8
Robbery	21	14.2
Burglary	21	14.2
Rape	26	17.5
Forgery	24	16.3
Narcotics	20	13.5
Assault with deadly weapon	8	5.4
Arson	6	4.1
Total	148	100.0

TABLE III
Age, I.Q., and Grade Level

	Range	Mean	SD	SE
Age	19-55	32.5	9.9	.81
I.Q.	85-130	107.7	13.0	1.06
Grade level	7-16	10.7	2.3	.18

TABLE IV
Ethnic Group

Ethnic Group	Number	Percentage
American White	105	71.0
American Mexican	23	15.5
American Negro	20	13.5
Total	148	100.0

Administration Procedure

Since the number of days available for testing was limited, it was necessary to test four men at a time. A medium-sized table was placed in each of the
four corners of the 24-foot by 24-foot testing room, and each man was seated
at a table in such a way that he could not see the other subjects. Then the three
H-T-P series were administered on an individual basis.

First each subject was provided with a number 2 lead pencil with an eraser
and a sheet of 8½-inch by 11-inch drawing paper.[3] He was then asked to draw
as good a House as he could. The paper was placed with the horizontal axis
the greater for this drawing. (The same position was presented when the subject drew a House with crayons and when he painted a House with watercolors). The paper always was placed with the vertical axis the greater for all
drawings of the Tree and the Person.

When a subject had completed the achromatic drawings, the pencil and the
drawings were removed; he was given a sheet of 8½-inch by 11-inch drawing
paper and a set of Jumbo Crayola Crayons[4] in 8 colors (black, blue, purple,
brown, red, orange, yellow, and green) and he was then told to use the crayons
to draw a House. If he asked whether or not he should draw the *same* House
that he had drawn before, he was told to draw it in any way that he liked but he
should draw as good a House as he could. The same procedure was followed for
the Tree and the Person.

As soon as the subject completed the crayon drawings, the crayons and the
last drawing were removed; and the subject was given a box of watercolors[5]
containing eight colors: black, blue, purple, brown, orange, red, yellow, and
green. He was also given a number 3 round brush, a number 7 round brush,
three paper towels with which to clean brushes if necessary, a small-flat water
container, and a sheet of 8½-inch by 11-inch drawing paper. The instructions
were to paint a House. When the House was completed, it was removed and he
was asked to paint a Tree. Upon completion of the Tree, he was asked to paint
a Person. If the subject asked about painting the *same* House, Tree or Person
which he had drawn before, he was told to proceed in the way he liked, but to
do as well as he could.

Time limits were not set. Each subject completed his drawing or painting in
his own time and to his own satisfaction. If he asked how he should draw or
paint, what kind of House, Tree or Person, or if his Person should be the whole
Person, he was told again to proceed in any way he chose, but to do as well as
he could.

The three phases of the test, achromatic, crayon, and watercolor were
completed at one sitting. The matter of rest periods was not mentioned, and

---

[3] The size of the paper was determined by departmental regulations.

[4] Jumbo Crayola Crayons, manufactured by Binney and Smith, New York, N.Y., are
sold by Woolworth Stores. It was assumed that the large size of the crayon would enhance
its associative value and more easily elicit childhood adjustment levels. No study has been
made by the writer of the difference between H-T-P materials brought out by the standard
size and the large size crayons.

[5] The watercolors used in this study are manufactured by M. Grumbacher, New
York, N.Y., and are sold by Woolworth Stores.

no one asked to rest or complained of fatigue. The subjects were permitted to smoke during the test and between the different test phases. Post-Drawing Interrogations were not made because of the lack of time.

Case Studies

The following cases are presented to illustrate how a chromatic H-T-P comprised first of crayons and then of watercolors can be used to produce more material than the achromatic-chromatic H-T-P, or any one of the 3 H-T-Ps by itself.

Case 1

The first case is a white, 22-year-old Protestant pedophile with an I.Q. of 103 and a seventh grade education. He was imprisoned for molesting girls under 12 years of age. Since he has been in prison, he has periodically engaged in homosexual activities of the "flip-flop" variety. He has been disciplined several times for minor infractions of the prison's rules.

There was no doubt clinically as to whether or not this subject's mildly euphoric condition with moderately manic overtones had serious underlying depressive features.

His manner of expanding upon his drawings and paintings seems to reflect some of his manifest manic qualities. The sun which he placed in the sky when he drew the achromatic and the crayon Houses, the warm colors which he used in drawing his crayon House (red and orange), and the bright flowers and path that lead to the doors of the achromatic and crayon Houses apparently represent his mild euphoria.

However, his watercolor House and watercolor Tree seemed to reveal rather marked feelings of depression: the watercolor House became dark, gloomy, and prison-like; its door was the barred door of a prison cell. There was no sun in the sky; no bright, gay flowers were painted; and the lawn became dank, swamp-like and uninviting. Similarily, the watercolor Tree became heavy, dark, and gross.

The odd and bizarre root and the inadequate branch structure of the achromatic Tree and the crayon Tree, the morbid quality of the watercolor Person, and his odd and incomplete achromatic Person with the over-emphasized ear suggest schizoid features with a paranoid coloring. That he suffers from painful, frightening fantasies which he struggles to control can be inferred from the abrupt flattening of the heavy foliage on his achromatic and crayon Trees.

The way in which he sees his father and mother is evidenced by his treatment of the Tree which he placed near each of his Houses. The relatively large Tree at the left or feminine side of the achromatic House suggests that he saw the mother as the dominant person in the home. In contrast, the crayon House has a small Tree on the right or masculine side with very little foliage. The watercolor House has a Tree on the right or masculine side which looks like a charred stump. The charred stump suggests a "burned out," impotent man, and this could be his view of his father.

Chimneys which are emphasized in the H-T-P are usually phallic signs; this is particularly true in this H-T-P protocol. The type of emphasis used here seems to reveal the subject's deep concern about the meaning and use of his sexual equipment. His identification difficulties and his tendency to play the sexual

Fig. 30, Case I (above)

Fig. 31, Case I (below)

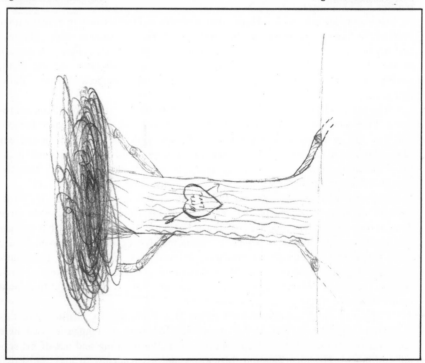

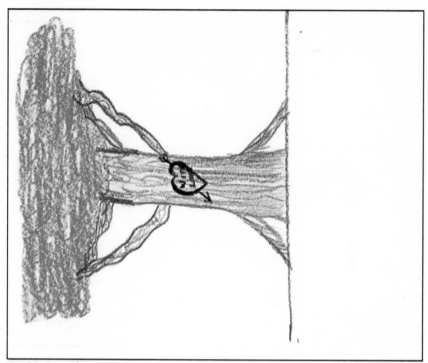

Fig. 32, Case I (above)

Fig. 33, Case I (below)

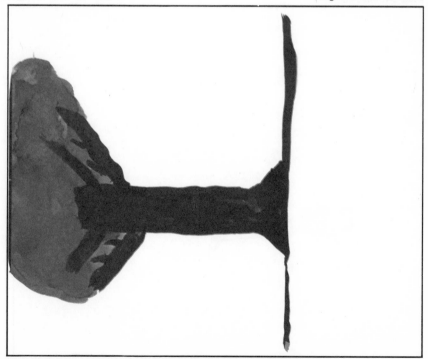

Fig. 34, Case I (above)　　　　　　　　　　　　Fig. 35, Case I (below)

role first of a woman and then of a man (flip-flop) is symbolized by the direction of the arrow[*] in the heart on the trunk of the achromatic Tree and the crayon Tree. On the achromatic Tree the arrow in the heart points to the right seeming to indicate his desire to love and be loved "like a man." The the arrow in the heart on the crayon Tree points to the left to signify his desire to offer and receive love "like a woman."

The story of his sexual vacillation is continued in his drawings and painting of a Person. When he drew the achromatic Person, he had trouble with the male's body, drawing the head only and displacing the signs of masculinity to the hair and the nose. Later when he was asked to draw a man with a body, he claimed that he could not do it, and in place of a complete mature male, he drew an odd-shaped, six-fingered, pre-genital boy.

For his crayon Person he drew a front view of a nude woman, and his watercolor Person was a front view of a woman without arms and legs. Apparently he is saying symbolically that sexually he tries to be a man but cannot, so he tries to be a woman. But neither can he be a complete woman. Rather he is a woman who lacks important anatomical features of the female. He appears to be deeply frustrated, to be caught on the horns of his sexual dilemma.

His struggle to contain his fantasies is indicated by the type of foliage that he draws on the achromatic and crayon Trees. However, the foliage on the watercolor Tree extends beyond the top of the page, suggesting that at times he succumbs to his fantasies. This regression is reflected to some extent by the gross,

Fig. 36, Case I

[*] Also, and more directly, by: (1) the penis-like-root (right) tentatively penetrating a gut-like tube, and (2) the intestine-like tubular root (left). Eds.

Fig. 37, Case I (above)

Fig. 38, Case I (below)

Fig. 39, Case I

crude, concrete qualities of the watercolor Tree and the absence of the heart and arrow that he drew on the trunks of his other Trees.

Case II

This subject is a single, 31-year-old, white, Protestant male, a surgical technician with a 12th grade education. He has an I.Q. of 115. He has been imprisoned three times for burglary. He claims to be an overt, aggressive homosexual who assumes the role of "jocker." He has had no serious diseases or injuries; there is no history of alcoholism, but he has used marijuana.

Reports from his supervisors seemed to indicate that he was suffering to some extent from delusions of persecution and ideas of reference. Clinically, he manifested no frank morbid symptoms.

In this case, the extension of the range of the H-T-P through the use of crayons and watercolors supplied additional clues to the underlying personality dynamics and made it possible to affirm the impression of the prison wing personnel, and to contradict certain statements made by the subject regarding his sexual role.

His achromatic H-T-P suggests that probably he is not the aggressive, "jocker" type of homosexual which he professes to be; instead he appears to be a drawn, slightly schizoid, anxiously insecure feminine type who is having difficulty in making satisfactory contacts with those about him. These inferences are drawn from the sketchy line quality of his drawings, the absence of a firm foundation and ground line for the House, the position of the House on the left side of the page, the transparency effect and distortion in parts of the House, the absence of a chimney and path, the poorly based Tree which has no branches in its thin diffuse foliage, and the female figure whose hands and feet are obscured. The relatively large size of the female figure compared to the size of the

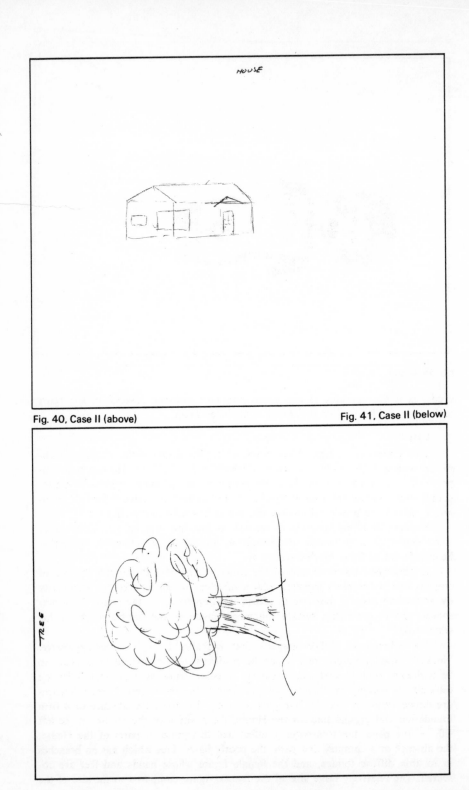

Fig. 40, Case II (above)   Fig. 41, Case II (below)

Fig. 42, Case II

Tree and the House faintly hints at the possibility of grandiose features. The belt emphasizes his sexual conflict. Also there is more than a suggestion that his view of women is highly ambivalent: he envies their power (over him) and yet bitterly resents it.

The crayon H-T-P extends these findings. For instance, the crayon House has a drastic tilt which appears to indicate a catastrophic loss of psychic equilibrium at an earlier age. The House tilts toward the left and the path approaches the House from the left suggesting that the narcissistic hurt has propelled him towards feminine identification.

The crayon Tree implies strongly that the narcissistic hurt was castrative in nature. As a result the subject has identified with the mother and assumed a passive-receptive attitude towards the father. The effects of the impact of the trauma are dramatically symbolized by the splintering and breaking off of the upper trunk, isolating it from the rest of the Tree and having it assume a horizontal, feminine position on the left or distaff side of the page. The broken part, however, is by no means a dead thing. Its bright yellow and green foliage suggests that this part, usually symbolizing the manner in which contact is made with the environment, is colorfully alive. He has isolated or broken off this part of his "self" and placed it in a feminine position.

It is possible that this dynamism of isolation is symbolized also in his achromatic and crayon drawings of a Person. He isolated these female figures by depriving them of hands and feet. Apparently the same theme is continued in the lack of branches in the foliage. The absence of branches parallels the absence of arms and legs from the females, but at a deeper level. None of his Houses has a chimney. By refusing to acknowledge this phallic sign he more completely isolates and encapsulates his feminine image.

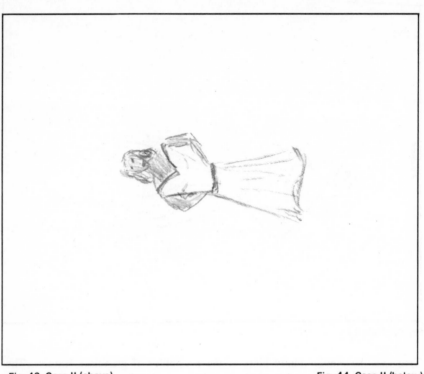

Fig. 43, Case II (above)   Fig. 44, Case II (below)

Fig. 45, Case II (above)   Fig. 46, Case II (below)

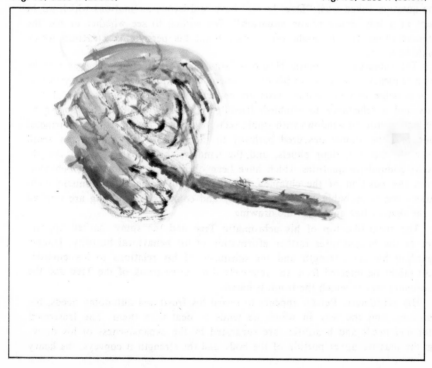

His crayon Person is, for the most part, a facsimile of his achromatic Person. However, he enlivened his crayon Person with blue, orange, yellow, red, brown, and black colors. This might mean that at the level to which he has regressed, he finds the feminine role to be more colorful, attractive and appealing.

The increase in the size of his watercolor figures supports earlier hints at underlying grandiose and megalomanic qualities.

The crotch-like spatial relationship of the two wings of the watercolor House is most unusual and offers further evidence of his sexual preoccupation. The segmentalization of the wings suggests an impending splitting of intellect and affect. Narcissistic tendencies are implied by the picture-windows which almost directly face each other. Although this House at first glance seems to be larger than the achromatic and the crayon Houses, closer inspection reveals that it, too, is a 2-room structure only.

The watercolor House offers confirmation of the already strong suspicion that basically this subject is predominantly feminine.

The huge eye tends to affirm most convincingly the reports from the ward personnel that at times the subject seems to have delusions of persecution and ideas of reference.

Case III

This organically healthy, white, 40-year-old, divorced, Protestant male who was the father of 5 children had been a soldier. He had killed a man in a street fight and was being considered for transfer to a minimum security institution. The question asked was, "Does he still have murderous inclinations which might erupt in a less secure prison situation?" We wished to see whether or not the extended-range H-T-P might offer clues about his personality structure which would be helpful.

The subject's achromatic House is large for the space and suggests that he has a tendency to respond to his environment with expansiveness and aggression. It is possible that his status needs are reflected also. Other indications of hostility and a reluctance to establish friendly relations with others are shown by the high, shuttered windows with small, sectioned panes, the closed, heavy-paneled door, and the almost obscured pathway to the door. In his tendency to detail the roof, chimney, door panels, and the windows, he reveals some of the obsessive-compulsive qualities which have been observed in his manifest behavior. From the position of the chimney, the presence of some exhibitionistic inclinations seems probable, and some anxiety and compulsive doubting are implied by the sketchy line quality of the drawing.

The spear-like top of his achromatic Tree and the spiny, barbed appearance of the foliage offer further affirmation of his behavioral hostility. Doubts regarding his ego strength and the adequacy of his relations to his environment might be inferred from the relatively diminutive trunk of the Tree and the inadequate way in which the trunk is based.

His achromatic Person appears to reveal his frustrated autonomy needs, his hostilities, and the way in which he tends to deal with them. The frustrated autonomy needs and hostilities are suggested by the expansiveness of his drawing: the massive upper portion of the body and the strength it conveys, the heavy head of hair, and the contempt expressed by the flared nostrils and the mouth. To curb and control his aggressive inclinations he tends to withdraw somewhat and assume a reserved and studied attitude towards those who populate his environment. This is symbolized by the profile facing the right side of the page. He takes out more insurance against his hostility and destructive tendencies by depriving his Person of legs. Under such conditions it would be impossible to charge out into his milieu to kill and subsequently be killed or imprisoned. This defensive system appears to be elaborated and extended by the pen and the glasses, and the emphasis which he gives to the ear. Apparently they represent socially acceptable means of dealing with disputes, i.e., by "seeing and hearing things more clearly and distinctly," and by writing pleas or writs to the proper authorities rather than resorting to force. In fact, this man had recently prepared a writ in at attempt to gain his freedom.

His crayon House is a child's fairy-land castle, and implies that he has strong needs to regress to the sheltered position of childhood. From his drawing this position is well sheltered—even well fortified. Its occupants are sealed off from the world by high, massive, impenetrable walls, tiny windows far up on the walls through which one may see out but no one could possibly see in. A heavy, solid door defies entry. The sharp spires lend a defiant quality to his withdrawal. It seems that he distrusted certain people with a vengeance. From the warm red, orange, yellow, and soft brown colors which he used to decorate this castle one might infer that he considered his fairyland castle a most pleasant place, perhaps almost as desirable as his mother's womb.

The crayon Tree speaks for itself. Highly decorated, it must be admired by all who view it. Well-potted, it need not worry about adequate satisfaction of its so-called baser needs. Gifts are scattered at its feet: as they lie there, they constitute a pseudo-tribute to the Tree; and when they are collected, the Tree can derive satisfaction as a surrogate giver.

He appears to stress symbolically his oral dependency needs in his crayon Person. Evidently the princess (his crayon Person) in the fairyland castle is his mother from whom he earnestly sought emotional satisfactions that she either could not or would not deliver. These inferences are based on the manner in which he emphasized the breasts (the source of supply for his oral dependency needs), then failed to give her the hands and feet which she needed to deliver the satisfaction. Without hands she cannot punish him physically (neither can she fondle him); without feet she cannot leave him (neither can she approach him). He greatly needs to render a female figure powerless.

Different aspects of his personality are tapped by the watercolors. His watercolor House suggests how he is when the "Sturm and Drang" subsides.[7] It is a quiet House. Conflicting forces are not excessively busy in it. It has a plain, undetailed, soft green roof with a gentle slope which is in marked contrast to the sharply pointed red spires of the castle and the excessively detailed roof of the achromatic House. His mind apparently has moments during which it is not crowded with obsessive ideas and feelings of hostility.

---

[7] And the subject has become temporarily drained emotionally by the cathartic effect of drawing the achromatic and crayon-chromatic H-T-Ps. Eds.

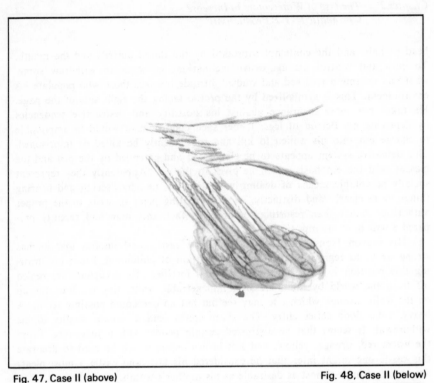

Fig. 47, Case II (above)

Fig. 48, Case II (below)

Fig. 49, Case III (above)   Fig. 50, Case III (below)

Merry X·mas!

Fig. 51, Case III (above)   Fig. 52, Case III (below)

In less stressful periods he could be a less pretentious and more congenial person. These potentials are suggested by the positioning of his comparatively plain watercolor House more to the right side of the page, a well delineated pathway to an open front door, and windows which are low enought to permit one to see into the House as well as out of it.

These inclinations are mirrored also in his watercolor Tree. The contour of the foliage has soft, round curves which present a striking contrast to the sharply pointed tops and spiny barbs of the foliage of his achromatic and crayon Trees. Again it appears to be indicated that even though the subject hates with a vengeance and has killed, he still has the capacity to be considerate and congenial. While the trunk of the watercolor Tree is not usually well delineated, based or rooted, it is a slight improvement over the trunk of the achromatic Tree which gives the impression of being suspended. The crayon Tree is not rooted or based firmly in the ground. It is set in a box, given artificial support, and is neither firmly based nor securely rooted in its natural environment.

The watercolor drawings, however, reveal more than this subject's more deeply repressed tender feelings. The watercolor Person shows with dramatic impact that the subject still ruminates about killing and being killed. There can scarcely be any other interpretation of the meaning of the death's head that he produced so dramatically.

Fig. 53, Case III

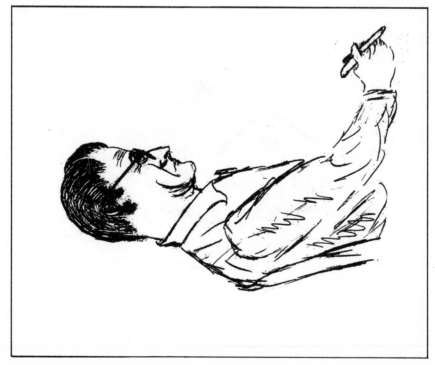

Fig. 54, Case III (above)   Fig. 55, Case III (below)

Fig. 56, Case III (above)   Fig. 57, Case III (below)

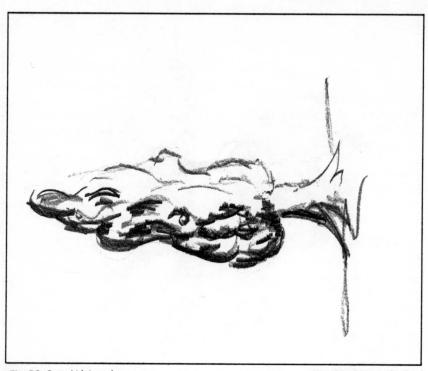

Fig. 58, Case V (above)

Fig. 59, Case IV (below)

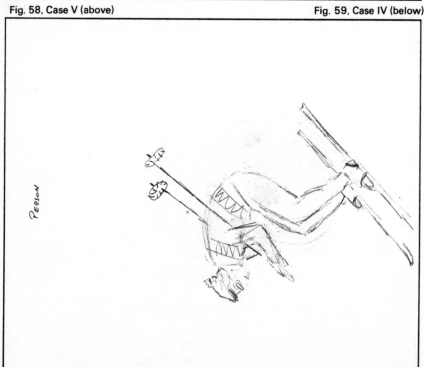

Case IV

This subject is a prison "bonarue" who had much to say about the problems of others in group psychotherapy, but adroitly skirted around his own
problems. When he was confronted with this, he became highly indignant and
stoutly and belligerently declared that he was saying all that there was to say.
His strong resistance led to considerable conjecture about the nature of his
underlying conflicts.

He is a 26-year-old, bright normal, civil service clerk with an 11th grade
education who never had been in trouble with the "law" before his conviction
for rape. He is referred to as a "bonarue" because of the unusual neatness of
his clothing and his person, and the meticulous, orderly way in which he carries
on his affairs both in work and at play.

The expansive, highly detailed achromatic House and Tree are splendid
portraits of his manifest aggressive and obsessive-compulsive defensive system.
Certain clues to some of his conflicts which probably made this defensive system necessary appear to be reflected in his achromatic Person.

The achromatic Person suggests that some possibility of "auxiliary regression" is present. The action in which he is involved is a downward plunge
to the left side of the page, much like a hasty retreat to a less mature level. Perhaps he is fleeing toward the relative safety of the preoedipal stage in which he
did not have to make painful decisions about his sexual roles. Note that the phallic
signs are tucked away: this could mean that he does not anticipate using them
soon.

Fig. 60, Case V

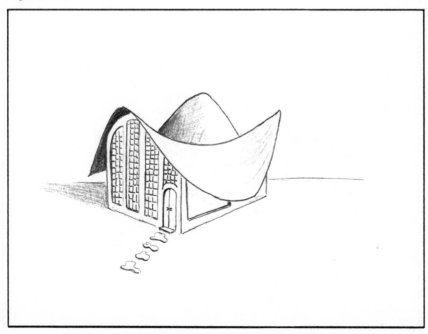

Fig. 61, Case IV (above)

Fig. 62, Case IV (below)

Fig. 63, Case IV (above)

Fig. 64, Case IV (below)

These phalli are sharp and connote a symbol of merged aggression and sexuality which reminds one of the offense for which he is incarcerated. His obsession with sexual ideas is also well expressed symbolically by the highly detailed roof and the excessively detailed chimney of his achromatic House.

His crayon H-T-P reveals more facets of his personality. His crayon House which has been reduced considerably in size, does not have the excessive detailing of the achromatic House, has but one small window, and a door to which there is no path and through which a dark, gloomy interior is seen. Black and brown crayons were used, suggesting the presence of an underlying depression.

It is possible that his vacillation between masculinity and femininity is hinted in the way in which he moved from the more rounded, feminine-like contours of his achromatic Tree to the more, angular, pseudo-masculine shape of the relatively fragile crayon Tree, which with its bright light may relate to his act of rape, the light on the Tree reflecting the demonstative element associated with "force" and his efforts to attain true masculinity.

The large, powerful, dominating female figure portrayed by his crayon Person seems to represent his mother who divorced his father when the subject was six years old. Since that time she has been both mother and father to him. He turns to her for advice and counsel. She is in part the destination toward which he feels he must rush for reassurance, relief, and desperately needed emotional supplies.

The rape for which he was imprisoned may have been a frantic last-ditch attempt to stay this retreat towards protective femininity, a kind of drastic last resort to salvage his manhood.

His watercolor H-T-P seems to extend and elaborate some of the above clues. For instance, the watercolor House, similar to a deserted House in a ghost town, takes over where the crayon House leaves off to tell how extreme his feelings of emptiness, desolation and abandonment are.

The watercolor Tree offers further evidence of his indecisiveness, obsessive-compulsive doubting, and the phenomenon of isolation peculiar to the obsessive-compulsive syndrome. These dynamisms are reflected in the fragmented disarrangement of the branches and the manner in which they are isolated from the trunk. The branches of the Tree symbolize the means by which an individual contacts his environment or reaches out to others. In this Tree, the branches convey the impression that the subject is deeply confused as to how or where to reach out to those about him.

When the crayon Tree and the watercolor Tree are considered in sequence, there is an indication that beneath the inadequate compensatory demonstrative masculinity implied by the crayon Tree, there are powerful conflicting feminine elements suggested by the more rounded contours of the foliage of the watercolor Tree and its fragmented, multi-directional branch structure.

Denial and isolation again appear to be manifested in the H-T-P protocol of this obsessive-compulsive individual as he offers a female head only for his watercolor Person. With the crayons he easily drew a broad-shouldered, forthright, dominating older female, but he could not deal with the body of a dependent, highly feminine young woman. Unadulterated femity is something with which he cannot cope. Evidently, a major conflict exists between his needs

Fig. 65, Case IV (above)

Fig. 66, Case IV (below)

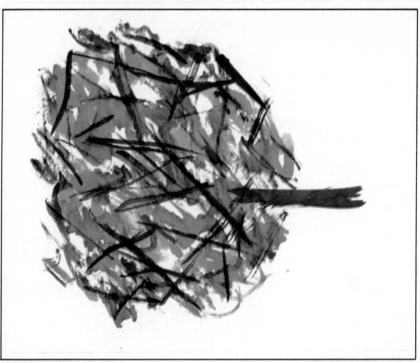

Fig. 67, Case IV (above)

Fig. 68, Case IV (below)

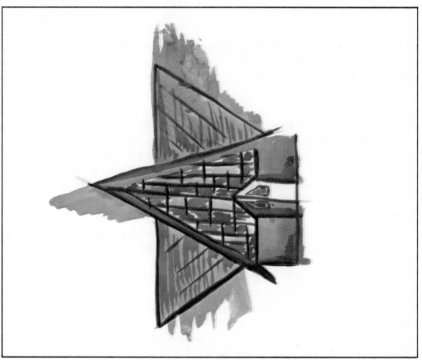

Fig. 69, Case V

Fig. 70, Case V (below)

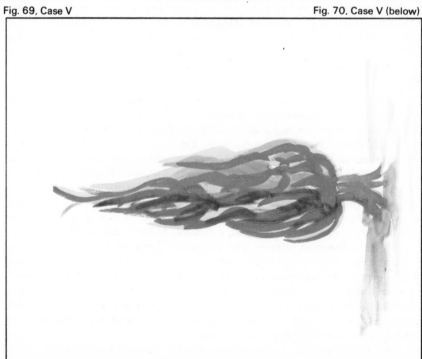

for a strong protective mother and a dependent receptive lover. He tried to resolve this dilemma by resorting to rape; an abortive declaration of independence and masculinity that failed miserably.

Case V

This subject is a white, 36-year-old, once married, once-divorced electrician with a high school education, who has been chronically addicted to heroin for the last 15 years. He has served two prison sentences for selling and using heroin. While he is in prison he works as a clerk and paints in oils as a hobby. There is no record of serious diseases or injuries. His experiences with traditional western-culture religions have been disappointing and he is now interested in Yoga and Buddhism.

His Houses seem to symbolize superego strivings. He offers an achromatic Buddhist temple, a crayon prison cell House, and a water color Protestant church of modern design. The architecture of the achromatic Buddhist temple has soft, rounded curves and suggests a structure related to the *anima,* the more feminine aspect of his superego. On the other hand, the watercolor church with its sharp points and acute angles apparently has to do with the *animus,* his superego's masculine characteristics.

Evidentally the *anima* is more tolerant, more accommodating and more effective than the *animus.* These qualities are suggested by the breast-like curves, the pathway leading to the door, the neat, well-defined form quality, and the solid appearance of the Buddhist temple. It is rather like an adequate mother who can tolerate and accommodate his archaic oral demands. The left sides of the roof, windows, door, and the temple as a whole are heavily shaded, suggesting that he has guilt feelings and anxiety regarding his regressive oral transgressions.

It may be assumed that his crayon prison is related to expiation and atonement for his oral transgressions. It seems that the oral indulgences condoned by the feminine component of his superego are condemned by its masculine counterpart. His subsequent guilt and anxiety are hinted at by the shading in the lee of the achromatic temple. However, the crayon prison has some very unusual qualities. It is a sun-lit, open-front cell House. The open front almost amounts to a welcome sign, and the bright sun-lit interior is not the atmosphere usually associated with mortification. It is possible that unconsciously he looks favorably upon the place which relieves him of his guilt-laden burden at the same time that it caters to his dependency needs, a dynamic factor in drug addicts.

In his achromatic, crayon, and watercolor Trees he presents a strikingly consistent picture of a highly egocentric, sensuous, pseudo-masculine individual who, whenever he can, refuses to interact with his environment. The impression of movement from the ground to the sky, i.e., from reality to unreality, is striking and unusual. He seems consumed in the flames of his emotional drives. It might be concluded that the rigid fixity of his concept of the basic self, reflected in all three Trees, is an unfavorable prognostic sign.

In the achromatic, crayon, and watercolor Persons he elaborates on the course that his use of heroin follows. The achromatic Person reveals how he justifies and rationalizes his addiction at the conscious level, putting on an act with which he tries to fool himself and others. He claims that heroin increases his ability to think, extends the range of his meditations, and releases his creativity.

For his crayon Person he used yellow, orange, and red to draw a flaming head to symbolize the "flash" or the "pop" which he experiences during the first moments of his "fix." Then, it seems he used the watercolors to depict his post-elation depression. During these depressions he realizes that he is a hollow shell of a man with false goals and fictitious motivations. He seems to realize that his course is fruitless and futile, and that he cannot travel the route of "flash" and "float" to fulfillment.

Summary

In each of the cases presented, the subject used watercolors to paint Houses, Trees, and Persons, most of which were different from those drawn with the crayons or the lead pencil. This provided more interpretive material and seemed to affirm the working hypothesis of the writer that "more H-T-P diagnostic and prognostic material is obtained when both watercolor and crayon media are used for the chromatic H-T-P." Watercolors apparently are more sensitive to certain strivings in certain personalities. The specific sensitivities vary from individual to individual. In one instance, the watercolors seem to reveal elusive

Fig. 71, Case V

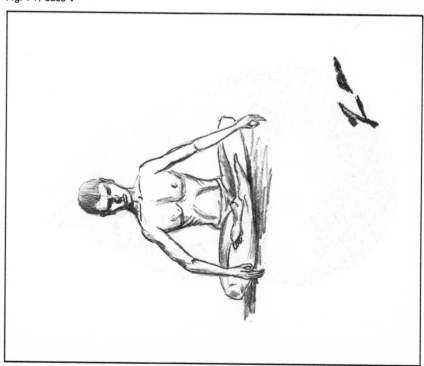

Fig. 72, Case V (above)   Fig. 73, Case V (below)

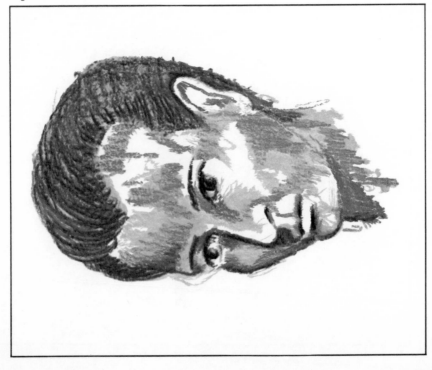

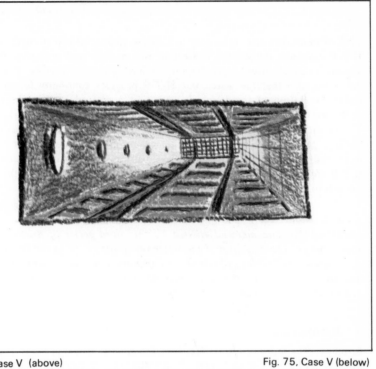

Fig. 74, Case V (above)

Fig. 75, Case V (below)

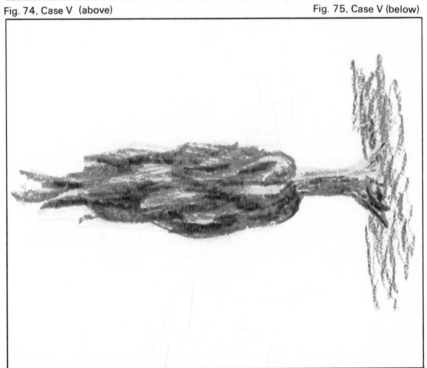

signs of morbidity and in another to indicate sources of ego strength. Watercolor H-T-P drawings suggest the content of ruminations and obsessive ideas, evoke obscure rationalizations, and magnify refined defensive devices. There is some indication also that the watercolor H-T-P provides continuity for the more extensive revelation of trends which were first expressed in the achromatic and/or the crayon phase.

In the H-T-P, as in other projective techniques, clues to the meaning of material brought out by items in the test or in the subtests must be obtained from and justified by the overall test pattern and personality configuration. H-T-P workers may soon be thinking of the different forms of the H-T-P as subtests in what might be called the H-T-P battery.

It is hoped that Mr. Spencer will continue his studies of his ingenious watercolor chromatic H-T-P, and that others will do likewise. It is not clear whether the additional dynamic material elicited by this third series of drawings is due to some inherent characteristic of the watercolors, per se, *or to the fact that another set of drawings has been obtained—and thus the longitudinal study of the subject has been extended. Further experimentation in this area is particularly inviting and should prove stimulating and productive. Eds.*

References

Birren, F. *The Story of Color.* Westport, Conn.: The Crimson Press, 1941.

Buck, J. N. The H-T-P technique: A quantitative and qualitative scoring manual. *Clin. Psychol. Monogr.,* 5; 1948, 1-120.

_____ *The House-Tree-Person Manual Supplement: Administration and Interpretation of the H-T-P Test.* Western Psychological Services, Beverly Hills, California, 1964.

Fenichel, Otto. *The Psychoanalytical Theory of Neurosis.* New York: W. W. Norton & Co., 1945.

Fromm, Erich. *The Forgotten Language.* New York: Rinehart and Co., 1951.

Hammer, E. F. *The Clinical Application of Projective Drawings.* Springfield, Illinois: Charles C. Thomas, 1958.

Horney, K. *Neurosis and Human Growth.* New York: W. W. Norton & Co., 1950.

Kris, E. *Psychoanalytical Explorations in Art.* New York: International Universities Press, Inc., 1952.

Napoli, P. Fingerpainting and personality diagnosis. *Genet. Psychol. Mongr.,* 34: 1946, 119-231.

Rapaport, D. *Organization and Pathology of Thought.* New York: Columbia University Press, 1959.

Waehner, T. S. Interpretations of spontaneous drawings and paintings. *Genetic Psychol. Mongr.,* 33: 1946, pp 70.

Randolph O. Boring received his Bachelor of Science degree from the University of Tennessee in 1936, and his Master of Science degree from Tulane University in 1952.

After serving in the United States Armed Forces, he was a Clinical Psychologist with the Veterans Administration from 1946 to 1952. He served as Executive Director and Clinical Psychologist in the Louisiana Mental Health Department from 1953 to 1957. Since 1957 he has been engaged in teaching, administration, and private practice in clinical psychology in Tennessee.

Robert C. Topper received his Bachelor of Science in Education degree from Ashland College in 1936; his M.A. from Ohio State University in 1937; and his Ph.D. from Indiana University in 1947.

For the past 16 years Dr. Topper has worked as a Consultant in Psychology to Management in the State of Texas.

Dr. Topper is listed in *American Men of Science, Leaders in American Science, and Who's Who in the South and Southwest*.

He is a licensed Clinical Psychologist in the state of Tennessee and holds the certificate in Clinical Psychology of the States of Texas and New York.

Chapter 3

The Topper-Boring H-T-P Variation

Robert C. Topper, Ph.D. and Randolph O. Boring, M.S.

The authors describe their "extended variation of the H-T-P" and define its role in the 3-item test battery which they use in the selection of personnel for industry. They discuss, pithily, but interestingly, their approach to the evaluation of the material gleaned by their battery, and they offer evidence of its validity.

In the late 1940s the writers developed "A Psychodiagnostic Screening Technique" [1] in connection with their work as Clinical Psychologists in a Veterans Administration Neuro-Psychiatric Hospital in Tuscaloosa, Alabama. Their efforts were to satisfy the urgent need for more rapid diagnostic procedures than were available at that time in the psychiatric setting. Their publication described a method whereby individual procedures devised by them could be administered to a number of patients at one time and yet the unique projective qualities of the individual tests could be retained.

The House-Tree-Person Test was an integral item in the Topper-Boring technique. However, following the drawing of a House, Tree and Person, three additional drawings were sought. After the testee had completed the "Person," he was instructed to draw "A Person of the opposite sex to the first drawn "Person." Following this, the testee was told, "Draw yourself." The last instruction was, "Draw anything you want to draw."

This extension of the H-T-P added significant projective stimuli to the range of the test battery. Other work by Topper and Boring during this time involved their using the H-T-P in the conceptual sense of the "Incomplete" item. On single sheets of paper, incomplete lines were given for the testee to complete into a House, Tree and Person, respectively, in any way that he desired. See Figure 76.

---

[1] Boring, R. O. and Topper, R. C., *A Psychodiagnostic Screening Technique*. Reproduced by the Veterans Administration for distribution to VA Clinical Psychological Services.

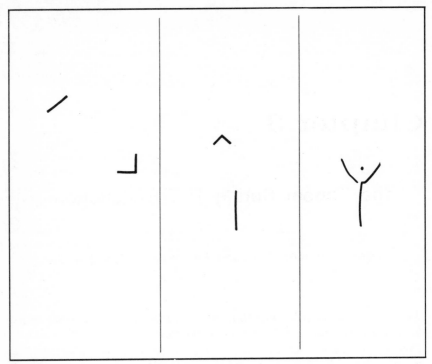

Fig. 76

This approach, they found, had merit in obtaining a brief sampling of the testee's basic thinking abilities, but it often limited the reflection of the personality dynamics.

The H-T-P Extension was used primarily in psychiatric testing situations until 1955, at which time the Topper-Boring technique was brought into the industrial setting. It has been used there since as a means of securing "depth" evaluations of personnel and applicants for employment ranging from truck drivers to corporation presidents.

The "depth" evaluation device now used by the authors has been narrowed to three items: The Bender Visual Motor Gestalt Test, the H-T-P Extension Test and the Boring Magic As-If Test (a verbal item found by the authors to have high projective valence).[2]

The intent of "depth" evaluation is to assist in the selection of desirable personnel for a given industrial position. It attempts to set forth valid and reliable statements referrable to a person's thinking and personality patterns. It seeks to reveal a person's success, or potential for success, in given areas of productivity. At the same time, it deals with the risks involved in keeping, or hiring, the person evaluated.

The formal evaluation report contains specific impressions obtained from

---

[2] The reader will find sample directions and a description of the 8½ x 11 Form Sheets in the Appendix to this chapter. Eds.

the productions of the testee on the above-named three tests. Impressions are organized around these areas: (1) Basic Ability to Think, (2) Ego Structure, (3) Emotional Patterns, (4) Insights Into Self, (5) Human Relations Skills, (6) Management Concepts.

Using the Bender and the H-T-P productions, the authors seek to provide answers to a somewhat schematic framework of questions:

(1) *Ability to Think:* What is the Person's actual thinking performance compared to his basic ability? How may the person vary from his shown ability or performance; e.g., is he imaginative as opposed to being able to work only at simplified, stereotyped levels? Does he perform best when he is led or when he is "on his own"? What are the causes of his lowered performance, if it is lowered? Answers to these questions are to be found in each of the three items of the Topper-Boring modification. Each item has been found to confirm and substantiate the other items in most cases. The H-T-P productions are highest in value in determining the dynamic factors operating in the producing personality. Thus, here they reveal the causes of lowered performance, lost potential, or poor judgment in thinking. The H-T-P productions reveal the person's intellectual drive or apathy, his spontaneity of ideation or his constriction of thought process. The H-T-P productions serve as a confirmation or refutation of the ability ratings which already have been derived from conventional personnel tests.

(2) *Ego Structure:* The goal here is to indicate some aspects of the person's functional strength, his capacity to confront and deal with reality. Here we are concerned with whether the person is retreating and withdrawing or dealing with reality in a confident manner. The person's grasp and control of reality is noted; his defenses and his compensations are sought. The H-T-P is sensitive to projections of these concerns, and it also reveals the "hurts" and traumatization which the person's basic Self has experienced.

(3) *Emotional Patterns:* What is the person's general emotional control? Is he mature or immature; does he tend to flair up or is he suppressive? Will he hold steady and be dependable under pressure? Is he flexible, stable and secure? Are there rich emotional experiences or is he a repressed "cold fish"? The indices on which to base impressions in this area are so abundant and so reinforcing in each of the three testing devices used by the writers that they feel that this is the easiest area to evaluate. Regressive, childish visual-motor controls shown by the Bender are very seldom unsubstantiated by the H-T-P productions. Persons of immature dynamics, even if they are of high thinking ability, invariably produce childish H-T-P figures and usually do so consistently for each of the six extended H-T-P items. In some cases the drawn human figures lay bare emotional immaturities in the most obvious, infantile manner.

(4) *Insights Into Self:* This area deals with the person's degree of self-orientation versus his sensitivity to the feelings of others. The highly self-centered person will not see his own strengths and/or weaknesses easily. He will not admit mistakes easily or readily be willing to improve himself. He will not recognize or appreciate the humor in life. Sensitivity to the feelings of others denotes empathy, a human quality which is of special value in management and sales relationships. To determine with any acceptable reliability a person's self-orientation and his usable empathy is frequently quite difficult. Simple imma-

turities are not sufficient evidence upon which to base a judgment of self-centeredness. It is often, however, in the three secured human drawings that the significant material is found which justifies this impression. For confirmation of judgments made in this area of personality, the authors rely strongly on the "verbal" projections given in the Boring Magic As-If Test.

The H-T-P's classical "paranoid" signs are, the authors' experience suggests, valid and reliable indices of the presence of a paranoid condition.

(5) *Human Relations Skill:* Here the industrial world is interested in the person's ability to assume leadership, his potential for effective and constructive influence, his capacity for the instigation of group action, his degree of spontaneity with others, his fairness to others and his availability for close, warm and healthy interpersonal relationships. Industry is concerned also with a person's adaptability within and to various socio-economic levels. Will the employee fit into the philosophies of the company? Is he "off the deep end" in some direction? Can he work with groups, but not with other individuals, or vice versa? The adequacy of any attempt to formulate the write-up from these questions depends largely upon the total pattern of the projective content of the person's productions. However, in many cases, single clues are sufficiently reliable for the determination of trends in human relationships. The psychopath, the paranoid, the passive-submissive, the immature, and the homosexual are, of all possibilities the ones most readily identifiable from their projections in the H-T-P. Negative interpersonal potentials appear to be more clearly projected than a capacity for positive relationships. The absence of untoward negative indices may be taken as evidence of capacities for positive human relationships. The spotting of leadership ability may pose difficulty, but inference for its presence may be made from combinations of factors such as spontaneity, ego strength, basic ability, empathy and positive interperson relationship capacities.

(6) *Management Concepts:* Under this heading the business world is interested in the person's reaction to authority, what he has to offer toward the development of others and whether or not he would be employee-centered or production-centered. Inferences here are made largely from the total pattern of projection, although discrete features may be more definitely shown in specific productions.

Following the accumulation of impressions gained in the above areas, the "depth" report includes a brief summary in which recommendations are made. Recommendations include an evaluation of the risks which will presumably be involved if the subject is employed.

The Bender H-T-P battery serves us as a clinical tool which provides leads to the evaluations and recommendations which are required in the industrial setting. These projections constitute material which appear to go beyond the yield of the conventional interview of the question-and-answer type. Following even an intensive personal interview, the interviewer often is left without sufficient data upon which to make an evaluation, even with numerous reservations. The "depth" tools remove *some* of the reservations, enable the interviewer's impressions to be confirmed or denied, and give the employer a more dynamically oriented picture.

The value in the business and industrial areas of the Bender H-T-P-derived

Impressions has been two-fold. First is our reassurance gained on the basis of our impression of consistent validity in predicting job success. The second is mechanical, one in terms of the administration of the techniques themselves. The usual practice is for the psychologist himself to administer the materials, but this is not really necessary. The blanks and directions for administration can, in the business world, be made available to branch offices and to personnel workers involved in wholesale recruiting campaigns. Adequate directions can be, and are, supplied. The personnel workers, with whom we work, are trained to make certain observations which aid in the interpretation of the material they obtain.

Perhaps it will serve to cite one company's experience, where reliable statistics have been maintained. This is a local trucking company, dealing almost exclusively with in-city driving. Since about 1959, all employees from vice-presidents to drivers have been screened with the projective materials. The driver population is the most significant since over 500 applicants have been screened.

At the beginning, all drivers in the company's employ were assembled in large groups, tested, and materials collected. From these, reports were written in an attempt to establish a usable categorizing or "labeling" system to expedite future screening. These initial reports were then checked against the driving records, the maintenance records, and the observational and empirical ratings of the management of the company. Categories established on this basis for this company were:

(1) Personality within "normal" limits	(7) Immature character
(2) Passive-dependent	(8) Psychopath
(3) Schizophrenic	(9) Senile
(a) Remissive	(10) Obsessive-compulsive
(b) Incipient	(11) Manic-depressive
(4) Hostile character	(12) Vague
(5) Homosexual	
(6) Inadequate personality	
(a) Basic	
(b) Neurotic	

Obviously, this "rounding" process loses some individuality, but it was introduced for speed in processing applicants, especially in view of the fact that reporting to the company has to be made by telegram from the diagnostician. (For applicants other than drivers, the full report, as described above, is used.)

A number of interesting results have followed from this process, despite the handicaps under which the psychologists work: such as, not seeing the applicant, having no information about the applicant other than the diagnostic materials, having to make an arbitrary statement with no chance for "qualifications," and the unavailability of the applicants so that no "better than" choices could be made, etc. Despite this, in a study of applicants over a period of 18 months, there was a 90% rate of success (that is, 90% of those recommended for employment turned out to be desirable employees). In a briefer study, applicants were employed who were *not* recommended, and none of these was later judged to be satisfactory.

Another interesting outcome of the total program was the finding that applicants who fell into the second category above (Passive-dependent) were the most desirable employees for one division of the company. The apparent reason for this seems to be the nature of their work. These men and women were under the very close direction of a dispatcher who, of necessity, had to keep issuing "orders" on when to go where.

One of the most significant results over the years has to do with insurance costs. During the time that the examining program has been in operation, the company has seen a drop of two-thirds in both accident frequency *and* accident severity. Both of these are highly significant to the company from the standpoints of profits and public goodwill. Much of these gains is attributed to the proper selection of drivers.

Boring feels that the H-T-P figures form the core which elicits the essential projection of the Topper-Boring projections. Boring, who is the basic interpreter, has administered and interpreted several hundred Rorschachs in the clinical setting. He finds that this Bender-H-T-P approach, however, is more reliable than the Rorschach. Not only is it a fruitful approach, it also makes projective interpretations available to a sphere of operations which, as yet for the most part, has not seen the advisability of using the more costly, individually-administered devices.

The editors regret that the authors did not see fit to illustrate this chapter with case material. Nonetheless, this chapter is presented because the editors wish to be as all-inclusive as possible in presenting the current variations of the H-T-P and because they feel that others may wish to use the Topper-Boring Technique and do research with it. Eds.

Appendix

DIRECTIONS

You have just been given eight sheets of paper upside down. In each case, follow the directions at the top of the front of the page; these are the only directions you can be given, other than what appear on this sheet. There is no time limit.

On each page, you should do the *very best you can*. What you do will be interpreted as the best you can do. Art ability, in itself, is not a factor. You should not use a straight-edge or ruler and you should not look ahead to the next card or the next sheet. You must use a pencil and you may erase if you like. Do not have any of the other pages underneath the one you are using.

On the first page, the one on top, write your name and indicate whether you are right or left-handed. Then, draw what you see on the nine cards you have been given, as indicated in the directions. Draw each as you see it—just the way you see it—the *very best you can!* Remember, make all drawings of the cards on the front side of that page only. Do not turn the cards around.

When you have finished all the cards on the first page, move the cards out of the way, turn your first page over and get it out of the way. Then take the rest of the pages, one at a time, off the top of the pile, turn each over and do what is asked. As each page is finished, turn it over on top of the previous one.

On the last page, fill in the blanks at the top and answer all the questions.

(Do not be disturbed when the Examiner checks the cards as he takes them; he is required to do this to make sure they are in a certain order for the next person.)

(On the last page, you are asked to give information about where you grew up, your sex, race and religion. In view of the Civil Rights Act of 1964, it should be explained that these are needed to keep from discriminating. The interpretations involved in this material are valid only if you are compared to people with like backgrounds. This is most readily seen in the sex factor; women and men draw differently and your sex is needed so you will be compared with others of your sex. The same principle is involved in the other questions. A person who grew up somewhere in the deep South draws differently from someone who grew up in Chicago; a Baptist draws differently from a Catholic; etc.)

Form 1

The next seven 8½ x 11" sheets are "headed" as follows:

Sheet No. 1

NAME . . . . Right . . . . or Left . . . . Handed
Draw what you see on these cards. After you finish the first, turn that card over and go to the second, and so on. (Make all drawings on *this side* of this page only.)

*   *   *   *   *

Sheet No. 2

NAME . . . . Draw a *House* . . . any house you want to draw.

*   *   *   *   *

Sheet No. 3

NAME . . . . Draw a *Tree* . . . any tree you want to draw.

*   *   *   *   *

Sheet No. 4

NAME . . . . Draw a *Person* . . . a whole person.

*   *   *   *   *

Sheet No. 5

NAME . . . . Draw a person of the opposite sex (opposite of the one you just drew) . . . a whole person.

*   *   *   *   *

Sheet No. 6

NAME . . . . Draw *Yourself* . . . your whole self.

*   *   *   *   *

Sheet No. 7

NAME . . . . Draw *anything* you want to draw.

Form 2

Name .... Where grew up .... Age .... Sex .... Race ....
Religion .... Company requiring tests ....
Are you an employee or an applicant? .... Position ....
Are you: Single ☐ Married ☐ Widow(er) ☐ Separated ☐ Divorced ☐ Divorced and
remarried ☐ Number of times married .... Age at first marriage ....
Age of spouse at time of marriage .... Spouse's age now .... Number
of children .... Education. ....
Experience .... (Do not write in this space: Verbal .... Non-Verbal ....)

THE MAGIC AS-IF TEST
(Just answer the questions truthfully; you want yourself reflected.)

1. If by magic you could be any person, dead or alive, in the world, whom would you
    choose? ....
    Give one reason for this choice: ....

2. If by magic time could be set back or set forward, which of the following conditions
    would you prefer? (Check one) ☐ Go back 20 years and start all over ☐ Go
    forward 200 years ☐ Keep status quo. Give one reason for this choice: ....
    ....

3. If by magic you had to choose to be an animal, what animal would you choose?
    .... Reason: ....

4. If by magic one of the following statements described most nearly a way of life
    suitable for man in this day and time, check your choice:
    ☐ "Ask and it shall be given unto you; knock and it shall be opened unto you."
       (This could mean that the world is one's oyster.)
    ☐ "Seek ye first the Kingdom of Heaven." (This could mean what profit it man if
       he does make a million dollars.)
    ☐ "Suffer little children to come unto me." (This could mean that the world is in
       your trust, and that you are your brother's keeper.)

5. If by magic happiness could be measured on a scale of from one to ten, with one
    ŗepresenting the least amount of happiness, check the amount of happiness in your
    life on the following:
    ☐ 1 ☐ 2 ☐ 3 ☐ 4 ☐ 5 ☐ 6 ☐ 7 ☐ 8 ☐ 9 ☐ 10

6. If you saw a bare-foot child step on a sharp nail, what would you immediately feel?
    (Check one)   # Concern for the child's welfare   # A squeamish feeling inside

7. Assuming equal salary, which one of the following would you rather be, if you had
    to be one of them?   ☐ Butcher ☐ Undertaker

8. Could you pick a kitten up by its hind-legs and dash its brains out against a brick
    wall? ☐ Yes ☐ No

9. Did you ever, or do you now, feel that you may have a special contribution for the
    world?   ☐ Yes ☐ No   If yes, what? ....

10. All men or women are at times "jackasses." Do you admit this to yourself?
    ☐ Often ☐ Once in a while ☐ Never

11. Can man really trust man? Check your own trust of others on the following scale (one meaning the least trust).
    □ 0 □ 1 □ 2 □ 3 □ 4 □ 5 □ 6 □ 7 □ 8 □ 9 □ 10
12. This little planet Earth whirling in space — do you find it (check one):
    □ Amusing   □ A sorry mess   □ The best of all possible places
13. Man's best bet in life is to (check one):   □ Keep a stiff upper lip   □ Have faith and do the best he can   □ Move straight ahead, remembering he won't get very far
14. On the following scale check the difference between the person you really are and the person you would like to be (one meaning the least difference):
    □ 0 □ 1 □ 2 □ 3 □ 4 □ 5 □ 6 □ 7 □ 8 □ 9 □ 10
15. The above test has made you (check one):   □ Think   □ Feel   □ Mad   □ Nothing

Solomon Diamond received his Ph.D. degree in psychology from Columbia University in 1936, and has been teaching at California State College, Los Angeles, since 1949.

Although he has had considerable experience in counseling, he has been interested in projective tests as devices for exploring problems of personality theory rather than as clinical instruments. His other articles dealing with projective devices of an experimental nature are: "Three impossibilities: a verbal projective technique" (*Journal of Psychology*, 1947) and "Sex stereotypes and acceptance of sex role" (*ibid.*, 1955).

His books include a general survey of personality theory, *Personality and Temperament* (New York: Harper, 1957), and *Inhibition and Choice* (New York: Harper and Row, 1963). The latter book deals with inhibition on a neurophysiological as well as on a behavioral level—a breadth which is reflected in the statement by one reviewer that it is "one of those rare books that should be read by every psychologist, whatever his particular interest." In writing it, Dr. Diamond has as collaborators his wife, Florence, who is a clinical psychologist, and a colleague and former student, Richard Balvin.

Chapter 4

The House, Tree, and Person
in Verbal Fantasy [1]

Solomon Diamond, Ph.D.

In an innovating step from the graphic to the verbal plane, Dr. Solomon Diamond provides us with an imaginative approach to the challenge of investigating the underlying meaning of the basic concepts in the H-T-P, the symbolic value of the House, the Tree, and the Person. By asking subjects to compose a story about these concepts in which they are given life, interact, and even speak, Dr. Diamond has devised a technique which falls midway between the H-T-P and the T-A-T, one which can be bent to basic research on the H-T-P or utilized as a modified tool in its own right. This technique combines (a) a somewhat freer, less threatened projection under the license of whimsy, with (b) the depth of material prompted forward by the relatively universal, meaningful, and personally-charged symbolic-valence of the House, the Tree, and the Person.

His approach carries heuristic promise.

I. Age and Sex Differences in Themes and Content

Part I of this chapter is based on the content analysis of 300 stories, which were written under the instruction to include three characters: a House, a Tree, and a Person. The method is obviously suggested by Buck's H-T-P technique (1948), and we shall assume that the reader has some knowledge of that method, as well as of Machover's related Draw-A-Person technique (1941).

---

[1] The editors express their appreciation of permission granted by the editor of the Journal of Projective Techniques to publish this material which appeared in slightly different form in that Journal in 1954 in Vol. 18, No.'s 3 & 4. Ed.

Subjects and Administration

All of the stories were written under classroom conditions. The adult subjects were 96 men and 81 women college students, with the age range in each sex from 19 to above 50, with the medians at about 24. Most of them were education majors enrolled in two sections of a course in Mental Hygiene, about 15 were students in a course in the Psychology of Personality, and 4 women were in a discussion group organized from another course. They were all given what was ostensibly a "test of social intelligence," one part of which had the following instruction:

"Write a story in which there are three characters: a Tree, a House, and a Person. All of these characters should have real personality. In fact, they should all have the power of speech, so that they can communicate their thoughts to one another. Let your story really tell what kind of Tree, what kind of House, and what kind of Person these characters are, and how they feel about each other."

The remaining subjects were 66 boys and 57 girls, pupils in the eighth grade of a public school in a middle-class community in the metropolitan Los Angeles area.[2] They received essentially the same instructions in writing, as an assignment for a classroom exercise in English composition. These children are described as ordinarily refractory to questionnaire tests which seek to probe their problems, even anonymously, but as having entered enthusiastically and unsuspectingly into this task.

PREFERENCE FOR PERSONS. Our principal interest will center on the themes which appear in the stories, but it seems advisable to present first certain other quantitative analyses, which will provide a basis for the reclassification of some of our subjects. In Table V, the stories are classified according to the kind of Person that appears in the principal human role. Stories written in the first person have been classified as having a Person of the same sex and age group as the author. Stories classified under "Family" are those in which it is not possible to select one of several family members as the principal character.

It will be worthwhile to recall some studies which relate to the problem of choice of Person, for the graphic H-T-P and the Draw-A-Person. Machover (1949) states that the choice of a Person of the opposite sex, for the first person drawn, is indicative of confusion in sex identification. Levy (1950) says that 87 per cent of adults draw their own sex first, and that of 16 known homosexuals, 13 drew the opposite sex first. These authors make no distinction with respect to the sex of the subject. (In the writer's experience with college students, women are far more likely than men to draw the opposite sex.) Jolles (1952), using H-T-P, found that about 20 per cent of boys and girls in elementary school draw the opposite sex, with little difference between the sexes at the younger ages, but a marked reduction in this tendency among the older boys. Weider & Noller (1953) using the Draw-A-Person, found that 70 per cent of the boys and 94 per cent of the girls in the third grade drew their own sex first. Granick & Smith (1953) found that among college students, about 12 per cent of the men and about 35

---

[2] The author wishes to express his appreciation to Mr. and Mrs. Robert L. Cox, whose interest led to collecting these stories.

per cent of the women drew the opposite sex first, but in neither sex was there any relation between this response and the M-F score on the MMPI; this led them to question whether the drawings can be regarded as primarily determined by identification, or self-portraiture. Giedt & Lehner (1951) studied the ages assigned to drawn persons by adult male subjects, and one may judge from their data that the use of aged and juvenile persons in such drawings is rare.

The most striking fact which emerges from the data of Table V is that a very large proportion of the female subjects, and very few of the male subjects, choose Persons of the opposite sex. This suggests the possibility of differentiating among women and girls, according to the sex of the Person chosen. (A similar differentiation among male subjects would be of equal interest, but is not feasible with the present data.) Differences with respect to the use of aged Persons and juvenile Persons also appear.

TABLE V
Choice of "Person"

	Men	Women	Boys	Girls
Same sex as author				
Adult, or no age	61	10	28	3
Old man or woman	7	6	9	5
Boy or girl	13	14	24	15
Opposite sex to author				
Adult or no age	4	27	1	16
Old man or woman	0	10	1	3
Boy or girl	2	9	1	9
Sex not indicated	7	4	1	3
Family	2	1	1	3
	96	81	66	57
Per cent opposite sex	6	57	5	49
Per cent old	7	20	15	14
Per cent juvenile	16	28	38	42

Null hypotheses rejected:

That men and women are equally likely to choose Persons of the opposite sex (.001).

That men and women are equally likely to choose juvenile Persons (.05).

That boys and girls are equally likely to choose Persons of the opposite sex (.001).

That boys and girls are equally likely to choose juveniles (.01).

That adults and children are equally likely to choose juveniles (.01).

RECLASSIFICATION OF FEMALE SUBJECTS. We propose to distinguish, in our further analysis, between those female subjects who, by an objective criterion, indicate an acceptance of their sex role, and those who indicate a rejection of it. With this intent, we shall establish groups to be designated as Gf, Gm, Wf, Wb, Wf', and Wm, defined as follows:

Gf includes all girls who have used feminine or "family" Persons, as classified in Table 1. Gm includes all those having male Persons, and those in which the sex of the Person is not indicated, except where the story is written in the first person.

Wf and Wm are similarly defined, except that the latter group does not include women who use boys as Persons. These constitute the separate group Wb. Wf and Wb together constitute Wf '. In other words, we regard the preference for a boy-person as constituting a rejection of the feminine role when it occurs in a story written by a girl, but not when it occurs in a story written by a woman. The justification for this difference in treatment will be given in the next section.

SOME SEX-LINKED CONTENT CHARACTERISTICS. For each story, the following determinations have been made.

(a) Is the concept of beauty present, in the use of such words as beautiful, lovely, graceful, shapely, pretty, handsome, etc.?

(b) Is there reference to building, whether of the principal House or any other?

(c) Is there any intimation of the Person's family, as by mention of a parent or child?

(d) Is the House given prior mention, as compared to the Tree? (For this purpose, no attention has been given to priority in the mere listing of the three characters in an opening sentence, without qualifying characteristics, as if echoing the instructions. When the first mention of either the House or Tree is made as part of a speech by the other of these characters the speaker is credited with prior appearance.)

In Table VI, the presence or absence of each of these content characteristics is indicated, for the stories written by each group of subjects, as defined in the preceding section. The last column of the table gives the probabilities based on the chi^2 values computed independently for each row. The population is non-homogeneous with respect to each of these content characteristics, as shown by these probabilities. However, it is not possible to establish a significant difference between Men and Women, taken as total groups, with respect to each of them. These total groups do not differ significantly with respect to use of the concepts "building" and "family." However, the sub-groups Wm and Wf are sharply differentiated in these categories, as well as with respect to prior mention of the House. In each case Wm more closely resembles Men. Thus, it appears that the difficulty in distinguishing between Men and the total group of Women, on these content characteristics, results from the heterogeneity of the Women, and this difficulty is largely removed when we discriminate between those women who choose male Persons and those who choose female Persons. Furthermore, we can readily see that throughout the Table, Wb closely parallels Wf, showing its affinity to the latter group rather than to Wm. Therefore, as already stated above, we shall combine Wf and Wb as Wf', the group of women whose choice of a Person does not indicate rejection of the feminine role. It may be admitted that this has been, in fact, a post facto justification, which was initiated by awareness of the "motherly" content of all the Wb stories. However, it is important that this procedure can be justified by criteria that are independent of the themes themselves, to the study of which we shall now turn.[3]

Major Themes

After a preliminary study of all the stories, the writer prepared a set of instructions for the judges, which included definitions of certain recurring themes. These definitions are reproduced here, since they can also serve the reader as a synoptic statement of the type of content commonly met in the stories.

---

[3] Additional evidence of the validity of the distinction between Wm and Wf groups can be found in the author's paper, "Sex stereotypes and acceptance of sex role," J. Psychol., 39, 1955, 385-388. (Editors)

TABLE VI
**Presence/Absence of Certain Content Characteristics,
and the Probability That the Population is Homogeneous
with Respect to Each**

	Men	Boys	Wm	Wb	Wf	Gm	Gf	P
Beauty	24/72	15/51	18/23	4/5	16/15	8/23	13/13	.01
Building	22/74	9/57	14/27	0/9	2/29	3/28	3/23	.01
Family	15/81	12/54	7/34	4/5	12/19	6/25	9/17	.05
Prior House	36/60	37/29	19/22	9/0	20/11	13/18	16/10	.001

COMPLAINT. An expression of resentment by the House, the Tree, or both, against neglect or abuse, or unfair disadvantages relative to the Person. Such stories generally have a misanthropic flavor, placing the Person in an unfavorable light.

DESTRUCTION. One or more of the principal characters suffers death or serious injury. The tone may be tragedy, pessimism, or cynicism.

ESCAPE. There is a threat or apprehension of serious injury, which fails to materialize or is at least minimized in its effect. Included here are stories in which death or injury does overtake wouldbe malefactors, and others in which injury is accepted in a spirit of martyrdom, to prevent harm befalling a loved figure. The main point of the story is "escape" from threat.

FRIENDSHIP. Friendly relations, motivated by a desire for fun or by positive feelings between the characters, who are essentially equal as companions, none being particularly dependent as compared to the others. Compare with HARMONY, LONELINESS, MATERNAL, for other types of relationship involving more than friendliness.

HARMONY. The characters live together cooperatively, rendering mutual service. The tone of these stories is often moralistic. The relationship is often utilitarian, a kind of "social contract" based on good sense rather than an expression of warmth.

INSPIRATION. The Person's life is in some sense redirected, or re-energized, through his or her perception of the "spirit" of the House or Tree. (This category does not include stories in which the misbehaving person is "taught a lesson" by a complaining House or Tree.)

LONELINESS. One or more of the characters expresses a need for companionship, or a feeling of insecurity based on introspective self-concern. A "happy ending," in which the insecurity is removed, does not change the classification, which is based on the need expressed in the theme.

MATERNAL. The House and/or the Tree take delight in their sheltering function. If there is a reciprocity of service, it does not seem to be based on an economic exchange, but on a spontaneous desire to give warmth and love, rather than to receive care.

REMINISCENT. Reminiscence of past events.

SUPERFICIAL. Stories in which the relationships seem merely casual, the conversation mere everyday chit-chat.

VALUATIVE. Evaluative discussion of the relative merits of the different characters, usually with a competitive or boastful orientation. A final moralistic resolution of this conflict does not suffice to place such a story in the category, HARMONY, where the competitive spirit is absent.

CONFLICT. There is a conflict of interest (not mere boastful rivalry) between the House and the Tree, such that the welfare of one is threatened by the other.

MISCELLANEOUS. Stories that do not include any of the above themes.

The 300 stories were prepared in typewritten form, with errors of spelling and many errors of punctuation eliminated, and without identification except by number. They were assembled in 15 groups of 20 each, each group containing six or seven stories by men, five or six stories by women, four or five stories by boys, and three or four stories by girls. Six graduate students each judged 100 stories, or five groups, in an arrangement such that each judge had one group in common with each other judge. There were thus two determinations of the major theme for each story. As would be expected, the different judges exhibited individual preferences for certain themes. One judge who made excessive use of the Inspiration category, as compared to the others, was asked to reread these stories, with some careful consideration of whether some of them might not better be placed in other categories. Another judge who made excessive use of the Miscellaneous and Superficial categories was similarly asked to reclassify the stories so judged, bearing in mind a phrase of the instructions, that the definitions of themes were "to be interpreted broadly, so that as few stories as possible shall be classified as "miscellaneous." The category Reminiscent was used much more rarely than had been anticipated, and each judge was asked to reclassify any story he had placed in this category, thus eliminating it from the tabulations. However, many significant differences between the judges remain. Thus, one female judge finds 26 stories of the 100 she read have maternal interest as their principal theme, while another finds none. These differences would make an interesting study in themselves, but it does not seem possible to discuss them without violating the deserved anonymity of the judges. They are mentioned here only as a factor which necessarily reduces the likelihood of coincident judgments by pairs of judges on each story, that is, as perhaps the major factor in reducing the reliability of judgments. This general problem is the subject of a recent article by Hammer & Piotrowski (1953).

Table VII shows the distribution of the 300 pairs of judgments, each story being entered once. In this and subsequent tables, the categories have been ordered so as to make more evident the relationships which are shown by these coincident judgments. For 129 stories, the two judgments were the same. For 66 others, the two themes selected are immediately adjacent as ordered in this Table, while for 48 more there is one intervening position. Thus 243 of 300 cases fall in 33 of 78 cells of this Table. A formal statistical test would be superfluous to show that the categories as established are meaningful. However, examination of the Table also shows the need for better definition of some of the categories particularly to differentiate Harmony from Valuative on one hand and Maternal on the other.

Preference for Themes

The 600 ratings were arranged in two series of 300 each, with each series containing a "split half" of the judgments made by each judge within each of the groups he read. Within each of these series separately, the relative frequency of each theme was determined for each major group of subjects, i.e., Men, Women, Boys, and Girls. The resulting frequency tables were quite similar, differing as they did only by chance, and each separately gave:

TABLE VII
Coincidence of Classification of Each Story by Two Judges, According to Major Themes

	1	2	3	4	5	6	7	8	9	10	11	12
1. Destruction	17	3	5	0	3	0	0	2	0	2	0	0
2. Conflict		4	4	4	1	0	0	0	1	0	1	0
3. Complaint			23	9	2	2	2	2	1	1	1	0
4. Valuative				11	3	9	2	3	0	1	1	0
5. Escape					9	7	2	4	1	4	0	0
6. Harmony						9	12	18	0	4	2	5
7. Friendship							15	14	1	2	3	5
8. Maternal								13	4	5	0	1
9. Inspiration									4	3	1	0
10. Loneliness										18	6	1
11. Miscellaneous											2	1
12. Superficial												4

TABLE VIII
Frequency of the Occurrence of Major Themes, as Determined by an Average of Two Series of Judgments

	Men	Boys	Wm	Wf'	Gm	Gf
Destruction	12	6	1.5	1	2	2
Conflict	5.5	1	1.5	1	1	1
Complaint	19.5	10.5	4.5	1	1	1
Valuative	11.5	3.5	4.5	1.5	3	3
Escape	2.5	6	3	2	7	2
Harmony	11	9.5	6.5	3.5	3.5	4.5
Friendship	7	7.5	2.5	13	2	4.5
Maternal	8.5	9	6.5	9	1	5.5
Inspiration	8	0.5	2	0	0.5	0
Loneliness	6.5	4	6.5	7.5	5.5	1.5
Miscellaneous	3.5	2.5	0.5	0.5	2.5	0
Superficial	0.5	6	0.5	1	2	1
	96	66	40	41	31	26

Table VIII gives the frequency of occurrence of the major themes, for each group of subjects, as determined by averaging the two series of judgments. In order to compute a chi^2 value for this Table, we have merged certain rows and certain columns, to avoid having too many cells with very small expected values. Specifically, we have merged Gm and Gf into one column, and we have merged the categories of Conflict, Inspiration, and Superficial with Miscellaneous, as one "greater miscellaneous" row. The resulting table has 9 rows and 5 columns, or 32 degrees of freedom. It yields a chi² sum of 61.43 (P <.01).   The major contributions of chi² arise from the following circumstances: in the category Complaints, Men have an excess, Wf and Girls a deficit; in the category Escape, Men have a deficit, Girls an excess; in the category Friendship, and to a lesser degree in the related category Maternal, Men have a deficit, Wf an excess. As a group, Wf makes the largest contribution to chi², while the contributions of Wm are quite moderate.

There is also appended to the Table a list of null hypothese which are rejected on the basis of chi² tests of appropriate four-fold tables constructed from the same data. For these tests, the customary correction for continuity has been deemed inapplicable, since the observed values are not limited to integral amounts, because of the averaging procedure by which they were obtained. It should be pointed out, however, that the probabilities given are based on conventional "two-tailed" tests, whereas the nature of these hypotheses is such that one-tailed tests, which would approximately halve the probabilities, would be justified.

Recurring Plots

Up to this point, we have dealt only with those results which have lent themselves to statistical treatment, and we have thus been limited to dealing with categories, whether of subjects or of stories, which were not too small. Ultimately, however, our interest is in the single individual, and in the unique fantasy production which helps us to understand him. Group differences, and statistics on major themes, are only of value as providing the background against which we can judge the meaning of the single story which interests us at a given time. However, between the individual story and the common theme there is another level, which we shall call here, for convenience, the recurring plot: the story which is found to recur several times, not often enough to permit statistical comparison of groups, but still often enough to impress us as a "type story." Such stories interest us especially because their uniformity supports an interpretation of the plot in symbolic terms. We shall give a brief synopsis of several such plots.

One of the most striking is the "learnt his lesson" story. In this story, the House and Tree complain to each other about the neglect and abuse which they suffer from the Person. They then conspire to "teach him a lesson," usually by withholding their favors of fruit and shelter, sometimes by direct scolding. The Person is often frightened, always contrite, and resolves to behave himself better thereafter. We can feel sure that the author of such a story has had strong conflict about the problem of surrender to parental authority. Boys write five such stories, and men ten; girls write none, and women only one that conforms strictly to the outline given above. However, women write two others which represent minor modifications, and as such give interesting expression to the feminine character. In one, a little boy is gently punished by the Tree, to stop him from tormenting the House by throwing his ball against it. Obviously, this is not the child's authority problem, but the mother's! In the other, the Tree and House conspire to teach an old man to be more friendly, but they conspire to do this through a demonstration of love and kindness, not through punishment.

It will be recalled that the concept of "building" occurs often in stories by men, and in group Wm, but rarely in Wf. It is interesting to observe that three of the Wm stories in this category have a common plot: a man selects a Tree from which to build his House, the Tree asks to be spared, the man explains the virtues of a House, and the Tree then, or the House after the transformation has occurred, expresses contentment with its fate. This seems to be a clear symbolic expression of the woman's renunciation of an original masculine protest.

Another interesting theme, which usually appears as a minor rather than principal plot, is an expression of worry by the Tree about its loss of leaves, or its uncertainty about bearing blossoms or fruit, which is met by reassurance from the House. This occurs several times in stories by both boys and girls, and seems to be an expression of adolescent concern about physical maturation.

Castration symbolism. We have at several points made the assumption, which we assume that the reader has willingly followed, that the Tree will more often be used as a masculine symbol, and the House as a feminine symbol. It is rare that feminine sex is specifically ascribed to either of these characters, although this does happen more often with the House. However, there can be little doubt that by and large they tend to have the expected qualities. A masculine-seeming House is certainly a rarity. A feminine-seeming Tree is more common, but still relatively less so than the sturdy masculine-seeming Tree.(Masculine House and Feminine Tree occur together in one of those few stories written by a man with a female Person). If we are prepared to accept the fact that the Tree will often by used as a phallic symbol, then we must expect that the vicissitudes of the Tree will often express castration anxiety. It is a fact that the Tree is far more often exposed to danger than either the House or the Person. Furthermore, the population is definitely non-homogeneous with respect to this content. Table IX shows the incidence of "Trees in danger" in the various groups. In deriving a chi² sum for this Table, we have combined Wb and Wf, and also Gm and Gf, to avoid small expected values. The result (14.38 with 4 degrees of freedom) corresponds to a probability less than .01. The major contributions to chi² arise from the circumstances that girls are more likely to use this content, and Wf' are less likely to do so. This outcome is consistent with the view that these stories are an expression of castration anxiety.

TABLE IX
Incidence of "Trees in Danger"

	Men	Boys	Wm	Wf'	Gm	Gf
Present	9	12	8	1	10	5
Absent	87	54	33	39	21	21

Many of these stories also enter the Escape category, which was used in our earlier analysis of major themes. It is a fact, as noted there, that boys and girls characteristically develop their stories in such a way that the danger to the Tree is averted, while adult subjects are more likely to permit the catastrophe to occur.

There is a notable small group of stories by boys in which the danger to the Tree is averted through violent retaliation against the threatening Man. These may be regarded as expressions of unresolved Oedipal hostilities directed against the father. This theme of violent retaliation does not occur in the stories by other groups, except that in one story by a girl, in which a young apple tree has been told that it will be turned into firewood if it does not produce fruit within the week, the timely and miraculous appearance of its golden fruit is immediately followed by a bolt of lightning which destroys the evil mistress and House.

There are several stories by girls in which the Tree takes a phallic role without any castration threat. In one, the Tree announces itself, to a boy, in a dream as "the root of life," in another, a boy "wished he were a Tree"—only to ask the House, a few sentences later, how it seemed to have people living inside one; in a third, a girl who has been warned by her parents against entering the forest and who nevertheless went there with her boy-friend, was frightened by the talking Trees. It is also appropriate to mention here that the reference to "forest" is more frequent in stories by girls than in those of other groups (P < .05), which suggests that they are often thinking in terms of a masculine enrivonment rather than a masculine identification.

Id and Superego. The Tree and the House have multiple potentiality as symbols. They are father and mother; they are masculine and feminine aspects of the self, they are also, in many stories, Id and Superego. The Tree offers itself readily as a symbol for "natural force," and the House as a symbol for socially established rules of conduct. Perhaps the most striking instance of this sort is in the story (by a woman) of a man who "imagined he had a House and a Tree living inside of him," with the Tree objecting that the House impeded its growth, while the House insisted that it was needed to hold the man straight. There are a number of other stories in which the Tree and the House represent conflicting ethical standards, with the Tree standing for free development of the individual, and the House for conformity to social expectation.

Summary and Conclusions

College students and eighth-grade students were asked to write a story whose characters included a House, a Tree, and a Person, all gifted with speech and giving expression to their feelings about each other. Quantitative analysis of the results led to a number of conclusions, relating to group differences in the preference for different kinds of Persons (see Table V), group differences in respect of other content characteristics (see Table VI), and group differences in respect to the themes of stories (see Tables VIII and IX). Examination of certain recurring plots gives further support to the view that the House and the Tree have certain typical, though not invariable, symbolic roles.

The writer has refrained from offering lengthy excerpts, which would illustrate in greater detail the projective possibilities of this instrument, which might be called the verbal H-T-P. Such illustrations would serve little purpose unless they were accompanied by clinical data about the subjects. Such data are available in a fair number of cases,   where the students have been seen by the writer for personal counseling, but they would be difficult to present without risking violation of the anonymity of the individuals involved. Suffice it to say, that in the writer's experience the use of this technique has been clinically rewarding, and professional friends who have used it independently, under clinic conditions, have confirmed this judgment.

If the technique is to attain maximum usefulness, there is need for more careful study of the symbolic roles of the House and the Tree. Furthermore, this is a problem which has great theoretical interest, aside from possible clinical application. It need hardly be added that results from any investigations with the verbal H-T-P should be studied in relation to experience with the graphic H-T-P (which includes verbal inquiry aspects), and with the Draw-a-Person technique, with the expectation that each of these methods can help to illumine the others.

II. Their Different Roles

Part I (1954) reported the theme and content characteristics, for child and adult populations of both sexes, in stories in which Houses and Trees appear as talking characters. This part reports a further study designed to delineate more clearly the different symbolic uses of the House and the Tree under such circumstances. In particular, interest attaches to the question whether or not all of the characters in such stories are to be regarded as self-portraits, as Buck (1948) assumes is the case in his graphic H-T-P, from which the suggestion for this method was taken. Rival hypotheses which were suggested in the earlier article are that the Tree and House may represent Father and Mother, or, on some occasions, *id* and *superego*.

Method

The subjects of the present investigations were upper-division college students in English composition classes or remedial writing classes. The stories were written as classroom exercises. Two forms of instructions were used, distributed randomly in each class, and differing only in the fact that where one read *House* the other read *Tree*. It appeared at the top of an otherwise blank sheet of paper, on which the story was to be written.

"Write a story about two characters, a House (Tree) and a Person. Both of these characters should have real personality. In fact, the House (Tree) should have the power of speech, just like the Person, so that they can communicate their thoughts to one another. Let your story really tell what kind of House (Tree) and what kind of Person these are, and how they feel about each other."

Tree stories were written by 14 men and 11 women, House stories by 13 men and 10 women. Most members of the small remedial class wrote on both themes, about a week apart. Personal interviews were had with some of the latter group.

A 50-item adjective check-list was prepared, to provide a basis for description of the "personalities" of the Houses and Trees. Most of the traits included were taken from Cattell's "list of variables constituting the complete 'personality sphere,' (1946). Perhaps the only items that do not have close synonyms in that list are *attractive*, *unattractive*, *strong*, and *weak*. The items were arranged alphabetically, without respect to pairing of opposites.

Copies of this check-list were given to two highly qualified raters [*], who had no previous acquaintance with this technique and no knowledge of the problem under investigation. They were instructed to use these to describe "personality" of each House and Tree. The raters worked from typewritten copies of the stories from which names had been removed. Errors of spelling, and grammatical errors which might interfere with ready comprehension, had been corrected. Each House or Tree received two independent appraisals.

---

[*] The author wishes to express his appreciation to Drs. Lucille and Bertram Forer, for their conscientious performance of a difficult task.

TABLE X
Correlations Between Composite Personality Descriptions

Trees by men vs. Trees by women 78
Trees by men vs. Houses by men 47
Trees by men vs. Houses by women 05
Trees by women vs. Houses by men 64
Trees by women vs. Houses by women 10
Houses by men vs. Houses by women 35

Results

The stories may be dichotomized according to type of instruction (Tree or House), and according to sex of author. Each group of stories is given a score on each of the 50 traits in the check-list, which is the number of times that trait was checked for all stories in that group. Taken together, these scores constitute a composite personality description for the Trees and/or Houses in that group. Correlations between these sets of scores are a measure of similarity between the composite descriptions, and they represent the principal data of this paper.

The correlation between composite descriptions applying to stories by men and those applying to stories by women is .82. This indicates that, taking the stories as a whole without regard to type of instruction, men and women project very similar personality characteristics into their characters. (This, it may be remarked parenthetically, would be less true with regard to the Persons in the stories). The correlation between composite descriptions of Trees and of Houses, without regard to sex of author, is .39. The fact that this correlation is so much lower than the one just mentioned (the difference being significant at the 1 per cent level) indicates that the Trees and the Houses are being used to project different personality characteristics. That is, they are symbols of different meaning, put to different uses.

Table V gives the intercorrelations of the trait distributions, or composite personality descriptions, of the stories divided both by types of instruction and sex of author. Regarded individually, two of these are significant at the 1 per cent level, and two at the 5 per cent level. Of the fifteen paired comparisons which can be made, to test the significance or differences among correlations, six are significant at the 1 per cent level, and three more at the 5 per cent level. Thus we have an indication that the four composite personality descriptions show differences which do not arise from chance. Comparing the correlations, one sees that the personalities projected onto the Trees are much more similar than those projected onto the Houses. Houses, in stories by men, bear more resemblance to Trees, in stories by either sex, than to Houses in stories by women seem to be unlike Trees by either men or women, but there is a suggestion that they are more like Trees by women than like Trees by men.

These relationships may also be seen in Table VI, which gives, for each category of story, the traits most frequently checked and those not checked at all.

Discussion

Our interpretation of the observed relationships is guided by the interviews which we had with four of the subjects, each of whom had written stories on both themes. At the opening of the interview, it was explained that the interviewer was conducting

Most Frequently Checked Traits and (In Parenthesis) Unchecked Traits in Each Category of Story

Trees by men	*Houses by men*
friendly	friendly
self-respecting	affectionate
masculine	assertive
assertive	contented
attractive	dependent
protective	feminine
strong	quiet
(demanding)	self-respecting
(inappreciative)	(inappreciative)
(unattractive)	(logical)
	(misanthropic)

Trees by women	*Houses by women*
friendly	friendly
feminine	demanding
self-respecting	dependent
strong	feminine
altruistic	affectionate
nurturant	grateful
(boastful)	selfish
(demanding)	(adventurous)
(hostile)	(cynical)
(inappreciative)	(misanthropic)
(selfish)	(suspicious)
(suspicious)	(wise)
(unattractive)	

a study of symbolism, and was especially interested in whether the subject could indicate any way in which his House or Tree was symbolic. None had any suggestion to make along these lines. The subject was then encouraged to dismiss the story from mind and to talk freely about himself. The interviewer's technique was primarily non-directive, but he also permitted himself such broad leads as "Tell me something about your childhood," or "Tell me some more about your mother." The guiding hypothesis with which the interviewer started was that in any individual case, the Tree and the House were most likely to be, respectively, symbols of father and mother. In each case, however, the conclusion seemed indicated that the Tree represented the self, often portrayed with ideal qualities, while the House did indeed represent the mother, and as such was as likely to be the target of hostility as of love. At the close of each interview series—with two of the subjects, two appointment hours were required—it was possible to state this symbolism in the tentative terms in which interpretations are customarily offered in counseling sessions. It met a surprised acceptance in three cases, and a rejection only in the one which was, clinically speaking, by far the most obvious! (From a counseling standpoint, it had been prematurely offered in this case).

A brief statement of one of these cases may be offered, not as evidence, but as an illustration. This subject is a young man who was raised on a farm in Tennessee. He lost his mother, who was then still a young woman, when he was twelve. He had had two unsuccessful marriages, and believes one can never feel as strongly about a wife as about a mother. *This subject's House was built by a young man to receive his bride. However, the bride died on the eve of the wedding, and the young man spent the rest of his years mourning before the hearth.* The subject is strongly attached to his daughter, who lives with the first wife. He writes regularly, takes her on vacation trips, and feels it his duty to transmit to her his own cultural interest. She is a tomboy, and has expressed the hope that she could live with him rather than with her mother. *His Tree is a giant coconut in a grove on a South Pacific island* (where the subject had seen military service). *The grove had been inherited by a young boy, who did not know the magic spell needed to lift the curse against transgressors, but the Tree takes a part in teaching the spell, removing the difficulty.*

The conclusion reached during these interviews is consistent with the results of the statistical analysis which was performed later. It appears that for both the men and the women subjects, the Tree becomes a symbol for self-identification. It is most typically a strong parental figure, tending to be paternal in the stories by men, maternal in those by women. Its faults are those which the author fears he has inherited. If the Tree is weak, this is an indication of strong self-depreciation. The House, on the other hand, is far more variable. It may be a self-ideal in the stories of some women, but it may also become a vehicle for expression of the hostility which is so common, beneath the surface, in the relations between daughters and mothers. It has a more companionate quality in the stories of men, although it continues to have primarily feminine qualities.

It cannot be affirmed that the relationships which obtain in this sample of stories, in each of which the Tree or the House appeared without the other, would be the same as those in stories in which both appear, along with the Person. However, this study leads to formulation of the following hypotheses, which may serve both as a frame of reference for interpreting individual productions and as the basis for further experimental test: *(a) The Tree, in verbal fantasy, is a symbol of the parental identification, and hence of the self, seen largely in ideal aspects, except where there is severe self-depreciation; (b) The House, in verbal fantasy, is most commonly a symbol of the mother, and is a self-image only when the author is prepared to accept a maternal role.* No evidence is offered as to whether the Tree and House play similar roles as graphic symbols.

These hypotheses also lead to the suggestion that, in clinical work, one may select either type of instruction, depending on whether one is most interested in learning about the unconscious self-concept or the unconscious attitude toward the mother.

Summary

College students wrote stories either about a Tree and a Person, or a House and a Person. By use of adjective check-lists, composite descriptions were constructed for Trees and for Houses, with attention to the sex of authorship. It is shown that Trees and Houses are not indifferent vehicles for projection, but that they have distinctive characteristics, which are tentatively defined.

References, Part I

Buck, J.N. The H-T-P technique: a qualitative and quantitative scoring manual. *J. clin. Psychol.,* 1948, 4, 317-396.

Giedt, F.H. & Lehner, G. F. J. Assignment of ages on the Draw-a-Person test by male neuropsychiatric patients. *J. Personality,* 1951, *19,* 440-448.

Granick, S. & Smith, L. J. Sex sequence in the Draw-a-Person test and its relation to the MMPI masculinity-femininity scale. *J. cons. Psychol.,* 1953, *17,* 71-73.

Hammer, E. S. & Piotrowski, Z. Hostility as a factor in the clinician's personality as it affects his interpretation of projective drawings (H-T-P). *J. proj. Techniques,* 1953, *17,* 210-216.

Jolles, I. A. study of the validity of some hypotheses for the qualitative interpretation of the H-T-P for children of elementary school age: I. Sexual identification *J. clin. Psychol.,* 1952, *8,* 113-118.

Levy, S. Figure drawing on a projective test. In Abt, L. and Bellak, L., *Projective Psychology, 1,* 257-297. New York: Knopf, 1950.

Machover, K. *Personality projection in the drawing of the human figure.* Springfield, Ill.: Thomas, 1949.

Weider, A. & Noller, P.A. Objective studies of children's drawings of human figures: II. Sex, age, intelligence. *J. Clin. Psychol.,* 1953, *9,* 20-23.

References, Part II

Buck, J.N. The H-T-P technique: a qualitative and quantitative scoring manual. *J. Clin. Psychol.,* 1948, *4,* 317-396.

Cattell, R.B. *Description and measurement of personality.* Yonkers, N.Y.: World Book, 1946.

Diamond, S. The House and Tree in verbal fantasy. 1. Age and sex differences in themes and content. *J. proj. Tech.,* 1954, *18,* 316-325.

Selma Landisberg, a graduate of Pennsylvania State University and Ohio State University, has worked as a clinical psychologist in mental hygiene clinics, institutions, hospitals, and community centers for the past twenty years. Presently she is in private practice and works as a therapist for the Community Guidance Service and the Lincoln Institute for Psychotherapy in New York City.

For the past 15 years, she and Dr. Emanuel F. Hammer have been conducting their own workshops in projective drawing techniques as well as under the sponsorship of various educational and professional organizations in the United States and the Dominion of Canada.

Miss Landisberg is the author of several papers on the H-T-P; she worked with John N. Buck during the early period of the technique's development.

The cases cited for illustration in this chapter were drawn from her recent experience as a supervising psychologist at the Staten Island Mental Health Center in New York.

Chapter 5

The Use of the H-T-P in a Mental Hygiene Clinic for Children

Selma Landisberg, M.A.

Miss Landisberg first defines the role of the H-T-P in the test battery employed in mental hygiene clinics. She then gives two excellent examples of the orthodox achromatic-chromatic H-T-P in action: she presents the cases at length and analyzes them in depth. These cases illustrate the relatively rich contribution which the P-D-I can make to the development of the total personality picture when the patient in question is willing and able to verbalize freely. Eds.

In the past ten to fifteen years, the H-T-P has been playing an increasingly vital role in the dynamic and diagnostic appraisal of patients of all ages evaluated and treated in mental hygiene clinics. Not only has this approach proved valuable as one of the media used by psychologists in achieving insightful understanding of an individual seeking help with his problems, but it has lent itself well as visual demonstration material of a patient's psychic state to the other members of the team or clinic colleagues who have also been engaged, through their own respective approaches, in the same study of the same patient. The H-T-P also has proven to be valuable as an instrument for checking progress in the treatment of individuals at various junctures as well as at termination, thus providing tangible evidence of the effects of the treatment.

The use of the H-T-P in one mental hygiene clinic which offers extensive diagnostic study and subsequent treatment of children and their families will be considered here. The initial service includes a developmental evaluation of the child, a detailed review of the history of the problem, a study of the family background, extensive psychological testing, and psychiatric examination, followed by a review of each case by the entire staff, consisting of social workers, psychologists, and psychiatrists, prior to the making of recommendations. Two cases exemplifying the contribution of the H-T-P to the diagnosis and treatment planning will be presented. In the first instance, the H-T-P offered confirmation of the impressions of other team members; in the second case, it produced a much clearer and more decisive picture of the patient's personality than was developed by other psychological tests or by the interview technique.

To offer as full a background as possible against which to study the H-T-P, the developmental histories, complaints, family background, and the psychiatrists' impressions in each case will be presented.

Case I

Mary T., age 10½, was referred by the family physician and the school psychologist because of her extensive daydreaming, poor school work (inconsistent with her reported I.Q. of 146), nail biting, diurnal enuresis, expressions of aversion against her mother, and the assumption of peculiar body positions because of fear that she might have an accident.

Mary's father, age 42, a college graduate, has held about a dozen jobs in the past 15 years, including that of merchant seaman, school teacher, short-order cook, public relations man, appliance salesman, and advertising editor for various small-town newspapers. Several of his job cnanges were precipitated on his part by his irresponsibility and his dishonest use of company funds. He is a Roman Catholic, but is not an active member of the faith.

Mary's mother, age 33, graduated from college one year ahead of her husband.

The Ts have been married 13 years and have lived in this community for the past 3½ years.

The oldest child in this family is Jim, age 12. Until recently, he wet his pants during the day. Next in age is the patient, Mary, age 10½. The youngest is Jean, 6 years old. Mary and Jean share their bedroom; Jim has his own room, and the parents occupy the third bedroom.

Mary is a nail-biter, daydreams considerably both in school and at home, fails to complete her school work, and displays a decided resentment toward her mother and her school teacher. She is considered to be of high intelligence and is in a special advanced class in public school, in the 5th grade. In the past six years, Mary has had diuresis two or three times each week. She shows poor toleration for frustration and tends to give up easily in her school work. She is reported to be a "light sleeper." When Mary attended Kindergarten at age 5, she suffered with separation anxiety, sat by herself and was very shy; finally she was withdrawn from the class after three months' attendance. In the first grade, she clowned, fooled around, and would not do her work. In spite of her poor school adjustment, however, she was able to obtain passing grades each year.

Because of the father's unstable occupational history, the family's economic distress, and the mother's admission to a mental hospital for two months, Mary was placed in a foster home from the age of 16 months until 28 months, and again was boarded out for four months to live with her maternal grandmother, and then with married friends of Mr. T. when she was 4½ years old. Presumptive evidence suggests significant sexual stimulation to be of causal importance. Both parents have engaged in acts of infidelity; the entire family joined nudist colonies for a few summer seasons until about three years ago. When she was around age 9, Mary was attacked by a group of boys who jumped on her and took off her clothes. Mary was considered a thin, ungainly child by the parents. Mrs. T stated that the family was not sympathetic to Mary when she became sick. Mr. T. admitted referring to Mary in her presence as "my happy little moron." Mary had a tonsillectomy at the age of 7 with considerable post-operative bleeding and subsequent vomiting.

The Ts have had a stormy and chaotic marriage. All three children often were present during the parents' arguments. The three T children were unplanned and unwanted. Mrs. T's pregnancy with Mary was uneventful and delivery was normal. Mary was described as the most beautiful new-born of the three children. She was breastfed for one month, then Mrs. T. developed mastitis. Weaning to the bottle was accomplished without difficulty. The Ts were in a difficult financial state at that time and lived with the maternal in-laws with whom Mrs. T. could not get along. Mary took to baby food at three months of age and was weaned fully from the bottle at 16 months of age. Because of poor in-law relationships, both Mary and her brother, Jim, were placed in a foster home for the following 12 months. Mary's toilet training began at 18 months and was completed by 2½ years for both sphincters. Teething began at 7 months; sitting by 13 months. Mary was described as a bright, alert child. The words "Mommie" and "Daddy" were spoken by Mary at 1 year and complete sentences at 2½ years. Mary had the habit of blanket-chewing up until 8½ years. When the Ts again took the children to live with them, it was noted that Mary behaved in a very shy manner around other children.

Because of Mr. T's frequent job changes, the family moved from one place to another in New England and upper New York. There were many arguments and occasional assaultive outbursts against Mrs. T. when Mr. T. was drinking. Many threats of separation were made by Mrs. T. when the situation appeared intolerable.

Mrs. T was the oldest of four siblings; there was one brother in the family. The maternal grandfather, a shop foreman, spent little time with the children and was considered a drug-store politician. The maternal grandmother had to work to help feed the family while Mrs. T. took care of her three younger siblings. At the age of 13, Mrs. T. was sent to live with a widowed and childless aunt in a western state for four years. She attended a university in that state for a year at the age of 16 and was a dean's list student. She returned to her home in New England to complete college with the aunt's financial support. Mrs. T. said she was under the impression that she was only going to visit the aunt for a few months at the age of 13 and implied that the visit was pre-arranged by her parents to last for a matter of years.

Mr. T. is the middle sibling of three children. His father is a druggist, described as a meek, passive person. Mr. T's mother was over-protective and seductive with him to the exclusion and antipathy of Mr. T's older brother and younger sister. Mr. T. said that his mother made a "sissy" of him and remarked that his mother was strict and seductive to the point "where she practically emasculated me."

Mr. and Mrs. T. consider their marital relationship to be an inadequate one and as was mentioned before, both have been unfaithful to each other since the marriage. Mrs. T. suffered a mental break, apparently of a psychoneurotic nature, and was placed in a state hospital where she received insulin coma therapy for a few weeks.

Both parents were extremely vague and guarded in regard to Mary's symptoms. Mrs. T. felt that Mary had improved so much in the past few months that a further evaluation of her was not necessary. Mrs. T. recently consulted an attorney about a legal separation and divorce from Mr. T. Mr. T., meanwhile, is unemployed, owes several thousand dollars, and recently had his car repossessed by the finance company. Mrs. T., who was probably quite attractive in her early adulthood, now is an unusually tense, anxious, and frightened woman. Her many years of marital stress are reflected in her distraught appearance. Mr. T. is a pleasant, jocular person, so preoccupied with sex that it was difficult to elicit information from him about his daughter, Mary.

In the psychiatric interview, Mary was described as an attractive well-groomed, slender girl. Initially she had a severe and tense expression on her face, was superficially poised, polite, and controlled. After receiving some support, she became extremely dramatic in her verbal, facial and bodily expression, but for the most part, she was tearful and depressed. She stated that her main trouble was that she was too young to date as her brother does and too old to get the consideration that her younger sister gets. She told of her brother as taunting and teasing her about his social life and how much better he was than she is; she told of her younger sister's teasing her and making her angry; and of her mother's always taking the part of her younger sister. Mary stated that she was very much afraid to express herself freely at home because she might hurt her mother's feelings and her mother might become sick and upset. Mary gave many examples of her younger sister's provoking her. The latter would mess up their room and then get Mary blamed for it; at night she would taunt and poke Mary from underneath. Mary stated, "I think that she really would like to kill me." Often her mother did not interfere because she was in bed and did not wish to be disturbed. Mary described her father as withdrawn and very strict. Whatever he says around the house is law. The children know that he means what he says, for on occasion, he has taken off his belt and struck them across the back with it.

Mary said the children in school all think that she is strange. They tease her and call her crazy. Mary feels that she simply cannot do things correctly at school; that she always makes "stupid mistakes." One or two girls in school do not tease her, but Mary has no close friends. She has a crush on a boy in her brother's class because he is handsome. She often daydreams about being in a beautiful forest alone with him with beautiful classical music playing in the background. She said that the other children call her a square because she prefers classical music to rock-and-roll.

In one of her daydreams, Mary has a fairy godmother who grants her three wishes: (1) to be beautiful and have lots of clothes; (2) to be brilliant; (3) to have a supply of wishes so that whenever she wants something like a sports car or an apple she can ask for it and get it. Mary mentioned that she has considerable difficulty falling asleep at night. Often she imagines that the clothes in the open closet are ghosts who will come out of the closet. Then she too will become a ghost. The ghosts will take over the whole world and soon there will be more ghosts than people, and after that everything will be peaceful. A frequent fantasy-nightmare is of being dressed in a leopard skin and talking to all the animals in the jungle who are her friends: then she is captured by cannibals and placed in a pot of boiling water. While the cannibals dance around her, her animal friends, especially the elephants, come to her rescue. At this time she is awakened by her mother or sister.

When she was asked if she had any fears, Mary became anxious and reticent, stated that she was afraid to collect rocks any more because if she did she would need to go down to the beach and the same thing might happen that occurred when she was nine, when the boys jumped on her and took off her clothes. In talking about this, she became extremely depressed and almost inarticulate. Her parents spanked her for going there, although, "They never told me not to go." Now she collects coins because "then you don't have to think about going out to collect them but can get them from your friends or by mail." When she was asked if she would ever get married, Mary said, "No," not if she had a choice. But her mother tells her that she should get married, that she is supposed to have three children. If Mary had a choice she would have no children, even though she likes baby things, has dolls, and takes good care of them. She mentioned that although she enjoys eating, she often has difficulty doing so. When she swallows food, she experiences a swollen feeling like having a balloon in her stomach; this feeling prevents her from eating any more. She has occasional stomach aches and nausea, also.

Obviously Mary has received excessive sexual and aggressive stimulation and has attempted to control her impulses through obsessive thinking, and hysteric and phobic symptoms.

A second psychiatrist's interview yielded the following additional information: Mary said that her mother scolds her a great deal and favors her older brother and

Fig. 77, Case I

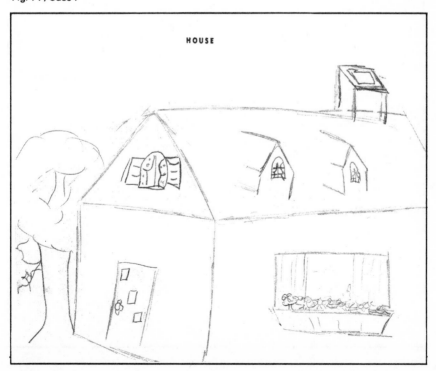

HOUSE

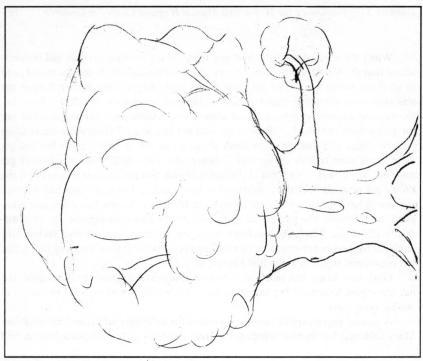

Fig. 78, Case I (above)

Fig. 79, Case I (below)

PERSON

younger sister. Her father favors the brother. Mary explained that she was "in the middle" and was not loved by either parent. She said that she would like to take a kitten with her to a desert island. She reads a great deal and enjoys science magazines which she understands, but which her brother does not understand. She smiled proudly when she said this, revealing her need to exceed her brother. She said that she had many problems and tearfully admitted that some of her worries were difficult to talk about. Again she said that her mother and father did not seem to understand her. The diagnostic impression of the second psychiatrist was that Mary had a phallic character with mixed neurotic symptoms. Both psychiatrists felt that psychotherapy was indicated for Mary and counselling for the mother. The father did not appear to be amenable to counselling.

Mary's H-T-P productions (Drawings, Drawing Sequence, and Post-Drawing Interrogation) are discussed in detail. The H-T-P, in this case, offered findings consistent with the data derived from the other tests in the battery and confirmed the psychiatric evaluations.

H-T-P Drawing Sequence

Achromatic, Patient is sinistral in handedness.

HOUSE
1. 15″. "What kind of house? I'll draw my grandmother's house."
2. Light strokes of roof area periphery.
3. Main wall.
4. Left side wall.
5. Reinforces roof.
6. "This doesn't look like my grandmother's house so it won't be my grandmother's house."
7. Door with windows and knob.
8. Dormer windows.
9. Tree – left.
10. Main window and flower box.
11. Chimney – reinforced.

TOTAL TIME: 5' 45"

TREE
1. Foliage perimeter.
2. Inner branch lines and foliage lines.
3. Downward trunk lines.
4. Roots. Two center.
5. Right side branch with foliage area and small branches.
6. Lower main foliage lines.
7. Bark lines and knot holes.
8. Additional inner foliage lines.
9. Adds left and right side roots.

TOTAL TIME: 1' 35"

PERSON

1. (Covers drawing page by resting right arm on desk around paper's top.)
2. Profile.
3. Mouth. Erases and re-draws.
4. Chin.
5. Erases whole profile.
6. Re-draws, enlarging profile area.
7. Mouth.
8. Erases and re-draws mouth.
9. Eye with pupil.
10. Eyebrow.
11. Hair outline.
12. Ear line of hair.
13. Inner hair shading lines.
14. Erases and re-draws mouth.
15. Ear outline.
16. Reinforces nose.
17. Neck.
18. Inner skeletal lines of upper torso and arms.
19. Right arm.
20. Left arm.
21. Body lines. Bust lines. Erases and enlarges body and bust lines.
22. "Wonder if that looks all right for her."
23. Erases right arm.
24. Blouse lines and left sleeve and left hand.
25. Reinforces blouse lines.
26. Right sleeve.
27. Blouse neck line.
28. Right sleeve and hand.
29. "Did I make her too big?"

TOTAL TIME: 9' 20"

Achromatic P-D-I

P1. Is that a man or a woman? A woman. I mean, teen-ager.
P2. How old is she? 16.
P3. Who is she? No – Reminds me of a girl; but I forget her name.
(Q) She was my baby-sitter for about a year.
P5. Whom were you thinking about while you were drawing? Of my baby sister. I think of my mother – brother and sister and my girl friend who taught me to make faces.
P6. What is she doing? Ice-skating.
Where? L.C. Park.
What is she looking at? At other skaters.
P7. What is she thinking about? Well – Thinking of how wonderful it is. Of her

boyfriend, maybe.

(Q) How much fun it is – to see beautiful scenery and everything.

(Boyfriend?) How she'd like to get him and he doesn't pay attention.

(Talk about?) Sports and science.

P8. How does she feel? She feels happy she's skating. Not very happy he doesn't pay attention to her.

Why? Wants him to like her.

(Q) Just like any girl would want a boy to like her.

T1. What kind of tree is that? Oak.

T2. Where is that tree actually located? In a park.

T3. About how old is that tree? It looks like – be about 50 years old.

T4. Is that tree alive? Yes.

T5. I (if subject says that the tree is alive)

(a) What is there about that tree that gives you the impression that it's alive? Has leaves and full growth on it.

(b) Is any part of the tree dead? No.

T6. Which does that tree look more like to you: a man or a woman?

Looks more like a masculine – as a man.

T7. What is there about it that gives you that impression? Looks strong and sturdy.

T8. If that were a person instead of a tree, which way would the person be facing? Facing me.

T9. Is that tree by itself, or is it in a group of trees? By itself. Others somewhere off – spread out.

T10. As you look at that tree, do you get the impression that is is above you, below you, or about on a level with you? On a level.

T11. What is the weather like in this picture? Clear and sunny.

What time of day is it? 4 P.M.

What time of year? Spring.

Temperature? Pretty moderate.

T12. Is there any wind blowing in this picture? Yes. Gentle breezes.

T13. Show me in what direction it is blowing. (Moves hand left to right around top periphery of tree)

H1. How many stories does that house have? 2 floors.

H2. What is that house made of? Of wood.

H3. Is that your own house? No.

Whose house is it? A house I made up. (Q) I have seen them – the parts like that. (Q) Doors. Split-level like this.

H4. Whose house were you thinking about while you were drawing? Something I might own.

H5. Would you like to own that house yourself? Yes.

Why? Looks so beautiful on inside and outside.

H6. If you did own that house and you could do whatever you liked with it:

(a) Which room would you take for your own? Upstairs. (Room with dormer windows).

Why? So nice.

(Q) To see. Look out on whole world.

(b) Whom would you like to have live in that house with you? My brother, father and mother. (Sister?) No. She makes a mess and says I did it. Why? I like them a lot. (Q) I don't know. I like my father. He's nice and strong. My mother is sweet and soft. (Brother?) He's–Maybe he does beat me up. He takes care of me. Teaches me how to dance. He's 12.

H7.   As you look at that house, does it seem to be close by or far away? About – Far away.

H8.   As you look at that house, do you get the impression that is is above you, below you, or about on a level with you? On a level.

H9.   What does that house make you think of, or remind you of? Of a nice, gentle, clear country. So quiet and peaceful. No buses rushing around. No beeping of horns. Nothing that's terrible. And no rock-and-roll singers.

H11.   Is that a happy, friendly sort of house? Yes.

H12.   What is there about it that gives you that impression? Looks so warm and peaceful and happy and friendly. If not friendly, it would be shabby; wouldn't look so good.

H13.   Are most houses that way? Yes. Why do you think so? They look good.

H14.   What is the weather like in this picture? Warm and sunny.

T15.   What does that tree make you think of, or remind you of? Not of anything. A park. Nice.

T16.   What else? (What happened to you of any importance when you were 3 or 4?) (N.B. Examiner's question based on age-level position of a lower right branch which juts out from the rest of tree). Mother went to a mental hospital. She wanted a rest. She was worrying all the time. I got lost in the hospital when I wanted to see her. I got my shoes stuck in the snow. She was away two months. My grandmother took care of me. (Q) She was worrying over me and worrying over Daddy. He lost his job again. A newspaper reporter. He's looking for a job now.

T17.   Is it a healthy tree? Yes.

T18.   What is there about it that gives you that impression? If not healthy, it wouldn't be strong and sturdy and have nice green leaves.

T19.   Is it a strong tree? Yes.

T20.   What is there about it that gives you that impression? How thick it is. Looks strong and sturdy and well-balanced.

P9.   What does that person make you think of, or remind you of? I don't know.

P11.   Is that person well? Yes.

P12.   What is there about her that gives you that impression: She looks happy. She looks nice.

P14.   What is there about her that gives you that impression? 'Cause she's having fun skating.

P15.   Are most people that way? Well, I don't know. Some are happy. Wouldn't say most are happy.

Why? Because of wars and Khruschev and taxes. Not enough money to pay for food.

P16.   Do you think you would like that person. Yes.
       Why? She looks like a nice sort of person.
P17.   What is the weather like in this picture? Sunny.
       What time of day is it? 2 P.M.
       What time of year? Winter.
       Sky; temperature? Cool. Breezy.

P18.   Whom does that person remind you of? Of my babysitter.
       Why? Looks that way. Liked her a lot. She was nice. Took care of us nicely.
P19.   What does that person need most? Well, I don't know. Think maybe she —
       A cat. Smoky.
       Why? 'Cause she likes Smoky as well as I do.
       (Q) My cat. She had 5 beautiful kittens. Mother doesn't like cats. We have
       a dog – Lady. I wish I had 15 cats – 17 cats.

T21.   Whom does that tree remind you of? Of my father. He's so strong and sturdy.
T22.   What does that tree need most? I don't think it needs anything.

H15.   Whom does that house make you think of? Of my mother.
       Why? So soft and gentle, friendly and kind.
H16.   What does that house need most? Needs proper care. And someone to live
       in it. Needs some nice furniture. Flowers need care. Needs painting.
       (Q) White with blue shingles.

HOUSE

(If Tree next to the House were a Person, who might it be?) Jack. My boy-
friend. Maybe he's ready to move in. He's walking by it.

She elected to draw her grandmother's house, where she was cared for while
her mother was in a mental hospital. Yet later, during the drawing, presumably
because of guilt feelings, she stated that it was not her grandmother's house. The
House gestalt is a large, capacious-looking structure, fairly open and friendly, with
outspread shutters and an inviting window-box with flowers. This feminine exhibitionism is countered to some extent by the ambivalent fear and desire to close off
herself expressed in the barring of the upper dormer windows which jut out from the
room that she would occupy if she owned the house. The marked emphasis on the
chimney, which is out of perspective and thrown forward to offer an interior view,
reveals her preoccupation with phallic matters. Her bird's-eye view of the House
suggests a feeling of superiority over the people in her home as well as a desire to get
away from the home. The transparent chimney reflects a lack of certainty that the
male or father figure can be relied upon to establish a realistic union with his family.
An unstable oppositionalism seems to be expressed in the roof and wall areas which
break into the right side of the page, although she made last-minute attempts to
correct this damage by drawing in the exterior line of the right wall of the paper's

edge. The gratuitously drawn tree on the left, 'though identified as "Jack, my boy-friend, ready to move in," on a deeper level may represent the feelings of rejection from the home, of being an outsider, which she experienced in earlier years when she was boarded in a foster home and cared for by relatives and family friends. This tree with its scrawly, downward-drooping branches suggests early depressive experiences; while its open vaginal-like center foliage area, which contains a large branch, reflects her sexual fantasy. The clinical impression thus far is that she is a precocious 10-year-old girl, who is excessively preoccupied with sexual matters, who wishes to be grown up, to exhibit and gain attention through her femininity, and is envious of the power of the male role. There is some defiance toward and feelings of superiority over her parents, which occasion fear and guilt since her ego foundation is not secure and she still has strong unmet dependency needs.

TREE

Her Tree also occupies much space. This fact, together with the anthropomorphic branch which appears to be an outstretched arm and fist, suggests her desire to dominate and defy. A marked fantasy investment is shown in the enlarged foliage area implying that she is a dreamer. The soft, feminine quality of the foliage in conjunction with the phallic branches suggests the focus of her dreaming. The age of 50 assigned to the Tree implies that she feels much older than her years and thus has experienced considerable trauma. The Tree's trunk, the index of ego strength, is stunted and knotted, and reinforces the impression of trauma and depression. However, the trunk's thickness and the large outspread roots suggest that she still has enough ego strength to keep in balance and obtain some gratification from her environment. Her identification with the male is decisively expressed in her P-D-I associations with the Tree. Undoubtedly she wishes to be "strong and sturdy" and is in fear of her passivity longings because of negative associations with the mother who, as is known, has shown weakness and breakdown in the past.

PERSON

Her drawn Person is a phallicized, seductive-looking woman – unusual in its mature conceptualization for a 10-year-old child. The underlying weakness of the female is implicit in her use of skeletal structural lines upon which to form the body outline. The fact that the torso is incomplete from the waist down seems to result from two factors: (1) possible sexual trauma or extreme sexual fear, and (2) her driving need to appear tall, mature, and capable, which causes her to overreach the bounds of a situation and to be impulsive, and subsequently to find herself in an insecure position without solid basing. Again she breaks out of the given space area and the phallicized arm reaches too far into the page's edge – revealing a defiance which is conflict-laden, for the hands have a closed-up mitten outline suggesting her fear of making contact with people and situations as they present themselves. She wishes to assert, but anticipates rejection or castration; this dynamic aspect is shown also by the blunted nose-end and the pulled-back mouth.

H-T-P Drawing Sequence (chromatic)

HOUSE
  1. "We did that last time."
  2. Roof—Black crayon.

3. Main wall outline – Black.
4. Door with windows. (Door outline – black. Fill-in – brown. Windows – blue).
5. Left side window with blue curtains.
6. Main window with green flower box and red flowers.
7. Main window curtains – green and light black vertical lines.
8. "Do you ever have any other visitors?"
9. Dormer windows – black outline.
10. "The top should be white; but since I don't have white, I'll do it in purple."
11. Purple shading of dormer windows.
12. Light purple shading of roof area.
13. Chimney with black brick outline and red inner shading.
14. Black outline of bricks in side and main walls.
15. "Not very good, is it?"
16. Adds red brick coloring to walls.

TOTAL TIME: 8'25"

TREE
1. Downward right and left side branch lines and trunk lines.
2. Right side branch outline.
3. Finishes lower trunk lines to base of paper.
4. Inner upper branch lines.
5. Bark lines.
6. Foliage perimeter – green.
7. Reinforces bark lines.
8. Green coloring of foliage area.
9. Brown coloring of trunk.
10. Brown knothole outline with black fill-in.
11. Green outline of right branch foliage area with green fill-in.

TOTAL TIME: 4'25"

PERSON
1. Profile – black.
2. Eye with pupil – brown.
3. Red mouth.
4. Brown hair area.
5. "I think I can do better in pencil though."
6. Black neck outline.
7. Inner skeletal lines – black.
8. Upper trunk and arm outline – purple.
9. Blue collar and scarf area.
10. Black outline of hands.
11. Purple upper trunk and sleeve fill-in.
12. Purple fill-in of upper torso.
13. Green hat.
14. Red pants outline and fill-in.
15. Brown shoes.
16. "He's rolling snowballs."

TOTAL TIME 5'30"

Chromatic P-D-I

P1.　Is that a man or a woman (or boy or girl)? That's a teenager. Boy.

P2.　How old is he? 13.

P3.　Who is he? No one in particular.

P4.　Is he a relation, a friend, or what? No.

P5.　Whom were you thinking about while you were drawing? Just thinking about the drawings.

P6.　What is he doing? (And where is he doing it?) Making snowballs. (Q) Might be in his backyard. (Looking at?) The snow. (Q) Just throwing snowballs at a tree. (Q) It's fun.

P7.　What is he thinking about? Well, I don't know. (Q) Uh–(long pause) How much fun it is.

P8.　How does he feel? Feels nice. Pretty good. Excited. Why? It's fun out in the snow. The first snow of the year. Been waiting a long time. (Hit tree?) It would be terrible to throw it at a man–hit him in the face. Would hurt it badly.

T1.　What kind of tree is that? An oak.

T2.　Where is that tree actually located? In Central Park.

T3.　About how old is that tree? 4 years old.

T4.　Is that tree alive? Yes.

T5.　(If subject says that the tree is alive)
(a) What is there about that tree that gives you the impression that it's alive? Leaves on it.
(b) Is any part of the tree dead? No.

T6.　Which does that tree look more like to you: a man or a woman? A man.

T7.　What is there about it that gives you that impression? Always strong and sturdy.

T8.　If that were a person instead of a tree, which way would the person be facing? Facing me.

T11.　What is the weather like in this picture? (Time of day and year; sky; temperature) Cloudy. Cool. (Q) 2 P.M. (Q) Summer.

T12.　Is there any wind blowing in this picture? Yes.

T13.　Show me in what direction it is blowing. (Moves hand from upper right to lower left of page).

T14.　What sort of wind is it? Breezy wind.

H1.　How many stories does that house have? Two.

H2.　What is that house made of? Bricks.

H3.　Is that your own house? No.
Whose house is it? Neighbor who lives across the street.

H5.　Would you like to own that house yourself? Yes.
Why? Looks nice. I like it. Picture window. Flowers on it.

H6.　If you did own that house and you could do whatever you liked with it:
(a) Which room would you take for your own? (Points to upper left–with dormer windows).
Why? Nice. Look out on world. Kind of fit into it. The room belongs to you.
(b) Whom would you like to have live in that house with you? May, Theresa,

Hope, Alice. My mother and father. (Girl friends)? Yes. They're nice. Sympathetic about your problems. (Mother and father?) They can protect me. My mother's very nice. I like her a lot. (Sister?) No. I sleep with my sister. I wish she wouldn't throw my things around. I'd lock my door so I won't lose my doll's bunting.

H7. As you look at that house, does it seem to be close by or far away? Close by.

H9. What does that house make you think of, or remind you of? My grand-mother's. It has a nice little farm. Nice but in the country. (Do you like where you live now?) I guess so.

H11. Is that a happy, friendly sort of house? Yes.

H12. What is there about it that gives you that impression? Just a happy, friendly – Isn't every house.

H13. Are most houses that way? Yes.
Why do you think so? Well, I don't know. Nice and neat. Why it looks happy and friendly. No paint chipping off.

H14. What is the weather like in this picture? Warm and sunny.

T15. What does that tree make you think of, or remind you of? My boyfriend, Jack. Looks like a gentleman. Nice and neat. Good looking.

T17. Is it a healthy tree? Yes, except for spots. Those spots do not remind me of Jack. Worm-eaten, old things. Old worries. The tree worried once. About all sorts of things. Like when the children kicked the young tree around. When it grew up, the men chopped on it with an axe on the other side. They wouldn't leave the poor little tree alone. (Q) Got to make furniture out of it. But couldn't chop through it. It's so tough.

T19. Is it a strong tree? Yes.

T20. What is there about it that gives you that impression? Wide. Sturdy.

P9. What does that person make you think of, or remind you of? A puppet. (Q) Being held by strings. Someone holding you and moving your arms and doing everything for you. When you try to do something, it won't let you do it. (Q) In school and at home. The teacher and some of the boys. (Q) Showing that I can't think as much. Think I'm stupid – a square. I do everything wrong. They like rock-and-roll and everything.

P11. Is that person well? Looks like might have got over chicken-pox.

P12. What is there about him that gives you that impression? Looks thin and puny.

P13. Is that person happy? Yes.

P14. What is there about him that gives you that impression? He's smiling.

P15. Are most people that way? Some people, I guess.
Why? Don't know. (Some not smiling?) 'Cause of taxes and everything.

P16. Do you think you would like that person? I don't know. Why? Don't know.

P17. What is the weather like in this picture? Cloudy. Ready to snow. Cold.

P18. Whom does that person remind you of? No one in particular. Why? He looks weak and puny.

P19. What does that person need most? Needs strengthening. Someone to – never mind – come with problems to. School.

T22.   What does that Tree need most? Needs someone to love him. Why? Because he's been kicked around and pushed around all his life.

H15.   Whom does that house make you think of? No one in particular.

H16.   What does that house need most? Someone to live in it.
Why? Empty (Q) Looks empty. People just moved out.

T23.   If this were a person instead of a bird (or another tree, or anything else
not a part of the originally drawn tree) who might it be? (Tree: Anything
happen at age 4?) The cows came through my clothes. Our clothes. Got
all muddy. Staying with grandmother in country.

HOUSE

In her chromatic House, the oppositionalism and the desire to escape from
the past, to move impulsively into new situations, are shown by the frontal breakthrough into the page's right edge and the forward jutting of the main wall. Her
need for superiority and aloofness come through in her use of purple (color of
power) in the dormer area. The entire concept is eroticized by: the vaginal-like
picture window seductively bounded by filmy curtains and red flowers; the red
brick wall and red chimney, showing body excitement and phallic interest. The
black brick outlining, hasty, and helter-skelter toward the center and bottom of
the wall (body image), suggests her attending guilt over her erotic feelings.

Fig. 80, Case I

HOUSE

Fig. 81, Case I (above)

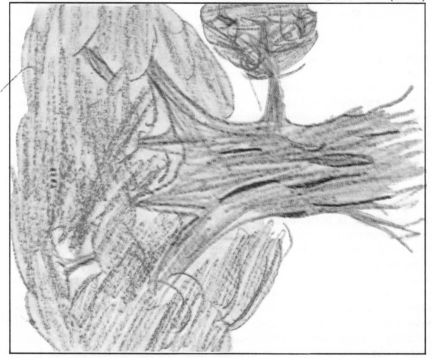

Fig. 82, Case I (below)

TREE

With color, an emotional excitant, her drawn Tree also bursts into the sides of the page. The heavy depressive quality of the overladen foliage in the achromatic drawing now is gone, and phallic defiance appears. The branches jut out boldly and exhibitionistically. The blackened center knot-hole bespeaks the trauma of her early years (i.e., the loss of the mother?) and reflects her guilt over her feminine sexual impulses.

PERSON

Given a second chance to draw a Person, she recovers from the impulsivity seen in her achromatic Person and draws a full figure. Vigorous activity and energy are reflected in the stance and the body positioning, and this Person's aim is to throw snowballs at a tree. But she added, significantly, "It would be terrible to throw it at a man – hit him in the face. Would hurt it badly." Here is depicted her near-conscious anger at her father. Her resentment at being overpowered by him (the history revealed that she has seen him as bullying the mother and strict with her) is revealed in her P-D-I comments that the Person "is a puppet being held by a string. Someone holding you and moving your arms and doing everything for you." She has been stimulated to act aggressively by her identification with the father, yet she feels restrained by external forces and by her own guilt. The figure is bent over, and there are black structural prop lines beneath the bold purple and red clothing, suggesting the underlying weakness of both her father's and her own social facade.

In sum, Mary seems to be a depressed, orally and sexually traumatized girl, trying hard, but not always with success, to deny and suppress dysphoric and hostile feelings by engaging in highly romantic, idealized and seductive fantasies of being loved and rescued from her intolerable home situation. She appears to force friendly affect when with people; often she struggles beyond her ego resources to achieve in a competitive, exhibitionistic manner, and to gain coveted attention and approval. Consciously she is trying hard, in a forced and strained way, to convince herself and others of the positive features of her parents (P-D-I: "I like them a lot. My father's nice and strong and my mother's sweet, gentle, soft and kind"); she wishes to identify with the imagined strength and achievement of the father and the seductive qualities of the mother, but these figures have been threatening, disappointing, and frequently inaccessible as supportive objects for her. The mother seems to have been experienced as overcontrolling and depriving and the father as sexually exciting, unstable, depressed, and destructive. In her associations to her drawn Person and Tree, she said, "He needs strengthening; someone to come to with his problems; someone to love him because he's been kicked and pushed around all his life." In an effort to make up for her felt deprivation and abuse (her chromatic Tree – self-portrait – was seen as "worm-eaten," "kicked around and chopped at when young"), much of her energies are shunted into highly romantic fantasies about male objects, apparently fostered by her father's sexually exciting and provocative behavior toward her. But as she experiences the father and other males as ambivalent toward her, turning critical, castrative, and abandoning her in pursuit of other women, she tends to take a very dramatic, attention-getting, forward role in an effort to capture and control the male. Her female Person drawing was of a seductive woman with large, phallically aggressive arms, who is thinking "of how she would like to get her boyfriend but he doesn't pay attention."

Her ego resources in terms of social sensitivity, fantasy capacity, richness of associations, potential impulse control, recoverability from regressive lapses, and overall intellectual ability are good. But at this time her low frustration tolerance, tendency to withdraw into wishful fantasy, inclination to invert hostility against herself as well as to project blame onto stronger objects, and her tendency to act seductively and regressively in forming relationships, serve to disturb her adjustment.

Unless there is therapeutic intervention she is likely to become more depressed, more fantasy absorbed, and inclined to act upon her fantasies in an impulsive way. The diagnostic impression is that she is a girl of superior intelligence with phallic character traits and depressive tendencies.

Case II

The second case required diagnostic clarification since there was uncertainty from the history and the psychiatric interviews about whether or not the patient was psychotic.

Mr. and Mrs. P. were referred by their family physician, whom they had consulted about their son, Michael, who refused to attend school. Michael had not been to school for several weeks prior to this referral. When the truant officer threatened to take Michael to court, the parents obtained a 30-day medical release from their doctor and asked the Center to make a study of Michael. The mother's attitude toward the referral was vacillant. On the one hand, she described the home atmosphere as an unbearable nightmare which could not continue; on the other hand, she felt that Michael's problem was one of adolescence and that "things will blow over."

The family consists of the father, age 40, a bus driver; the mother, age 37, a housewife; Michael, the patient, age 14, in the 9th grade in a public high school; and three younger brothers, whose ages are 11, 9, and 5, respectively. The family moved into the community two years ago, after being forced to move from their previous home which was to be razed, as it was on the approach line to a new bridge. Michael has his own room; the three younger boys share one room but occupy separate beds. The family is Roman Catholic and attends church regularly. For the past year, however, Michael has not attended church. Previously he knew Latin well enough to serve as an altar boy from the age 10 to 12 years.

Michael has had spotty school attendance since the family moved. Before the end of the 8th grade at a parochial school, he said that he was not returning to school because his teacher picked on him and the pupils thought he was a bookworm. Mr. P. tried to use force to take him to school, but Michael, a tall husky boy, was simply too big and resisted his father successfully. However, the principal was able to persuade Michael to return to school to finish the term and Michael passed with flying colors. He enrolled in a parochial high school, but stayed home a few days each week and failed two subjects. He complained that he had too much homework. It would take him 6 hours to complete a 3-hour homework assignment. He worked off his frustration on his family by cursing, throwing books, and telling everyone to be quiet. The parents, thinking that public school might be easier for him, suggested that he transfer. After his first day at public high school, however, he came home and said that he had made a mistake, for there were too many children in the school and he did not like changing classes from room to room. Pleading and coercion were of no avail. Whenever he was pressed to return to school, he would throw things around the house, break glasses, milk bottles, ash trays, curse and beat his fists on the wall.

Michael can not endure physical pain. If he has a stomachache or toothache he will thrash around in bed and scream. Until recently, when he was placed on stelazine, he seldom slept at night, and when he did sleep, he had nightmares. He would usually fall asleep at 4 or 5 in the morning and sleep until 4 or 5 in the afternoon. He fights constantly with his younger brothers and orders them around. He keeps himself isolated from his former school friends and if they come to see him, he goes to his bedroom, telling Mrs. P. to say that he is sick. He used to enjoy fishing, an activity which his father put off doing with him. Now if Mr. P. offers to take him fishing, he says, "Go yourself." Michael often curses Mrs. P., telling her that it is all her fault because she yelled at him and threatened him with reform school when his problem started. At one time, Michael said, "Please get me some help. I can't help myself." But this reaction later was followed by his saying that he would speak with no one and did not wish his parents to go to the Center. Since he has been treated medically on an emergency basis, he has been able to sleep at night, feels better, and the entire household has been calmer.

The Ps trace Michael's difficulty to the time they moved. Before that, he did what he was told to do. Even when he wanted to have his own way, they were able to manage and control him. After the age of 13, he became rebellious and was always ready to pick a fight with his three brothers. From the start, the boys in the neighborhood and at school, who had already formed groups, challenged him as a newcomer. He claimed that he made an effort not to appear bright when he moved to the new school because he feared that the pupils would look down on him as a bookworm. By the time he reached 8th grade, he decided not to study so that he would be at the same level as the other boys, since being friends with them meant so much to him. The teacher complained that he was not paying attention but was fooling with the girls who seemed to like him. Expressing regret, Mrs. P. said that at that time she was pushing and yelling at him to study harder and did not realize that he was neglecting his studies so that he could become acceptable and popular. By the time he reached high school, he had quite a few friends. But he had trouble with the children in his neighborhood. When he would defend his younger brothers against aggressive children, he would usually be beaten up by the bigger boys. When Michael began to stay away from school, Mrs. P. aided and abetted his truancy by stating on the slips sent home by the school that Michael had been ill.

In regard to his early behavior, the Ps revealed that 'though he was outwardly manageable, he always had been a problem in the home and had been subjected to many traumata. Two months after birth, he had exzema and was an extremely difficult baby to handle. Mrs. P. believes that he might have been affected by her emotional behavior. She always was excited, easily upset, yelled, and usually "ran around in a stew." He was on a special diet until the age of two years, at which time his rash subsided. Before then, nothing relieved his itchiness and irritability. The Ps would take turns in walking him at night to try to stop his screaming, but to no avail.

At that time they lived in a one-room apartment. Michael had become so conditioned to not sleeping that even after the exzema subsided he hated to go into his crib. If he were allowed to do so, he would stay up and play until midnight. Mrs. P. permitted him to stay up with her to keep her company when Mr. P. worked at night. When Michael was 16 months old, he was able to climb out of his crib and his parents had to keep putting him back in. "He would cry with a resistance like no other child."

When Michael was 3 years old, his brother James was born and Michael had to share a room with him. From the age of 3 to 5 years, Michael received very little attention from Mrs. P. as James was birth-injured and had osteomyelitis of the maxilla. James required medical care at home and had to be taken to the doctor's several times a week. Then a third child, Steven, was born when Michael was 4½ years old. Michael slept in the same room with James until he was 10 years of age and during that time, from 3 to 10 years, he had nightmares. When he had his own room, however, the nightmares stopped. While James was ill, Michael was "an extremely good boy." Michael had had friends since he was 2½ years old; he had gone out to play and had eaten well. After James was cured and Mrs. P. stopped devoting all her time to him, Michael began to act up and required all her attention. The more attention she gave him, the more he demanded. He felt that he was too big to play with his brothers.

Michael lasted two months in Kindergarten; he would come home crying and Mrs. P. would feel sorry for him. He went "wonderfully" to the first grade but at the same time he developed "nervous habits," did not sleep well at night, and yelled during his nightmares. If he fell at school, he would scream all the way home. His first grade teacher said that he grimaced and made nervous gestures. He did well in his work but was anxious and upset about his homework. When he had trouble with homework, he would cry and Mrs. P. would help him. Other than these lapses, he was a "model child." He joined the Boy Scouts. He was an altar boy at church. When he was with his parents, however, he always was fresh, impudent, and argumentative. Mr. P. never interacted pleasantly with Michael and put off taking him out with him alone. Mr. P. was constantly after Michael about little things, and if Michael wrangled with his brothers, Mr. P. would take the side of the brothers and would hit Michael with his hands. Today, Mr. P. believes that he should have "spoiled" Michael, instead of showing his temper and hitting him. He talks to Michael only when the latter first talks to him and usually does not bother with him.

Michael was conceived 3 months after the P's married. Mr. P. wanted a boy; whereas Mrs. P. wanted a girl because she had been the only girl among four brothers and thought that having a girl would be a change. She would have "something to dress up and admire." Mrs. P. was in poor health during the pregnancy; in the third month she hemorrhaged so much that she almost miscarried. Nausea was present during all her pregnancies. Labor was normal and lasted 13 hours. There were no complications, 'though it was a forceps delivery. Michael was born head first in very good condition, and weighed 7 pounds, 5 ounces. The mother and infant were in the hospital 6 days. "I wanted to breast-feed, but I didn't know where to begin and the nurses in the hospital didn't want to be bothered." He was a very hungry baby and took the bottle well, but never seemed to be satisfied. Because of his exzema at two months of age, a specialist took him off all foods but milk and then placed him on a diet. When a certain food was introduced, they would wait for his reactions to that food. One week Michael got fruit; the next week, a vegetable, etc. Several foods finally were eliminated and this diet lasted two years. Since then he has eaten everything, although the rash has recurred in mild form from time to time.

Michael teethed at 5 months; sat at 6 months; and walked at 12 months. Bowel training started when he was 8 months old and he was placed on a baby toilet seat. He did not take to it. It was begun again when he was 18 months old and completed in two months' time. Bladder training also was begun when he was 18 months old and by the time he was 23 months of age, he was dry day and night. He did not resist training and actually seemed to like the idea of accomplishing. He had no illnesses other than an allergy until he was 6 years old and in school. He had a severe case of mumps at 6; and when he was 8, he had measles which caused earaches. Also when he was 8, a boy hit him in the stomach while they were wrestling and Michael had to be hospitalized for stomach spasm and a high fever. While he was in the hospital, his parents stayed near him as he disliked doctors and would not accept "needles" or medicine. When he was 10 years of age, he was hospitalized again with a stomach virus and pains resembling those of appendicitis. At 12 years of age, he was sick with chicken pox and was out of school for two weeks. During the past few years, he has had a chronic stomach condition which the doctors said he would outgrow.

In grammar school, Michael did well academically, averaging grades of from 80 to 90. He loved baseball, fishing, and swimming; but Mr. P. did not care for sports. The most Mr. P. would do by way of playing with his sons would be to allow them to ride in his bus with him for a few hours.

Both Mr. and Mrs. P. tend to demand obedience of their children by shouting and screaming, with Mr. P. doing most of the hitting, and Michael being the most frequent target. When he was 13 years old, Michael began to rebel against "everything" that his mother and father stood for. He wanted his parents to suffer with him and he delighted in provoking them.

From the foregoing, Michael's behavior suggests the presence of a severe emotional disturbance, marked by difficulty in concentrating, withdrawal, ideas of reference, and primitive acting-out. As the oldest child, he has borne the brunt of his parents' neurotic tendencies; the father has been critical, avoidant and punitive in his reactions, probably because of fear that Michael might be more favored than he; the mother has unconsciously rejected Michael's masculinity and has been burdened with guilt over her hostile reactions.

The following is excerpted from the psychiatric interviews:

Michael was a greasy-looking but well-dressed 14-year-old boy who entered the room with a great deal of hesitation. He talked about his fear of school teachers, particularly those who made fun of students who made mistakes and caused the students to "feel foolish." He complained about both his parents, saying that when he does things wrong, his mother nags him about it all day and constantly preaches to him. She tells his father, and then Michael is beaten. Michael complains that his father keeps beating him for the same thing for the rest of the day. This has been going on for as long as Michael can remember. He recalled, with some embarrassment, that one time his father chased him outside the house brandishing a broomstick. Michael also is aware to some extent of his own difficulties. He explained that he loses his temper at trivial things, and when he does so, he loses all control of himself and does not know what he is doing. He expressed shame over this behavior.

When he grows up, he would like to become a clerk at a bank. At one time he had wanted to become a doctor but he realizes that "there is too much schooling involved." His three wishes were: (1) to be rid of his present difficulties and be in better control of himself; (2) to be wealthy; (3) to have an important position, sitting behind a desk like a lawyer and having a hundred people working for him. He began the session evasively, appearing suspicious and hostile. When he warmed up, he was able to smile appropriately and relax somewhat. Early in the session, his associations seemed to be difficult to follow and his affect was constricted. At the end of the session, he stated that he now knew what the Clinic was like and would not hesitate to return. He asked how long it would take to be helped and stated that he did not wish to return to school.

His affect reflected no definite psychotic qualities; the conflicts of adolescence appeared to be very intense in him.

One psychiatrist felt that Michael had a number of character problems along passive-aggressive lines with some obsessional traits. Another diagnosed him as an obsessional neurotic with possibly a borderline psychosis.

The discussion of Michael's H-T-P follows. The chromatic P-D-I was not adminstered because of a lack of time.

Fig. 83, Case II

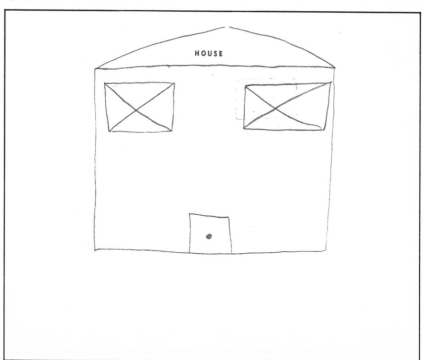

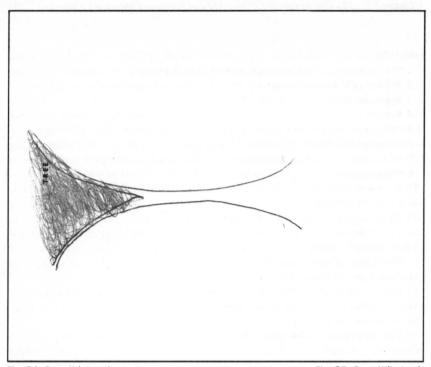

Fig. 84, Case II (above)   Fig. 85, Case II (below)

HOUSE
1. "Never did much drawing, anyway. How long do I have?"
2. Top line of wall drawn slowly.
3. Right wall line.
4. Roof-lines.
5. (Turns page to side) Wall baseline.
6. (Turns page to original position) Left wall line.
7. Stares at production for about one minute.
8. "Not an artist."
11. Door with knob.
12. Upper left window.
13. Upper right window.
14. Cross lines in both windows.
15. Erases left window and redraws, enlarging it and attempting to match size with size of right window.
16. Cross lines in left window.
17. Erases right window.
18. "Wouldn't happen to have a ruler, would you?"
19. "Oh – free-hand."
20. Redraws right window – enlarging.

TOTAL TIME: 6'

TREE
1. "Not a drawer – I'm telling you."
2. Downward right-and left-side branch and trunk lines.
3. Inner V-shaped branch lines.
4. Dark foliage fill-in.
5. Erases foliage area.
6. Erases entire tree.
7. "Any more drawings involved in this test?"
8. Upward outlining of trunk and main branches. Enlarging over original.
9. Inner V-shaped branch lines.
10. Erases left branch and redraws.
11. Foliage curlicues straight across top touching upper branch ends.
12. Foliage fill-in – heavy swirling lines.
13. Reinforces foliage.

TOTAL TIME: 3'30"

PERSON
1. "Oh" (Long pause. Stares.) "Want the whole person?"
2. Head outline with nose extension
3. Eye.
4. Brows – reinforced.
5. Erases eyes and brows.
6. Redraws eyes and brows – enlarging.
7. Erases right eye and redraws.
8. Mouth.

9.Erases mouth.
10.Redraws mouth.
11.Right ear.
12.Erases right ear.
13.Redraws right ear.
14.Erases chin line.
15.Body and arm outline.
16.Left arm erased.
17.Redraws left arm.
18.Bottom of body and legs.
19.Erases right leg and redraws.
20.Erases left leg and redraws.
21."I can't draw. Lopsided –everything."   TOTAL TIME: 11'15"

Achromatic P-D-I

P1.   Is that a man or a woman? It's a man.
P2.   How old is he? 20-30.
P3.   Who is he? A common man.
       (Q) No.
P4.   Is he a relation, a friend, or what? No.
P5.   Whom were you thinking about while you were drawing? No.
P6.   What is he doing? Standing.
       Where is he doing it? Inside.
       Looking at? Picture.
       (Q) Marine. (Q) Boat out in the sea.
P7.   What is he thinking about? He'd like to own a boat himself.
       (Q) Like to go fishing.
P8.   How does he feel? Content.
       Why? He's looking at the picture.

T1.   What kind of tree is that? (Mumbles).
       (Q) I'm talking to myself. A peach tree.
T2.   Where is that tree actually located? Florida.
       (Q) Along the beach.
T3.   How old is that tree? 3-4-3 years old.
T4.   Is that tree alive? Yes.
T5.   (a) What is there about that tree that gives you the impression that it's
       alive? The peaches on the tree.
       (Q) The leaves. Branches are standing straight. Not looping over.
       (b) Is any part of the tree dead? No.
T6.   Which does that tree look more like to you: a man or a woman?
       A man, I guess.
T7.   What is there about it that gives you that impression? Shape of the face –
       of the tree.
       (Q) Posture is straight.
T8.   If that were a person instead of a tree, which way would the person be
       facing? I'd say facing me.
T9.   Is that tree by itself, or is it in a group of trees? In a group of trees.

T10.   As you look at that tree, is it above you, below you, or about on a level with you? Above me.

T11.   What is the weather like in this picture? Cool.
        (Q) Time of Day? P.M.
        (Q) Time of year? Summer.
        (Q) Sky? Blue.

T12.   Is there any wind blowing in this picture? No.

H1.   How many stories does that house have? One-story. Two-story.

H2.   What is that house made of? I'd say brick – all right.

H3.   Is that your own house? No.
        Whose house is it? Next door.
        (Q) 2-story.

H4.   Whose house were you thinking about while you were drawing?
        Nobody's in particular.

H5.   Would you like to own that house yourself? No.
        Why? Because I like a back door to the house. It only has a front door.
        (Back door?) So could use the main entrance for – If you don't want to
        come in front door. Feet are dirty.

H6.   If you did own that house and you could do whatever you like with it:
        (a) Which room would you take for your own? Up right.
        Why? Be upstairs. Near the scenery.
        (b) Whom would you like to have live in that house with you?
        My family.
        Why? Usually have a family.
        (Q) Like to take care of them. Let them live in the house.

H7.   As you look at that house, does it seem to be close by or far away?
        Close by.

H8.   As you look at that house, do you get the impression that it is above you,
        below you, or about on a level with you? Level.

H9.   What does that house make you think of, or remind you of? (Home?)
        No. A place where you sleep – live.

H11.   Is that a happy, friendly sort of house? Yeah. I guess so.

H12.   What is there about it that gives you that impression? A door to the house.

H13.   Are most houses that way? I'd say so.
        Why do you think so? Because of the outside. The way a house looks.

H14.   What is the weather like in this picture? Summertime.
        Time of day? Morning.
        Sky? Few clouds.
        Temperature? Warm.

T15.   What does that tree make you think of, or remind you of? Scenery.

T17.   Is it a healthy tree? I'd say yes.

T18.   What is there about it that gives you that impression? Branches are straight.
        Bark of tree is nice.

T19.   Is it a strong tree? Yeah. Strong tree.

T20.   What is there about it that gives that impression? Fat tree.

P9.   What does that person make you think of, or remind you of? Happy
       person.
P11.   Is that person well? I'd say he does look well.
P12.   What is there about him that gives you that impression? He has a nice
       complexion. Not pale. Not ill.
P13.   Is that person happy? I guess so.
P14.   What is there about him that gives you that impression? Smile. Slight
       smile.
P15.   Are most people that way? Don't know about – Maybe most.
       Why? Because everything's going their way. A job. House. Family.
P16.   Do you think you would like that person? Maybe.
       Why? Not too sure. Guess so. Nice face.
P18.   Whom does that person remind you of? (Mumbles) Of a man.
       Why? Nobody in particular.
P19.   What does that person need most? Glasses.
       Why? Eyes are squinting. Hard for him to see without them. Maybe he
       doesn't know he needs them. Always sees like that and doesn't think he
       needs them. Things aren't too clear. He thinks they are – has got used to
       looking that way.
T21.   Whom does that tree remind you of? No.
T22.   What does that tree need most? Sun.

Fig. 86, Case II

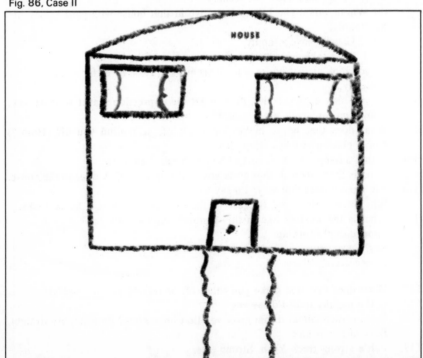

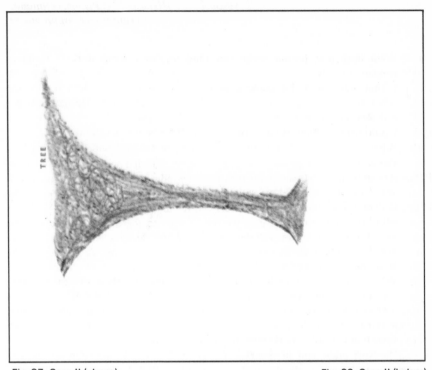

Fig. 87, Case II (above)

Fig. 88, Case II (below)

H15. Whom does that house make you think of? People living in it.
H16. What does that house need most? A walk. So can walk up to the house. They have mud. No cement walk. Get all muddy and drag it into the house.
H17. If this were a person instead of a tree, who might it be?
(Q) (House) What are the cross lines in the window? Curtains.

HOUSE

The immediate impression is one of regression and withdrawal. The face-like character of the House (with the crossed window lines that look like closed-off eyes, and the buttoned-up, mouth-like quality of the door) expresses the paranoid nature of the withdrawal. The central placement of the door knob has an umbilical implication and may express a wish to regress. From the window treatment, it may be assumed that he anticipates being closely watched and does not want to be seen. His ego has a brittle, hollow quality, as is suggested by the one-dimensional, facade effect and the unfilled spacing of the wall. The absence of a chimney reveals his felt emasculation. In place of the chimney, there are the unjoined apex roof lines. This is a pathological sign, for the openness indicates poor ego boundaries with vulnerability in regard to impulses from within and to stimuli from without. Ideas of persecution and reference probably are present and invade his thought processes and fantasies.

The high placement of the House suggests his fear of the environment and his desire to keep himself physically at a distance. Yet the House is fairly large, centrally placed, and the windows are enlarged. These signs reflect his continued need for egocentric display as he keeps himself encapsulated. The straightness of the lines and the striving for symmetry suggest that he is struggling to keep himself stabilized within reality through obsessive-compulsive mechanisms.

In his verbal associations, we recognize his impaired thinking and projective tendency for he says that he would not like to own the House since it does not have a back door — yet he presents only the front view of the House. His feeling of being unwanted by and undesirable to his family is expressed in his concept that his feet would be dirty and therefore he would be expected to use the back door. His desire for power and his concomitant need for protection are expressed in the P-D-I by his statement that he would "let (my) family live in the House . . . Like to take care of them".

TREE

His Tree is a splitting affair, with the two large branches veering off in opposite directions — suggesting the beginning of a breakdown of the personality. His inner tension and mental confusion come through in the heavy, swirling lines of the foliage — which presents a small tornado effect. His feminine identification, which undoubtedly frightens him, is seen in the vaginal-like appearance of the upper Tree. His ego fragility is reflected by the thinness of the trunk. The Tree is not toppling or falling apart, so it may be assumed that his pathology is of a slow-moving and insidious type.

PERSON

The distortion in judgment, degree of regression and readiness for impulse outbreak are apparent in his Person drawing, which is a primitive, hollow, bizarre production, with the profiled nose out of relationship with the head-on eye placement. The fusion of the head (control area) with the body (impulse area) suggests that he has much trouble controlling himself. The beady eyes and the accented ear orifices indicate visual and auditory suspiciousness, respectively. The huge mouth tells of his oral demandingness and its clam-like one-dimensionality reflects the fact that he is withholding and ungiving, so great is his need to be filled up and gratified. The displaced nose to the left suggests his fear of castration. The whole body conveys an impression of immobility and we can assume that he feels stuck, helpless, and vulnerable. The club-like nature of the limbs reflects the crudity of his contacting and his readiness to defend himself by primitive attack. In his verbal associations he reveals that he is unsure of his perceptions and may even doubt their reality. "Things aren't too clear. He thinks they are – has got used to looking that way."

H-T-P Drawing Sequence (chromatic)

HOUSE
1. Main wall outlines – black.
2. Window outlines – black.
3. Door – reinforced.
4. Door knob.
5. Roof outline.
6. Brown curtain outlining.
7. Pathway.

TOTAL TIME: 2'11"

TREE
1. Downward lines of branches and trunk – brown.
2. Branch and trunk fill-in – brown.
3. Foliage curlicues straight across top touching upper branch ends. Brown.
4. Foliage fill-in – circular lines across, going methodically from top to bottom. Brown.

TOTAL TIME: 3'40"

PERSON
1. Head outline including nose extension. Black.
2. Purple eyes.
3. Black eyebrows.
4. Black mouth.
5. Black ears. Reinforces right ear.
6. Black body and limb outlining, reinforcing upper right torso line and end of right arm.

TOTAL TIME: 5'3"

His chromatic drawings are essentially the same as the achromatic. His extensive use of black and brown indicates his felt depression. His House is the only chromatic drawing that shows some change from the achromatic. The windows are now open and curtained; and there is a walk-way, suggesting that if he were given a warmer and more protective setting he might become a little more trusting and accessible. The fact that the chromatic Tree is of the same character as the achromatic, points up the unlikelihood of any major disruptions taking place in the near future. The markedly inappropriate purple eyes of his drawn Person reinforce the impression of paranoid reactivity.

The total clinical picture is that of a slowly decompensating, regressing, obsessive-compulsive boy, who is full of anxiety and confusion as he enters adolescence. He is caught between two opposing drives: he desperately desires to present a facade of adequacy and achievement, yet simultaneously he wishes very strongly to withdraw and isolate himself from people who might hurt and overpower him. He seeks to compensate for his lack of great achievement and prestige by indulging in magical fantasies. He feels rejected by his family, but since he has had experiences which make him feel that his demands will be satisfied, at times he may well throw himself forward and insist upon having his way. He is frightened by his passivity and feminine identification; the expectations of approaching adulthood tend to overwhelm him. The consistently childlike character of the drawings indicates that there has been an early arrest in growth.

Though there is an indication of his having been indulged, his overriding experience has been one of excessive frustration and deprivation. His ego is becoming fragmented by his anxiety impulsivity, his wish to withdraw, and his paranoid reactivity. His ego is being buttressed by obsessive-compulsive defenses, but they are weakening fast. The diagnostic impression is borderline schizophrenia. Though he may improve in a residential treatment center, he probably will need supportive therapy for many years to offset the possibility of prolonged hospitalization.

The foregoing case examples provide evidence of the widened scope, depth, immediacy, and sensitive detailing of the clinical problems afforded by use of the H-T-P. They illustrate, also, the integration of the H-T-P-dervied data with the developmental, historical, interview, and other material available on the patients studied.

Harold Michal-Smith, Ph.D., is Professor of Clinical Psychiatry at the New York Medical College, and Director, Division of Psychology, Department of Pediatrics, of the Flower and Fifth Avenue Hospitals where he has been actively engaged for the past fifteen years in the problems of mental retardation and the neurologically impaired. Dr. Michal-Smith has lectured extensively both in the United States and abroad on these subjects. He is the author of four books and over fifty articles in scientific journals. Dr. Michal-Smith is visiting lecturer at Teachers College, Columbia University and special consultant to the National Institute of Neurological Diseases and Blindness. In addition to his services as a clinician, he has been actively engaged in research on mental retardation.

Murry Morgenstern, Ph.D., is the Chief Psychologist at the Cerebral Palsy Clinic and School in Roosevelt, Long Island, N.Y., and is Associate Chief Psychologist at the Flower and Fifth Avenue Hospitals, Mental Retardation Clinic. He is Supervising Psychologist at the Clinic involved in training psychologists in the field of mental retardation. He has published papers and chapters on the special child and on learning disabilities. Together with Dr. Michal-Smith he is co-author of a forthcoming new volume on retardation to be published by The Charles Thomas Company. Dr. Morgenstern has had considerable experience in the treatment of the retarded and is recognized as an authority in the field of the emotional rehabilitation of the retarded.

Chapter 6

The Use of the H-T-P with the Mentally Retarded Child in a Hospital Clinic

Harold Michal-Smith, Ph.D. and Murry Morgenstern, Ph.D.

The authors describe the development, from primitive and schematic to complex and realistic, of the "normal" child's graphic presentation of his concept of House, Tree, and Person, which parallels the child's physiological and psychological development. They outline many of the frustration-producing problems faced by the retarded child as he attempts to explore his environment and derive satisfaction from it. Drs. Michal-Smith and Morgenstern illustrate their discussion with many achromatic drawings and give their qualitative analyses in condensed form.

The authors' findings that the drawings of white, Negro, and Puerto Rican children are essentially undistinguishable as to line of descent, native language, etc., will be of special import to those engaged in cross-cultural research, and to all those interested in the racial issues which have been activated by today's civil rights movements.

Drawings may be said to have become as closely identified with projective techniques as astronauts are with space ships. One is almost inconceivable without the other. A drawing, be it of a Person, a House, or a Tree, like an astronaut, is a recorder of what is felt, experienced, and observed. It is a graphic communication, creatively expressed, of an individual's relationship to himself and to the world around him.

To understand the mentally retarded child and the reflective aspects of his drawings, the following comments are necessary.

The need to make, to do, or to express one's self whether in a utilitarian production or in an abstract painting is a universal urge set in motion by inner drives and feelings which are the roots of dynamic behavior. However, the need for self-expression which eventuates in a recognizable final form is slow and follows specific patterns of growth similar to the human child's physical development.

Once the young child's fine-muscle adaptation is adequate to the task of holding a crayon or pencil, he has reached the first step toward drawing. Initially his early experimentation results in purposeless scribbling, or large joined but meaningless strokes, which serve as a release for his need for muscular activity. From this rudimentary graphic expression he moves to circular scribbling and finally to a combination of both which results in new patterns, zig-zag lines, and eventually the inchoate loop, which lay the groundwork for drawing. During this early stage he has begun to use the linear or straight line and the sweeping circular stroke which ultimately becomes the circle. Developmentally, the straight line (both vertical and horizontal) and the completed circle usually are incorporated into the child's voluntary activities by the time he has reached 3 years of age.

As yet the child cannot draw what falls within his range of vision. He responds only to what he understands and knows. As Luquet (1913) states, "The child draws what he knows and not what he sees". In our culture, the child's experiences center in the primary group, his family in the home. A dependent little creature, he is bound to his parents, most particularly his mother, in a circumscribed area, the home. His drawings at this age commonly represent the key figures in his life and he uses the circle, his first developmental graphic expression, to represent his mother or other family members. Gradually the linear line is added for the upper and lower appendages which he frequently joins to the head. Straight line appendages depict both legs and arms, the legs are drawn at right angles to the body, and the arms in sloping lines which extend downwards and outwards. The hand, if it is included, may be only a short cross line at the end of the one-dimensional arm line.

Between 5 and 6 years of age, when the geometric figure, the square, has been mastered, the young artist tends to utilize this skill in his representations. Boxlike, square hats appear on top of the head; noses may become more differentiated and may take on a squarish or rectangular shape. Characteristically, at this stage, hair is represented by spiral or zig-zag lines. Since the child draws only what he understands and not what falls within his vision, he utilizes certain basic forms repetitively. His drawings are formalized, conventional and stereotyped. Inherent weaknesses due to developmental limitations, weak analytical and observational powers, and poor drawing techniques restrict his graphic representations. Persistently, his drawings may be oversized, transparent, incorrectly synthesized and oriented. As the child matures mentally, his drawings become less formalized and more naturalistic or representational. Representational or naturalistic drawings depend on a well-developed memory, an ever expanding grasp of sharp observations, an understanding of part-whole relationships, and good visual-motor coordination.

When the child is between 8 and 9 years of age, experimentation with the profile begins and as the child matures, he succeeds in drawing the profile which is directionally well-oriented.

The House (or home) which like the human members of the primary group makes up the young child's world, has been found by various investigators (Griffiths, 1935; Eng, 1954) to be his second favorite drawing theme. Like the human figure, the House evolves through may developmental stages. The very young child, as soon as he can grasp a block adequately, becomes pre-occupied with House building. Block construction of the House may be a precursor to, or concurrent with his graphic expression. As soon as the square developmentally has become a familiar pattern, the child can move more comfortably to drawing a House. The circle which may have served as the symbol for House in his previous developmental stage is now discarded for the simple square arrangement. Fortuitous alterations may follow which eventually produce an elongated square House or a rectangular one. Regardless of side length and the size of lines, however, the House is characteristically a trapezium. In the early stages, the House is an object consisting of four lines only; it is without details or perspective. By the child's seventh year of age, more and more details appear and the House takes on a more finished look. Windows, whether rectangular, circular or square, dot the front facade; doors, similar in shape or more recognizably rectangular, are also added. Like the hat on the Person, the square chimney with its spiralling smoke makes its appearance. As the child acquires a greater understanding of spatial relationships and form perception, the house is drawn with two walls and eventually, during adolescence, in realistic perspective.

The Tree, which is frequently included spontaneously in the child's early drawings of the House with the sun shining overhead, follows its own discernible developmental pattern. In the embryonic or initial stage, the Tree has a one-dimensional, vertical line for the trunk, and a few wispy strokes that radiate from the top, like single-line fingers drawn on the human hand, for the branch structure. In the second stage, the single-line, finger-like projections cover a larger area of the trunk. Linear lines project from each side of the trunk from its top to its bottom giving the Tree the appearance of a veined leaf. Straight lines, so important in the first two stages of Tree representations, are discarded in the third stage, and in their stead, a dark mass of circular scribbles resembling shading appears on top of the long lined trunk. The general appearance of the Tree is much like that of an old fashioned hat pin with its central thin line and solid top knot. This form, interestingly enough, also delineates the flower when it enters into the child's drawings. The final or last stage of the Tree is a two-lined trunk which is the incipient representation of breadth. Projections or branches likewise begin to show more than one dimension and are lobe-like protuberances. Perspective comes in adolescence at the time when understanding of abstract concepts is a developing verbal skill.

In general, the young child's drawings during his early developmental stages tend to be crude and disproportionate. The head of the Person, the central organ and the one the child is most familiar with—possibly because it is experienced as the center of his own activities or possibly because it is the first meaningful object in his life—is often oversized. Often too, an eye may be drawn larger than the mouth or an arm. The drawings are stiff, mechanical, and puppet-like without any recognizable movement. Movement is described verbally rather than represented pictorially, or is indicated by line extensions, like the balloon devices used in comic books. Thus, a line drawn from a hand to a square object in space may be used to denote movement: "This is a lady pushing a baby carriage." The drawings of early childhood tend to resemble one another since there are few distinguishing characteristics to set off a particular expression or discriminatory differences in figures.

As was stated, children's drawings show weaknesses because of developmental limitations: the inability to analyze, to conceptualize, and to relate facts. If the weaknesses, such as disproportion, transparency, confused orientation, incorrect synthesis, etc., which are typical of childhood, persist long after the developmental milestones have been passed, close scrutiny must be given to causation. What is characteristic for the young child must be suspect in the pubertal or adolescent child.

The mentally retarded child's drawings characteristically reveal the typical weaknesses of early childhood. Developmentally the retarded child's growth is not consonant with his age. Physically he may continue to grow and keep abreast of average children, but biologically he lags behind them in many areas of behavior. Historically his background may show either genetic or environmental factors which are etiologically responsible for his mental retardation and/or for his impaired central nervous system.

The retarded child's delayed biological growth processes fail to follow the timing and patterning of "normal" sequential, orderly change and may, as a result, affect his speech, language and verbal facility, his motor skills and coordination, his mentation and his social relationships.

Delayed development and poor intellectual endowment may in childhood set the retarded child apart from other children and in later life from adults around him, but at the outset or in early childhood, he is subjected to the same forces that ordinarily converge to form the foundations of personality and adjustment.

Like his better endowed brothers and sisters, the retarded child has the basic needs for feeding, care and shelter, affection, and intimate mother-child rationships. His parents' concern and their other reactions to his inability to crawl or speak, or meet their anticipated goals begin to bear upon his role, status, self-esteem, self-reliance, and feelings of security. He feels overwhelmed, defenseless, and vulnerable.

As he continues to grow older, the retarded child experiences great difficulty in attaining social-emotional maturity since this depends on the growth of earlier patterns. New desires and new emotions arise which he cannot gratify, as a result he suffers a loss of self-respect and lacks willingness to venture forth and involve himself in the environment.

Like every other child, the retardate encounters pleasant and unpleasant experiences, stresses, and frustrations, but because of his delayed developmental milestones in mentation, coordination, and sensory adaptations, he tends to see himself as different, off the beaten track, possibly even as damaged and helplessly vulnerable to "the slings and arrows of outrageous fortune." In the past decade research has gone a long way to show that a person's feelings about himself can influence profoundly his self-concept, his physical, psychological and mental functioning.

A low self-opinion whether based on internal developmental delay or objectionable outside forces or the interaction of both, may lead to the lowering of the adaptive functioning of the ego, as well as the lowering of other ego functions, and even to a frank breakdown. In the retarded child, the ego is weak and tends to fail in its integrative task. Too dependent and too helpless to engage in greater activity to secure gratifications, originally provided to him by the parent or by the outside, the retarded child cannot differentiate between the ego and the non-ego and for the most part has only a tenuous relation to outside reality.

With regard to thought processes, one of the ego functions, the mentally retarded child is closer to his primary thought processes than are his "normal" contemporaries. Illogical or at times even autistic or irrational thoughts which are evidence of the normal state of development in the young child appear to be atypical in the older retarded child whose ego functioning indicates arrested development. The normal child is capable of abstract thinking, but the retarded child can cope with concrete content only.

Again, the defenses available to the retarded child's immature ego are less stable and more primitive than are those of the "normal" child. His responses to pain, the unpleasant, or to danger may vary widely and result in dramatic behavioral differences ranging from head-banging, loud, vociferous screaming, and trance-like behavior to rage reactions. The retarded child with his immature ego development finds it difficult to cope with impulses and drives, to learn substitute gratifications, to organize and plan, to formulate his ideas, to grasp abstract ideas, and to utilize the abilities he possesses.

Assessment of his problems and of ways to help him utilize his potentialities requires procedures which will present a picture of his dynamic behavior, his conscious and unconscious attitudes, in brief, a portrait of his outward and his inner behavior.

Comparative studies of the mentally retarded assume a "blanket" category —the "mentally retarded child" or the "brain injured mentally retarded child" —an assumption of similarity which, it seems to the authors, is quite untenable in the face of the widely varying nature and severity of the retardation and/or brain damage in individual children.

In dealing with mentally retarded children it has been stressed frequently that one should not lose sight of the fact that they are, first and foremost, *children* with the common basic needs of all children for the satisfactions necessary for personality growth and development.

While this is undoubtedly true, in trying to gain insights into the course of personality growth of the mentally retarded child, one should bear in mind some of the factors which tend to separate these children in experience from their more normal peers and, for that matter, from children who have become retarded later in life because of brain damage or injury and who for a period of life have experienced "normality".

First, mentally retarded children have lived and probably will continue to live with their condition all their lives. Secondly, the condition of retardation causes irregular rates of physical growth and development–late walking, late speech, slow perceptual integration–all of which probably alter the orderly course of personality development and make it more difficult for the child to relate to his world. Furthermore, many of these children encounter minor separations, hospital and clinic experiences (often with traumatic consequences) which the "normal" child seldom is called upon to face. All these experiences are superimposed on the very real difficulties of the mental retardation itself which interferes with the retardate's relationship to his environment.

Finally, since early personality maturation is patterned in terms of the child's relationship with the mother or mother-figure, it is important to recognize that the parents through whom these children have to relate and develop are the parents of a mentally retarded child. Those whose work brings them into contact with these parents are keenly aware of the emotional difficulties experienced by these parents in finding ways of coming to terms with the reality of having brought such handicapped children into the world–intense feelings of anxiety, resentment, and guilt which must be dealt with at a time when the young child's paramount need is for secure and accepting parent figures with whom to relate.

Consideration of ego strength and ego weakness plays a prominent role in the personality evaluation of all children. Obviously not all projective instruments or any specific projective technique can delineate unfailingly the child's personality *in toto*, whether the child be retarded or "normal". However, much can be gleaned about the personality and development of the retarded child from the H-T-P technique despite some investigators' contrary findings that no projective approach is reliable or revealing of dynamic behavior.

Psychological thinking maintains that conscious and unconscious drives are the roots of all behavior; that conscious drives predominate in some types of behavior and unconscious drives in others. Conscious factors are the foundation of ordinary behavior, the commonplace activities of daily living, and unconscious factors the foundation of neurotic or pathological adaptations. To understand the why of behavior or what makes an individual behave as he does, both the conscious and unconscious must be assessed, but the knowledge of the unconscious is crucial to the understanding of maladjustment.

The H-T-P is one of many efficacious tools used in tapping the unconscious painlessly and pleasantly. Children, particularly, find drawing a pleasurable activity in and of itself and are less likely to resist it or to erect barriers to defend themselves against revelation. The H-T-P is especially effective with the retarded child who cannot formulate his ideals well or engage freely in spontaneous conversation. Limited abstract ability may preclude questioning which if comprehended would be resisted stubbornly. The H-T-P test is relatively free of many of the attributes of the usual testing procedure such as spoken language or verbal communication, concentration on questions and responses, and an anxiety provoking atmosphere. Even the most diffident and reticent mentally retarded child almost always will attempt the H-T-P test.

The H-T-P is especially fruitful with children whose verbal proficiency may not be equal to the demand of comprehensive self-expression, or free enough to engage in spontaneous conversation. Drawings consequently have special applicability to the young child, the aphasic child, the mentally retarded child, and the foreign-language-speaking child.

Buck (1950) maintains that "each drawn whole, the House, the Tree, and the Person is to be regarded as a self-portrait . . . ". The House, the Tree, and the Person fall within the child's experiences, and presumably have symbolic meanings which reflect the individual's mental, psychological and physiological status.

In the home, the child's earliest dynamic environment, happy and stressful events occur; in the home the socializing process begins, and the earliest relationships are shaped and molded. The House then is something that each child knows, and developmentally it is something that he can portray as soon as he has learned to go beyond the scribbling stage. Each child's drawing of the House contains much of himself: his feelings, attitudes, fears, wishes, and fantasies.

The House, whether it is a large circle or an ill-formed square, becomes a symbol of the child's experiences and the way in which he has experienced them. Every detail, every addition or omission, every distortion is a graphic imprint of his conscious or unconscious attitudes. Like a motion picture flash-back, the House sets the stage for all that has gone before in the child's life: the atmosphere, the social situation, and the role which the home has played in his first encounters with others. This drawing may pull together early associated ideas about his earliest experiences, but may not represent the House as it actually existed in the past or as it now exists in reality. The House may be a dream image, a fantasy picture of what it should have been or should be. In general, the underlying rationale is that the House reflects the individual's life role and the satisfactions or dissatisfactions gained from his home environment. Other related aspects of the personality also can be gleaned from this drawing, such as the individual's sense of reality, his ego strength, and social accessibility.

The Tree, a relatively simple figure, can give a dramatic graphic appraisal of the individual's unconscious concept of himself. The trunk, psychologically, points to the individual's estimate of his basic strength and prowess; the branches, the individual's potential for deriving environmental satisfactions.

The Person, on the other hand, is considered to reflect the body image and to offer a self-portrait with special emphasis on physical inferiorities, attitudes toward sexual roles, and the overall attitude toward other people. It is true that many clinicians feel that the self-portrait concept has been uncritically acclaimed. Nevertheless, the drawing of the Person carries with it special features which have significance to the individual and reveal his feelings and attitudes.

The H-T-P test, then, as used by the clinician is a projective tool which is thought to reflect the personality characteristics of the individual, whether "normal" or retarded. Interpretative analysis is based on what has been portrayed, how it has been portrayed, what has been left out of the portrayal and what elements have been exaggerated, underemphasized or distorted. In the main, interpretation rests on proportion, placement, perspective, details, line quality, and the quality of the details and their distortion. The dynamic personality indicators of the retarded are based on the same sources. The retarded child, like the "normal", has needs, fears, wishes, anxieties, and fantasies which express themselves symbolically in his drawings.

The authors' experiences at the Clinic for Mentally Retarded Children at Flower and Fifth Avenue Hospital in New York City with a subject population comprised of a large percentage of Puerto Rican and Negro children indicate that the drawings of these children are not greatly modified by cultural differences. The traditional patriarchal structure of the Puerto Rican family and the eventual change of parental roles in this country, the harsh and rigid methods of child discipline, the large family constellation, the family tensions, and the poor living conditions of the Puerto Rican children, like those of the Negro children, are all reflected in their drawings, just as such factors are presented in the drawings of similarly situated white retarded children. The drawings of white, Negro, or Puerto Rican retarded children all show poor perception, poor line quality, absence of details, poor judgment, and weak or undeveloped egos. Low self-esteem, inordinate dependency on external support, feelings of rejection and isolation, etc. (the end results of deeply felt inferiority feelings) are characteristic of the retarded child regardless of his line of descent, native tongue or place of birth. One trend, however, in the Puerto Rican adolescent girls' drawings is the presence of details revealing sexual awareness and interests.

In an unpublished study conducted by the authors, three certified and highly qualified psychologists independently examined 69 samples of House-Tree-Person drawings made by retarded subjects, who were from 8 to 16 years of age and had I.Q.'s ranging from 42 to 71, for discrimination of ethnic background. The results indicated that, in the raters' judgments, ethnic background cannot be determined by a qualitative method of drawing interpretation. However, when these drawings were subdivided by age and sex, the raters were able to identify the adolescent Puerto Rican females to a significant degree.

The interpretation of drawings, even those of the retarded, is not a simple matter and calls for a broad and deep understanding of child development, dynamic behavior, and mental retardation. The retarded child's drawings are unlike those of his "normal" like-age peers, but in general they show similarities to those of other retardates. However, within group commonalities, there are individual differences which make for a unique personality picture.

Representative drawings of the retarded from the Flower and Fifth Avenue Hospitals' Mental Retardation Clinic will be presented and discussed. It should be borne in mind that no single feature *per se* can carry the weight of the interpretation. Drawings, like other projective techniques, must be considered within the framework of the total Gestalt and must be integrated with all other available data. For purposes of this discussion however, interpretation of the test material is based solely on the drawings. The reported I.Q.s are from either the Binet or the WISC.

Perspective

Perspective is a difficult concept for even the average child to grasp: it is far more difficult for the retarded child. Spatial relationships such as distance and closeness simply are too abstract for his limited capacities. Poor perception of the spatial relationships involved in his drawings often causes the retarded child to place individual details with little regard to objective reality. Often the House, for example, is drawn as a three-walled figure with the parallel endwalls narrow or uneven and with little or no indication of depth.

As a rule the retarded child is at a loss to know where to start when he is confronted with a large white sheet for his drawings. Placement of the drawing is in

no specific quadrant although many use the upper half of the left side. This placement may be atttributed not only to spatial difficulties but also to the psychological problems of failure to recognize one's own place in the family or group
with consequent feelings of isolation and withdrawal. Unable to act on his own
initiative, the retardate's tendency is to hug the margin as if desperately clinging
to a crutch for support (Fig. 89). It is not unusual to find the immature retarded
child making use of the upper left side placement. Machover (1949) maintains
that the left side reveals the individual's close ties to, and dependence upon, the
family. Occasionally the retarded child's inability to handle space is shown also
in the facial features: For example the facial features may be displaced; the eye
may be drawn below the mouth, or the nose on the same horizontal plane as the
eye.

Body imbalance, which is frequently experienced by the retardate, may show
itself graphically in completely skewed figures which look as if they were float-
in space. There is no anchorage, nothing to maintain the object in an upright
position. Such representations reveal the retardate's feelings of body inferiority.

Symmetry, which indicates balance and control, generally is poor in the
drawings of the retarded. This disturbance may be due to confusion in lateral
dominance, motor incoordination and cortical problems, conditions which are
found commonly in retardates with central nervous system dysfunctioning. The
imbalance may be so extreme that the drawings look as if they are disintegrated.

Fig. 89

Proportion

The relative size of objects often is an undeveloped concept in younger or more related children, just as the comparative form of adjectives is misunderstood by them. For example, if animals or people are presented in the drawing of a House, either or both may tower above the House.

In disproportionate drawings of the Person, the head most commonly is large, whereas the trunk and the appendages are short and thin, or even omitted altogether. Over-emphasis of the size of the head frequently is found in the drawings of young "normal" children of from 3 to 6 years of age (Fig. 90). For the older retardate, head disproportion seems to be more usual representation indicating immaturity and developmental lag, and according to analytical theory, the oral dependent stage.

It should be remembered that the higher the intelligence level of the retarded child and the better his adjustment, the less striking will be the atypical characteristics of his drawings.

Like the drawings of the "normal" child below the age of 7 years, the retardate's drawings, usually are small. Occasionally, however, the other extreme is seen and the page cannot contain the entire graphic production (Fig. 91). It is not uncommon to find the retarded child drawing a small Person with overly-large, irrelevant details such as a ball, rope, etc., drawn close by.

The older retardates, like older "normal" children, come closer to drawing larger figures. Irrelevant details again may be outsized, however, which illustrates graphically the retarded child's poor judgment.

A small upright House may set the tone for all the other objects and the Tree as well as the Person may be almost microscopic in size. Constricted drawings, whether drawn by the retarded or by the "normal" child, suggest feelings of inferiority and frustration.

Details

Awareness of what happens around one and the recognition of environmental stimuli generally are reflected in drawings by the number and appropriateness of the details. Details are to drawings what colorful description and expressive narrative are to literature. They give life, color, and tone to what is depicted.

The retarded child's drawings, by and large, are bare of details. This paucity can be seen in the House, the Tree, and the Person. The House may be doorless, roofless, and/or windowless. The Tree may have no branches or be merely a small, dried-up stump; the Person, a rigid disproportionate series of circles and a line or lines.

The human figure may lack facial features, appendages or sexual characteristics. The male and the female figures are drawn alike. A large round head, eyes that are circles without pupils, perhaps another circle for a nose, short appendages, and large buttons frequently constitute the Persons portrayed by younger defectives.

The use of circles to represent details suggests the orally arrested development of the retardate who must be buoyed up by the outside and directed step by step to learn to see and regard external stimuli. Dependence on the key figure,

Fig. 90 (above)

Fig. 91 (below)

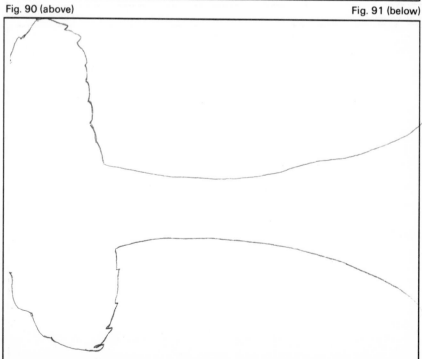

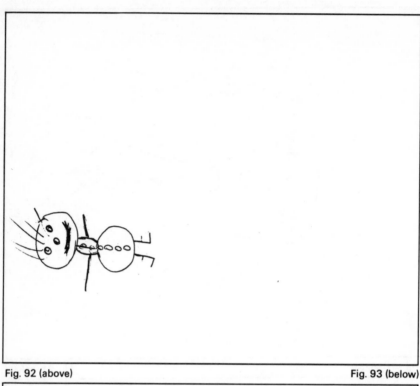

Fig. 92 (above)

Fig. 93 (below)

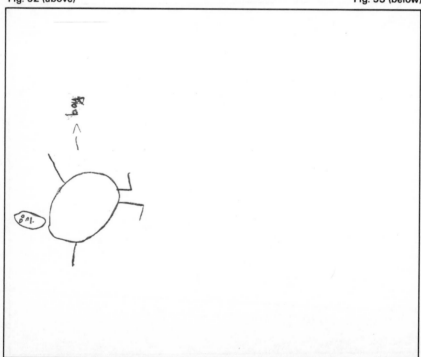

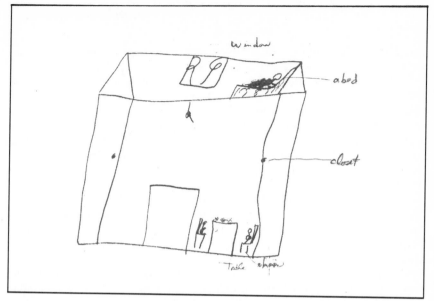

Fig. 94

usually the mother, is excessive. It is the mother who, figuratively speaking, keeps the wheels turning by assisting, guiding and pointing out the directions (Fig. 92).

Facial expression is drawn rarely. Faces drawn by the retardate tend to look alike, are without contour, empty, unseeing, and have little recognizable character. Differentation may be seen primarily in the mouth. Usually the appendages and the neck are one-dimensional.

Frequently the retarded child is unable to join the appendages to the body or the branches to the Tree. *Disjointed detailing is common among retardates with brain impairment* (Fig. 93).

Transparency also is seen frequently in their drawings. A diaphanous skirt or a pair of trousers may be drawn on a figure but it allows an interior view of the legs, undergarments, etc. The walls of a House may be transparent and show the interior (Fig. 94). Such a transparency usually is drawn by the more retarded child who cannot follow concepts and in general has poor judgment and poor reality testing.

A thin, shrunken, one-dimensional Tree trunk with a paucity of branches shows the individual's feelings of a lack of basic power and inner strength. The human figure most likely will reflect similar feelings if it is thin, weak, and without many details, and the lines are light in pressure.

Line Quality

Frequently the line drawn by the retarded child is tremulous, quavering and/or jerky in quality. Actual breaks in the line where the pencil has wavered because of jerkiness or incoordination are discernible; these all suggest poor motor control and poor motor adaptation. As in the retarded child's reproductions on the Bender, there may be wavering lines instead of clearly defined lines. This incoordination and jerkiness may be related to brain impairment with associated mental retardation. The lines also may show heavy pressure, and appear to have been drawn swiftly and impulsively.

The following are illustrations and discussions of retarded children's drawings. The first presentation (Figs. 95, 96, 97, 98, 99) indicates a few developmental stages of H-T-P drawings. However, the personality development of this patient is considered to be atypical. Gregory is a boy who wishes to reach out and manipulate, but wiil do nothing which does not give him what he desires. He tries to organize himself and will go to extremes to achieve order. He denies hostility, but expresses it verbally. It is suspected that he experiences his mother as punitive and demanding.

In Fig. 95, Gregory uses the circle, the earliest developmental stage in drawing that is commonly achieved by the three-year-old. His chronological age at the time was 6-6 and his Intelligence Quotient was 69. This circle, however, does not portray a Person but a House, a representation frequently observed in the House drawings of young children who have not yet mastered the techniques necessary to convey their concepts correctly graphically. Basically this production is an anthropomorphic House, shaped like a human head; it shows conflict areas: inferiority feelings, inaccessibility, and fearfulness of contact.

His Tree (Fig. 96) combines the circle and the linear line for the trunk. Again a sense of incompleteness and feelings of emptiness are highlighted.

At a later date, when Gregory is 8-9, his drawing of the Person (Fig. 97) is reminiscent of that of a younger child's. Its placement and size indicate Gregory's

Fig. 95

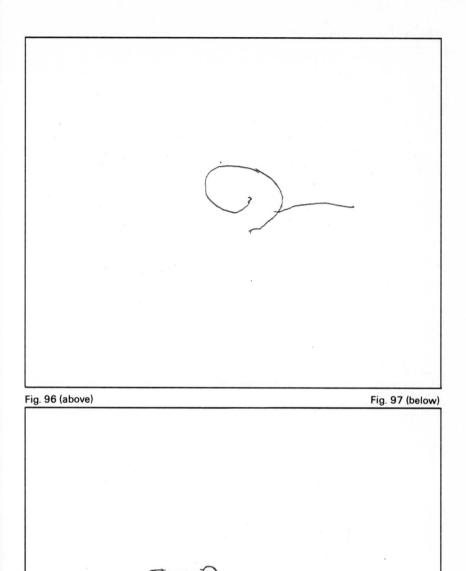

Fig. 96 (above)

Fig. 97 (below)

Fig. 98 (above)

Fig. 99 (below)

difficulties in social adaptation. Withdrawn and remote, he appears hypersensitive and at a loss to know what is happening around him. His feelings of distance and isolation are forcefully expressed in his tiny, inaccessible, and misshapen House (Fig. 98).

By the age of 12 years Gregory's drawing of the Person (Fig. 99) is radically different; it has become more expansive, but in essence, he still is close to his earlier modes of graphic expression in his continued use of circles and straight lines. Standing out prominently in this retarded boy's development are: his infantilism, dependency, conflict in communication areas, and difficulty in coping with criticism. Although he is no longer as withdrawn and remote as he was, he does not appear to have gained more or better understanding of ways with which to cope with the environment or establish contact with it.

Marie, C.A. 15-5, I.Q. 55

PERSON (Fig. 100)

Much obsessive thinking seems to be going on within this youngster, who is highly sensitive to her intellectual limitations. Marie attempts to compensate for her limitations by glamourizing herself. Her concern with approval (and suspicion that others always are looking at her critically) is exaggerated. She attempts to present herself as a "good" girl although her negativism can be very strong.

She is aware of and concerned about sexuality, but tries to deny and hide her sensuality. She denies her impulses and very likely her responsibility for her misbehavior which incurs disapproval. She can be very stubborn in her denials and in the hostility evoked by criticism.

A rigid family background is suspected. Her family's emphasis on control and Marie's feelings of inadequacy in respect to the amount of ideation and impulsivity which she has to "sit on" suggest that considerable pressure for conformity to family doctrines has been exerted upon Marie.

Oversized head—awareness of intellectual limitations.[1]

Profuse head detailing—obsessive thinking.

Facial features (amount of space given to hair, glamourized eyes)—sexual interests.

Ears—concern with opinions of others.

Stance, tensely inactive—"I do nothing that can be criticized."

Self-conscious mouth—determined line of negativism—when combined with stance.

Little girl figure, with glamourized head, blank spaces of costume—denial of sexuality.

Amount of ideation (in lieu of action and/or spontaneity)—rigid family background.

TREE (Fig. 101)

The Tree suggests the emotional emptiness which Marie experiences but reveals her feminine identification, also established in the Person drawing. The

---

[1] The authors present in shorthand fashion at the conclusion of their discussion of each drawing what they regard as the most significant qualitative points therein (in italics) and their interpretations thereof (conventional type). Eds.

Fig. 100 (above)   Fig. 101 (below)

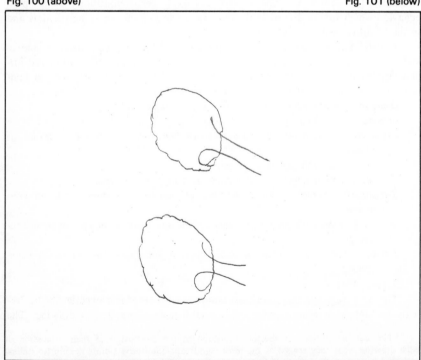

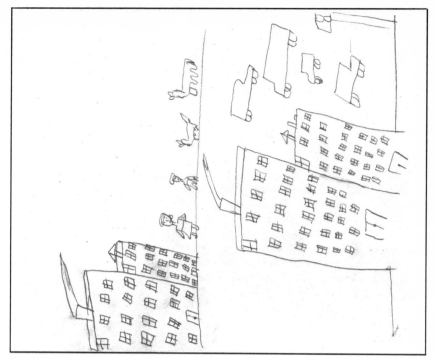

Fig. 102

Tree shows her sense of inadequacy and insecurity much more intensely however, since in this drawing she does not exercise the social controls and learned social defenses which were revealed in the Person. There is the same denial of impulse life, though, and some capacity for a rather broad kind of humor which she uses as an attempt to mask her depression and doubt. The two Trees may relate to her family background; she may have been so over-protected that she was never alone and now feels comfortable only as part of a family or group. She needs such support and cannot perform (or is not used to performing) without it.

Size, without roots or baseline—insecurity and inadequacy.

Empty figures—denial of impulse life.

Body of Tree superimposed on trunk and not truly continuous with it—reinforces impression of ideation, sitting on top of impulse life.

HOUSE (Fig. 102)

The compulsiveness shown here testifies to the rigidity already shown in the Person drawing. In addition, the fearfulness engendered by the fast-moving, high pressured nature of the world she experiences is suggested. A sociable child, Marie is dependent on social contact but also uses activity and busyness to ward off the fears, depresssion and anxiety which are activated in her when she is alone or unoccupied. She is very much aware of her need for external controls with which to supplement her inadequate internal controls. She also is made anxious by the overstimulation exerted by her large family and its activities.

Excessive details, repetitive similarity—rigid concreteness.

Filling in of empty spaces—obsessiveness which serves as a defense against suppressed feelings and ideation.

People, animals and windows—dependence on social contact, fear of anxiety aroused when alone or inactive.

Stoplight at extreme right—need for external controls.

Clinical History

Marie's parents have been separated for more than six years. Her father is blind and is provided for by welfare. Marie is the third child in a family of six children, five of whom are supported by the Aid for Dependent Children and by the older sister's voluntary contribution of $45.00 a month.

Marie, an unhappy child, is solitary and must provide her own recreation and leisure activities: these are primarily listening to records and looking out the window. She would like to go out and do things on her own, but she has no friends. Any outside excursion, even to a neighborhood store, becomes an expedition, since Marie is too fearful to travel by herself. Her mother is anxious about her, because Marie may not remember what she starts out to do.

Marie greatly admires boys and would like to have a boy-friend, but this wish has not materialized. The mother complains that Marie is garrulous at home but silent as a tomb when outside the home. Marie attends a junior high school and is in a class for the mentally retarded.

She is not interested in a work training program because she is fearful that work, like school, will prove to be an unsatisfactory experience.

Alexander, C.A. 14-6, I.Q. 56

PERSON: (Fig. 103)

This youngster has more serious problems than his mental retardation. In fact, his emotional problems may be exaggerating his degree of retardation. He feels immobile, impotent, and incomplete. He has no feeling of ability to deal actively with his environment with which he has no real interaction. His difficulty with sexual impulses is so great that he denies them entirely.

Often his ideation is irrational and individualistic. His reasoning is illogical and possibly contaminated by his associations. His distance from reality seems to be increasing. The presence of self-absorption that may have delusional trends is suggested.

Alexander has been criticized harshly, rejected, and punished for his limitations.

Absence of legs—immobility and feelings of incompleteness.

Squarish shape—individualistic approach.

Eyes—self absorption.

Protrusions that might be arms—aborted contact with environment, impotence, inability to deal with environment; could also be displaced phallic representation.

Protrusions in combination with cutting off of figure at waist—severe sexual anxieties. The cutting off suggests punitive treatment.

HOUSE (Fig. 104)

He is isolated from and insulated against his environment. To need to erect such defenses, Alexander must feel both vulnerable and helpless. Withdrawal from reality is indicated. Some perseverative trends are a possibility when he is

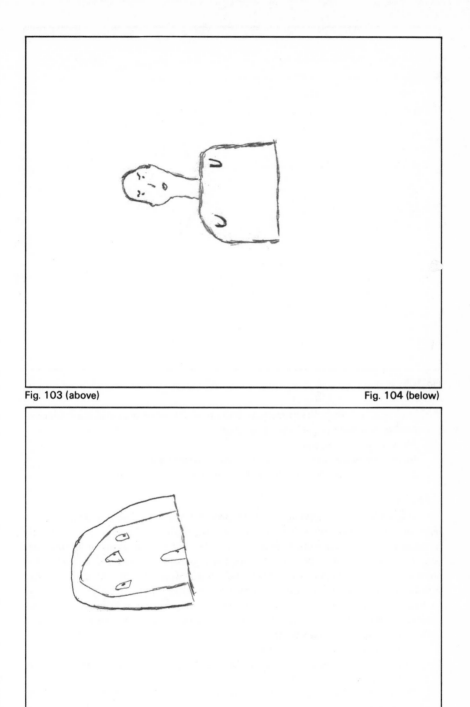

Fig. 103 (above)   Fig. 104 (below)

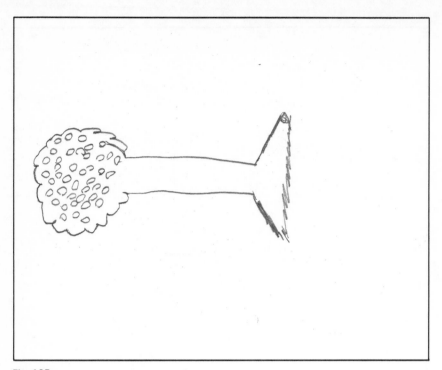

Fig. 105

forced to respond. Impulsive reactions also are likely when his isolation is pierced.

Double boundaries—feelings of isolation.

Placement—withdrawal.

House, windows, doors, all same shape—perseveration.

Occurring in openings to environment—forced responsiveness.

TREE (Fig. 105)

Alexander is very anxious about his security and feels quite unstable. He also feels that acceptance, achievement, and the realization of his desires are an unlikely eventuality. He is immature in psychosexual development (analysis of all drawings suggests that there may be some frightening adolescent impulses mixed in with a greatly retarded and confused general psychosexual development). An active fantasy life is indicated as being possibly repetitive in nature and certainly immature in content. Alexander is not always able to control his ideation or keep it on the track he intends. His thoughts sometimes seem to him to have independence or an existence of their own, apart from his control.

Shaded roots—insecurity and anxiety.

Distance of leaf area from ground (tall trunk with no way to climb it)—acceptance and own desires unavailable.

"Fruit," repetitive, open shapes, crowding one another—lack of control of ideation.

Ruth, C.A. 14-1, I.Q. 61

PERSON (Fig. 106)

Ruth may be an overdisciplined child, held down by fanatical rules and regu-

Fig. 106

lations. She anticipates criticism, rejection, and abuse in fantasy or in reality (one suspects that it is in reality). She is extremely anxious and frightened about her sexual impulses, but at the same time, she cannot prevent her attempts to display and express them. The possibility exists that she has had sexual experiences. Her insecurity is obvious and there is evidence of instability in regard to her feelings of being accepted and belonging. Her family probably has threatened to punish her by sending her away from home. She begs for affection like a very young child, but does so mechanically as though she does not expect to receive it.

She is quite alert to her environment, although she often is at a loss as to how to react to it or deal with it. Ruth has difficulty in knowing how to express herself spontaneously and has been offered little chance to do so.

She feels physically trapped, incoordinated, and vulnerable, and has fears about her physical well-being and safety.

She is aware of her intellectual (and other) limitations and attempts to compensate for them by doing as little on her own as she can. She waits for instructions and directions in order to avoid behavior which might result in punishment. She also is aware of her dependency which is on a level much less mature than her years.

Thin neck — overdisciplined.

Shaded hair (restricted to one side of head only), treatment of lower trunk, and double line of dots delineating sexual area — anxiety about sexual impulses.

Shaded eyes — fright and anxiety.

Extended arms — need for affection.

Position of lower part of body — held down, trapped.

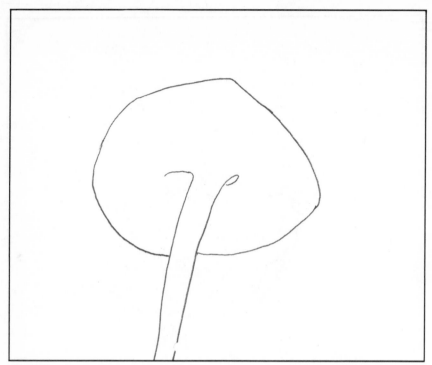

Fig. 107

    Facial expression, inactive extension of arms and immobilized body — anticipation
      of criticism, etc.

    Buttons — immature, emotional dependency needs.

    Presence of "contact features" — alert to environment.

HOUSE (Fig. 94)

This House also points to isolation, overdiscipline, and possible sexual activity. She feels quite apart from the other people in her world and experiences this separation as punitive. Ruth feels inadequate to meet most of the day-by-day demands made of her. She has little emotional relatedness and is not critical of her judgment of reality or of her behavior.

    Bed and anxiously shaded figure in it — possible sexual activity.

    Transparency — poor judgment.

    Bed in attic — feels apart, little relatedness.

    Tiny figure, large table — feels inadequate to meet every day demands.

    Closet — uncritical of own behavior.

TREE (Fig. 107)

Ruth feels depressed and emotionally empty. She experiences no sense of productivity in her life. She has few emotional resources upon which she can draw. She is not sure of her acceptance by and security within her family. She exercises little self-assertion in seeking satisfactions or in building goals for herself. She is too passive in her acceptance of her emptiness, depression, and mistreatment by others.

    Barren tree — emptiness, no productivity.

    Lack of roots — insecurity, lack of resources.

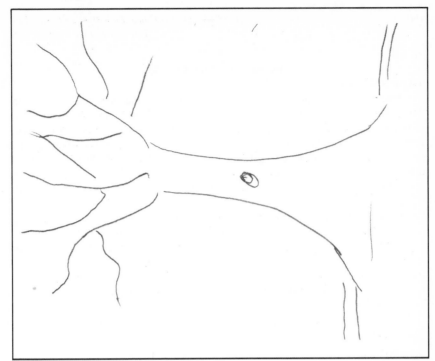

Fig. 108

Overlapping branches and trunk — passivity.
No shading or elaboration — too readily accepting.
Turned page — negativistic passivity as the "fight" in this youngster.

Nelson, C.A. 14-4, I.Q. 70

TREE (Fig. 108)

This Tree has many more qualities of a schizoid youngster's drawing than that of a retarded child's! A capacity for sensitivity appears here which is uncommon in the intellectually limited child. There also is an expression of feelings of fragmentation or lack of cohesiveness with which he must content. Emotional warmth from his family, as well as from others, is lacking. Feelings of loneliness and isolation are exaggerated. A tendency to withdraw from social demands to seek satisfactions in fantasy is shown. The schizoid behavior pattern (possibly related to or intensified by severe emotional rejection or other trauma in early childhood years) increases this child's lack of responsiveness to intellectual stimulation and makes it unlikely that there ever will be a full development of his intellectual potential.

Flow of branches — sensitivity.
Separation of trunk and limbs — fragmentation.
Expansiveness of branches — fantasy.
Scarring and trauma — loneliness, lack of affection.
Distance to limbs — loneliness.
Separation of limbs — isolation.
Line quality — sensitivity.
Most activity in upper branches — withdrawal to fantasy.

Wayne, C.A. 15-0 F.S.I.Q. 50

TREE (Fig. 109)

Wayne has periods in which he feels disoriented and disorganized. His impulses flow without control or refinement. This variability is suggested by his initial attempt at structure which was overcome by his impulses. His disorganization may be precipitated by fatigue and depression. There are suggestions that he uses ritualistic ways of trying to deal with his problems. He feels isolated and does not relate well to his environment. He is so confused by inner and outer promptings that he fails to differentiate his feelings from environmental stimuli.

Agitated lines — disorientation and disorganization.

Inability to confine lines to Tree's outline — loss of structure.

Specific symbols — ritualistic tendencies superimposed on agitated lines.

Sequence, line quality, and emptiness — "empty spaces" create depression, which in turn leads to agitated reaction, and this in turn to ritualistic attempts at control.

"Branch" area precariously balanced on top of overly long trunk — isolated, does not relate well.

Overlapping of trunk line and agitated lines — failure to differentiate feelings from environmental stimuli.

HOUSE (Fig. 110)

This House is much better integrated and organized than the Tree. However,

Fig. 109

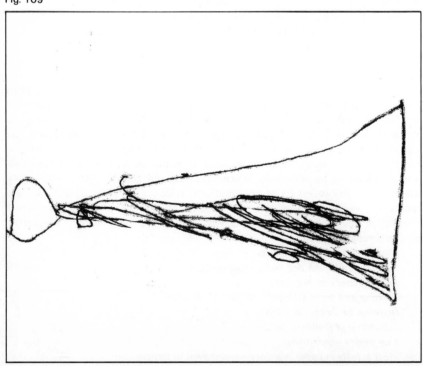

it also shows depressive moods as well as a sense of isolation from reality, family, and society. Wayne feels most secure when he is isolated and withdrawn. He seems anxious about his mental processes and also feels compelled to rely more upon feelings than upon rational processes. He does not make much productive use of his energies or resources.

    Placement — isolation.

    Tilted roof (tilted on one side, bulging out on other) — anxiety about intellectual processes.

    Windows at top only — isolation.

    Emptiness in majority of figure — depression.

Arlene, C.A. 17-11 I.Q. 56

PERSON (Figs. 111, 112)

    Arlene is extremely immature for a 17-year-old girl; she lacks the bodily awareness one would expect her to have developed 10 or 12 years earlier. She is full of impulsive hostility which, once aroused, continues in a perseverative, compulsive way. Having been verbally abused, she reacts hostilely. She is self-absorbed, has poor control of impulses, and shows little motivation to learn control. Arlene is more likely to respond by verbal tirades than by physical outbursts which would be followed by guilt reactions. She denies any misbehavior and blocks out her awareness of her misdeeds. She is hyper-reactive to criticism or correction.

Fig. 110

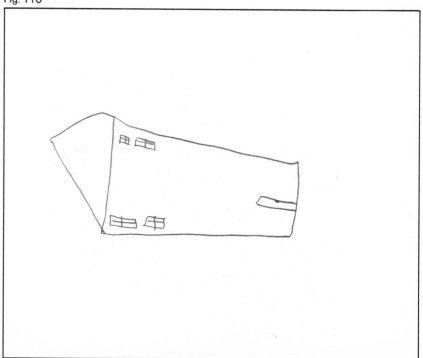

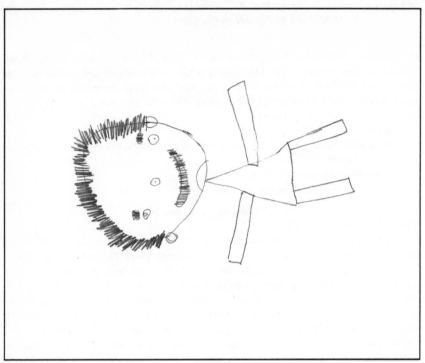

Fig. 111 (above)
Fig. 112 (below)

Arlene exhibits emotional dependence at a very young level – that of the child who demands and demands but has no concept of giving in return. In fact, she is emotionally unresponsive except to her needs and demands.

She feels rejected (and probably is), insecure, uncertain of environmental security and/or stability. She also is aware of her intellectual inadequacy, and her infantilization may be, in part, a defense against this.

Head precariously balanced on body – aware of intellectual limitations.

Agitated, hostile "hair" treatment; outlining of head – rejected for these limitations, anxious and hostile about them.

Mouth and teeth – impulsive hostility, perseverative verbal aggressiveness. (Verbal hostility of this kind rarely is seen except in children who have been verbally abused. Also, note that the "teeth" slash through and sew-up the mouth.)

Eyes – self-absorption.

Eyelash, brow – concern with social events relating to her body.

Absence of neck – lack of control.

Slant of body – unsure of stability.

Feet – uncertain of environmental security.

Ears – sensitive to criticism.

Oversized head, body proportions, inclusions and omissions – immaturity.

Hands omitted in Fig. 111 and circled in Fig. 112 —denies misbehavior.

Fig. 113

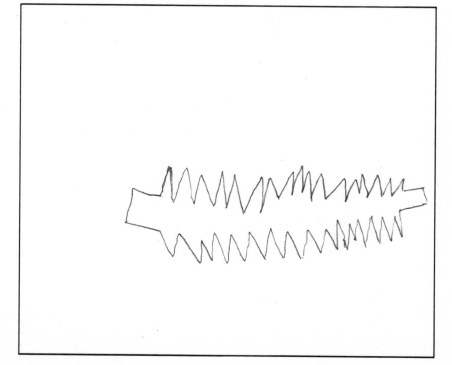

Fig. 114 (above)

Fig. 115 (below)

TREE (Fig. 113)

Arlene is aggressively hostile. She feels no relatedness to others on any level. She has no sense of belonging. Her concerns are primarily with her needs. She tries to control and limit her hostility, possibly because of a fear of retaliation and the unfulfillment of her needs. She has few personal-emotional resources to draw on, with resulting dependence on and demandingness from others.

Angulated leaves —aggression and hostility.

Entire figure in one closed segment and continuous pattern of branches — attempts at control.

Completely cut-off figure on all sides — no relatedness.

HOUSE (Fig. 114)

Arlene feels very much controlled by authority. She does not feel really welcome in her home, but is so frightened by everything outside it that she clings to home contacts exclusively. The conflict between her dependency and her hostility toward those upon whom she depends is constant and absorbs most of her emotional energies.

Afraid to grow up, she is made anxious by demands that she perform for herself and develop independence. She is afraid of new or unknown experiences.

Sun and cloud —authority figure and anxiety.

Absence of walk —no accessibility.

Grass —dependency.

Double line and door —absence of welcome in home.

Shading of "grass," sun, etc. —frightened by everything outside home.

All the agitated activity —afraid of the new, etc.

Building actually in the air —isolates it from environment. Protective of this source of security and fearful regarding its stability for her.

Kenneth, C.A. 14-7, I.Q. 62

PERSON (Fig. 115)

This adolescent probably is in the 5- to 6-year-old developmental stage. Inextricably tied to the umbilical cord, he clings to support for the anchorage and underpinning which he must have for such limited emotional mobility. Without backing, he is helpless and vulnerable. His interest in the vast outside world is minuscular. Events, objects, and people pass before and around him, but he has little understanding of what they are or what they mean. Closely bound to home ties because of his dependency and deeply experienced feelings of insignificance and inferiority, he does not try to involve himself with others or participate in activities with his contemporaries. His engagement appears to be only in the family group which apparently does not provide all the gratification he demands. In psychoanalytical terms, he is at the oral dependent and demanding stage. The wish to be sustained, nurtured, and loved is all compelling but unrealized.

Boys and girls are dimly perceived by Kenneth to be different individuals, but his perception of this fact is superficial and based on external appearances only. His emulation of others seem to follow the female pattern; probably he is

Fig. 116 (above)

Fig. 117 (below)

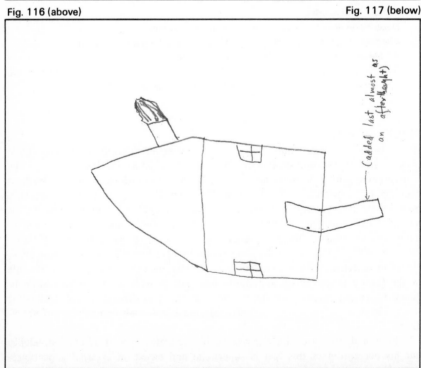

(added last almost as an afterthought)

more attuned to his mother's feminine ways than to his father's masculine behavior, since he is more identified with his mother than with his father. He has many angry and oppositional feelings, the expression of which he successfully suppresses.

Closed eyes — lack of outside interest.

Placement — tied to home.

Size — feelings of inferiority.

Lack of hands — no active involvement with outside.

Evangeline, C.A. 14-9, I.Q. 65

PERSON (Fig. 116)

Evangeline shows few signs of complicating pathology. She is in the midst of adolescence. She is provocative, but in a controlled way. She feels extremely awkward and unsure when she tries to exert herself in the environment. Often she would like to deny responsibility for the things she does. She exhibits some striving for power and position.

Her imagination is limited. Her ideas and identifications are slightly immature, but her social development does not appear to be as seriously retarded as her intellectual development, although she does not extend herself readily. The impression formed is that she has higher intelligence than she has demonstrated.

Hands on hips and depiction of hair — provocative.

Hair contained and kept to one side; small hands; emphasized neck — control.

Stance — feeling of awkwardness.

Poor joining of lines — lack of responsibility.

Shoulders, plus length of arms — striving.

Separation of arms from body — awkward about exertion in environment.

HOUSE (Fig. 117)

Her House has the physiognomonic quality often seen in drawings of young children. Both the organization and the integration of details are good. The House depicts much emptiness. It also shows some feelings of a need to be guarded in initial relationships with others. Evangeline socially is interested and responsive but places strict limits on how far she is willing to go in her responsiveness.

Placement — center of page suggests responsiveness.

Only two side windows — feeling of emptiness.

Door-size, placement, presence of knobs and walk — accessibility and responsiveness.

Walk cut off at bottom — limits how far willing to go in responsiveness.

TREE (Fig. 118)

This drawing shows an anxiety about her abilities which is not as clearly revealed here as it was in her other drawings. She feels angrily anxious about her origins and beginnings. Her anxiety about her future is more uncertain and less hostile. Here too, she tries to control and limit how much she will deal with at any time. She begins aggressively but becomes increasingly uncertain as she recognizes the difficulties of the task which she has undertaken.

Meshed branches — anxiety.

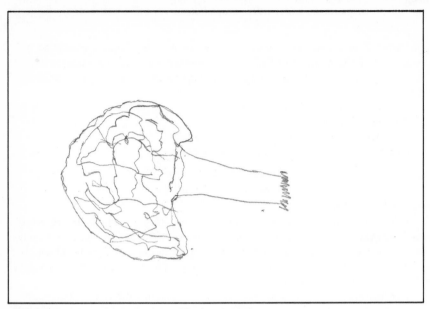

Fig. 118

Shaded and pointed roots — anxiety and anger.

Faint line quality and emphasis upon leafy area — uncertainty of future.

Closed-in leafy area — control (the lines indicating anxiety are carefully contained within the boundaries).

Variations in line pressure — she becomes increasingly uncertain as she realizes the difficulties of the task she has undertaken.

Summary

The material presented in this chapter is a brief summary of the authors' cumulative experiences gained through many years of work with retarded children. Admittedly the focus here has been circumscribed and many aspects of mental retardation have been untouched. The authors, however, are primarily concerned with the H-T-P test as an appropriate projective tool for the evaluation of personality dimensions of the retarded. In their opinion, children's graphic forms (whether they are produced by the bright or by the retarded) reflect affective attitudes, interpersonal relationships, ego strength, and self-concept, and consequently are useful and discriminatory in the field of mental retardation.

One pitfall to avoid in the analysis of any projective technique is to be careful not to exaggerate interpretation. This tendency must be kept in mind to prevent extravagant and excessive analysis. Also, it should be recognized that what may at first be presumed to be evidence of mental deficiency may instead be signs of maladjustment. Frequently the H-T-P drawings highlight conflict areas and stress situations accompanied by anxiety, and throw light upon incipient conditions precursive of future problems. As with other projective techniques, the H-T-P drawings direct attention to the emotional significance of an individual's experiences or to tension areas. Whereas pathological signs may suggest problems, the reverse does not follow: that is, the absence of atypical features does not necessarily imply that there is a wholesome adjustment.

There is always the temptation to agree with findings emanating from related disciplines, but the authors mindful of their observations and investigations in this field find no evidence from the drawings which distinguish retardates who come from different cultures. The H-T-P drawings of the retarded, whether white, Negro, or Puerto Rican, show much in common, 'though the personality pictures of the individual subjects vary.

The visual evidence presented here can be assessed independently by the professional reader who is encouraged to form his own conclusions, remembering of course, that the quantitative and qualitative study of the same drawings may lead to different interpretations, particularly when the test is used by clinicians who have been oriented and trained along different theoretical lines. But even here, one becomes aware quickly of the large area of overlap in the interpretation of the H-T-P by clinicians of different theoretical orientations.

References

1. Buck, J. N. *House-Tree-Person (H-T-P) Manual Supplement,* Beverly Hills, Calif., Western Psychological Services, 1950.

2. _____ *The H-T-P Technique.* A quantitative scoring manual. *J. of Clin. Psychology,* Supplement No. 5, 1948.

3. Eng, H. *The Psychology of Children's Drawings.* London, Kegan Paul, Ltd., 1954.

4. Griffiths, R. A. *A Study of Imagination in Early Childhood.* London, Kegan Paul Ltd., 1954.

5. Gunzburg, H. D. Maladjustment as expressed in drawings by subnormal children, *J. of Ment. Def.,* 57, 1952.

6. Hammer, E. F. *The Clinical Application of Projective Drawings,* Springfield, Ill., Charles C. Thomas, 1958.

7. _____ *The H-T-P Clinical Research Manual,* Beverly Hills, Calif., Western Psychological Services, 1955.

8. Harris, D. B. *Children's Drawings as Measures of Intellectual Maturity,* New York, Harcourt, Brace and World, Inc., 1963.

9. Jolles, I. *A Catalogue for the Qualitative Interpretation of the H-T-P,* Beverly Hills, Calif., Western Psychological Services, 1952.

10. Luquet, G. H. *Les Dessins d'un Enfant,* Paris, F. Alcan, 1913.

11. Machover, K. *Personality Projection in the Drawing of the Human Figure,* Springfield, Ill., Charles C. Thomas, 1949.

12. Michal-Smith, H. Identification of Pathological cerebral functions through the H-T-P technique, *J. of Clin. Psychology,* 9, 1953.

13. _____ *The Mentally Retarded Patient,* Philadelphia, J. P. Lippincott, 1956.

14. _____ and Morgenstern, M. Psychodynamics of the Brain-Injured Child, in *The Special Child: Diagnosis, Treatment, Habilitation,* Helmuth, J., Ed., Seattle, Bureau of Publications, 1962.

15. Morgenstern, M. Psychological Problems of the Cerebral Palsied Child in *Special Child in Century 21,* (Hellmuth, J., Ed.), Seattle, Special Child Publications, 1964.

16. Schilder, P. *Contributions for Developmental Neuropsychiatry,* (Bender, L., Ed.), New York, International Universities Press, 1964.

Herdis L. Deabler received his Ph.D. from Boston University. He was Chief of the Psychology Service at the Veterans Administration Hospital, Gulfport, Mississippi, 1949-60; Area Chief Psychologist, Veterans Administration Area Medical Office, Boston, Massachusetts, 1960-1964. From 1964 to the present time, he has been Chief Clinical Psychologist, Veterans Administration's Out-Patient Clinic, Boston, Massachusetts.

Dr. Deabler is a Fellow in the American Psychological Association and a Diplomate in Clinical Psychology of the American Board of Examiners in professional Psychology.

Chapter 7

The H-T-P in Group Testing
and As a Screening Device

Herdis L. Deabler, Ph.D.

Dr. Deabler outlines the specific advantages which the H-T-P has been found to have as part of an admission screening battery. He describes the "trimmed" method of administration and offers statistical evidence of the H-T-P's validity (in terms of scope) in this more limited usage.

The author lists in detail the diagnostic indices for the presence of psychoneurosis, psychosis, organicity, and character disorder which he and his colleagues have gleaned from more than 3,000 H-T-P productions. (Eds.)

For the past fifteen years the House-Tree-Person (H-T-P) projective technique has been administered to nearly every patient entering the Gulfport (Miss.) Veterans Administration Hospital, a 915-bed psychiatric hospital. The H-T-P has been a major test in the hospital's admission screening battery (Cowden, et al, 1955). It is also being found useful in the intake evaluation of patients in the Mental Hygiene Clinic of the Boston (Mass.) V.A.'s Out-Patient Clinic.

I. Specific Advantages of the H-T-P

The H-T-P has been found to be a clinical instrument possessing several advantages:

1. It is simply administered, it can be used with a wide variety of patients, including those of low mental ability as well as those of high or average mental endowment. The individual patient may utilize whatever ability he has.

2. Its major approach to personality evaluation is non-verbal, which makes it appropriate for use with patients of varying language, cultural background,

and levels of education. Its non-verbal nature makes it especially valuable with psychiatric patients, many of whom are blocked on a verbal level and frequently exhibit muteness or retardation of speech.

Patients who are verbally unresponsive often are able to express themselves facilely in the H-T-P drawings.

3. Pertinent information is gained about the personality dynamics of patients which readily can be used in subsequent psychotherapeutic sessions. Relevant data on self-concept, body image, psychosexual identification and conflict, immaturity and regressive trends, and general attitudes towards the environment usually are obtained from the patient's H-T-P productions.

4. The H-T-P is distinctively time-saving when compared with other projective devices. A wealth of clinical data can be obtained from it with the expenditure of a relatively small amount of time. Even more strikingly is this true when the test is administered to a group.

II. Group Administration of the H-T-P

The H-T-P, with its simple instructions and uncomplicated performance, easily lends itself to use as a group projective test. In addition, there is a marked motivational advantage to be gained in using it with patients in a group setting. A fearful or resistive patient, who might render a poor or scanty production if tested alone, may be stimulated by seeing other patients present accept the task and he will willingly engage in creating the requested H-T-P drawings. We have found, in the main, that the drawings produced in a group situation compare favorably, qualitatively and quantitatively, with those obtained through individual administration of the test[1].

The interrogation or inquiry after testing that is usually given after individual H-T-P administration, generally is lacking in group testing unless group interrogation forms are distributed. However, using the H-T-P as a group procedure enables one to obtain clinical data on a much larger number of patients than otherwise would be possible, and for purposes of screening large numbers, the post-drawing-interrogation often is not greatly missed.

Our testing groups have not been large in number, never involving more than twelve patients, with the usual group containing from six to ten. Small individual tables were constructed for use in group testing; the table tops were 18" x 36" in size. Testing sessions usually were scheduled for the first hour of the testing day so that the patients would be relatively fresh and rested. Usually one staff psychologist and one advanced trainee worked with such groups. Seldom were behavior problems exhibited in these group testing sessions. Seriously disturbed patients were scheduled for a later period in their hospitalization when their behavior would presumably be more stabilized.

In out-patient clinic work, the H-T-P usually is administered individually by the clinical psychologist on intake day.

---

[1] In fact, Hammer (1958) finds, because of the greater emotional and physical distance between subject and Examiner, the less felt need for defensive maneuvering, and the reduced contamination introduced by the Examiner's personality, age and sex as relatively strong influencing variables, that group administered H-T-Ps often provide richer and more openly expressed graphic materials than individually administered H-T-Ps.

III. The H-T-P As a Diagnostic Screening Device

The H-T-P has been found to possess definite value as a diagnostic screening device. In the clinical appraisal of patients entering a psychiatric hospital or appearing at the Out-Patient Clinic, the staff is interested in an early screening evaluation to obtain an answer to four main assessment questions:

1. Is the patient neurotic?
2. Is he psychotic?
3. Is there evidence of organic involvement?
4. Does the patient exhibit a character or behavior disorder?

We have found the H-T-P helpful in our attempts to make preliminary, tentative classification of patients in these main diagnostic groups. Patients in each of these categories have been observed to exhibit certain characteristics in their H-T-P drawings which are considered to be diagnostic indices. These indices usually are then checked and compared with data obtained from the other tests in the admission battery: the Bender-Gestalt, the Sentence Completion Test, the Modified Thematic Apperception Test and the Shipley-Hartford Vocabulary Test (Cowden, et al, 1955). From the H-T-P drawings and the other test data, a general diagnostic statement is then formulated and written.

In a research study utilizing a sample of 200 alphabetically selected cases there was agreement in 71.5% of the cases when the diagnostic impression gained and reported from the admission battery was compared with the diagnostic conclusion of the psychiatric staff after a complete workup of the case had been made in diagnostic staff conferences. Partial agreement was found in an additional 17.5%. The screening report was part of the staff conference when the final decision was made on the diagnostic classification and therefore some contamination may have occurred, since the report itself presumably influenced the diagnosis. However, the screening report was but one source of information at such staff meetings. All other available data, such as the psychiatric and social history, laboratory reports, ward behavior reports, admission clinical report, individual psychological testing, psychiatric interviews, etc., also entered into the final diagnostic appraisal.

The agreement of the screening report with the final evaluation appears to be significantly high and worthy of note. In arriving at the diagnostic impression incorporated in the admission testing report, it is our experience that the H-T-P-derived data when compared with data derived from other tests in the battery gives the most valid diagnostic leads.

The more important H-T-P diagnostic screening indices used are:

A. Psychoneurotic Indices

Psychoneurotic patients rarely, if ever, give bizarre productions on the H-T-P. Reality sense is not impaired and irrational distortions of the basic figures are not found. In neurotic patients, there is an unevenness of quality of productions. A neurotic may produce a fairly good House, a fairly good Tree, but produce a poor Person, often erasing or exaggerating parts of the Person drawing, and in so doing, indicate or suggest the personal conflict involved in his disorder. This unevenness of production tends to show disturbance only in certain areas of adjustment with only partial involvement of personality functions,

whereas with the psychotic or the organic patient, total involvement and relatively poor productions in all drawings are found more usually. With regard to
specific types of neuroses, the anxiety neurotics often use heavy lines and/or an
excessive amount of shading; obsessive-compulsives over-accentuate details
of the drawings, expending considerable time on doors, windows, siding, side-
walks, etc.; and hysterics on the chromatic H-T-P frequently use more than an
average number of colors, usually selecting the bright colors.

B. Psychotic Indices

Psychotic status is indicated where bizarre productions are made, where
major distortions of basic figures appear, and where illogical, unrealistic figures
are formed and allowed to pass. With the exception of fairly well integrated
paranoid cases, schizophrenic disorders are identified without difficulty on the
H-T-P. One or more of the following distinctive characteristics appear in their
drawings:

(1) The double-perspective House – an attempt to show three or more sides
simultaneously.

(2) Transparency – both the inside and the outside of a House are shown in
a single drawing and/or in drawings of the Person, body parts are shown through
the clothing.

(3) House drawings placed considerably above the ground or baseline,
reflecting a loss of contact with reality.

(4) House drawings made entirely of the roof which suggests excessive
fantasy states.

(5) House drawn with the end chopped off which implies a break with reality
and a fear of the extension of the self into the environment and/or possibly into
the future.

(6) House drawn with no windows or doors (or if they are drawn, they are
usually placed high). This suggests inaccessibility and a lack of a desire for contact with the environment and the persons in it.

(7) House drawn with the end wall larger than the main wall, especially if
the patient is of average intelligence or above.

(8) Trees drawn with the branch structure reduced or minimal in size, which
suggests a lack of satisfactory contact with the environment and the presence of
withdrawal tendencies.

(9) The Tree drawn with a split trunk, reflecting an inner splitting or disorganization of the personality.

(10) The typical schizophrenic profile of the Person: no hair, a mask-like
face, and a thin, rigid, emasculated physique.

(11) Ambivalence of profile for the Person: the body facing in one direction
and the head in the opposite direction. This is perhaps symbolic of or concrete
evidence of the homosexual trends frequently found in paranoid schizophrenics,
or it may present the general confusion and feelings of disorientation which
schizophrenics experience.

(12) The accentuated eye (a classical paranoid sign). Absence of an eye (or
eyes) frequently is found in the drawings of catatonic schizophrenics.

(13) Over-accentuation of the ear, or omission of the ear, often is indicative

of the presence of auditory hallucinations.

(14) Omission of the clothing and over-accentuation of the sexual organs seldom are found in drawings produced by those who are not schizophrenic or suffering with character disorders. This reveals a marked break from the mores of society and/or reflects regressive mechanisms.

(15) Omission of major body parts such as the hands, feet, arms, neck or shoulders—sometimes even the head, the pelvis, or the entire body—reflects a lack of wholeness of the personality and/or weakness, impotence, or complete inability to cope with the problems of life.

Depressed patients tend to draw much smaller figures with the size of all the drawings being reduced. This characteristic, also, is found at times in the drawings produced by catatonic schizophrenics. Depressed patients use very light strokes in making drawings, and they do not draw many details. They frequently place their drawings low on the space provided. In the chromatic series, the color they most frequently select is black.

The combination of black and blue frequently is employed by schizo-affective patients. Manics tend to make overly-large drawings for the space provided. Their lines are heavy strokes, with little attention being given to details, although much extraneous material is introduced; pages frequently are filled with other drawings or scribblings of one kind or another. It has been observed that black and red are the colors most frequently used by manics. This color combination is also employed by psychotic epileptics.

C. Organic Indices

In cases where there is a cerebral involvement, patients are found to do much erasing with little improvement or even worsening performance upon redrawing. Organics seldom try to produce more than side-view, simple, concrete figures. Figures frequently are drawn with broken, sketchy, irregular lines (the line quality suffers markedly with organic involvement). Epileptic patients often draw their Persons with slanting postures, probably as an index of their feelings of impending loss of bodily equilibrium. The drawings made later in the series usually are of poorer quality than earlier ones, probably due to susceptibility to fatigue. Drawing angles especially are difficult for organic patients to draw; for this reason House drawings reflect organicity more readily than do Tree or Person drawings, although usually there is organizational difficulty in producing all three drawings. The drawings frequently are smaller— size reflecting feelings of the loss of or the reduction in mental potential that organics consciously or unconsciously experience. Considerable stereotype or perseveration is noted in the drawings of organics. In the achromatic-chromatic H-T-P, which calls for two Houses, two Trees and two Persons, the same pattern often is repeated in each of the two figures. Organic patients find it difficult to make a shift, to vary their drawings in any significant way; their rigidity is marked. Integrative ability, the capacity to organize parts of figures into a well-formulated whole, is markedly impaired; along with this deficiency, organics complain that they are unable to do the simple tasks requested.

D. Character Disorders

The H-T-P does not seem to be quite as sensitive in picking up psychopathic or character disorders. Nevertheless certain distinguishing tendencies are found in the drawings of this group. Psychopaths usually do not draw any more than is minimally necessary. In Person drawings, for instance, they frequently draw a stick man. In their House or Tree drawings, there seldom is any shading. Occasionally, however, psychopaths engage in the embellishment of their drawings, especially Person figures, reflecting an exhibitionistic and/or narcissistic trend. Psychopaths at times degrade their drawing concepts as by putting a privy by a large House; by having an animal urinating on the Tree; or by drawing a grotesque, nude female. They frequently draw their Persons in aggressive postures, or in action using guns, swords, or other instruments of aggression. Their immaturity is reflected in their production of cowboy and other childhood fantasy figures. In the chromatic series, empirical evidence is that Yellow is the color frequently chosen by them.

The concepts and interpretations of the originator of the H-T-P, John N. Buck (1948a, 1948b, 1951a, 1951b, 1964), the validation and summary studies of Isaac Jolles (1952a, 1952b, 1953, 1964), the writings of Emanuel F. Hammer (1954, 1958) and Karen Machover (1949) have been used in interpreting the H-T-P drawings obtained in admissions testing. The indices listed above evolved from their writings and out of our extensive use of the H-T-P. The H-T-P was administered to more than 3,000 newly admitted psychiatric patients, and interpretative concepts were revised and sharpened as additional drawings were studied and compared with other diagnostic data and subsequently observed behavior.

There is definite need, of course, for intensive statistical validation of the more widely held "classical" interpretations. The diagnostic hypotheses of the H-T-P have been based, for the most part, on empirical data and clinical observations. As Hammer (1958) has pointed out, no single sign can be conclusive evidence of the presence or absence of a given disorder or personality characteristic. Of course, a Gestalt frame of reference, that is, interpreting the drawings as a whole, is more reliable than using a single deviation in performance as a pathognomonic indicator. One also is safer in using techniques, such as the H-T-P, predominantly as screening devices, for impressions gained and reported in screening settings usually are accepted as hypotheses to be checked further through additional observation, testing, and examination. However, such screening hypotheses, although they are only tentative impressions or opinions, are needed in clinical work for they indicate the direction for further necessary investigation. Not infrequently, however, the overall data are so clear-cut and definite in the H-T-P that further investigation is not indicated, especially when other known data are in accord with the H-T-P performance.

As a screening procedure, it may be concluded that the H-T-P is a helpful and relatively rich diagnostic instrument. It has stood the clinical test of continued use. Statistical verification, however, must be awaited.

References

Buck, John N. The H-T-P test. *J. Clin. Psychol.,* 1948, 150-159.

_____. The H-T-P technique, a qualitative and quantitative scoring manual. *J. Clin. Psychol.,* Monograph-Supplement No. 5, Oct. 1948.

_____. Directions for administration of the achromatic-chromatic H-T-P. *J. Clin. Psychol.,* July 1951, 274-276.

_____. The quality of the quantity of the H-T-P. *J. Clin. Psychol.,* Oct. 1951, 352-356.

_____. *The House-Tree-Person (H-T-P) Manual Supplement.* Beverly Hills, Calif.: Western Psychological Services, 1964.

Cowden, Richard C., Herdis L. Deabler, and J. Harry Feamster. The prognostic values of the Bender-Gestalt, H-T-P, TAT, and Sentence Completion Test. *J. Clin. Psychol.,* July 1955, 271-275.

Hammer, Emanuel F. Guide for qualitative research with the H-T-P. *J. Gen. Psychol.,* 51, 1954, 41-60.

_____. *The Clinical Application of Projective Drawings.* Springfield, Ill.: Thomas, 1958.

Jolles, Isaac. A study of the validity of some hypotheses for the qualitative interpretation of the H-T-P for children of elementary school age: I. Sexual identification. *J. Clin. Psychol.,* 1952, 113-118.

_____. A study of the validity of some hypotheses for the qualitative interpretation of the H-T-P for children of elementary school age: II. The "phallic tree" as an indicator of psychosexual conflict. *J. Clin. Psychol.,* 1952, 245-255.

_____. A study of the validity of some hypotheses for the qualitative interpretation of the H-T-P for children of elementary age: III. Horizontal placement. IV. Vertical placement. *J. Clin. Psychol.,* 1953, 161-167.

_____. *A Catalogue for the Qualitative Interpretation of the H-T-P.* Beverly Hills, California: Western Psychological Services, 1964.

Machover, Karen. *Personality Projection in the Drawing of the Human Figure.* Springfield, Ill.: Thomas, 1949.

Abraham Levine received his undergraduate and Master's degrees at the City College of New York and his Ph.D. at New York University. He completed his psychoanalytic training at the National Psychological Association for Psychoanalysis and now is a member of the Institute for Psychoanalytic Training and Research.

From 1955 to 1964, he was Director of Psychological Services at Hillside Hospital, Glen Oaks, New York. He also served as Associate Editor of the Journal of the Hillside Hospital. In addition, he supervised the psychological programs of the Jewish Community Services at Jamaica, Long Island, New York and the Pride of Judea in Brooklyn, New York. In addition, he served in both advisory and consultant roles for other agencies and institutions.

Prior to going to Hillside Hospital, Dr. Levine had been employed at Mount Sinai Hospital in New York City from 1949 to 1955, where he served as Senior Clinical Psychologist and Research Assistant in Psychiatry.

Dr. Levine has authored and co-authored over a dozen papers, including "Observations on the House-Tree-Person Drawing Test Before and After Surgery," with Dr. B. Meyer and Dr. Fred Brown. Dr. Levine has conducted workshops on the Bender Gestalt and the Rorschach projective techniques.

He is a Diplomate in Clinical Psychology of the American Board of Examiners in Professional Psychology and a Fellow of the American Psychological Association and the Society for Projective Techniques.

Dr. Levine currently is engaged in private practice in New York City.

Allan Sapolsky received his M.S. degree from the City College of New York in 1953 and his Ph.D. from Adelphi University in 1958. In 1961 he began psychoanalytic training in the New York University Postdoctoral Program.

For six years he was a Senior Psychologist at Hillside Hospital, Glen Oaks, New York. He is now an Assistant Professor in the Psychology Department of Brooklyn College of the City University of New York.

Dr. Sapolsky is the author of a number of scientific publications; he is a Diplomate in Clinical Psychology of the American Board of Examiners in Professional Psychology.

Chapter 8

The Use of the H-T-P As an Aid
in the Screening of Hospitalized Patients

Abraham Levine, Ph.D. and Allan Sapolsky, Ph.D.

The authors present a vivid picture of the wealth of diagnostic and prognostic material which can be derived when a single achromatic drawing of a House, a Tree, or a Person is interpreted by highly skilled clinicians of long and wide-ranging experience.

This single picture approach (not intended for clinical usage, of course) has two legitimate applications: (1) to demonstrate the worth of a projective technique sampling; and (2) to appraise the ability of a student or an applicant for a psychological position to make qualitative analyses in depth and with accuracy.

The H-T-P has earned its place within the diagnostic battery of psychological tests; it is within such a battery that this projective instrument is most validly employed. Circumstances sometimes will dictate other usage of the H-T-P, however. The relative ease and speed of H-T-P administration, coupled with the problems of under-staffing and the pressure of referrals, frequently result in the H-T-P's being selected as the projective test to be used for the rapid screening of hospitalized patients. On such occasions, the H-T-P has been found to be useful in highlighting specific psychopathology, in providing hypotheses concerning personality dynamics, as well as in singling out those cases which may require more immediate intensive examination.

Furthermore, the H-T-P is of value in assisting in the development of treatment plans for patients hospitalized within a setting which offers psychotherapy and utilizes its milieu therapeutically. Such an approach to the H-T-P will be illustrated in this brief chapter by an intensive analysis of selected typical draw-

ings of voluntarily hospitalized patients. Subtle nuances in these drawings will
have to be neglected, but an effort will be made to identify those major aspects
which have contributed to the interpretations. (For this we must presuppose
some familiarity with both H-T-P interpretation and psychoanalytic theory on
the part of the reader.)

Fig. 119

HOUSE (Fig. 119)

House A (drawn by a male, age 54) displays a number of interesting characteristics: (a) it is relatively small and placed within the upper left quarter of
the page (tending toward the type of drawing frequently produced by depressed and withdrawn patients); (b) it is drawn in emphasized perspective (reliance upon intellectual defenses in an effort to gain distance while seeking to
understand the self in relationship to others); (c) the roof (ideation) is not completely enclosed by boundary lines (inability to distinguish inner fantasy from
outer reality can lead to delusional thinking); and (d) it is drawn without concern for lines meeting (difficulty controlling impulses, as well as feelings of inner instability with fears of imminent collapse). This, then, is a basically depressed,
anxious, withdrawing individual whose defenses are in the process of fragmen-
ting. His control over impulsive expression is waning and he is in danger of
developing delusional thinking.

At this juncture in his life, the patient's immediate difficulties appear to
center about his inability to express or channel his aggressive impulses successfully within socially provided modalities (the lines are drawn in a slashing man-

ner without concern for their going beyond the realistic boundaries of the building). The difficulties he has in instituting conscious, volitional, intellectual controls result in an impulsive and unrealistic expression of affect, whereas internalization of his anger leads in the direction of withdrawal and depression.

This type of House, with perspective used in this manner, begins to approach the typical coffin-like Houses drawn by some hospitalized patients. In such cases it is generally a sign of suicidal depression. In this instance the aggression is gaining some external expression, which would mean that the depression has not as yet fully crystalized in terms of there being a need for immediate concern about his suicidal propensities. Hospital personnel must be alerted, however, to the likelihood that if his depression were to intensify clinically, it would probably activate a strong suicidal potential.

The patient wishes to show that there is some life in the House, some warmth (smoke in the drawing), which may be interpreted as deriving from his relationship to the mother (the House often is symbolic of the mother). But the intensity of the aggression (the manner in which the smoke lines are drawn) suggests that considerable ambivalence is attached to his needs for warm, nurturing relationships. It appears that he seeks to burn up, in the realm of aggressive, phallic (chimney) fantasy (rising from the roof, or ideation, area) much of his anger toward women (mother substitutes).

He has drawn one window in the roof (ideation), and this without crossbars. This suggests that, despite his efforts to appear mature (crossbars in other windows, use of perspective), it may be oral level material (open window) which determines his fantasies and underlies his personality problems. The oral-dependent aspects of his personality probably are not acceptable to him, and he may seek to present himself in a stronger, more mature kind of self-sufficient role. An awareness of his underlying needs will be helpful to the hospital personnel when they are confronted by his aggressive, seemingly mature, intellectual facade. While this facade represents a utilization of ego strengths, sometimes it may successfully belie the intensity of his anxiety and fears, as well as cover his internal fragmentation. If this happens, environmental demands then may put too much expectation upon independence, or too great a premium upon compliance with rules and regulations. Since his intellectual defenses are only tenuously organized at this point, his efforts at repressing or inhibiting affective expression can become so weakened that unpredictable aggressive outbursts may be precipitated (sharp lines at back base of House go out toward the right (environment). His efforts to counter the direct expression of aggression presumably will take the form of withdrawal into oral and aggressive fantasies, which may lead to: (a) his feeling exceedingly inadequate, with all his anger directed against the internalized mother figure, leading to possible suicidal activity; and/or (b) defensive projection of the aggression, resulting in a paranoidal, delusional orientation.

Therapeutically, then, the point of emphasis in his hospitalization would be to assist him to direct his anger externally. Although some of this does take place at present, it occurs pathologically because he lacks sufficient controls. Psychotherapy must be related to his inability to deal with affect expression, especially aggression. A therapeutic milieu program designed to strengthen his decompensating intellectual defenses could shore up his obsessive-compulsive defensive structure and enable him to gain greater control over his impulses.

The foundation of the House has gaps and unconnected lines, suggesting that there is a basic ego weakness stemming from his early years of development. This would indicate that any encouragement of regression within the hospital setting would be likely to decompensate him further. Psychotherapy, therefore, should be of a non-probing type, directed mainly toward dealing with his aggression while avoiding direct examination of his libidinal impulses.

Although an exaggerated doorknob is drawn, the door itself is not consistently touching the foundation. He strives to appear amenable to outside contact, as if he were a ready participant in the environment. In truth, however, he is in the process of withdrawing, with intensified feelings of being inadequate and inferior (the perspective of the House goes off exaggeratedly into the background and not toward the environmental (right) side of the page). When he does seek contact, he will want a passive, dependent relationship, which would serve only to decompensate him further. Such an oral-dependent attachment to the hospital is a distinct possibility, suggesting that treatment plans should focus upon a short-term hospitalization. This patient is likely to begin to feel comfortable within the hospital setting and to become more and more frightened about leaving. Taken from left (home, the past) to right (environment, the future), the House starts relatively large and becomes sharply smaller as it goes toward the environment. It might be helpful if, soon after admission, some activities and/or work were prescribed outside the hospital.

Although he seeks to make the House three-dimensional, the chimney is drawn in two dimensions, only, indicating that his phallic, masculine aspects are felt to be only a "show", covering up deeply felt inferiority and inadequacy in this area. His participation in group activities and sports should be structured so as to support and enhance his feelings of masculinity, while serving also to dilute any overdependent attachment which could develop in his relationship to his therapist. Again, pyschotherapy should avoid dealing directly with his feelings of masculine impotence, but should be focused instead upon reality testing (to counter delusional formation) and his difficulties with expressing aggression.[1]

The most striking aspect of House B (Fig. 120) which was drawn by a male, age 38, is its transparency. Such transparencies frequently are drawn by psychotic patients who believe that other persons know what they are thinking. This type of patient does not bother to close the door when he appears for an interview since privacy is not possible when others can read your mind. Such patients are likely to discuss personal matters inappropriately with anyone, but they will not talk about or discuss such matters during treatment sessions because they assume that the therapist already knows their thoughts and feelings.

---

[1] These one-drawing analyses in depth are presented to show the great amount of useful diagnostic and prognostic information that can be gleaned from a single drawing by skilled clinicians with extensive experience with the H-T-P. The Editors wish to reinforce the remarks of the authors in cautioning against any general use of this type of analysis and in particular against placing undue credence upon the information so derived until it has been reinforced by other test analysis and/or by observation.

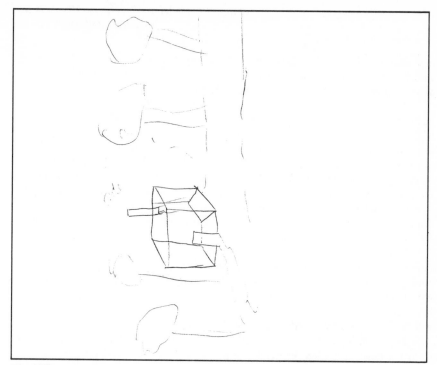

Fig. 120

This bizarre presentation of a House, the inside of which is observable through the walls, denotes extreme difficulties in differentiating internal from external stimuli. Such a gross break in reality testing reveals the primitive character of his thinking along with the marked impairment in his judgment. By displaying the inner barrenness of the House (the inside is clearly devoid of persons or things), he emphasizes his lack of identification, empathy, or relatedness with others. He reveals severe regression, withdrawal, and feelings of alienation from the world. In dynamic terms, he lacks inner objects, implying a withdrawal of cathexis from, and fragmentation of, the inner representations of the parental figures, leading to a regression and fragmentation of his ego.

An intense, fearful dependency is suggested by the number of Trees (mother symbols) with which he has had to surround himself. This is consistent with the infantile, regressed position noted above. He drew the Trees quickly using a light line, suggesting that he will not be eager to talk about his dependency needs, his felt helplessness, and his need for protection. In fact, the long, disproportionately large chimney (phallic symbol) reflects his desire to be viewed by others as a strong, potent male. But the chimney is poorly anchored to the roof and seems to be floating in almost a disconnected manner, demonstrating further his lack of cathexis and identification with the father figure.

His three-dimensional House indicates efforts to appear stronger, healthier, and more mature than he actually experiences himself to be. The attempts at perspective further suggest some positive efforts at mobilizing his energies to see and understand himself in relation to the world. Unfortunately, his House is of such bizarre quality, his judgment is so poor, and his currently available resources are so limited, that he does not achieve any true stability from these efforts.

His desire to grow and to become a strong, phallic person can serve as a positive motivation in undertaking hospitalization. Yet, although the door appears to be open (actually he does not have a door to close), and since there is an absence of inner objects, it is apparent that he cannot be reached easily in treatment. Nevertheless, it will be necessary to contact him therapeutically by way of the home (the pathway from the door goes directly to the home (left) side of the page): that is, as a parental figure. Although he is likely to cast the therapist in a maternal role anyway, it is important to recognize the fearfulness and withdrawal which is likely to result if the therapist attempts to bring reality clarification too soon or too abruptly into the relationship.

A major goal in hospitalization will be to arrest the regressive process by building up object cathexis and by strengthening his tenuous hold on the public conceptions he does have of himself. His reality testing will require considerable improvement, but he must be offered some degree of oral gratification to bring about some relaxation within the hospital setting. His dependency demands will be exceedingly marked, and he will be unable to tolerate being confronted with his infantile position. Group activities may prove successful in drawing him from his lonely isolation, especially if he can gain some security from a giving group leader. The activities chosen should be those likely to afford him some success so that eventually he can experience acceptance and comfort within the group. Nursing personnel might well be instructed to offer him additional attention until his regressive process can be reversed. The reconstruction of his ego will be a slow process and long term hospitalization must be envisaged.

TREE (Fig. 121)

Tree C (Fig. 121) was drawn by a male, age 37. This drawing is an example of what is called the "split-Tree": that is, there are no lines connecting the left and the right sides. In such a rendition, the examiner can draw a line through the Tree from the bottom to the top without intersecting any line of the original drawing. It is as if the left side were one Tree and the right side another. Such a split-Tree reflects a lack of ego organization or integration, a lack of ego oneness, and generally is diagnostically pathognomonic of chronic schizophrenia.

Another striking feature of this Tree is that the branch lines run over the edges of the paper and graphically illustrate this man's lack of impulse control. Although he does try to drain off much of his aggressive impulses (sharp, pointed branch lines) in fantasy (upper part of page), nevertheless he is capable of uncontrolled, aggressive reactions in the home (left side of page run over) and in the environment (right side of page run over). Probably he has been openly aggressive and assaultive, since he lacks the ability for prolonged inner control and discipline. The question arises as to his suitability for an open hospital setting.

Note that efforts have been made to give the Tree an appearance of connectedness (the innermost branches of the left and right trunk lines almost touch, serving to obscure the basic split-Tree characteristic), and suggesting that only through close, careful clinical interviewing will a thinking disorder (schizo-

Fig. 121

phrenia) be detected; and without such close scrutiny of his thinking processes he can be identified mistakenly as having an impulse disorder only. The branches (ideation) running off the top of the page suggest also that he will have thoughts which he will keep hidden from his therapist, and it will require more intensive psychological testing before their nature can be ascertained. This patient should receive immediate, careful and complete evaluation if he is to remain in the hospital for other than custodial care or chemotherapy.

The wide base of the Tree's trunk suggests a deep-seated, oral-dependent hold on the mother (mother earth). However, this is not so clearly displayed here as in other drawings which accentuate elaborate, grasping root systems. These wide lines, indicative of a passive oral-receptiveness, are aggressed, negated, and hidden by his strange rendition of grass. The authors have found empirically that grass drawn with single, vertical lines is usually correlated with excessive masturbatory activity. Here the grass lines are drawn so large, so aggressively, and so impulsively that one wonders whether this patient has indulged in irrational sexual activities. One can speculate that when his oral longings are aroused, he reacts defensively with a sexualized, aggressive, uncontrolled, and irrational expression of "masculinity". Thus during his hospitalization, he will have to be watched carefully if he does engage in aggressive and bizarre sexual activity.

The Tree is of relatively large size, encompassing a considerable area of the page. Its size and placement suggest, for this patient, a complete self-centeredness and self-preoccupation. He feels that he should get what he wants when he wants it, and he will respond aggressively when his needs are frustrated. This will present problems for the hospital personnel in terms of his expectations and aggressive demands. He will see himself as the most important person on the ward and will encounter marked difficulty in sharing with others and in restraining himself in a group setting. What he has to say will be the most important thing; and what he wants will have to get primary attention.

The Tree is devoid of foliage. This reflects not only his inner barrenness but also the lack of ego organization that he needs to provide him with a sense of productivity or an ability to think in terms of the future. He will probably engage in hedonistic fantasy against whose pressure he has only limited delaying or impeding mechanisms (that obsessive-compulsive delaying mechanisms are non-operative is indicated by the lack of leaves).

This patient will need a highly controlled, organized, and minutely scheduled day. Everything must be planned and rigidly set forth for him. He will need to learn to internalize the rules and regulations which are spelled out for him. At first this will require explicit external controls, coupled with firm, consistent, and benevolent enforcement, in the hope that such structuring will facilitate the beginning development of his internal controls. If he responds positively to such a regimen, intensive, long-term hospital treatment can be considered seriously. Especially helpful should be group activities and participation in group therapy where other members of the group would be able to sit on him, acquaint him with his true impact upon others, and thereby assist him to institute inner controls which would permit more harmonious participation with others. A

Fig. 122

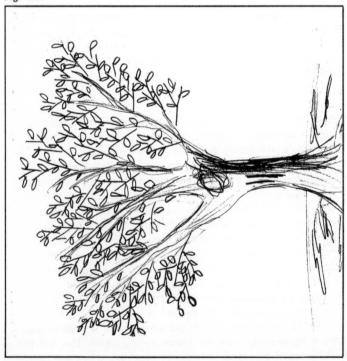

supportive, reality-testing form of psychotherapy, designed to aid in his identi-fication with a male therapist, could serve to solidify his ego development and provide the opportunity to internalize objects with a consequent development of impulse control.

The extensive area of the page covered by Tree D (Fig. 122), which was pro-duced by a female patient, age 18, alerts one to this adolescent's need to occupy a large part of her environment. Also, the abundance of leaves points toward a concomitant need to appear as a fruitful, alive, and highly productive person. This profusion of branches and leaves (ideation) also suggests that the patient is a hyper-ideational individual, with possible manic-like trends. The painstaking effort expended in rendering the countless number of leaves reflects the strong obsessive-compulsive component within her personality. Overtly this may be expressed in efforts to be highly intellectual, organized, and accomplishing, while dynamically it points to strained efforts toward countering the strong push of unacceptable im-pulses and needs seeking expression. Despite her desire to be precise, many of the leaves and twigs are not attached to the branches. This, together with the essentially uncontrolled rendering of the shading on the trunk and the somewhat peculiar depiction of a knothole, illustrates the process of decompensation of her obsessive-compulsive defensive structure.

It may be conjectured that the crystallization of the anal, obsessive-compulsive defensive system arose from her inability to negotiate successfully her Oedipal con-flicts and felt castration (knothole, scar lines on the Tree's trunk). Note that the trunk is darkened on the right (environmental) side, suggesting that the sun (warmth) is perceived as coming from the home (left) while the environment is ex-perienced as cold and ungiving. Furthermore, virtually all of the branches (ideation) tend to reach back toward the home side, suggesting that much of her hyperidea-tion will have a backward slant, and is likely to be highly colored with Oedipal longings for the father (often the sun is symbolic of the father).

The shading lines drawn within the Tree's trunk (body) indicate a reliance upon somatization as a defensive mechanism. In this case, heavy (aggressive), dark (depressive) shading appears predominantly on the environmental side of the trunk (if the entire trunk were so covered, it would suggest the presence of an agitated, somatic depression). This raises the hypothesis that the anger which first was ex-perienced toward the mother (emphasis upon obsessive-compulsive defenses focus-es the analytic spotlight upon the mother-daughter relationship during the anal period), who demanded compliant, productive behavior, was later displaced from the home (no shading on the left side of trunk) onto the environment. In order to control the expression of this unacceptable anal-aggressive rage, now displaced to mother substitutes in the environment, she has related in terms of intense somatic complaints. That this characteristic mode of defense began early in childhood is indicated by the shading at the base of the trunk (the beginning).

A strong oral component within her personality is inferable from the wide base of the trunk, while narcissistic elements are suggested by the size of the Tree and her placement of it in the foreground of the page (the ground line is used to give a perspective which emphasizes the foreground placement). The trunk line at the left goes to the bottom edge of the page (reality, objectivity), but the right trunk line is not so placed in the ground. From earliest childhood then, she has attempted to remain reality-rooted and objective in her relationship to the home, but she could not permit her subjective reactions and her feelings and fantasies to influence her behavior within the home. It is in the environment that her primary danger of losing control occurs. It is suspected that while she has been unaware of her anger at the mother figure, she has found it difficult to establish tranquil relationships with mother figures outside the home; in defending herself against expression of her anger, depressive and somatic symptoms have arisen.

Apparently her need to achieve and produce (in order to be loved by her mother) was too strongly instilled with phallic qualities for her to be able to accept her femininity fully, and she has been unable to experience and express, and thereby free herself from her binding anger at the demanding mother. Much of the Tree does have a feminine quality, however, reflecting basic strengths which have not yet matured or solidified. Psychotherapy directed toward reestablishing her controls, clarifying and strengthening her relationship with the father figure (so that her femininity can become more acceptable to her), and examining her rage at the mother figure can serve to free her for further emotional development. Group activities accentuating femininity, and occupational therapy projects for release of aggression without the concomitant need to produce a finished product, can assist the psychotherapeutic endeavors.

Fig. 123

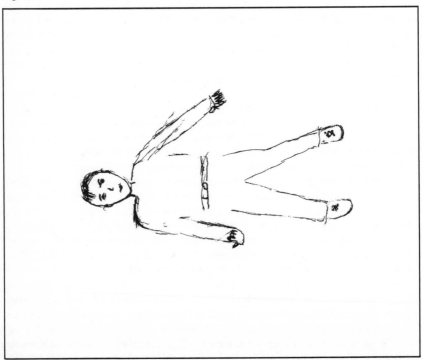

PERSON (Fig. 123)

Person (Fig. 123) was produced by a 27-year-old man. Its placement, fullfaced, in the center (willingness to confront the world), and toward the bottom of the page (reality based, objectivity) reveals that this patient is a man who places considerable emphasis on being realistically, objectively oriented (having his feet on the ground). He wants to meet the world in a strong, firm, solidly planted position, with an attitude of self-assertion and rational, intellectual knowing. That this broad-based stance is essentially defensive in nature is suggested by the emptiness of the figure, by the varied line pressures, and by the fact that there are parts of the body that do not seem to have any peripheral line at all. Behind the veneer, then, he feels disorganized, ill-defined, and non-assured.

The differences noticeable in the shoulder line (left compared to right) reflect the inner doubts which he experiences regarding his strength and masculinity. The shoulder on the right side of the page is a little lower than that on the left and is off balance, indicating that when he goes into the environment his masculinity is most keenly threatened. The small additional lines on this shoulder give it a "chip on the shoulder" quality; it is as if he must prove how strong, aggressive, and masculine he is, an orientation offering inherent difficulties to him as he attempts to adjust and adapt within the interpersonal hospital environment.

The strong, heavy mouth line indicates that he will be carefully selective of the words he uses. He will wish to seal his lips or just talk in a simple, rational, assertive way (it is a sharp, dark line). His psychotherapist's probing for ideation is likely to be countered and frustrated, since it will be experienced as tending to undermine an important defensive position which he maintains only tenuously. Its fragile character is suggested by the number of other light lines around the mouth, probably intended to represent lips, suggesting that at times words do emerge from his mouth beyond his control. This may indicate that he is aware that things are not right with him, and that if he felt less threatened he might become highly motivated to confide his fears and reveal his weaknesses, with the hope of gaining help from the therapist.

The weakness and lack of line around the waist and buttocks, when combined with his difficulty in rendering the shoulders, permits the hypothesis of the presence of a marked homosexual problem. In this connection, the firmness of the ear lines and the peculiarly drawn ear on the left side (as contrasted to the right), point toward probable paranoid manifestations of the homosexual problem. It seems likely that he will suspect that people are saying things about him, that people are seeking to "screw" him or alluding to him as a homosexual. As a consequence, he is likely to protest offensively that he is a man who is fully aware of the intentions of others, and that he is a smart, alert man. Yet there is such a disordered quality to his thinking (as represented by the disarrayed hair) as to suggest felt decompensation in his intellectual capacities with increasing doubts about himself. The numerous lines around the shoulders and the double line around the chin reveal that a decathectic process (primarily from the father figure whose masculinity we must question) is beginning, and that depersonalization dimensions have been reached (in the sense that he is not very clear about his identity or ego boundaries). Defensively he struggles to remain objective, emotionally uninvolved, and clearly masculine in his posture, thereby striving to retain a hold on reality and counter the decompensating, withdrawing trend. But when he seeks to move out into the environment, he has difficulty maintaining contact with others because of his fears and suspicions about their intentions toward him.

It will be noted that his treatment of the shoelaces and the fingers reflects an obsessive-compulsive quality which is not evident in other areas of the drawing. But the hands are drawn in such a peculiar manner and the shoe (to the right) is not really connected to the leg, revealing the inadequacy and weakness of his present obsessive-compulsive defenses. Activity planning must include concerted efforts at shoring up and reconstituting these defensive operations.

The hand toward the "home" side of the page initially was drawn longer and then shortened (previous lines not erased), offering a graphic illustration of his being caught reaching out, and at the same time pulling away from contact with the parental figures. An important long range psychotherapeutic goal would be to clarify with him his identification problems within the context of his relationship with his parents. Success in this area would be likely to reduce his paranoid fears and tensions, and enable him to counter his withdrawal and relate to others. But such a psychotherapeutic endeavor must be preceded by a strengthening of his masculine self-image by experiences obtained in a carefully prescribed milieu program designed to offer him the experience of masculine acceptance and accomplishment. This can be undertaken within the context of a variety of specific men's social groups and sporting activities, as well as activities wherein his efforts to be intellectual can become better established. It must be expected that his relationships with persons in the hospital will have highly peculiar accents to them (both hands, but especially the one toward the environmental side of the page, are pulled in in a very strange and unusual manner), and his standoffish, argumentative, suspicious, sullen, hostile attitudes will make him unpopular. It would be well to aim for his participation in patient government to enhance his ability to accept and identify with authority without feeling that he is being attacked or that advantage is being taken of him.

The patient's rendition of a belt serves to give some semblance of continuity to a body which is actually separated from the legs. This is an effort to make the world think that he is still intact and a male who has masculine accoutrements and still wears pants. The inclusion of a circular belt buckle (unconnected) suggests an orally dependent, umbilical attachment to the mother figure which he wishes to deny and rationalize (there are no other usual indicators of overt dependency needs, such as buttons, pockets, open mouth). While the hospital situation is likely to offer some covert gratification to his dependent, infantile needs, he may be impelled to fight against this gratification (closed mouth). This patient is too fragile at this time to admit or confront any inner weakness, and one may expect difficulty in treating him because of his inability to allow himself to become dependent upon or close to a therapist. For this reason, and because of the homosexual threat that such closeness would entail, the therapist will need to constantly be on the alert to maintain a proper distance. It will be best to avoid the dependency area in hospital psychotherapy, concentrating more upon helping him to establish clearer ego boundaries by examining and clarifying his relationship to authority (father and father substitute) figures. Reality will have to be clarified for him, especially as it is related to his paranoid characteristics, but always in a manner which cannot be construed by him as attacking him.

The process of regression to an oral-umbilical tie with the mother probably is a reactivation due to his inability to maintain himself at the phallic level and his inability to retain an identification with the father figure. This probably has had specific precipitants (the entire figure looks as though it had been punctured and was collapsing). It should be the goal of hospital treatment to reinforce the patient's masculinity and to raise his self-esteem so that he can begin to relax his defenses. The emptiness at the crotch suggests that part of him is inclined to accept a castrated position but he must counter this with an air of bravado. His belligerent, defensive, suspicious posture will be difficult for the hospital staff and other patients to endure for long, but it does appear that with the suggested therapeutic approach he will be able to relax this stance somewhat.

The Person's body is unintegrated and empty, pointing toward either an inner emptiness or the expulsion of an internalized object (likely the father). The former would be reflected in depressive qualities, while the latter would be manifested in a delusional, paranoid manner regarding the expelled father fig-

Fig. 124

ure. This remains to be worked out further from the other H-T-P drawings and more substantial test procedures.

PERSON (Fig. 124)

Person F (Fig. 124) was produced by a female, age 18, who had not been able to crystalize a feminine identification or to achieve satisfactory relationships with those about her. Efforts to appear overly feminine, sensual, and sexually available (the hair is on the environmental side of the page; the bust is large, the waist narrow, and the legs are wide apart), together with a tendency to relate to others on the basis of giving (the peculiar emergence of the arms from the bust), suggest the likelihood of frantic sexual acting out (difficulty with impulse control is suggested by the line breaks in the skirt and the lack of a barrier such as a collar or a necklace between the body and the neck). But the strange virtual fusion of the arms (avenues of interpersonal contact) with the body (again suggesting that she relates to others in terms of her body) indicates that she is actually quite withdrawn (as does the lack of pupils in the eyes). The aggressive "X-ing" at the waist (possibly intended as a belt), which also seems to bind the arms to the body, implies that she is in marked conflict over her sexual activity and that such behavior may be experienced as compulsive and partially ego-alien. The fact that she draws the entire body in the shape of a keyhole permits the speculation that she experiences an inner void which prevents her from feeling complete unless she has a man (key).

To a considerable extent her identification has not solidified because of her inability to accept a feminine, maternal role (fear of pregnancy reflected by "X-ing" at waist), and her inability to overcome her reaction to the lack of a penis (the heavy emphasis on the shoes (phallic symbols), especially the boot-like shoe on the environmental side, which is not connected to the leg; also the light, single dot for a nose). A part of her wishes to protest that she has no penis, while voyeuristic components are inferable from the keyhole rendition. This suggests a potential for homosexual activity in which she would wish to see the "female's penis" in order to bolster the denial of her felt castration. Another avenue for expression might be overly-feminine exhibitionism, whose unconscious roots would be the desire to display her "penis".

Within the hospital she will require structure and close supervision to assist her in the development of control functions which are presently unsuccessful and debilitating. However, the heavy reliance placed upon denial mechanisms, the basic withdrawal, and the feelings of helplessness in the face of her impulses, all serve to make her availability for treatment questionable. This matter will have to be evaluated further by more intensive psychological examinations.

In conclusion, an attempt has been made to demonstrate how a single piece of important data, *i.e.* an individual H-T-P drawing can be used to obtain both a structural and a psychodynamic understanding of the hospital patient. We wish to reiterate that we are not espousing the routine utilization of the H-T-P by itself. It is our conviction that it is only when the H-T-P is thoroughly and independently analyzed that it achieves a truly contributory place within the clinical psychologist's psychodiagnostic test battery.

Interpretations advanced for individual drawings must be substantiated by analysis of the complete H-T-P, as well as by other diagnostic battery test data, before one can give them credence. The authors, of course, had access to other data, which offered support of the "blind" analyses presented here. A high rate of correspondence also was generally found between the H-T-P interpretations and the clinical pictures presented (where specific comparative information was available). Thus, for example, patient A was described as having been unable to hold jobs because of his argumentativeness and outbursts of anger. He entered the hospital in a state of depression which was accompanied by a strong desire to die, but he had made no overt suicidal attempts. Delusions of persecution and grandiosity regarding his capacities also were present.

Patient B's life adjustment was described as megalomanic. When dependency gratification was not obtained, he was characterized as displaying irrationality, a loosening of thought associations, mounting anxiety, and feelings of being persecuted.

Patient C had a central nervous system disease (not detected in the interpretation of the Tree) with aggressively labile and histrionic affect. There was a diagnostic question of an underlying schizophrenia.

Patient D was hospitalized because of unmanageable, over-active behavior. She was hyperideational with delusional content and was openly belligerent and argumentative toward her father. Her uncontrollable behavior alternated with withdrawal and excessive feelings of isolation and depression. Although she suffered from a heart disease which had required surgery in early childhood, and she later suffered from various allergic reactions, no verbalization of hypochondriacal ideas was evident during her hospitalization.

Patient E entered the hospital with feelings of confusion, depression, and what he called "fogginess in thinking". He was found to have delusional thoughts with a paranoid flavor, including ideas of reference. Transfer to another hospital was necessary after he became assaultive.

Patient F, an unmarried female, developed a psychotic depression following a therapeutic abortion. Her typical reaction under stress was to retreat and withdraw. She derived but little benefit from her hospitalization.

George Rex Mursell received his B.A. in Social Work at Boston University, and his M.S. and Ph.D. in Clinical Psychology at Ohio State University. He studied under Arps, Goddard, Maxfield, Pressey, Burt, and Renshawe, and received his first job-training in clinical work from Goddard, Wells, and Kuhlmann.

He has worked as a psychologist in state hospitals, state institutions for the retarded, state prisons, correctional institutions for juvenile delinquents, schools for the deaf and blind, and in public school and court settings.

He served in the U. S. Army in World War II as a Consulting Psychologist and was demobilized with the rank of Colonel.

He had been Director of Psychological Services for 14 years at two state schools for the retarded in Oregon and Iowa, when he retired in November, 1963. He came out of retirement in September, 1964, to serve as Supervisor of Clinical Training in the Department of Psychology of Rainier School, Buckley, Washington.

Chapter 9

The Use of the H-T-P with the Mentally Deficient

George Rex Mursell, Ph.D.

Dr. Mursell stresses the often overlooked fact that the mentally deficient individual is more than a person merely handicapped by inadequate intelligence.

In support of his contention that, in practice, a projective technique must be administered to every suspected mental deficient (above the idiot level), the author offers three convincing case illustrations. The achromatic H-T-P drawings are analyzed from the standpoints of quantity, quality of the quantity, and quality, and the P-D-I is considered at length.

The H-T-P of case three is of special interest because the presence of organicity, which is only suggested by the drawings, is demonstrated dramatically by the P-D-I (the exact reverse of the relationship ordinarily found between the drawings and the P-D-I where organicity is concerned).

While he was Director of Psychological Services at the Fairview Home in Oregon and the Glenwood State School in Iowa, the writer examined several thousand mental defectives with the H-T-P and trained a number of psychologists in its use. At both institutions the technique was used routinely with all subjects who could do more than scribble, and their drawings, insofar as possible, were analyzed both quantitatively and qualitatively. The H-T-P technique was added to the battery of tests used at the Rainier School, Buckley, Washington, when the writer joined the staff in September 1964, and it is rapidly proving its utility to the professional staff.

The technique is both a quantitative and qualitative instrument, and those who use it for only one of those purposes do not extract its full values.

Unfortunately, however, there never have been quantitative norms published for ages below 16 years, even where (as in the Seattle Public Schools) the H-T-P is used routinely as one of a battery of tests. With the many thousands of cases examined by use of the H-T-P, cases distributed over a wide geographic area and covering all ages and levels of intelligence, ample data exist upon which to establish such norms.

Since there are no objective norms for subjects below age 16, the writer has tried various means to derive such norms from Buck's tables and scoring system, including extrapolation by regression equations, comparison with subjects' scores on other tests, expansion from the Goodenough norms by extending the ratio of actual versus possible scores on the Person to the House and Tree, and utilization of the 1937 Stanford-Binet norms at age 16[1].

Qualitative scoring and analysis of the H-T-P and its use as a projective technique are well documented by Buck (1948) in his Manual, and Hammer (1958) in his *The Clinical Application of Projective Drawings* (especially in chapters 2, 3, 8, 9, and 24) and require no discussion here.

In applying the H-T-P technique to the mentally deficient, one should keep in mind that they are "children" in mental development and their judgment, system of values, and personalities are conditioned by their lower intellectual capacities which are not analogous to those of "normal" adults. Also one has to be aware that they have been conditioned into having certain attitudes by the frustrations they have experienced in society while trying to compete with those of greater mental capacities. For instance, the H-T-P drawings of most mental defectives will show feelings of inadequacy and inferiority; too much stress should not be placed on this recurring theme (recognized, yes, but not elaborated upon as unusual). Buck, in his paper read at the September 1950, meeting of the American Psychological Association divided the mentally deficient into two groups— *organic* (endogenous *and* exogenous) and *functional* ("pseudo," transistory, or reactive); it is to the *organic* group that the above remarks apply.

The term "mentally deficient" is used in this chapter rather than the newer term "mentally retarded." There are styles in semantics, as there are in hair or dress, but to the writer, "mentally retarded" suggests (1) persons with a temporary, transitory, or reversible process, and (2) the hope that by some means of maturation, learning, or teaching they can be helped to "catch up." This may be true for the *functionally* retarded but not, in our present state of knowledge, for the *organic* mentally deficient. Perhaps chemotherapy may provide such a miracle, but certainly it will not be psychotherapy.

---

[1] None of these methods is statistically sound. But if, for instance, a subject with a C.A. of 9-10 makes an I.Q. of 52 on the H-T-P, one can find the M.A. (7-10) for I.Q. 52 at age 16 on the Binet tables, and looking up the I.Q. for M.A. 7-10 at C.A. 9-10 find an I.Q. of 80 for his age, of 9-10. This is better than recording his I.Q. as if he were 16, 'though one recognizes that there is a large probable error from such a method, as there is no doubt a large probable error in Buck's adult norms. Even the best intelligence tests have probable errors, and since the H-T-P is rarely used alone but usually as part of a battery, and the H-T-P quantitative scores have their chief value for "Within-test" analysis, not too much is lost by such extrapolation, and there is some gain.

Administration

In the administration of the H-T-P to the mentally deficient, as to all children, the writer believes that it is essential that the examining room be free of cues, such as pictures on the wall, picture calendars, etc., and that the subject be seated so that he cannot see out a window to copy visible trees or houses. Occasionally subjects use the examiner as a "model" for drawing the Person, and there seems to be no way of controlling this without interfering with the spontaneity of the drawing unless the examiner is not seen by the subject. This is not desirable, since it creates an artificial testing atmosphere and deprives the examiner of a clear view of the S's emotional responses and of the drawing process for purposes of recording sequence, latencies, time, etc. . .

In the drawing of the Person, the writer frequently has found it necessary to use instructions which avoid the term "Person", since some subjects do not know what this means, saying instead, "Draw a man *or* woman, *or* a girl; draw just one of these". Some examiners add, "Whichever you (want), (wish), (like)," but this may compel a choice to be made on an emotional basis, since a subject may interpret this to mean that he is to draw the one he wants the most, or likes the best.

As was mentioned, it is the writer's practice to use the H-T-P with any subject who can do more than scribble. True, many productions so obtained do not lend themselves to much analysis, quantitative or qualitative, but some reasonable or supportive interpretations can be made of any graphic-expressive movement.

Even subjects who can only scribble usually enjoy the test. Since it is the writer's purpose always to use the H-T-P as the "ice-breaker" of a battery, it serves as an essentially non-threatening introduction[2] to a strange situation and to a new person or authority-figure.

The H-T-P's Worth

Some clinicians may reject the H-T-P as having no value and argue that all that is obtained from it is the examiner's projections. Perhaps these persons have not read Buck's *Manual* (1948) and *Manual Supplement* (1964), or Hammer's *The Clinical Application of Projective Drawings* (1958). They also are urged to read the article by Jacob Sine in the November, 1964, issue of the *Pyschological Review* entitled, "Actuarial Experiential Validity," as undoubtedly some of these clinicians might deny the validity of any projective technique or any expressive movement.

On the other hand, there are some who are too compliant and uncritical toward all projective techniques and swallow, "Hook, line, and sinker" (and perhaps would swallow the rod too, if they could get at it) the claims made about projectives.

One must be alert to the fact that examiners often project their biases into their interpretations, even if unconsciously, as all of us project ourselves into our communications. One also must guard against uncritically accepting all inter-

---

[2] An excellent usage; other clinicians prefer to use it as the concluding member of the examining battery to take advantage of the fact that at the least, the patient is somewhat fatigued by then. J.W.B.

pretations offered by the authors and proponents of any projective technique.

It is necessary to be careful not to read into the H-T-P drawings more than is there; this is particularly true in reference to the drawings of the mentally deficient. A compulsion to justify use of the technique by an elaborate interpretation of a few details is worse than overlooking valuable existing cues. If there is nothing or very little of diagnostic or prognostic significance in the drawings, it is best to say so.

One also should be aware that any set of drawings is temporal and may be reproduced differently from time to time or setting to setting. This may be due to mood swings or in rare instances to forgetting to include a detail. Very few subjects will produce exactly the same drawings from one examination to another. To determine what is accidental and what is significant requires clinical judgment. For instance, recently a male subject drew a male Person consisting only of a head (with facial features) and the legs; a week later he drew the head, with features, and the legs, and then added arms to the head; while a week after that he drew two Persons (male and female); the female figure had a head and features, a triangular body, legs, and arms again attached to the head; the male figure was the same as the female, except that it had *no body.* The omission of the arms from the first drawing may have been accidental, but the omission of the body from the last male figure certainly was not.

One possibly can get along without using the Post-Drawing-Interrogation (P-D-I), and rely solely on quantitative and qualitative analysis of the drawings. Under pressure of time and work this frequently is done, even though one recognizes that significant interpretative cues thereby are sacrificed. Not all clinicians have time to use the Chromatic phase of the H-T-P. However the P-D-I is a projective adjunct and should be used whenever possible, especially if one keeps in mind that Buck's questions in the P-D-I serve only as a framework, and additional questions need to be inserted to secure elaboration of some answers and extract deeper feelings and attitudes. In using the P-D-I with the mentally deficient, however, one should not be disappointed if only a few responses seem significant; in fact, to find more than a few is the exception, but if these few are followed up, one frequently obtains insights not revealed by inspection of the drawings only.

As illustrations of the use of the H-T-P with the mentally deficient, three cases (identified only as Edward, Andrew, and John for the sake of anonymity) are presented. The case of Edward is presented in full, including the P-D-I questions and answers, to show how feelings of rejection and guilt are assumed from the drawings.

Edward: Report of Psychological Examination

Name: Edward *Born:* 10-27-47 *ADM:* 8-20-64 File: xxxx X
Age: 17-0 *M.A.:* 8-6 *I.Q.:* 47 *Date Exam:* 11-5-64 *Examiner:* GRM

Diagnosis: Encephalopathy due to post-natal injury; kernicterus, moderate mental deficiency; mild personality imbalance.

Reason for Referral: Evaluation for institutional programming. Edward was admitted because of overt sexual approaches to female relatives, including his mother.

Recommendations (brief): Continue academic training. Place on part-time work assignment. Encourage group activities to include females. Assign to psychologist for group and individual psychotherapy.

Tests Administered		C.A.	M.A.	I.Q.
9-29-57	Stanford-Binet (L)	9-11	5-10	59
6-23-59	Stanford-Binet	11-7	7-2	62
11-5-64	Wechsler-Bellevue II	17-0	8-6	57 (VIQ 64, PIQ 57)
11-5-64	Bender-Gestalt	17-0		(organicity plus other)
11-5-64	H-T-P Projective Drawings	17-0		(emotional rejection)
11-5-64	Jastak Wide Range School Achievement			(Rd. 1.8, Sp. 2.2, Ar. 2.9)

Background Data: Edward was reported to have been an Rh-negative baby and to have had blood interchanges 2 or 3 times after the first day. A maternal aunt and cousin are said to be mentally deficient. The patient has one brother and one paternal half-brother, both older than he. At about one year of age he was in a car accident, suffered a concussion, had 6 ribs broken near the spine, and fractured both clavicles. His left leg is shorter than the right and there is a slight weakness in the left hand and arm. A vague report was made of mild infrequent seizures, but Edward has had none here.

Test Behavior: While he was verbally affable, there was an under-current of negativism which became overt during interrogation after the projective drawings were completed. His effort was optimal, but he was unable to tolerate "pushing" and showed resentment of questions concerning his feelings and attitudes.

Test Analysis: Scores from previous tests of intellectual ability in 1957 and 1959 were comparable in general to those now obtained. An increase of one year in mental age from 1957 to 1959 may be explained partly by the assumption that the Stanford-Binet used in 1959 was a different form from that used in 1957, although even if the same form had been used the practice effect would have been minimal.

There has been a further increase in intelligence since 1959, but it is apparent that his curve of development has flattened considerably, since his increase in mental age has been only one year, four months, in the past five years. This is quite a decrease in the ratio of mental development when compared with the two-year period from 1957 to 1959 and suggests that he has reached his maximum mental capacity.

On the Wechsler-Bellevue, Form II, he obtained a verbal I.Q. of 64, a non-verbal I.Q. of 47, and a full scale I.Q. of 57. His lowest scores were on Arithmetic (3 raw) and Picture Arrangement (zero raw) and his highest on Comprehension (7 raw) and Object Assembly (16 raw). However, his score on Block Designs in reality was as high as that on Object Assembly since on two of the more difficult designs using 9 blocks he succeeded in completing the designs in slightly over the prescribed time limits.

So far as his present functional level of intelligence is concerned, his mental age is about eight and a half years (8-6) with an I.Q. of 47. However, if one assumes

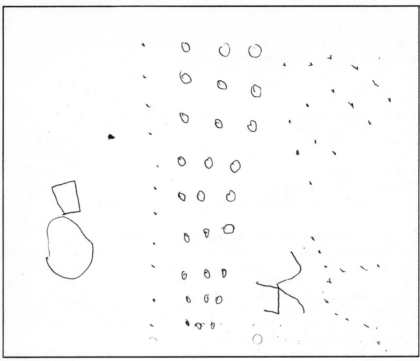

Fig. 125 (above)

Fig. 126 (below)

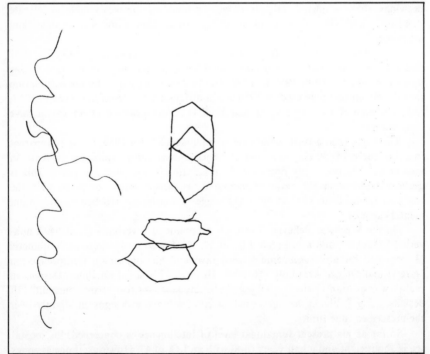

Fig. 127

that his two highest scores approximate his potential mental ability, then his mental level could be around ten and a half years (10-6) with an I.Q. of about 70. (This is what he achieved on the "percent raw G" of the H-T-P.)

His Bender-Gestalt reproductions (Figs. 125, 126) showed difficulty with angulation, some rotation of parts, and distortions. His reproductions of design 3 and 8 were from right to left, although he is right-handed, and his reproductions of designs 1, 2, and 5 became progressively larger. In general, however, he reproduced the essential Gestalt formation. Organicity, is suggested, but there is also some personality difficulty, especially in the organization of his interaction with his environment. For instance, Edward drew a large Design A, below it No. 1, 2, and 3, then to the right of A he drew No. 4, below it No. 5, squeezed in No. 6 between 3 and 5, and at the bottom of the sheet drew No. 7 and 8, partly rotated.

On the Wide Range School Achievement Test he reads at grade level 1.8, spells at grade 2.2, and performs simple arithmetical functions (only addition and subtraction) at grade level 2.9. This pattern of ASR is, according to Jastak, a modified non-reader pattern frequently associated with social maladjustment such as lying, truancy, stealing or sex.

Post-Drawing Interrogation (Figs. 127, 128, 129)

P1. Is that a man or a woman? Boy.
P2. How old is he? Eight years.
P3. Who is he? My school mate on dormitory.
P4. Is he a relation, a friend, or what? Friend.

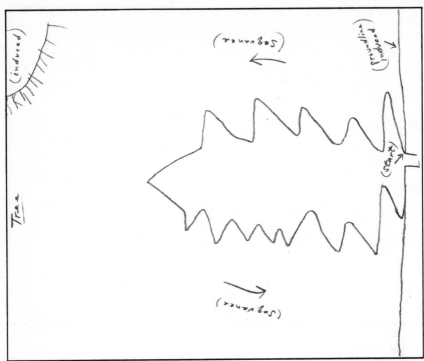

Fig. 128 (above)

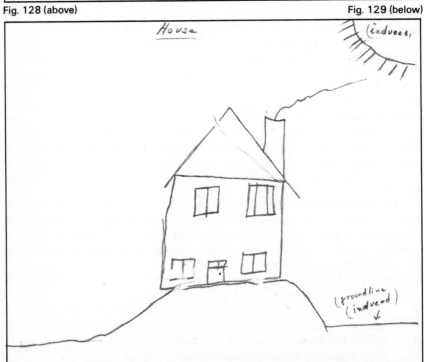

Fig. 129 (below)

P5.   Whom were you thinking about while drawing? Friend.
P6.   What is he doing? Holding out his arm. *Why?* To hang onto other kids. *Where?* Behind building.
P7.   What is he thinking about? What games to play. *What else?* Nothing.
P8.   How does he feel? Feels, oh, happy. *Why?* 'Cause he's playing games.

T1.   What kind of tree is that? (long pause) Older tree. *What makes you think so?* (no response)
T2.   Where is that tree actually located? (long pause) Towards a park. *You mean in a park?* No, towards it.
T3.   About how old is that tree? (long pause) Between 8 and 90.
T4.   Is that tree alive? Yes.
T5.   (a) What is there about that tree that gives you the impression that it's alive? It's still standing up.
      (b) Is any part of that tree dead? No.
T6.   Which does that tree look more like to you: a man or woman? (very long pause) Man.
T7.   What is there about it that gives you that impression? Men enjoy trees. *Why?* (long pause) 'Cause they stand up.
T8.   If that were a person instead of a tree, which way would the person be facing? Towards me, instead of against me.
T9.   Is that tree by itself, or in a group of trees? In group now.
T10. As you look at that tree does it seem to be above you, below you, or about on a level with you? On level with me.
T11. What is the weather like in this drawing? Nice sunny day – fall – warm (this reflects the weather prevailing at the time of the examination and probably has little or no significance).
T12. Is there any wind blowing in this picture? No.

H1.   How many stories does that house have? Two.
H2.   What is that house made of? Wood.
H3.   Is that your own house? No. *Whose house is it?* Parent's house.
H4.   Whose house were you thinking about while you were drawing? My parent's house.
H5.   Would you like to own that house? No. *Why?* Like it a little different. *How?* All on one floor.
H6.   If you did own that house and you could do whatever you liked with it:
      (a) Which room would you take for your own. Living room.
      (b) Whom would you like to have live in that house with you? One of my brothers. *Why?* I liked one brother better (long pause) I really like them both and would have both of them live with me.
H7.   As you look at that house does it seem to be close by or far away? Close by.
H8.   As you look at that house does it seem to be above you, below you, or about on a level with you? Above me – up on a hill.
H9.   What does that house make you think of, or remind you of? House my grandparents had.
H10. What else? (no reply)
H11. Is that a happy, friendly sort of house? Yes.

H12.   What is there about it that gives you that impression? It could look like it was a friendly house.

H13.   Are most houses that way? Most are not. *Why do you think so? (bitterly)* In some of them people go out and drink beer and do things bad.

H14.   What is the weather like in this picture? Nice sunny day.

T15.   What does that tree make you think of or remind you of? Nothing. *Does it make you think of a woman or man?* (no response, but his face got red)

T16.   What else? (became negativistic and mildly antagonistic and squirmed around in his chair and sweated).

T17.   Is it a healthy tree? Yes.

T18.   What is there about it that gives you that impression? Makes me feel like it's growing.

T19.   Is it a strong tree? Yes.

T20.   What gives you that impression? 'Cause it's standing up.

P9.   What does that person make you think of, or remind you of? Wish I was with him. *Why?* (pause) To play games.

P10.   What else? (no reply)

P11.   Is that person well? Yes.

P12.   Why do you think so? Goes outside and plays.

P13.   Is that person happy? Yes.

P14.   Why do you think so? He's happy 'cause he's at school. *Do you mean in school?* No, I mean here at this school, on my dormitory.

P15.   Are most people that way? Yes. *Why?* (no reply)

P16.   Do you think you would like this person? Yes. *Why?* 'Cause I do.

P17.   What is the weather like in this picture? Sunny.

P18.   Whom does that person remind you of? Friend. *Why?* (no reply)

P19.   What does that person need most? That I couldn't tell you. *What do you need most?* Shirts to wear.

T21.   Whom does that tree remind you of? (pause) No one. *Your mother?* (long pause, red face) Yes. *Why?* (no reply)

T22.   What does that tree need most? Water and someone to care for it. *Why?* So it can stand up strong.

H15.   Whom does that house make you think of? Grandparents.

H16.   What does that house need most? People to live in it. *Why?* Looks like it's empty now.

On the House-Tree-Person projective drawings his "weighted flaw" I.Q. was 45, his "weighted good" I.Q. was 45, his "percent raw G" I.Q. was 70, and his "net weighted" I.Q. was 45. Using Buck's "Quality of the Quantity" analysis his ratio of good to flaw scores was in the moron range for details, in the low imbecile range for proportion, and between imbecile and moron for perspective. This would suggest that his ability is highest in dealing with the concrete aspects of everyday life, poorer in evaluating his environment and his relation to it, and poorest of all in solving immediate everyday problems with emotional connotations. His ratios for the House and Tree were in the borderline to dull average range, but for the Person were in the low imbecile range. This ratio of good to flaw scores on the Person was in part the result of his "stick-man" drawing; but analysis of his P-D-I indicated that his use of a stick-man also was a reflection of his inability to obtain satisfaction from interpersonal relationships. (His use of a stick-man could be too, an unconscious reflection of his loss of body-imagery due to the physical insults his body suffered in infancy).

Time consumed in drawing was five minutes on the House, two minutes on the Tree, and one minute on the Person. Voluntary comments during the drawing phase were scant and chiefly associated with erasures and redrawing. Most comments were verbal criticisms of his drawing: "That looks pretty bad;" "That don't look right, so I'll change it," etc., but sometimes he did not change it, and even when he did, there was little improvement.

Analysis of the drawings indicates:

GENERAL

Some organizational difficulty in all three drawings and poor use of details in Tree and Person suggest functional depression in interpersonal relationships. Placement of the whole below the midpoint of the page reflects insecurity and inadequacy with a generalized depression of mood. The partially shown sun implies his feeling of a cold environment and a poor relationship with his family.

HOUSE

The groundline sloping down from both sides implies feelings of isolation and exposure probably with concomitant internal dependency needs. The accentuated chimney (in relation to the size of the windows and the door) suggests phallic preoccupation with exhibitionistic tendencies and/or over-concern with succorance (emotional warmth). The small door may indicate a feeling of inadequacy in social situations. The placement of the House as if it were above him indicates a feeling of rejection from the home and/or of striving towards a home situation that he feels he is unable to attain. Emphasis on the eaves suggests an overly defensive and suspicious attitude. The weak peripheral boundary of the left wall reveals his feeling that factors in the past have lessened his personality strengths. The midline vertical bar on three of the four windows indicates fixation on the female sex symbol.

TREE

The unshaded branch structure with the spike-like presentation suggests a feeling of emotional isolation and the presence of oppositional or hostile tendencies. The overly large branch structure with a tiny trunk indicates feelings of basic insecurity and inadequacy. The relation of the branch structure to the trunk (short and slender) indicates a precarious personality balance because of over-striving for satisfaction. The Tree is of the type known as Nigg's Tree (for the psychologist who first identified it) and is said by Buck to be drawn usually by patients with encapsulated personalities; patients who frequently are hostile.

PERSON

The "stick-man" Person suggests evasion and a poor body image. The Person's thin arms imply feelings of weakness and futility, but with some striving referable to the future since the arm on the right side is longer than the arm on the left side. (Edward's *left* arm is the weaker arm.) The absence of feet reveals his feeling of a crippling lack of autonomy. The large mouth may indicate strong oral needs. The lack of hands indicates his feeling of "castration" perhaps more social than sexual; the long thin neck suggests poor coordination between body drives and control thereof; and the lack of a trunk shows a loss of body imagery, especially since the neck is separated from the trunk by a break in the line.

The most significant responses from the Post-Drawing-Interrogation (P-D-I) were:

HOUSE

"Two (stories) wood." He did not want this House because he wants his House all on one floor. He chose the living room for his room and would "arrange" it differently. He would want one of his brothers to live with him (but after a long pause, he expressed guilt by changing his, "I like one brother better," to, "I really like them both." He sees the House as close by but up on a hill. It reminded him of his grandparents' home. It's a friendly House, because, "It could look like it." But he revealed his feelings by saying bitterly, "Most are not (that way)," because, "In some of them people go out and drink beer and do things bad." The House needed people to live in it. (The weather was a direct reflection of the weather at the time of the examination.)

TREE

(Many latency pauses on this.) It is an "Older Tree." He did not elaborate under questioning as to why it looked older even when this question came up again later. The Tree was located, "Towards a park" (not *in* but *towards*). It was alive because, "It's still standing up." It looks like a man because, "Men enjoy trees" (*very* long pause). If it were a person, it would be facing, "*Towards* me instead of *against* me." Edward became negativistic on T15 and refused to say of what the Tree reminded him. He said the Tree was healthy and strong because, "Makes me feel like it's growing 'cause it's standing up." He said that the Tree needs care but would give no reason why.

PERSON

(His "stick-man" presentation was as sterile in the P-D-I as in the drawing.) The Person is a boy about eight years old, a school mate on his dormitory, a friend holding out his arms to hang onto other kids, playing games, thinking about what games to play, happy because he's playing games. He's well because he goes outside and plays; he's happy. " 'Cause he's at school" (further probing showed that what Edward meant was that the boy is happy because he's at this institution). When he was asked what that Person needed most, he replied, "That I couldn't tell you." And to, "What do *you* need most?" he said, "Shirts to wear."

CONDENSATION FROM THE H-T-P

Edward shows feelings of insecurity and inadequacy with an accompanying depression of mood. The general environment is seen as cold and hostile. There is over-concern with sex. His home and family seem to him to lack psychological warmth. His striving for interpersonal acceptance is futile. He has guilt feelings over his Oedipus complex with bitterness over rejection by his mother. He has many hostile and oppositional tendencies largely internalized. His body image is poor.

He has a poor personality balance because of over-striving for satisfaction. Feelings of emotional isolation and exposure are present. He has strong dependency needs. As he sees it, the future in society holds no hope for him, but he claims to be happy in the situation. (*Note:* The examiner tried to interpret the H-T-P without reference to sexual matters, but so many signs pointed in that direction that they simply could not be ignored.)

GENERAL SUMMARY

This boy functions in the moderately retarded range with an intellectual potential in the borderline to mildly mental defective range. He reads at grade level 1.8, spells at grade level 2.2, and performs simple arithmetic functions at grade level 2.9. This is the non-reader pattern frequently found in those with problems of a social nature. Organicity appears to be present, but it is not as strong an efficiency-depressing factor as are Edward's emotional problems. His personality structure currently is weak because of feelings of rejection from home, guilt over an Oedipus complex, feelings of futility and emotional isolation, and defeatistic attitudes. However, in spite of, and perhaps because of, his needs for dependency, protection, and autonomy, he feels happier and better adjusted in his present institutional setting. These constitute a strength which it is hoped can be utilized in his growth and training towards his eventual return to an open society.

RECOMMENDATIONS (full)

Continue his academic training. Place him on a part-time work assignment on the institutional grounds with explorations into his job interest and capabilities. Prepare him for his eventual return to community living, not necessarily in his own home, but perhaps, as a start, in a sheltered workshop. Encourage more companionship and interaction, under supervision, with the opposite sex. It is not expected that he will become self-supporting without considerable help and supervision; but if he can be brought to semi-independent status, it will be better for him and his family.

The second case is Andrew. This case is presented to illustrate how the H-T-P drawings sometimes indicate the presence of psychotic process, when no clear signs of a psychosis are seen in day-to-day behavior.

Andrew: Report of Psychological Examination

Name: Andrew *Born:* 3-1-51 *ADM:* 8-18-64 *File:* xxxx Y
Age: 13-7 *M.A.:* 6-6 *I.Q.:* 48 *Date Exam.:* 9-29-64 *Examiner:* GRM
    Diagnosis: Idiopathic encephalopathy; moderate mental deficiency; possible psychotic process.
    Reason for Referral: Evaluation for institutional programming. Andrew was committed as unmanageable at home and in school.
    Recommendations (brief): Enroll in school program. Begin training in work assignments. Refer for psychiatric examination.

Tests Administered:		*C.A.*	*M.A.*	*I.Q.*
8-26-57	Wechsler Childrens Scale	6-6	(?)	54 (V 58, P 58)
8-26-57	Leiter International	6-6	2-6	38
8-26-57	Goodenough Drawing	6-6	(?)	(?) (no score)
10-18-60	Goodenough Drawing	9-8	6-3	65
10-18-60	Peabody Picture Vocabulary	9-8	6-2	64
10-18-60	Jastak W. R. School Achievement	9-8	(Read gr. 1.2, Arith. gr. 1.1)	
10-18-60	Wechsler Childrens Scale	9-8	5-6	54(V 57, P 58)
5-25-64	Wechsler Childrens Scale	13-3	(scores below norms)	
9-19-64	Goodenough Drawing	13-7	7-0	52
9-19-64	Wechsler Childrens Scale	13-7	5-6	41 (V 47, P 46)
9-19-64	Jastak W. R. School Achievement	13-7	(Read 1.3, Sp. 1.0, Ar. 1.4)	
9-19-64	H-T-P Projective Drawings	13-7	(Psychotic-like-drawings)	
11-16-64	Peabody Picture Vocabulary	13-9	8-0	67

Background Data: Delivered by instruments, he has had seizures ever since, although they are now infrequent and medically controlled. He makes frequent threats to kill members of his family when he is frustrated and cannot have his way, often attacks a younger brother and hits at adults. He has not, however, ever harmed anyone. He had been in special classes in public and private schools, but was expelled as aggressive and unmanageable. His mother is overly-protective and his father overly-stern; they quarrel continually.

Test Behavior: He was exceedingly friendly and cooperative during the examination and his effort was good. He showed no signs of frustration and his mood was expansive.

Test Analyses: The Wechsler Childrens Scale administered in 1957 was inappropriate for him: he was then six and a half years of age with a mental age of not much above three years. The Leiter International Test also was not appropriate, since it was much too difficult for his mental level. On the other hand, the Picture Vocabulary Test, adminstered in 1960, was too easy and too specific, since only one type of response was called for and it measured only one type of ability.

On the Wechsler Childrens Scale now adminstered, he obtained a verbal I.Q. of 47, a non-verbal I.Q. of 46, and a full-scale I.Q. of 41 (extrapolated). This is equivalent to a mental age of five years, six months (5-6) on the Stanford-Binet. He made weighted scores of zero on Vocabulary and Block Designs, and a raw score of zero on Comprehension; however, his significantly higher scores on Similarities, Picture Completion, and Object Assembly suggest that his potential is at least two years higher when efficiency-depressing factors in his personality are ruled out.

There is a noticeable tremor (fluttering) of the eyelids when he is faced with a new question or task, but this quiver ceases when he becomes absorbed in the task. However, if he finds the task too difficult, the tremor is exaggerated. When the task is completed to his satisfaction, his eyelids quiver again, he hugs himself, and he quivers all over like a "pleased puppy."

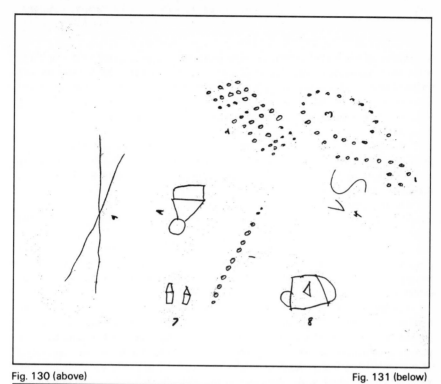

Fig. 130 (above)

Fig. 131 (below)

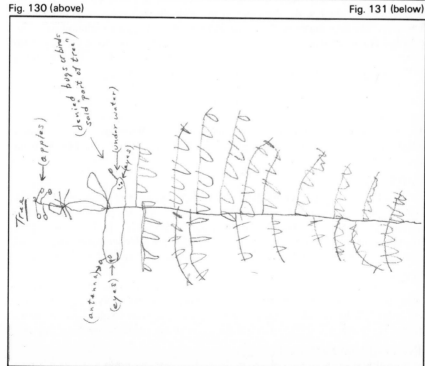

Many of his verbal responses were incoherent, disassociated, and rambling; some were incomprehensible. If he is not diverted externally, he rambles on and on incoherently with words and phrases which make sense, but are not integrated into meaningful wholes. This was especially noticeable on the Vocabulary subtest, which had to be discontinued because of his "flight of ideas" and confabulations.

Although his score of only one on a practice item of the Block Design probably can be associated with brain-damage, his inability to perceive meaning in the designs or to copy any after many demonstrations seems to point just as readily to disassociation from reality.

On the Jastak Wide Range School Achievement Test he scored at grade level 1.3 in reading, 1.0 in spelling, and 1.4 in arithmetic. This is practically the same as he did on this test in 1960. He recognizes the letters of the alphabet, and can read a few words such as "see," "cat," and "milk." His spelling consists of printing his name. On the arithmetic items he counts dots to 15 with one error, recognizes all single digits and some two digit numbers, but can neither add nor subtract.

On the H-T-P projective drawings his productions were, to say the least, bizarre. He "spoiled" all three drawings for quantitative scoring purposes by adding many irrelevant (to the examiner) details, but presented a definitive picture of a schizophrenic process by the nature of those details. It was significant of his underlying higher level of intelligence that he not only drew clouds, but, what is seldom found in the drawings of the mentally deficiency, rain descending therefrom. The eyes drawn on the Tree and the Person suggest paranoid ideation, while his House clearly was indicative of extreme fantasy (a flying House). Also it was noteworthy that he confused animate and inanimate objects by combining his "Superman" and aeroplane into one anthropomorphic unit.

In the interests of economy of space, Andrew's P-D-I is not given in full. A number of his answers were—as might have been expected from his graphic productions—highly irrelevant. At least one was frankly bizarre: in reply to, "Is there any wind blowing in this picture?" he said, "Blowing down!" At times he exhibited a hypomanic tendency to embellish his answers by flitting from topic to topic.

SUMMARY

This boy functions at a moderately mentally deficient level (M.A. 6-6, I.Q. 48). There are many signs of a schizophrenic process shown in his test behavior and in his test responses. His formal education is now stabilized at the first grade level, although he has the basic intellectual capacity to attain a higher grade. His mental disturbance, however, is a formidable bar to any practical utilization of his intelligence.

The probability of organicity (brain-damage) was explored, but his ability to concentrate on some tasks and not on others, his general affability under stress, his facility with drawing, and his fine motor coordination, all suggest that if brain-damage is present it is diffuse and not the cause of his apparent psychotic process.

RECOMMENDATIONS (full)

Enroll him in the school program, more for companionship and socialization

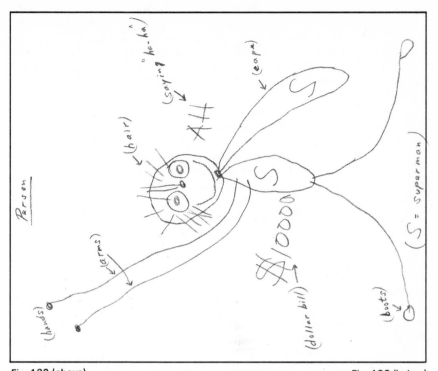

Fig. 132 (above)

Fig. 133 (below)

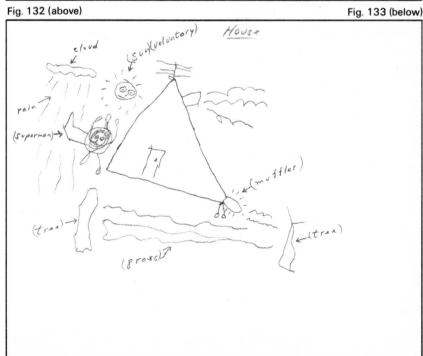

than any expectation of academic learning. Try him in occupational therapy in an effort to train him in concentration. Refer him for psychiatric examination to corroborate the impression of schizophrenia. Begin training in work assignments on his dormitory.

(Later Note): Psychiatrist reports he found no behavioral signs of psychosis except great indulgence in fantasy, inability to keep attention fixed on anything, and the neurological sign of quivering of the eyelids. Andrew is not withdrawn; he does not seem to have delusions or hallucinations. His dormitory attendant reports that all efforts to get him to work are futile as he cannot concentrate long enough to begin any job, let alone finish a job; as the attendant expressed it, "He's way out on Cloud 9 all the time."

John is presented to illustrate instances in which the H-T-P drawings throw relatively little light on the specific problem while the P-D-I and other tests and/or observations are more meaningful.

John: Report of Psychological Examination

Name: John   *Born:* 6-30-53   *ADM:* 2-28-64   *File:* xxxx Z
Age: 11-3   *M.A.:* 5-4   *I.Q.:* 47   *Date Exam:* 10-10-64   *Examiner:* GRM

Diagnosis: Mental deficiency due to uncertain cause with the functional reaction alone manifest; moderate mental deficiency on a functional basis; possible aphasia; possible schizophrenia.

Reason for Referral: Re-evaluation for possible change in program.

Recommendations (brief): Refer John to speech and hearing consultant for examination for aphasia; refer to psychiatrist regarding possible schizophrenia; refer to medical department for EEG; enroll in full school program.

Tests Administered:		*C.A.*	*M.A.*	*I.Q.*
2-4-63	Wechsler-Bellevue	9-7	– –	55 (V 50, P 61)
2-4-63	Bender Gestalt	9-7	(cortical impairment)	
10-10-64	Wechsler Childrens Scale	11-3		43 (V 40, P 57)
10-10-64	Time Appreciation Test	11-3	(unrelated responses)	
10-10-64	Bender Gestalt	11-3	(brain-damage?)	
10-10-64	H-T-P Projective Drawings	11-3	(organic, with schizoid reaction pattern, with feminine identification)	
10-10-64	Jastak W. R. School Achievement	11-3	(R. 4.9, Sp, 4.2, Ar. 3.8)	
10-16-64	Peabody Picture Vocabulary	11-3	5-4	47

Background Data: John's parents were divorced; both have remarried since. His mother is said to be schizophrenic; her present whereabouts are unknown. He has twin sisters who are younger than he and reportedly normal. He has no spasticity; there is no history of seizures. His vision is normal. He has a mild conductive hearing loss but of no significant degree. His EEG varies from normal to uncertain. He started using words at five or six years of age, but never used sentences until he went to live with a grandmother two years ago. He did not play with children in his early years and is reported as always having been unsocial and withdrawn. He was moved from one home to another. Both parents are reported as having been promiscuous while the boy was in the home (many "friends" of each parent coming and going). He was in special classes, but recently was dropped because of his inability to understand what was said to him or to communicate intelligently. He has many feminine characteristics (his penis is only 4.5 cm in length): his mannerisms, walk, and gestures are girlish.

Test Behavior: For the most part his effort was good and at no time did he show negativism. However, rapport was superficial only and all his interaction was on the surface. Underneath this facade of conformity he seemed to be removed and in a world of his own. His articulation was very good and no speech difficulty was noted, despite reports to the contrary in previous examinations.

Test Analyses: The reports of previous examinations on the Wechsler-Bellevue cannot be accepted at face value, since his verbal I.Q. was reported as below the norms used, and no comments were made as to subtest evaluations.

Current examination on the Wechsler Childrens Scale quantitatively was unsatisfactory, and the scores, as such, almost meaningless. On the Verbal Scale his responses were extremely below the norms. One cannot say, however, that his responses were totally unrelated to the questions even though they were not scorable as correct. For instance, to the question, "From what animal do we get milk?" he replied, "Water," and to, "From what store do we get sugar?" he replied, "For cereal mush"; while to the question, "What should you do when you cut your finger?" he replied, "Say *ouch*"; and to, "What should you do if you lost the ball of one of your friends?" he replied, "Gymnasium." However, he gave three instantaneously correct responses on the Information subtest, one on Similarities, and five on Vocabulary. His total weighted score on the Verbal Scale was only 2, far below the norms and equivalent to an extrapolated I.Q. of 40.

On the non-verbal scale his responses on the Picture Completion subtest were unscorable as correct, although not totally unrelated. On the other four subtests (none of which required a verbal response) his scores ranged from 4 to 22 with mental age levels from 5½ to 11½ years. On Block Designs, supposedly an index of brain damage, John scored slightly above the normal expectations for his age. He might have scored even higher, for at one time he reproduced design #5 correctly, but before indicating that he had completed the task, he rearranged the ninth block (incorrectly). He seemed to be experiencing some sort of an attack (a momentary aberration which was similar to a petit mal seizure and something like schizophrenic anger). After that, he attempted Designs #6 and 7 in a desultory manner. His total weighted score on the nonverbal scale was 19, which gave him an I.Q. of 57. (Later in this session an attempt was made to readminister the Comprehension subtest, but he resisted with angry responses of, "No, No!" to each item).

The adminstration of Buck's Time Appreciation Test was unsuccessful in the sense that none of John's responses were correct; he did respond to each question, however, and all answers were relevant 'though incorrect.

His reproductions of the Bender-Gestalt Designs appear to be more psychotic than organic, although signs of both conditions are present. He started far from the left margin and produced such large circles in Designs 1 and 2 that he soon

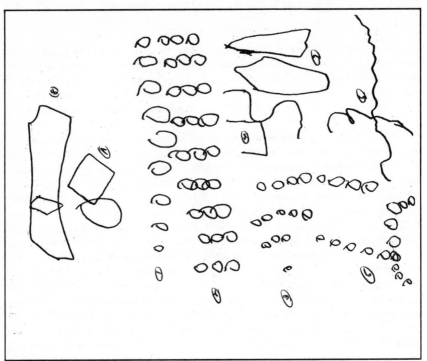

Fig. 134 (above)

Fig. 135 (below)

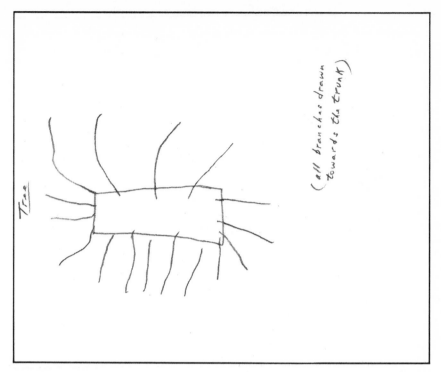

(all branches drawn towards the trunk)

Tree

Fig. 136

ran off the right margin. The same wide left margin also was noted on the Spelling test of the Jastak. In general, he produced circles for dots, showed an inability to close circles, meticulously but erroneously counted the dots for designs 2, 3, and 5, showed some overlap, and had difficulty with angles. He was unable to reproduce the essential design on #7, but all the others were recognizable configuration reproductions. The fact that he filled the entire sheet has the same significance as his writing and figuring which show the same largeness. This may represent personality expansiveness, organic impairment, or a compensatory reaction to his mentally deficient functioning, or a combination thereof.

Post-Drawing Interrogation: John

P1. Is that a man or a woman (or boy or girl)? Woman.
P2. How old is he (she)? 10 years.
P3. Who is he? Friend.
P4. Is he a relation, a friend, or what? Friend.
P5. Whom were you thinking about while you were drawing? Fight.
P6. What is he doing? (and where is he doing it?) Woods. *Where?* A hand.
P7. What is he thinking about? Head, an ear.
P8. How does he feel? Bad, got sore ear. *Why?* Stomach-ache.

T1. What kind of tree is that? Chop wood, saw.
T2. Where is that tree actually located? Right there. (pointed to page)
T3. About how old is that tree? 10 inches.
T4. Is that tree alive? Alive.
T5. What is there about that tree that gives you the impression that it's alive? Matches.

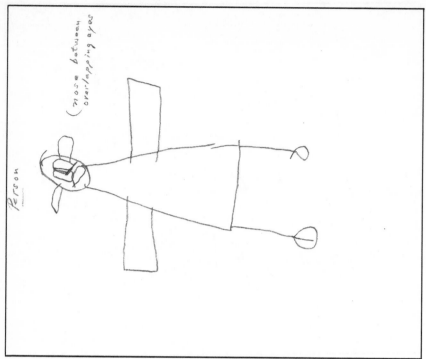

(nose between overlapping eyes)

Person

Fig. 137

T6.   Which does that tree look more like to you: a man or a woman? Girl.
T7.   What is there about it that gives you that impression? Children. *Why?* Nice.
T8.   If that were a person instead of a tree, which way would the person be facing? Against the wall.
T9.   Is that tree by itself, or is it in a group of trees? A room.
T10. As you look at that tree, do you get the impression that it is above you, below you, or about on a level with you? One tree.
T11. What is the weather like in this picture? Rain.
T12. Is there any wind blowing in this picture? In the air—sunshine.
T13. Show me in what direction it is blowing. Swish (waving arms around).
T14. What sort of wind is it? (no reply)

H1.   How many stories does that house have? 3.
H2.   What is that house made of? Roof. *Q?* (patient blocks).
H3.   Is that your own house? Yes.
H4.   Whose house were you thinking about while you were drawing? A ceiling. *Q?* A chimney.
H5.   Would you like to own that house yourself? A door.
H6.   If you did own that house and you could do whatever you liked with it:
      (a) Which room would you take for your own? Book. *Why?* Wall.
      (b) Whom would you like to have live in that house with you? Right there (points to the lower right).
H7.   As you look at that house, does it seem to be close by or far away? Far away—street.

H8.   As you look at that house, do you get the impression that it is above you, below you, or about on a level with you? Several roads.
H9.   What does that house make you think of, or remind you of? This is on a hill.
H10.   What else? (no reply)
H11.   Is that a happy, friendly sort of house? Green *Q?* Red.
H12.   What is there about it that gives you that impression? A *W.*
H13.   Are most houses that way? A *H. Why do you think so?* A *X.*
H14.   What is the weather like in this picture? A *W.*

T15.   What does that tree make you think of, or remind you of? Capital *T.*
T16.   What else? Trying make it blow.
T17.   Is it a healthy tree? Sick tree.
T18.   What is there about it that gives you that impression? Has headache.
T19.   Is it a strong tree? Cut.
T20.   What is there about it that gives you that impression? Road in.

P9.   What does that person make you think of, or remind you of? Capital *P.*
P10.   What else? A *W.*
P11.   Is that person well? Keep out.
P12.   What is there about him that gives you that impression? Start with *S* – sick.
P13.   Is that person happy? *H* – starts with *H* – sad.
P14.   What is there about him that gives you that impression? Head here.
P15.   Are most people that way? Eat – *E.*
P16.   Do you think you would like that person? Start with *L.*
P17.   What is the weather like in this picture? Start with *F.*
P18.   Whom does that person remind you of? Start with *M.*
P19.   What does that person need most? Start with *B.*

T21.   Whom does that tree remind you of? Start with *K.*
T22.   What does that tree need most? Cut. *Q? C.*

H15.   Whom does that House make you think of? Start with *Z.*
H16.   What does that house need most? 2 years. *Q? Y.*

Analysis of the Drawings (Figs. 135, 136, 137)

HOUSE

The lack of a chimney connotes a feeling of a lack of masculinity and/or psychological warmth within the home. The dormer peaks with no joining roof area imply a felt lack of ability to obtain satisfaction in intellectual activity or in fantasy. The twin peaks imply a deep-seated nurturance need. The poor organization of details within the whole suggests an equivalent inferior organization of the total personality.

TREE

The Tree with its one-dimensional roots dangling above the ground implies poor contact with reality. The one-dimensional branches express strong feelings of inadequacy. There is no branch-to-branch organization (implying a deep feeling of inability to derive satisfaction from the environment) and some branches are not connected to the trunk (suggesting that John may feel less and less able to cope with his environment). John drew each branch in the order of tip-to-trunk, thereby expressing, it would appear, his feeling that the environment essentially is hostile to him. The only hopeful prognostic sign is the substantial trunk of the Tree.

PERSON

The overemphasis on the ears suggests possible auditory hallucinations and certainly a hypersensitivity to criticism. The eyes shown as hollow sockets reveal hostility, self-absorption, and a minimal interest in those about him. The overemphasis upon the broad arms indicates an over-concern with strength and his great need for striving. The position of the arms expresses his feeling of vulnerability and his great need for warmth and affection, which he seems to feel he can get only if he assumes a non-threatening posture. The omission of fingers and hands implies feelings of castration and a paralyzing ineptness in dealing with the more refined psychosocial relationships. The one-dimensional legs bespeak his awareness of a crippling lack of autonomy.

All three drawings suggest that John tends to identify with feminine figures (see "Background Data" for an account of his feminine physical characteristics). All three drawings clearly show the difficulty that John experiences in organizing his concepts. The House and the Person contain an admixture of functional and organic components with the former predominating; the Tree, on the contrary, is almost typically organic.

It seems apparent that John's organicity does not involve the motor area to any appreciable degree, at least insofar as hand control is concerned. It seems apparent also that he is functioning at an intellectual level well below his potential and is suffering from acute feelings of inadequacy, ineptness, and frustration.

Analysis of the Post-Drawing Interrogation

The Administration of the P-D-I was frustrating because almost all of John's answers seemed, *at first*, to have only a tentative relationship to the questions asked, and even to be bizarre at times. Later and after more careful inspection of his replies, it became apparent that while his graphic productions had identified many of his psychological dynamics, the P-D-I had given invaluable insight into the mechanics of the expressive-associative difficulty which handicaps John so greatly.

John's first four answers (P1 through P4) seemed relevant. Starting with his answer to P5 ("Whom were you thinking about while you were drawing?"), he began to show his associative disorder, for he replied, "Fight".

To T1 ("What kind of Tree is that?") he answered, "Chop wood, saw", presenting a tangential association. When he was asked how old the Tree was, he answered, *"Ten inches,"* showing clearly how difficult it is for him to maintain contact with the original auditory stimulus: by the time he had uttered the word *ten*, the matter of *age* had disappeared for him, and he remembered only that some measure had been sought—hence *inches*, instead of *months* or *years*.

He carried this a bit further with his answers to T8 and T9. To, "If that were a Person instead of a Tree, which way would the Person be facing?" he replied, "Against the wall". Then to the next question, "Is that Tree by itself, or is it in a group of Trees?" he associated not with the question, but with his own previous reply and continued with "A room".

To some questions concerning the House, he replied in segmental fashion.

For example: to, "Whose House were you thinking about while you were drawing?" he replied, "A ceiling?" and to the examiner's follow-up question, he said, "A chimney". To the immediately subsequent, "Would you like to own that House yourself?" he answered, "A door".

As he fatigued, he began to perseverate in almost single-letter fashion. For example: to, "What is there about it (House) that gives you that impression?" he answered, "A *W*, abstracting the first letter from the word *what* at the beginning of the question. To the next question, "Are most Houses that way?" he replied, "A *H*". (First letter from the word *House*). And in his answer to the immediately subsequent, "Why do you think so?" he associated with the *sound* of the word *why* (Y) and answered, "A X."

When he was asked "Is that Person well?" he answered, "Keep out," associating, one assumes, with a previously received warning against the danger of falling into *wells*. To P12, "What is there about him that gives you that impression?" he replied, "Start with *S* –sick." Here we have the word *start* beginning the reply to P12; then it, in turn, becomes the stimulus and (still perseverating on the first letters of words) he continues with *S;* then that, in its turn, becomes the stimulus, and produces the word *sick* –reversing the previous order of word, then first letter.

Ultimately he became so single-letter-bound in his replies that it was impossible at times to deduce what had stimulated the production of the single-letter he used.

Perseveration of this sort certainly is organic.

From the P-D-I responses it appears that John has a very limited memory-attention span, is highly stimulable, and can abstract in a way which no basically mentally deficient individual could be expected to do.

From the drawings and the P-D-I it appears that this expressive-associative difficulty has an organic etiology, and has produced painful feelings of ineptness and inadequacy in John.

In spite of John's low score on the structured tests of intelligence (Wechsler and Time Appreciation Test), his scores on the Wide Range School Achievement Test and the Block Designs clearly show that basically he is of normal or near-normal intelligence. His present reading grade is 4.9, for both "word recognition" and "word meaning"; his spelling grade is 4.2, and his arithmetic grade is 3.8. The reading level for his life age would be 5.3, but one should remember that he has been educated only in special classes.

Since his mental level was not clearly indicated by the WISC, the Peabody Picture Vocabulary was administered as a further check. His score of 51 thereon gave him a mental age of five years, three months (5-3) and an I.Q. of 47. However, the nature of the Peabody is such that persons with associative disorders (due either to aphasia or to personality disturbance) would be expected to do poorly on it.

The question of aphasia was considered, and an attempt was made to administer Eisenson's Test for Aphasia. However, this examiner was unable to tell positively from John's responses whether he was aphasic or not, or if aphasic, of what type. He named all colors from sight, but when he was asked to point to green he said, "Green hand"; when he was directed, "Show me red", he replied,

"Cat," etc. He named pictures of common objects on a card such as fork, pencil, knife, scissors, and comb, but when he was told, "Show me the one we eat with," he replied, "Food." And when he was instructed, "Point to the one we cut with," he said, "Saw." He named a series of printed numbers, but did not point to any when named. He read sentences by separate words, but could not read a four-word sentence as a sentence or tell its meaning. To the question, "What do people wear on their heads?" he first replied, "Hair," and then changed it to, "Coat." To, "What do birds move when they fly?" he said, "Tree." This is the type of responses he gave on the verbal scale of the WISC. He also showed some echolalia.

All this suggests some kind of "associative" aphasia rather than purely "receptive" or "expressive" aphasia. He does not show the usual incoordination, clumsiness, and poor manual dexterity often seen in expressive aphasia, but he does show an inability to express ideas in speech or in writing which is common to expressive aphasia. However, this also is common in schizophrenia[3].

Summary: Although his intellectual level, as computed from the objective scores on intelligence tests, presents him as mentally deficient, his performance on Block Designs was above his age level and his reading, spelling, and arithmetic were at or near his age level, indicating little if any mental deficiency.

Although many of his verbal responses seem bizarre and unrelated to the verbal stimulus they are not solely or truly schizophrenic. His behavior does not fit a psychotic pattern only, since his withdrawal and "aloneness" can be explained just as readily as being due to his communication difficulties.

He presents many signs of "expressive" aphasia or if there were such a category, "associative" aphasia. He has no difficulty in speaking or writing separate words, but he cannot put them together to express ideas despite his fairly high level of intelligence. It would be inexact to say that he is mentally deficient, but functionally he is. For a specific diagnostic category to be given, the clinician can only say that John is a "puzzler". Further studies are needed.

Recommendations (full): Refer John to the speech and hearing consultant for examination for aphasia; also refer him to the psychiatrist for exploration of the presence of a psychosis; request an EEG study; enroll him in a full school program and encourage his participation in all group games and activities; assign him to the psychologist for individual and group psychotherapy. (*Later Note:* To confound the issue, his EEG varies, the speech consultant is uncertain about the presence of aphasia, the psychiatrist says that John is not psychotic, and the psychologist still is in doubt about his diagnosis.

This chapter dealt with the psychodiagnostic use of the H-T-P. It should be remarked parenthetically that psychotherapy can be effective with the mentally deficient, as has been described in the literature and demonstrated in practice. But a discussion of psychotherapy is not within the scope of this chapter. However, one basic management consideration needs to be mentioned: the concept of "mental age". Too much emphasis has been placed on the I.Q. without regarding it as an artifact produced by the relation of chronological

---

[3] If an associative-expressive difficulty of this magnitude were due to schizophrenia, the H-T-P drawings and P-D-I would be bizarre. *(Ed.)*

age to mental age. If one keeps in mind the mental age of any mentally deficient individual, the full comprehensive program of control, discipline, training, education, and placement is simplified. If for instance, one sees a mentally deficient twenty-year-old with a mental age of five years throwing a temper tantrum and kicking and screaming, one needs only to remember that this behavior is a common and reasonable reaction for a "normal" five-year-old under certain circumstances.

Realistic understanding of mentally deficient persons and their treatment and management must be based on a full recognition of their feelings of insecurity, inadequacy, rejection, dependency, the futility of striving, and a lack of psychological warmth. All or many of these feelings frequently are expressed by the mentally deficient in their drawings and this should occasion no great surprise, because mental defectives in addition to having deficiencies in intelligence usually have emotional and other personality problems. Because of their frustrations resulting from competing in the home, school, and community under the handicap of limited intelligence, they tend to develop more emotional and personality problems than those who have no similar intellectual limitations. To grasp the severity of their problems and delineate the areas in which they occur, it is necessary to include in the psychologist's armamentarium a variety of tests, techniques, or devices which can uncover and identify the problems of the mentally deficient.

The tests or techniques used for this purpose should be easy to administer, non-threatening, and productive of response from those of limited intellectual abilities, those who are severely disturbed, and those who have difficulties in verbal communication. *The H-T-P is such a technique.* It has proven its usefulness empirically in the total evaluation of the mentally deficient, who in the H-T-P project their feelings, attitudes, and problems just as others do. The vehicle of projection for the mentally deficient must be adapted to their communication and intellectual levels, yet be sufficiently stimulating to bring forth their unexpressed frustrations. The writer has found the H-T-P to be one of the best instruments for this purpose.

References

Bielauskas, V. J. *The House-Tree-Person (H-T-P) Research Review.* Beverly Hills, California, Western Psychological Services, 1963.

Buck, John N. The Time Appreciation Test. *J. App. Psychol.,* Vol. 30, No. 4, 1946, 388-398.[*]

_____ The H-T-P Technique, a qualitative and quantitative scoring manual, *J Clin. Psychol.,* Monograph Supplement No. 5, Oct. 1948.

_____ *The House-Tree-Person (H-T-P) Manual Supplement.* Beverly Hills, California; Western Psychological Services, 1964.

Hammer, Emanual F. *The Clinical Application of Projective Drawings.* Springfield, Illinois: Thomas, 1958.

Jolles, Isaac. *A Catalogue for the Qualitative Interpretation of the H-T-P.* Beverly Hills, California: Western Psychological Services, 1964.

Sines, Jacob O. Actuarial methods as appropriate strategy for the validation of diagnostic tests. *Psychological Review,* 17, 1964, 517-523.

[*] Now published and distributed by Western Psychological Services.

Isaac Jolles received his M.A. degree in Psychology from Ohio State University in 1940.

From 1940-1941 he served an internship in the Ohio Bureau for Juvenile Research. From 1941-1943 he was Clinical Psychologist at the West Virginia Industrial School for Boys. He was Senior Psychologist at the Indiana State Prison from 1943-1945. From 1945-1955 he served as Staff Psychologist for the Illinois Department of Public Instruction. From 1955-1958 he was a School Psychologist in the public schools of Quincy, Illinois. He served as School Psychologist for the South Suburban Public School Cooperative Association of Cook County, Homewood, Illinois, from 1958-1963. Since 1963 he has been School Psychologist for the Thornton Township Special Education Association of Harvey, Illinois.

Mr. Jolles is a member of Divisions 12 and 16 of the American Psychological Association; a member of the Illinois Psychological Association; and a Fellow of the American Association on Mental Deficiency.

He is the author of the book *A Catalogue for the Qualitative Interpretation of the H-T-P*. He has published some twenty articles in various professional journals.

He holds the certificates of Registered Psychologist of the State of Illinois and Qualified Psychological Examiner of the Illinois Department of Public Instruction.

Chapter 10

The Use of the H-T-P
in a School Setting

Isaac Jolles, M.A.

Mr. Jolles compares the practice of psychology in a school setting with the practice of our profession in other settings, and in the process points up the principal differences. In this context, he emphasizes the importance of employing the H-T-P in the attempt (1) to identify the psychological problems handicapping school children and (2) to devise methods for their amelioration.

Mr. Jolles presents the achromatic-chromatic H-T-P's—analyzed in depth—of three children who present typical but quite different problems. Eds.

Before discussing the ways in which the H-T-P may be useful to the school psychologist, it is appropriate to consider briefly the work of a psychologist in a school setting to see how it differs from that of his colleagues in a community clinic or in the various institutional programs. Because the functions of a school psychologist vary considerably from one school district to another, it would be a prodigious task to cover the gamut of the professional roles of school psychologists. Therefore, emphasis will be placed here only on diagnostic and consultative work, for it is in these areas that projective devices are used to a considerable degree. A few therapists are employed by public and private schools, but their interest in the H-T-P would be similar to that of psychologists in clinical settings.

The great majority of school psychologists are asked to make diagnoses of personality and behavior disorders. Frequently they work closely with the school social worker who, in turn, may serve as a counselor, working directly with the child or with the family, or may refer the family to some other community agency. In this respect the school psychologist's work resembles that of the clinical psychologist, but with one important difference: the school psychologist usually works independently of psychiatrists. The school depends entirely upon the psychologist to diagnose the problem and to help the social worker in the development of a treatment program. There are occasions when the type of treatment required necessitates referral to a psychiatrist or a physician; but it is usually the psychologist's diagnosis which determines this.

When a school district employs a school social worker, this worker usually provides the psychologist with a social history. There are times, however, when a school district does not employ a social worker, and then the psychologist must make his diagnosis of emotional problems without benefit of a social worker's complete family history. His knowledge of a child's family background frequently is limited, therefore, to unreliable impressions formed by teachers during their contacts with a parent. Under such circumstances, the psychologist must rely greatly upon projective techniques to derive a relatively sound understanding of the dynamics operating within the child's family.

Occasionally, the psychologist is consulted by the speech therapist. This usually occurs when the speech therapist has worked for perhaps a year without noting much progress in a pupil's speech. Under such circumstances, the speech therapist may wish to determine whether or not emotional factors prevent the child from developing more mature speech. Such a study may involve making a differential diagnosis to determine whether the speech problem is emotional or organic in origin.

Similarly, remedial reading teachers in the school may request a differential diagnosis for some of their pupils who have severe reading problems. The writer has found the H-T-P to have considerable value in making this differentiation.

This same problem may arise in connection with another type of learning disorder. During recent years there has been an increase in the establishment of special classes in public schools for children having some kind of cerebral dysfunction. In many cases such dysfunction can be detected through psychometric studies, but there are times when objective tests do not reveal perceptual problems: However, such deficiencies often are readily detected in the drawings made by the pupils.

The following cases illustrate these various uses of the H-T-P. Only those aspects of the H-T-P which tend to demonstrate its usefulness with specific types of cases are presented—not all the data in each case are given.

Case No. 1: Sigma Phi; age 5 years, 6 months.

This child was referred by the school social worker. The worker's attention had been called to this case because of the child's immature social behavior and poor control in kindergarten. An EEG was part of the neurological examination. Some slight but inconclusive evidence of cerebral dysfunction was detected. However, the neurologist declined to make a diagnosis of brain damage and suggested referral of the child to a psychiatrist. Because of financial limitations, however, the parents did not follow this recommendation, but consulted the school social worker instead. This case illustrates the advantages of using the H-T-P with very young children: it proved productive where other projective devices offered little insight into the child's personality.

Post-Drawing Interrogation [1] (Figs. 138–143)

P1.   Is that a man, a woman, a boy, or a girl? Man.
P2.   How old is he? Old as my dad.
P3.   Who is he? My dad.
P5.   What is he doing? He's at work.

T1.   What kind of tree is that? A regular tree.
T2.   Where is that tree? Next to the house I bought.
T3.   About how old is that tree? 40 months.
T4.   Is that tree alive? No.
T5.B.   (a) What do you think caused it to die? Chopped down.

H1.   Does that house have an upstairs? Yes.
H2.   Is that your house? Yes.
H3.   Would you like to own that house? Yes.
H4.   a. Which room would you take for your own? (Subject points to the very top room.) Why? Looks kinda high.
       b. Whom would you like to have live in that house with you? One sister and one brother and one mommie and daddy.
H5.   As you look at that house, does it seem to be close by or far away? Far away.
H6.   Does it seem above you, below you, or about even with you? Even with.

T6.   Does that tree look more like a man or a woman to you? Woman.
T7.   If that tree were a person, which way would that person be facing? (Away from subject.)
T8.   Is that tree by itself or in a group of trees? By itself. Would it like to be with other trees? Yes.
T9.   Looking at that tree, does it seem above you, below you or about even with you? Even with.

P7.   What is he thinking about? He wish he had another brother.
P8.   How does he feel? Fine.
P9.   Of what does that Person make you think? My daddy.
P10.   Is that person well? Yes.
P11.   Is that person happy? Yes.
P12.   What is the weather like in this picture? Summer.

T10.   What is the weather like in this picture? Summer.
T11.   What kind of weather do you like best? Summer.
T12.   Is any wind blowing in this picture? No.

H7.   Of what does that house make you think? My own house.
H8.   Is that a happy, friendly sort of house? Yes.
H9.   What is the weather like in this picture? Windy. Which way is the wind

---

[1] Jolles' modification designed specifically for use with children. J.N.B.

blowing? (Subject indicates from right to left.)

H10.   Of which person you know does that house make you think? (No response.)
H11.   Has anyone or anything ever hurt that house? No.
H12.   (Subject instructed to draw the sun.) Suppose this sun were some person you know—who would it be? My mom.

T15.   (Subject instructed to draw the sun.) Suppose this sun were some person you know—who would it be? My dad.
T16.   Of what does that tree make you think? The trees in my house.
T17.   Is it a healthy tree? Yes.
T18.   Is it a strong tree? Yes.

P13.   Of which person you know does this person remind you? Myself. Why? Looks like my age.
P14.   What kind of clothing is this person wearing? Summer.
P15.   What does that person need most? A daddy and mama.
P16.   Has anyone ever hurt that person? Yes.
       a. How? Not being friends with him.
       b. How old was that person when it happened? About my age.
P17.   (Subject instructed to draw the sun.) Suppose that sun were some person you know—who would it be? One of my friends.
       (Subject instructed to draw groundline.)

Fig. 138, Case I

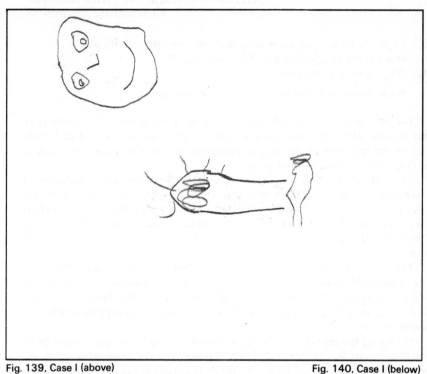

Fig. 139, Case I (above)   Fig. 140, Case I (below)

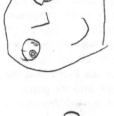

T19.   Of which person you know does that tree remind you? My dad.
T20.   Has anyone or anything ever hurt that tree? No.
T21.   What does that tree need most? Water.

H14.   What does that house need most? Made very good.

The line quality in the achromatic drawings gives evidence of considerable inner tension. The child also manifests concern about his ego control as is indicated by the heaviness of the lines depicting the wall of the House, the trunk of the Tree, and the trunk of the Person.

The manner in which the arms of the Person are depicted is suggestive of considerable impulsivity. His responses to the P-D-I question, "What does that House need most?" was, "Made very good." This was an indication of his effort to maintain control in spite of the control problem suggested by his House being off balance. This could be an important factor in the generalized tension noted above.

The high placement of the House and the Person on the drawing sheet suggests considerable fantasy activity, and this is further indicated by the narrow vertically elongated House and the overly large head on the Person. It is conceivable that such fantasy activity may be at least partly a defense against his poor impulse control.

In view of the results of the EEG, it should be noted that such control problems often occur in children with brain damage, and the manner in which the arms of the Person are joined to the trunk is a typical organic manifestation. Furthermore, there is some degree of segmentation in the drawing of the House, and this too is typical of the drawings of organics.

Additional evidence of this child's ego weakness is his precarious reality contact, noted in each achromatic drawing and in the chromatic House drawing. (Note the distance between the groundline and the drawn whole.) He manifests adequate interest in every day events, however, for in all the achromatic drawings the essential details are present except for the chimney on the House. This child seems to be somewhat aware of his ego weakness and his tendency to regress under environmental pressures because of the inability of his ego to cope with those pressures. This was learned from his statement in the P-D-I that the wind was blowing from right to left (i.e. he feels pushed back into the past).

Sigma's regressive tendencies are manifested by his dependency upon his parents and by his oral eroticism. The former is borne out by his response to P15 in the P-D-I and the latter by the paneless windows of the House. It should be noted that this evidence of oral eroticism disappears when warmth is experienced, as indicated by the presence of window panes on the chromatic House.

This child feels completely rejected by his mother. (See his responses to T6 and T7 of the P-D-I.) The lack of warmth in this relationship may be an important contributing factor to his immaturity. This is vividly portrayed by the House which is falling over and away from the sun which he identified as his mother. In contrast, he feels very close to his father (see the answer to T15 of the P-D-I and the drawing of the Tree itself) and strongly identifies with him. (See the reply to P3 of the P-D-I.) Despite his feeling of being rejected by his mother, his response to H4b indicates that he maintains his ties to her and to the rest of the family. There is no evidence of sibling rivalry; his response to P7, in fact, suggests that he has a desire for another brother.

This boy has problems in interpersonal relationships as is indicated by: the poor quality of the drawn Person, the ineffective manner in which he drew the hands of the Person, his response to T8 which implies social isolation among his peers, and his response to P16 which reveals his difficulties in making friends.

He has a tendency to react to stimulation or excitement in social situations as is shown by the adequate size of the chromatic Person when compared to the smallness of the achromatic Person. This tendency, however, is handicapped by his poor impulse-control. He has suffered trauma through rejection by his peers (P16). But in spite of his feeling isolated socially, he has not yet become asocial (T8).

On the surface he appears to be adequately assertive, but on a deeper level, he has a desire to withdraw: this is indicated by the comparative size of the drawings of the achromatic and chromatic Trees as well as by the vertical placement of each on the page. He apparently experiences psycho-social castration, and finds that he has little capacity to reach out to his environment for satisfaction (note the absence of the arms from the chromatic Person and the limited branch structure of both Trees). Hence, he depends a great deal upon fantasy activity to gratify his emotional needs. There also is reason to believe that these fantasies are a source of anxiety and possibly of guilt. This is suggested by the heavy black shading on the roof of the chromatic House. Feelings of guilt and hopelessness are also suggested by the dead Tree (T4). There is evidence of anxiety at the reality level: this is manifested by the manner in which he uses shading for the groundline. However, it is encouraging to note that he attributes his difficulty to his environment rather than to something deep within himself (T5B).

It can be concluded that Sigma has grave problems in his relationships with his mother and with people in general. His social problems seem to be related chiefly to his uncontrollable impulsivity and his tendency to over-react to excitement during play. This also could be the source of much of his problem with his mother. Furthermore, this personality pattern is suggestive of some cerebral dysfunction and this has added significance in view of the marginally positive EEG.

The H-T-P derived data provide the school social worker with a clearer picture of the family dynamics with which she must deal, and at the same time alerts the teachers to this child's control problems so that they can use those special remedial measures which are often effective with the over-active child with brain damage.

Case No. 2: Alpha Beta; age 13 years, 11 months

Alpha was referred for psychological study for a diagnosis of her reading problem. Reading tests revealed inconsistencies which suggested that this adolescent girl experienced stress in her interpersonal relationships. For example she performed better on group tests than in individually adminstered tests. She had great difficulty expressing ideas to the examiner, a man; she was therefore, referred to the speech therapist, a woman, for further diagnostic study. These symp-

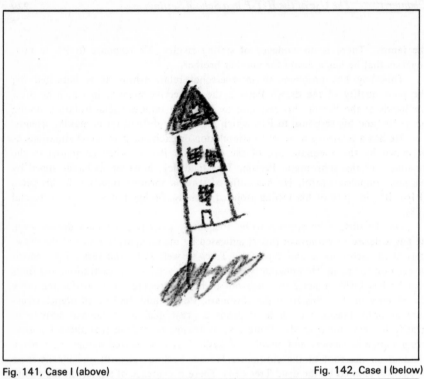

Fig. 141, Case I (above)

Fig. 142, Case I (below)

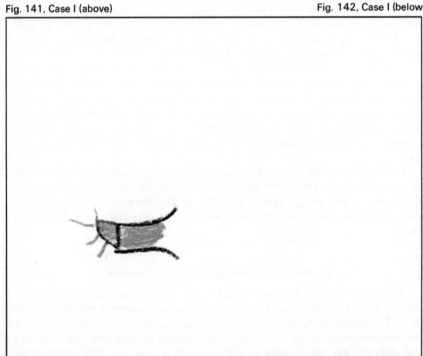

Fig. 143, Case I (above)   Fig. 144, Case II (below)

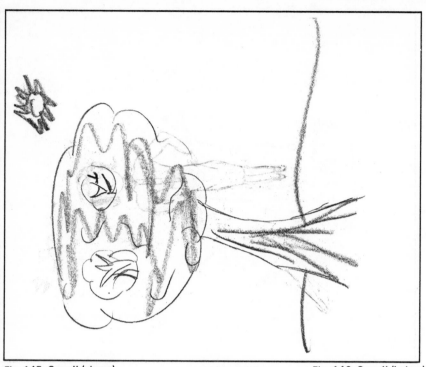

Fig. 145, Case II (above)

Fig. 146, Case II (below)

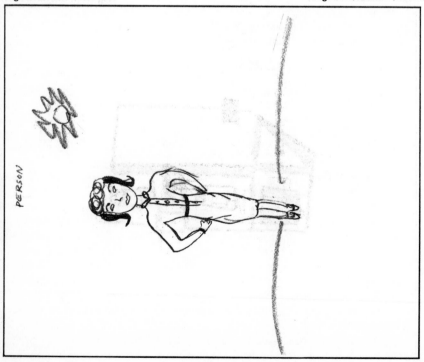

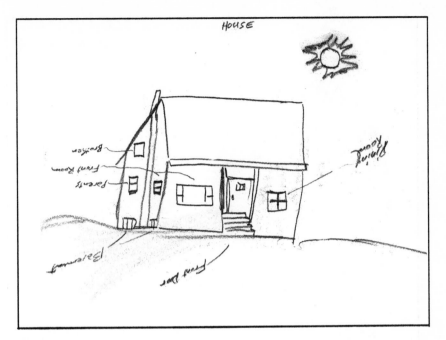

Fig. 147, Case II

toms did not appear when she worked with the speech therapist. This indicated that Alpha underwent particular stress in her relationships with males. This finding suggested the presence of specific emotional problems. The first technique to be used in the investigation of these problems was the H-T-P. Since the major findings in this case were derived from the drawings, the P-D-I is omitted.

The achromatic drawings reveal a generalized tension. Her manner of using shading in the drawings of the Tree and the Person reveals the anxiety which presumably contributes heavily to this tension. The seriousness of her emotional state is depicted vividly by her Tree. Note the achromatic drawing of the Tree in which the trunk seems to crack at the mid-point, and when this is considered with the chromatic Tree which is almost toppling over, an impending serious breakdown is to be anticipated. One might note further her defensiveness as revealed by the eaves of the achromatic House: this is given even greater stress in the chromatic House drawing in which she colors the eaves, even though little color is used on this House as a whole.

Alpha's problems in the sexual area are revealed in several ways. On the achromatic House she draws a very tall, transparent chimney which bends peculiarly near the top: on the chromatic House the chimney is heavily shaded with black. On both drawings of the Person, Alpha uses heavy shading to depict the belt, thus indicating her concern over repression of her sex drives. Finally, the achromatic drawing of the Person portrays a rather mature young woman, whereas the chromatic drawing of the Person depicts a young girl. This suggests that Alpha tries to appear mature, but underneath she is still a child in her psychosexual development.

The amount of space employed for the roof of the House, and the disproportionately large head of the achromatic Person indicate over-emphasis upon fantasy

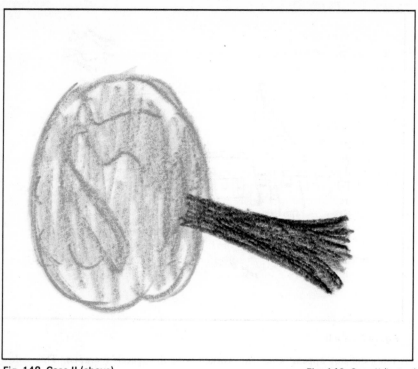

Fig. 148, Case II (above)   Fig. 149, Case II (below)

activity. This probably serves to absorb much of her emotional energy. It is apparent that this girl has a tendency towards free emotional expression, which conflicts with her striving for control. This is indicated by the leaning of the Tree towards the right, the heaviness of the lines of the walls of the House, her rigidity is depicted by the stance of both drawn Persons. All these factors could contribute to the tension observed clinically in this girl.

Alpha was referred to the school social worker who attempted to work with the family. But within two months Alpha had a breakdown at school which lead to her referral to a psychiatrist for psychotherapy.

The H-T-P in this case quickly confirmed the seriousness of this girl's personality problems. When Alpha was first referred to the psychologist, there was no indication of any problem other than reading. Through the use of the projective H-T-P technique, however, a deeper personality picture was revealed. As a result, when this girl had her breakdown at school, her teachers, the social worker and the school nurse already were prepared for it so the girl received psychiatric attention with a minimum of delay and no opposition from the family.

Case No. 3: Delta Rho; age 8 years, 3 months

Delta was referred for psychological study to determine her eligibility for placement in a special class for the educable mentally handicapped. A report on the use of the H-T-P in the public schools would be incomplete without the discussion of such a case, for, in the majority of school systems, determining eligibility for special classes probably is the psychologist's principal function. Determining eligibility may have been the principal reason for this particular examination, but secondary factors here were important also. If a child is to benefit from special class placement, he must be helped to make an adequate social adjustment. Therefore, it is important that the psychologist provide the teacher with insight into the child's personality dynamics. Delta Rho had had periods of moodiness in which she had been defiant and even malicious. She had done such things as spit at children, pull chairs from under them, and lie about their behavior.

Post-Drawing Interrogation (achromatic)

P1.   Is that a man, a woman, a boy, or a girl? Boy.
P2.   How old is he? 3.
P3.   Who is he? Dick.
P4.   Who is that? A boy. Is it someone you know? Friend.
P5.   What is he doing? Walking.
P6.   Where is he doing it? Home.

T1.   What kind of tree is that? Peach.
T2.   Where is that tree? In our yard.
T3.   About how old is that tree? One year old.
T4.   Is that tree alive? No.
T5.   B. a. What do you think caused it to die? We don't feed it.
          b. Will it ever be alive again? Yes.

H1.   Does that house have an upstairs? Yes.
H2.   Is that your house? Yes.

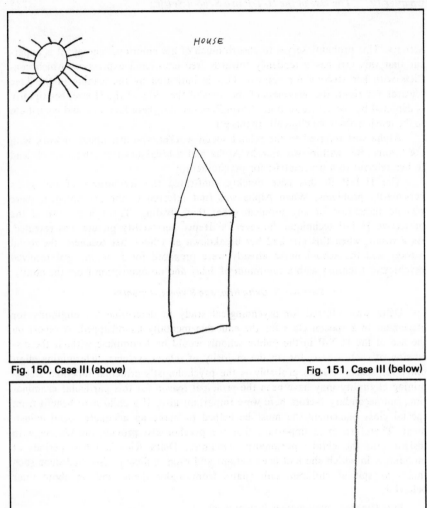

HOUSE

Fig. 150, Case III (above)

Fig. 151, Case III (below)

TREE

Fig. 152, Case III

H3. Would you like to own that house? Yes.
H4. a. Which room would you take for your own? Downstairs. Why? You can look at TV.
b. Whom would you like to live in that house with you? My sister. Anyone else? No.
H5. As you look at that house, does it seem to be close by or far away? Far away.
H6. Does it seem above you, below you, or about even with you. Even with.

T6. Does that tree look more like a man or a woman to you? Man.
T7. If that tree were a person, which way would that person be facing? (To subject's left.)
T8. Is that tree by itself or in a group of trees? By itself. Would it like to be with other trees? Yes.
T9. Looking at that tree, does it seem above you, below you, or about even with you? Even.

P7. What is he thinking about? That he's playing.
P8. How does he feel? Happy. Why? He want to play.
P9. Of what does that person make you think? He'll make you mad.
P10. Is that person well? Yes.
P12. What is the weather like in this picture? Hot.

T10. What is the weather like in this picture? Hot.
T11. What kind of weather do you like best? Hot.
T12. Is any wind blowing in this picture? No.

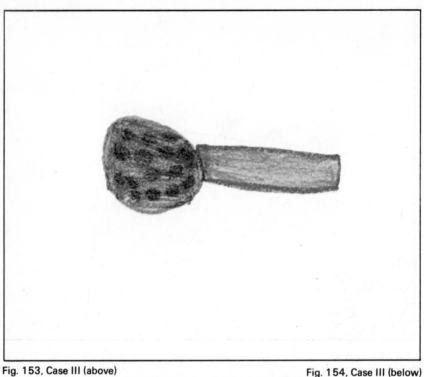

Fig. 153, Case III (above)   Fig. 154, Case III (below)

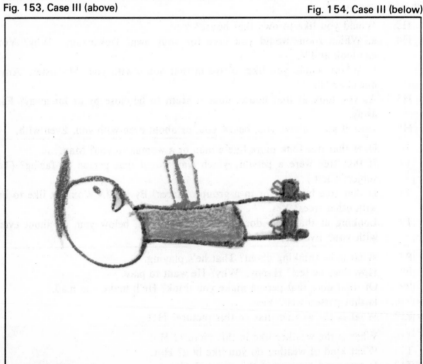

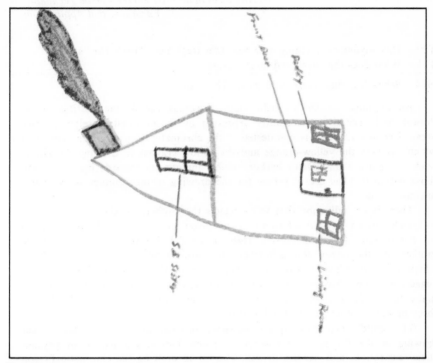

Fig. 155, Case III

H7. Of what does that house make you think? It's windy. Which way is the wind blowing? Left to right.
H8. Is that a happy, friendly sort of house? No.
H9. What is the weather like in this picture? Bad.
H10. Of which person you know does that house make you think? Dick.
H11. Has anyone or anything ever hurt that house? Yes. How? They saw it.
H12. Suppose this sun were some person you know—who would it be? Jane. Who is she? A girl.
(Subject instructed to draw the groundline.)

T15. Suppose this sun were some person you know—who would it be? Sally. Who is she? A little girl.
(Subject is instructed to draw the groundline.)
T16. Of what does that tree make you think? That it's sunny out.
T17. Is it a healthy tree? Yes.
T18. Is it a strong tree? Yes.

P13. Of which person you know does this person remind you? Mother.
P14. What kind of clothing is this person wearing? Pants.
P15. What does that person need most? Food.
P16. Has anyone ever hurt that person? No.
P17. Suppose that sun were some person you know—who would it be? Father.
(Subject instructed to draw the groundline.)

T19. Of which person you know does that tree remind you? Sally.

T20.   Has anyone or anything ever hurt that tree? Yes. How? They saw it.
T21.   What does that tree need most? Grass.

H14.   What does that house need most? The doors.

An appraisal of Delta's achromatic drawings reveals the hostility, withdrawal, and general inaccessibility expressed by the enclosed, unrelieved space areas. Her hostility also is manifested in the chromatic drawings: the manner in which she uses the yellow-orange and the yellow crayons in drawing the House tends to indicate that Delta harbors much antagonism towards her home and those within it. (The use of yellow for the drawing of the chimney is extremely unconventional.)

There is an indication that Delta rejects the mother, for she assigns a room to herself and a foster-girl referred to as her sister, and to her daddy, but no room for her mother. Her responses to H4b of the P-D-I reveal a rejection of the mother *and* the father; this is further substantiated by her responses to H5 in which she also indicates rejection of her home itself. An unhappy home life is suggested by her answers to H8 and H9, too. It can be concluded that Delta has many emotional problems arising from her home situation; it is very likely that these problems contribute to her hostility.

This child's problems in interpersonal relationships are revealed in her drawing of the Person. The absence of hands indicates a feeling of psychosocial castration, and the use of yellow-green in drawing the chromatic Person is a further reflection of her hostility toward people. The use of the purple crayon as a pencil could be indicative of her need to develop power over others, and one might conclude from this that Delta would use aggressive behavior to accomplish this.

Delta's erotic needs are vividly depicted in the chromatic Tree where she uses red most unconventionally and even employs rose-pink for shading the trunk. Note the difference in the presentation of the achromatic and chromatic Houses. The former reveals much withdrawal and inaccessibility, but in the latter windows appear, which suggests a basic willingness for social interaction. This child will respond more favorably when she experiences warmth. The lack of warmth at home probably is responsible for much of her immature emotional development. In answer to T4 and T5 of the P-D-I this child attributes her maladjustment (her Tree is dead) to a lack of gratification of her oral needs. Then in response to P15, there is further indication of oral needs.

Once we understood the problems that this child had at home and the effect which these had had upon her social relationships, it was possible to take interrelated steps to improve the home situation by referring the family to a Counselling Center. Play therapy was recommended for the child in the hope that this would alleviate the intensity of her need for overt expression of her hostility. At the same time, her teacher was placed in position to provide this child with a feeling of warmth as soon as she entered the special class with the hope this would enable her to be more responsive.

It is important to note how much can be derived from the apparently simple drawings of a young retarded child along with this child's simple responses to the P-D-I. In cases like this, projective devices such as the Rorschach and the

Thematic Apperception Test tend to be relatively non-productive because of the paucity and limited expressiveness of such a child's responses.

The H-T-P is also of great usefulness in the public schools in the screening of pupils. The drawings may be obtained easily through group presentation and because of this the H-T-P technique can provide much information about a large number of children within a short period of time. For example, the H-T-P was used 15 years ago in the Joliet public schools while we were attempting to set up an experimental class for the education of brain-damaged children. Although we used a number of screening devices, the H-T-P proved to be the most effective in detecting organicity. It is conceivable that school social workers could be trained to use this device in an effort to identify children in need of treatment of emotional problems.

Elizabeth Maxwell entered the fields of guidance and psychology via the teaching profession. She secured her B.S. in education, with a major in English, from the University of Pennsylvania in 1941. Her first teaching assignment in the public schools of Philadelphia called upon her to teach mathematics, music, and something called hygiene. It was natural, therefore, that she eagerly accepted an appointment as Counseling Teacher, under an imaginative program inaugurated by the Department of Pupil Personnel and Counseling of the Philadelphia Public Schools, for the training of elementary school counselors. The training program offered during her three years as a Counseling Teacher prompted her to begin graduate study for an M.S. in guidance at the University of Pennsylvania; a program which was dropped unceremoniously when she secured her "Mrs." instead of her "Master's." The pull toward counseling was strong, however, and after teaching for several years in Connecticut after her marriage, she obtained her M.A. in guidance at the University of Connecticut, and accepted an appointment as guidance counselor in Clark Lane Junior High School, in Waterford.

As the increasing need for psychological services at the elementary school level became more and more apparent, Mrs. Maxwell returned to the University of Connecticut to enter a program developed by Dr. Thomas W. Mahan, Jr., leading to a Certificate of Advanced Graduate Study as a psychological examiner. She is presently serving the six elementary schools of Waterford as Guidance Consultant, with responsibility for the standardized testing program, psychological evaluations, consultation, and referrals.

Chapter 11

The Use of the House-Tree-Person Technique with Elementary School Underachievers

Elizabeth S. Maxwell, M.A.

Mrs. Maxwell outlines concisely and succinctly the particular difficulties faced by the school guidance consultant in determining, in instances of the most frequently referred problem, whether a child's failure to achieve academically is due to the presence of an emotional disturbance, a basic intellectual flaw, some organic disorder, or some combination of these complex factors.

The author presents several most interesting cases to illustrate the role placed by the H-T-P in the establishment of a diagnosis and a prognosis for the non-achiever. The facile flow of Mrs. Maxwell's phraseology produces a striking three-dimensionality in the vivid and colorful word portraits she paints of her subjects, their backgrounds, their problems, and their projective behavior. It might well be said of her (as it was of William James) that she is a psychologist who writes like a writer. Eds.

As guidance consultant for the elementary schools of a medium-sized New England town, I am expected to be something of a generalist: not so much a highly trained expert in any one field as a person of broadly based, if not intensive, professional training, who can function in many areas to help children, parents, and teachers to solve problems which contribute to learning disabilities. Our school system, like most in the area, operates on the assumption that academic progress cannot be separated from total functioning, that all behavior is multiply caused, and that learning cannot, therefore, be dealt with in "cook book" fashion as a simple mechanical process. Nevertheless, because we are school people, with a deeply ingrained awareness that the school's primary obligation is to educate, and that the first criterion of our effectiveness is the academic progress of our pupils, school achievement is the primary focus of concern for most teachers and administrators.

It is not only inevitable, but fortunate, that this is true. To sift out for special consideration the children with problems, many of which have little apparent connection with the three R's, *non-achievement in the classroom* is one of the best indicators we have at our disposal. Although alert teachers can frequently identify -the child who has serious personal problems even when he is a high achiever, about 90% of the youngsters with difficulties calling for guidance services do have learning disabilities. So our teachers are asking a significant question when they ask, "How can we help this child to learn?"

By far the most frequent call for my services begins, at least, as a request for an appraisal of mental ability. Intelligence is difficult to define and easy to misjudge. Conscientious teachers who try every stratagem at their command to help an underachiever without success usually find themselves, sooner or later, wondering whether or not he is retarded. There is even a certain pressure on our teachers to consider this possibility, because Waterford, Connecticut, our base of operations, is the home of Seaside Regional Center, a remarkable institution for retarded children, with a truly pioneering approach to the problems of the mentally handicapped. Because Seaside's children are entitled, by state law, to instruction in our public schools, if they are capable of profiting by a school program, Waterford has developed an unusually comprehensive program of special classes for retarded children of various ages and different degrees of mental deficiency. Retardation, therefore, is highly visible in our town, and teachers who once would have despaired of helping them have learned that mentally handicapped children can learn, and happily, in classes tailored to their special needs. Small wonder, then, that a teacher faced by an apathetic or rebelliously unhappy child who does not learn in spite of her best efforts often thinks first of retardation—even, perhaps, with hope, because for the retarded, opportunities for help are abundantly available!

It is usually my sorry fate to have to tell such teachers that another answer must be found. In many cases, of course, the teacher is fully aware that this is likely. Although many youngsters manage with almost incredible shrewdness to conceal a high level of ability behind dull eyes and a lifeless manner, teachers can be as shrewd as their charges, and the children's best disguises are often penetrated by teachers who know that many psychological problems can masquerade as scholastic slowness, and who detect evidence of a lively intelligence in youngsters who become dull only when there is school work to be done. Many referrals for testing are, therefore, requests for insight into a child's personality, rather than for a simple estimate of cognitive capacities. "What," the teacher then asks, "makes this child tick? What does the world look like to him? How can I get through to him in that world?" It is in attempting to answer these questions that projective techniques are most valuable. Experiences with the H-T-P has shown that it has many advantages over other projective approaches to children of elementary school age.

One of these advantages, I find, is expressed in the old Chinese bit of folk wisdom, "One picture is worth a thousand words." Often a teacher can get a better "feel" for what bothers a child from viewing his H-T-P productions than from my best efforts to communicate in words what I have been able to learn about him. The obstreperous, rebellious little fellow who acts "too big for his britches" and practically asks for the disapproval and irritation he so often calls forth looks a bit different to his teacher if she sees his picture of himself in his drawings: small, huddled at the bottom of the page as if seeking firm ground under his feet, with arms helplessly outstretched and a placating, clownlike smile that sheepishly reveals his feelings of defenselessness. Instead of "that impossible child", he may become in his teacher's eyes, "that poor little kid", and one giant step has been taken toward providing him with more "good growing weather" in the classroom.

With primary grade children particularly, the H-T-P provides for me, as well as for teachers, glimpses into their inner world which their verbal responses do not reveal. Betsy, for example, was referred because she was withdrawn, uninterested, did not complete written work, and took little part in oral group activities. Amazingly, this second grade child began to talk quite freely almost immediately as we set to work. She asked me why I had chosen her to play with, and when I answered that I wasn't exactly playing, but had been asked to help her because she did not seem to be enjoying her school work, Betsy looked at me intently and said, "I'm *not!* —Not at all!" Thereafter, the difficulty lay not in getting her to talk, but in getting her to stop. She was quite aware of having a problem, and convinced that she knew what it was: she was unhappy because she had no friends in her present class, though she had had friends, and had enjoyed herself, the previous year. Transferred to a new school in September, she found none of her former playmates available.

As to the reasons behind her difficulty in reaching out more confidently for new friends, it was the H-T-P which provided the clues. Her House drawings were efforts to reproduce her own home, and revealed in their details and in her conversation about them that Betsy was a very "family-oriented" child. She spoke warmly about her parents and siblings as she drew, but made it clear, nevertheless, that she thought five brothers and sisters were too many. Betsy, the third of six children, had been "pushed off the perch" at 15 months by the birth of a sister. It appeared that she felt acutely the need for a greater display of love and attention than had been her lot in this large family. And her Tree and Person drawings were transparently revealing of the all-important event which had probably triggered her current hostility and insecurity: the birth, in September, of her mother's sixth child. Betsy's Trees, otherwise unremarkable, both contained large squirrel holes, complete with tenants. Her achromatic Person, which she identified as herself, was decorated by a huge black circle over the abdomen. Asked what this was, Betsy smiled slyly and said, "It's a big, black circle!" Pressed a bit further, she silently drew smaller dots all over the figure's dress, as if to insist that the "big, black circle" was simply an oversized polka-dot.

The most disturbing of Betsy's drawings was her chromatic Person. Her response, when requested to draw a Person with crayon, was to ask whether she could draw a picture of a "great big plastic lady" her father had recently brought home so he could "play a joke on his workmen." Told that she could choose her own subject, she giggled in embarrassment and said "She's bare!" As she drew, at the same time telling how she and her brothers and sisters played with the "plastic lady," it was difficult to determine from her confusing statements exactly what the "plastic lady" was, and what it meant to her. (I later discovered that it was a department store window dummy which Betsy's father had bought cheaply, in order, just as she had said, to have some fun with the workers in his small business.) Again, the advantages of graphic expression over verbalization were apparent: the figure Betsy drew was of fascination and terror. Done in purple, red, and yellow, it resembled a puppet from the waist down, but the upper part showed an aggressive female, featuring long, clawlike red fingernails. It appeared that Betsy's concern about sex and birth, brought to the fore by the arrival of the new baby, had been intensified by the play with the dummy to an uncomfortable pitch of curiosity, guilt, and aversion. In conferring with her mother, I learned that the youngsters had been dismembering the dummy, carrying it about the house and setting it up in unexpected corners to "scare" their mother, who had gone along with what she regarded as harmless fun by emitting gratifying screams upon seeing it. When she realized the effect of this play on Betsy, she decided to insist that her husband remove the dummy from the house, and to seek opportunities to satisfy Betsy's curiosity and allay her anxieties. Several months later, a follow-up inquiry revealed that Betsy had come out of her shell quite noticeably in the classroom, had made some friends, and was taking part in class activities with more enthusiasm.

Not all elementary school children enjoy drawing, by any means. Fortunately, however, even with youngsters who would rather do long division than draw – and there are some –the drawings still can be very revealing. The child whose pictures are bland and empty tells as much by what he omits, at times, as another tells by what he includes. A dramatic instance of this occurred at my first meeting with Karen, a first grader who liked neither the drawing nor anything else she was asked to do, 'though she was so maddeningly polite in her attempt to conceal this that I despaired, for a time, of seeing anything but a placating smile, or hearing anything but fulsome remarks. Having assured me that I was "the most beautifullest lady in the world," even "beautifuller" than Mrs. D., her teacher, and also that it was very nice of me to "help" her, Karen sighed deeply, folded her hands, and awaited her fate.

As we worked, a few cracks began to show in the enamel, and when these were acknowledged calmly, Karen began to emerge bit by bit from behind the facade. But it was not until I unwittingly called her attention to an omission in her chromatic House that there was a real breakthrough. Karen had added a good bit of environmental detail to her narrow, empty little brown box of a House (Figure 158). One feature was a garden, with flowers arranged, obviously by design, in groups of four. As she had been talking about her two sisters and her brother, with clear though covert hostility, during the drawing of her achromatic series, I commented, in an attempt to mine this vein a bit more, "You have the same number of flowers as you have in your family." Frankly, the omission of parents had not occurred to me, until, with instant alarm, Karen pointed to one of the gaps between her groups of flowers and said, "But my Mommy and Daddy aren't dead!" I said that I had meant the four children, but Karen's anxiety was not easily allayed: she said, "But if there are only four stems, my mother and father would be dead, huh?"

This bit of unexpected drama paved the way for further revelations by Karen —ending with "I really like everything except me . . . I hate myself!" It also served as the much-needed kick which alerted me to look for something more deep-seated than the reactions of an insecure child to the pressures of her first year in school. Subsequent events bore out my opinion that psychotherapeutic help was needed, and Karen's parents accepted a referral.

Another advantage of the H-T-P, particularly with very anxious, over-controlled children who have erected strong defenses against their unmanageable feelings and impulses, is that it provides an opportunity for release without the necessity for verbalization—procedure often extremely threatening to them. Such a child seems, often, to experience a lowering of his anxiety level while drawing. This next may make it possible for him to communicate verbally as well as graphically.

Robert was such a child. Referred for an evaluation of mental ability, he was so anxious, placating, and unwilling to verbalize during the administration of the Peabody Picture Vocabulary Test that it seemed invalid to attempt a WISC. Asked whether he liked to draw, he responded eagerly in the affirmative, perhaps as a welcome escape from further testing. Almost as soon as he had begun to draw the achromatic House, however, Robert began to talk about his own house, his family, and his worry about having to move soon to a new house in another town, leaving all his friends behind. Although he remained somewhat tense and insecure, there was a breakthrough into verbal communication. A relationship was established in which Robert began to trust himself, and me, sufficiently so that he could perform on the WISC which was later administered.

Not all defensive, inhibited children are non-verbal. Douglas, like Robert, was referred because of low achievement and evidence of insecurity. Although he verbalized very freely, much of his talk constituted a smoke-screen rather than a view. He discussed at length, his worry about his low achievement, going so far as to express his fear that he might be unable to get into a good college (his choice was Harvard) if he did not improve. As Doug was in the third grade at the time, worry about college moved his concern to a safer distance. Most of his conversation was indicative of acute anxiety, at the pseudo-sophisticated level of a child highly aware of and much influenced by the concerns expressed by parents or other significant adults. His talk was laden with detailed explanations of his difficulties, many having a strong flavor of "alibi". At times he would switch to a near "pie in the sky" solution: the future would be fine, and the present was to be ignored.

Douglas went into considerable detail in explaining the reason for the illegible handwriting on which, in turn, he blamed all his other learning problems. An injury to the little finger of his right hand the previous year had necessitated splinting for some time, and had left the finger stiff. I might have questioned whether the injury had any deep meaning for Doug, had he not drawn both of his own-sex

Persons with a finger missing from the figure's right hand. His House and Tree drawings were relatively unrevealing, but his Persons showed not only that the injury had symbolic meaning, but that personal maladjustment was probably severe. Each was a bloated, empty figure with a tiny head and weak extremities, crowding the page at top and bottom as if cramped by a constricting environment. Although both were identified as males, they had shapeless lower garments which looked more like skirts than pants. (See Figures 156 and 160.) In addition to the general impression of some feeling of depersonalization and weak, badly-threatened ego-controls, here was evidence of conflict with regard to sex roles and sexual activities. The advisability of a referral for a psychiatric evaluation, to which Douglas's other performances pointed, was firmly established by the drawings.

Robert and Douglas both presented, in their behavior during testing and in the classroom, aspects of what seems to be the most common syndrome presented by the underachievers whom we are called upon to test: that of the quiet, over-polite, conforming child whose only method of rebelling against whatever is bothering him is to manage, somehow, not to achieve in school. These are our "para-lyzed compulsives." Often they appear unresponsive and uninterested in achieve-ment, and the common description of them by teachers is highly likely to include the words "lazy," "immature," and "unmotivated." But under their apparent apathy and endless dawdling, one often uncovers a compulsive need to accomplish, a tendency toward perfectionism, and a big emotional investment in achievement

Fig. 156, Douglas

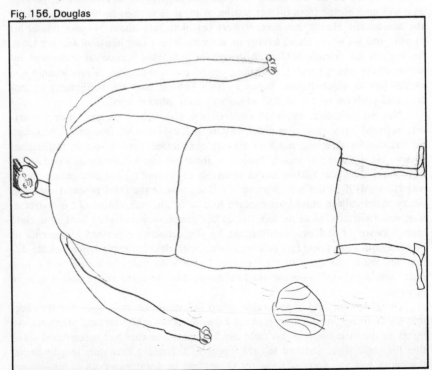

as representing the only way in which they can demonstrate that they have any value. Overwhelmed by pressure for achievement, both from significant adults and from within themselves, they are caught in a paralyzing conflict between powerful desires to succeed and a strong need for rebellion. The obviously "nervous" ones like Douglas are often quickly recognized by their teachers as something other than lazy and uninterested. Those who are more controlled are not so easy to understand. It is often helpful to a frustrated teacher, when I can demonstrate the inner conflicts through the content of a child's drawings and his verbalizations about them, to show that he is a *passive resister*, rather than a *drifter*. Perceiving that a child is reacting intensely, though negatively—that his engine is racing 'though the wheels of learning spin uselessly—gives the teacher hope of finding a way to provide the traction that will get him moving.

The compulsive non-achievers are often the products of good homes , of conscientious, striving parents whose own achievement-related anxieties have "rubbed off" on their children. Intelligently concerned, and often possessed of considerable insight into their children's difficulties on an intellectual level, these parents are sometimes able, with some support and guidance from the school, to modify their own behavior and expectations sufficiently to enable their children to function more comfortably and more efficiently. It is often possible on the basis of the H-T-P productions, to discriminate, among the non-achievers, between those who can be helped by ordinary measures taken by parents and teachers and those who require psychotherapy. More often than not, it is the Tree drawings which are most helpful in this respect.

An example of this usefulness of the Tree drawing occurs in the case of David, a youngster whose behavior showed many signs of the "paralyzed compulsive" syndrome previously described. He was controlled, conforming, unresponsive; signs of maladjustment were numerous, but slight. It would have been difficult, without the Trees, to get a clear picture of the extent of his disturbance. The achromatic Tree (Figure 157) was rather horrifying. Two carefully truncated limbs were so placed as to be obvious representations of arms. Above these were two more limbs; one of them spiky and aggressive and the other a weak, shaky limb with tiny round "leaves." Above these was the top of the Tree, and it, too, was a "stump." The chromatic Tree (Figure 159), done entirely in brown, was a somewhat simplified version of the achromatic. David commented, as he drew, "No leaves . . . this is a winter tree." His remarks about the achromatic Tree were even more revealing. He chose the feeble branch, whose sparse, tiny leaves may well picture his impoverished emotional life, as its worst feature. Asked what was best about his drawing, David pointed out the neat, careful way in which his hands had been cut off!

David's Person drawings had hands, though they were rather weak ones. He did chop off the top of each head with a flat horizontal line reminiscent of the tops of the Trees, but this off flatness was quickly disguised by the addition of hats. Here was a dramatic example of the power of the Tree to get beneath the surface defenses. Without it, the attempt to "chop off" the turbulent thoughts and fancies in David's poor head might have been missed, and I should have had no indication of the intense guilt and fear associated with his hands.

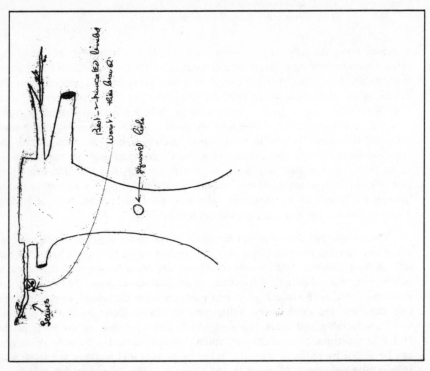

Fig. 157, David (above)

Fig. 158, Karen (below)

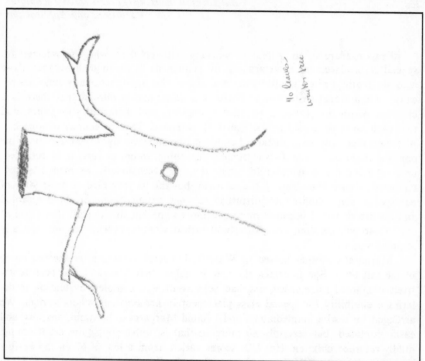

Fig. 159, David (above)

Fig. 160, Douglas (below)

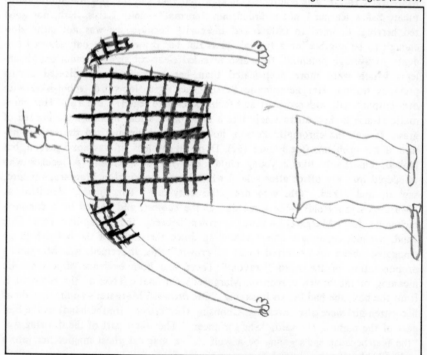

Drawings are often helpful in working with children who are referred for special class placement as retardates, by helping us to distinguish between those who are really limited intellectually and those who are functionally retarded because of emotional disturbance. There is a naive notion abroad that there is a clear-cut distinction between retarded youngsters and disturbed youngsters, and that each must be placed in the "correct" category. This, of course, is nonsense. Although there are many disturbed children who show no signs of retardation, the opposite is far from true. It is extremely disturbing, in our culture, to be retarded, or even to be a non-achiever for other reasons. Occasionally we meet a sunny-tempered, secure child among the retarded, but this is very rare: at least 90% of our special class children are disturbed to some extent. Some are both retarded and disturbed, but it becomes more and more apparent to our staff that some of our "retarded" children are seriously disturbed youngsters who are not basically retardates at all.

Margaret's mother moved to Waterford several months after the beginning of the fall term. She informed the new Principal that Margaret had been tentatively diagnosed as retarded, and had been awaiting a complete evaluation to determine eligibility for special class placement in her previous school system. We arranged for testing immediately, and I found Margaret to be timid, anxious, and easily confused, but certainly no more so that is, unhappily, quite usual among mildly retarded children. Her I.Q. scores varied, from a low of 67 on the Performance Scale of the WISC to a high of 92 on the Goodenough Draw-a-Man. Until Margaret's H-T-P was completed, it appeared that she was just one more unfortunate "slow learner," not retarded, not "normal"—neither fish, flesh, nor good red herring, doomed to failure and insecurity because she was not quite slow enough to be eligible for a special class. But her drawings not only showed evidence of average potential; they also revealed clear-cut signs of emotional problems which were more deep-seated than her behavior had indicated during previous testing. Her achromatic Person was rigid, lop-sided, robot-like, with over-emphasized, widened eyes and feeble stick-like legs (Figure 161). Her chromatic House looked distressingly like a houseboat, afloat in an undulating sea of grass. It was the chromatic Person, however, which dramatized the serious nature of her problems (see Figure 162). Done all in black, it was not a person, but looked remarkably like a young child's drawing of a kitten. (A teacher who wandered into my office after school while I was working on Margaret's record, saw it, and asked, "Oh, who drew the kitty-cat?" This figure, identified as "Margie, 8 years old"—the same age as the subject, and named by a common nickname for "Margaret"—wore a crown between the kitten-like ears. One hand, a rigid, inanimate object extending down the center of the body, held an elongated object also referred to as a "crown," this, it seemed, was Margaret's pronunciation of the word "crayon." There had been evidence of a symbolic meaning of the brown crayon on Margaret's chromatic Tree: as she removed it from the box, she had kissed it, saying, "Oh, *brown!*" Margaret's comments about her kitten-girl were also revealing. Choosing the "crown" (in the hand) as the best part of the picture, she said, "She's a queen." The worst part of the drawing was "the feet because she's gonna be a wolf . . . a magical ghost magics her into a wolf. She'd rather be a queen."

We were saved some time and Margaret, perhaps, was saved additional pain by what I saw in her H-T-P. For Margaret's mother, a pleasant, competent woman (so completely cooperative that this in itself should have been a warning signal, but we often forget to be suspicious!) had described her daughter as retarded and had provided information supporting her opinion, but had mentioned nothing whatever of suspected emotional disturbance. Yet she immediately agreed to apply for an evaluation at the Child Guidance Clinic, and two weeks later, while expressing some irritation because she had not already been given an appointment, she admitted that she had "already had experience with another guidance clinic, and had not found them very efficient." It is possible that she will not find the local clinic to her liking, either, but the school staff might now have the advantage of any advice or information which the clinic provides to help us to serve Margaret better.

The Case of Cheryl

This case is presented as an outstanding example of the advantages of drawing techniques with children who are unable to verbalize. Cheryl, a beautiful 12-year-old girl with deep blue eyes and silky brown curls, neat as a pin and carefully groomed, had chosen drawing as her medium of expression. She stuttered badly, often with complete blocking so that her whole face was distorted in the attempt to form words which would not come. With her peers, she was usually able to communicate easily, but she labored under a crippling degree of anxiety when speaking to adults. Her parents and teachers had observed that her problems were compounded because she did not know how to "let go," but always kept her feelings bottled up. At our first meeting, she struggled to respond to questions in spite of her inner fear and rage, but no spontaneous speech was possible until she began to draw. The drawings themselves were revealing; even more astonishing was the way in which, as she drew, she was able to forget her anxiety, at least intermittently, and speak quite naturally.

Cheryl, invariably shy and quiet in the classroom, had always had difficulty in keeping up with her classmates academically. She had been retained an extra year in first grade, and though this had seemed to result in some progress, she had never managed to do more than barely make the grade. During the school year previous to her referral, her teacher, believing that some of her difficulty resulted from inconsistent, over-indulgent home training, had conferred with her parents. He had recommended various changes in their management of things in the home. Both parents were eager to cooperate, and hoped that their new regime, a more demanding one, would help Cheryl to settle down to business in school. Its effect, unfortunately, was the opposite, and Cheryl's tensions increased to a degree which convinced her parents that her problems were beyond solution by any efforts they could make. The referral for psychological evaluation occurred after their conference with the school principal about the advisability of seeking professional help.

Tests administered included the WISC, the reading portion of the Wide Range Achievement Test, the Goldstein-Scheerer Cube Test, designs VII to XII, and the H-T-P drawings. Cheryl's reading skill was more than one year retarded; the I.E. scores she attained on the WISC were: Verbal, 91; Performance, 94. These quan-

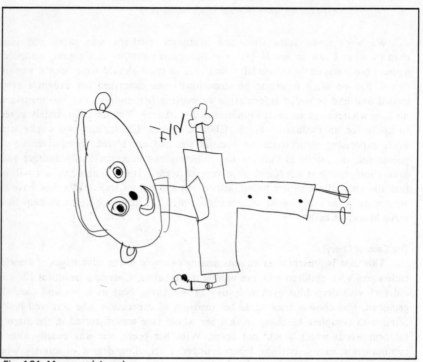

Fig. 161, Margaret (above)

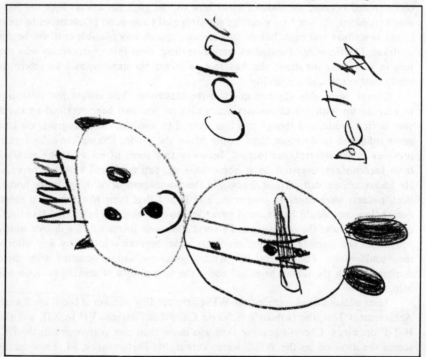

Fig. 162, Margaret (below)

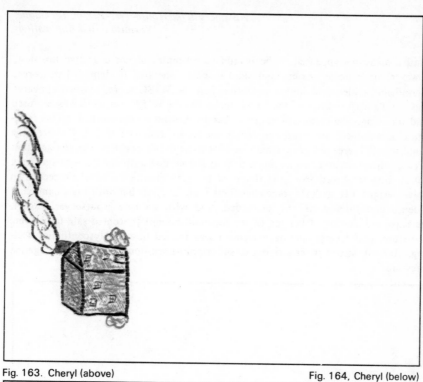

Fig. 163. Cheryl (above)   Fig. 164, Cheryl (below)

titative measures appeared to be invalid as estimates of her cognitive function, however, since acute anxiety and rigid defenses operated to depress her scores. Significant evidence of higher potential than the WISC scores showed appeared in Cheryl's performance on the Kohs blocks. On the WISC, her work was confused and fumbling. She expressed anger at her frustration as she worked. "This is almost impossible!" she protested. After she failed designs 1 and 2, I offered the Goldstein-Scheerer designs, remarking that these didn't count on the test and that I could therefore give her as much help as she needed until she "caught on" and, lo! A miracle! Freed from the threat of the test situation, Cheryl proceeded to solve designs VII to XII, somewhat fumblingly at first, but with increasing confidence and interest as she succeeded, and with no help whatsoever, except, perhaps, my sharing of her joy in her accomplishment! It seemed safe to assume, therefore, that Cheryl's non-achievement was related to strongly conflicting feelings about it: strong inner striving versus crippling self-doubt and rebellion against pressure.

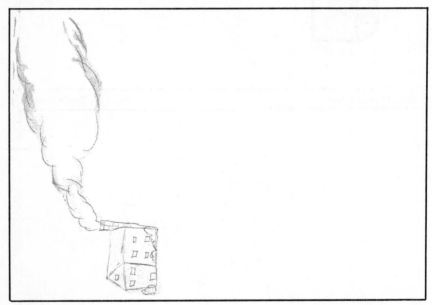

Fig. 165, Cheryl
Achromatic Drawings
HOUSE (Figure 165)

Cheryl's little "dream cottage," which was scarcely more than 1½ inches square, was sketched quickly but carefully with light, short strokes which required some reinforcement for the outline, though all details were added with sure, quick strokes and no fussiness was shown about complete symmetry. Place in the upper left-hand corner of the page, the cottage had an appropriate but transparent addition of shrubbery, but no ground line. Its outstanding feature was a large, emphasized chimney, with a tremendous volume of smoke billowing from it as if blown across the page by a stiff breeze.

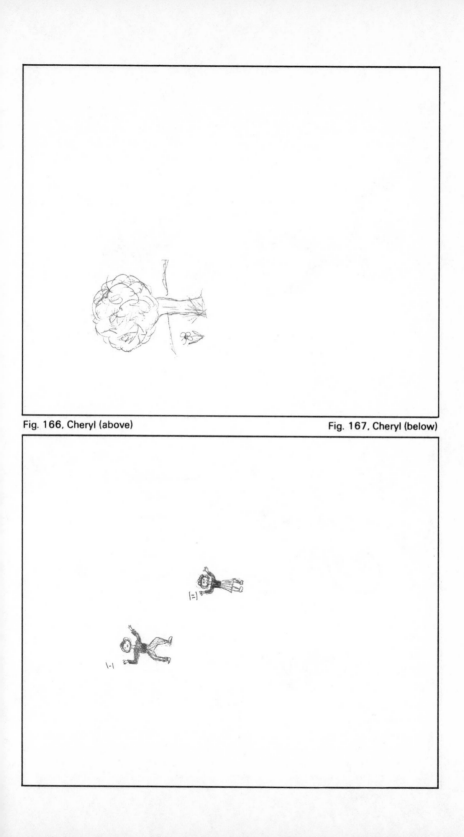

Fig. 166, Cheryl (above)

Fig. 167, Cheryl (below)

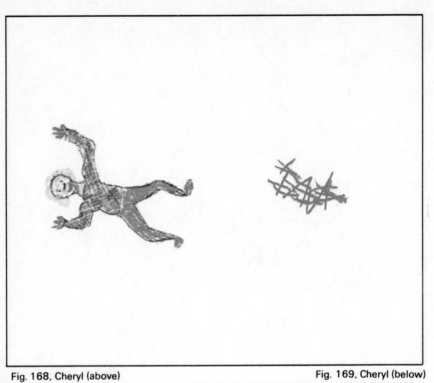

Fig. 168, Cheryl (above)   Fig. 169, Cheryl (below)

TREE (Figure 166)

Placed, like her other drawings, in the upper left-hand corner of the page, the Tree was drawn rapidly, with a sturdy trunk which met the ground rather abruptly, a symmetrical, crowded mass of leaves, and some tall grass sprouting by the base of the trunk. A single flower grew nearby. Aside from the small size — about 3 inches — and retreated placement, the Tree had a healthy look, but there was a niceably excited quality about the stroke in the crown of the Tree, which is full of sharp little lines giving an impression of unrest and activity.

PERSONS (Figure 167)

There, for the first time, Cheryl showed great anxiety as she drew. Having made her figures too tiny to permit the good execution noted in the House and Tree — they were scarcely more than an inch high — she struggled with details, made many erasures, and used much shading. Her first figure was intended to be a girl in slacks, but it turned out to be a boy. The second figure was almost identical from the waist up, but wore a pleated skirt, and it was even smaller than the male. Although Cheryl commented amost continuously on her difficulties and dissatisfaction with her work as she drew, the two tiny figures emerged well-proportioned and fairly adequately detailed, except for the uniformly 3-fingered hands. Both Persons, however, had a helpless, floating quality; the girl, in particular, had the aspect of a toddler coaxing her daddy to pick her up. There was even a hint that the figures were not living children, but two little puppets with no motive power of their own.

Chromatic Drawings

HOUSE (Figure 163)

Cheryl's second House was almost a replica of her first, except that the door faced toward the center, rather than off the page, the large chimney was partially concealed and window placement was disorganized. Neatness of execution in this more difficult medium was achieved by precise, careful handling of the crayons. The impact of color did little to loosen Cheryl's rigid defenses.

TREE (Figure 164)

The chromatic Tree was apparently intended to be a replica of the pencil drawing, but it is a considerably less stable Tree. The trunk ends more abruptly, and there are no ground lines. The tall grass sketched in the achromatic drawing becomes a bushy clump, rounded at the bottom and exactly centered below the trunk, cradling it. The overall effect is that this is a mushroom-shaped figure resting on a rounded base, much like those of the "roly-poly" figures children like to bat about, but which always end up erect despite the buffeting.

PERSONS (Figures 168 and 169)

Faced with the problems of human figure drawing in this frustrating medium, Cheryl could no longer draw miniatures. Her first chromatic Person was 4 inches high. This "girl" is dressed in slacks, and except for the lower legs and feet, which are small and weak, she is quite muscular, with bulging, masculine shoulders and heavy arms. This portrayal of strength is contradicted, however, not only by the weak underpinnings but by the bulging, babyish stomach, the figure's toppling toward the right, and the bent knees. Here, along with the suggestion of a toddler asking to be carried, we have a hint of the attitude of an infant in a crib, reaching out to be lifted into her mother's arms. Or perhaps, like the achromatic Persons, this figure is a marionette with no capacity for independent action.

In drawing her male chromatic figure, Cheryl lost her rigid control. Beginning this figure, like the female, with the legs, she made three false starts, obliterating each one vigorously with red and complaining of its ugliness. At my suggestion, "Draw an ugly boy, then," she succeeded in completing a 5½-inch figure which was, for Cheryl, very uncontrolled. The musculature noticed in her female is greatly exaggerated; the male is all bulging muscles, though the general effect is that of an inflated balloon rather than one of strength. The overemphasized, hunched shoulders and the arms which end in fists turned inward toward the body give an ineffectively aggressive appearance to the figure, suggesting that the aggression is turned inward against the self. The figure's twisted right foot, short legs, elongated neck and over-sized head complete the picture of a rag doll or a padded dummy with no real life of its own. The choice of color was as deliberate as it was bizarre (see Figure 169). Here for the first time is a creature of fantasy rather than an attempt at a realistic representation.

In summary, we have here a series of small, neatly executed drawings, "up in the air" but reality oriented, with rigid defenses being reasonably well maintained until, on the final drawing, Cheryl's controls collapse and a fantasy figure results. That her control was costing too much was apparent in each picture, but this was displayed blatantly only in the chromatic male, and then only after Cheryl received the permission implied in my comment, "Draw an ugly boy, then."

Verbalizations About Drawings

While drawing the achromatic House, Cheryl was able for the first time, intermittently, to speak in a normal voice with no stuttering. In response to inquiry, she chose the smoke as the best part of her House, the windows as its worst feature (a plausible response, as they were hastily drawn, and less symmetrical than other features) and the attic room as her choice if this were her own house. "This isn't my house, though!" She went on to say that in an attic room she would be able to keep her two-year-old sister, Sally, out of her things, and followed this by complaints, restrained in tone but heartfelt, about Sally and her seven-year-old brother Billy, both of whom bother her, get into her possessions so she cannot keep them neat, and follow her around when she wants to go off with her own friends. She cannot get the younger children to leave her in peace, Cheryl said, " . . . until I finally yell at them." She added, "Our house is hardly ever quiet, with Billy and his friends all over, and me and my friends, and Sally getting into things, and breaking things all the time."

Cheryl's Tree drawings inspired relatively little comment from her, but while engaged in drawing them she seemed more at ease in general conversation, mostly about surface matters. There was little of the intermittent tightening up and return to stuttering which had occurred during the drawing of the achromatic House. A double advantage of the Tree was demonstrated: it not only calls forth unconscious projection with less interference by the social defenses which may influence House or Person drawings, but is "safe" enough as a concept to reduce anxiety in an over-controlled subject. For the achromatic Tree, Cheryl chose the leaves as the best feature, and the fact that the trunk met the ground too abruptly, with no evidence of a root system, as the worst part: "A tree doesn't just *end* like that!" she said. Yet on the chromatic Tree, she not only exaggerated the rootlessness, but did not give it a firm meeting with the ground. She chose the trunk as best part this time, and as the worst feature, the absence of "roots going into the ground."

During the production of her achromatic Persons, Cheryl's comments were almost wholly about the difficulty of drawing people and her dissatisfaction with her work. Typical remarks were, "Shoes are the worst . . . Sometimes I can draw them, when I'm lucky." "Now comes the worst part, the hands . . . I don't like to draw hands." When she had completed her first figure she said, without inquiry from me, "It looks like a boy; it was meant for a girl, though . . . I'll make the legs skinnier and shorter—girls don't have long, fat legs like boys!" When she had completed her erasure and correction, Cheryl was still not satisfied that it looked like a girl, so I suggested that she let it be a boy, and draw a girl next. This figure, even smaller than the boy, was conventionally dressed in a skirt, though Cheryl complained, "I can't draw skirts very well." She chose the shirt (the figures had almost identical treatment of the upper body) as the best part of each figure, and the pants of the boy, and legs and skirt of the girl, as their worst features. In response to inquiry, she stated that the male was four years old, and the female was five.

As Cheryl worked on her first chromatic Person, she accounted for the deep orange hands and feet by saying, "Orange hands because there's no tan." Suddenly she exclaimed, "Oh, look! One hand . . . one arm is longer!" Indeed, it was, and she showed some irritation at the impossibility of erasing, but with no return of her earlier stuttering. The best part of this figure was the face; the worst, "Hands, feet, and hair." (Here, for the first time, Cheryl's choice of "best part" does not seem to be based on her artists eye for the best *drawn* features; the face is rather primitively drawn.) Asked what the girl needed, Cheryl said, "Buttons; when I inquired what she was doing, she answered, "Standing there . . . waving, I guess." Asked to whom she was waving, Cheryl responded, "To a friend, I guess . . ." in a dying voice, and then, in a whisper, " . . . or Mother."

Cheryl's final drawing, following her three obliterated attempts and my "permission" to draw an ugly boy, was drawn hastily, with evidence of tension. But she did not lose control, in any global way, either of her feelings of her reality-testing capacity, even in this highly-charged atmosphere. Her verbalizations had fantasy elements, but her manner showed that she was aware of the fantasy, not adrift in it. She commented, as she finished, "He's a boy that just came out of a washing machine, or something . . . a grinder." I asked how he got in the machine, and Cheryl responded, with a hint of a smile, "I don't know; maybe he just wanted a bath!" Asked for the worst feature, she said vigorously, "I hate the whole thing!" Pressed for a choice, she said, "Neck, legs, arms, shoulders, hair, face . . . the whole thing!" When asked what her boy needed, Cheryl grinned and said, "A lot! . . . A new shirt and pants, and to smooth himself out and twist his foot (the figure's distorted right foot) back the right way." Asked whether he could smooth himself out, she answered that he was "going to stay that way, I guess, unless a miracle happens."

Interpretive Notes

As can be expected to an observant, over-controlled child, Cheryl is in contact with reality in spite of evidence of fantasy elements in her inner world. Note her realistic choice of the windows as the worst part of her achromatic House, her accurate observations about the root systems of trees, her plausible way of accounting for the bright orange hands and feet of her chromatic female, her reality-based reason for preferring the attic room—even the faintly mocking air as she described her "ugly" boy. Whatever one might read into them in terms of her inner dynamics, one must also agree that Cheryl's verbalizations (except for some comments about the chromatic Persons) are all quite defensible on a common sense basis. Her control has both advantages and disadvantages. She can tolerate an amount of anxiety which might overwhelm a more volatile child, and still function after a fashion, but the strong defenses erected against overt expression of her feelings have boxed her in. She has built stout walls for protection and now finds herself trapped within them.

There is much evidence that Cheryl is approaching the limits of her toleration of internal and external pressure. Her stuttering and inability to achieve are the main symptoms in the classroom. Her choice of the enormous billows of smoke as the best part of her Houses, and the restless, excited interior of the crown of her achromatic Tree, which threatens to escape from the fully enclosed but cloud-like and permeable outer boundary, both show how much inner turmoil is crying for release. Information secured from a conference with the mother revealed that Cheryl's behavior at home has changed, during the past year, in ways indicating that her controls are breaking down. For the first time, she has begun to rebel at doing assigned chores, to "talk back" when corrected, to show constant hostility and oral aggression toward her brother, and, to a lesser extent, toward her sister.

That some of the smoke Cheryl drew represents environmental stress is clear in her verbalizations and in other aspects of the House drawings: her preference for the attic room, the need for tranquility reflected in the green so prominent in the chromatic House, and the wind which sweeps the smoke across the page. It is clear that her pattern of non-achievement is not a reaction only to school failures and current parental pressures, however; Cheryl has internalized her family's values, and her growing need to rebel pulls against an almost equal need to conform. The House taps deeply-rooted disturbances in Cheryl's relationships with her parents, and shows a problem of holding on and letting go, possibly stemming from the anal stage of development. Cheryl holds on to her possessions, her privacy, her feelings: in her Houses she carefully reinforces the walls and roof. Her mother described her as always having been a "very good" child; so much so that when she began to show rebellion openly the mother was not so much angry as astonished. Her manner, as she spoke of Cheryl's rebellious behavior, was one of almost amused tolerance, with perhaps an undertone of approval in spite of her genuine concern.

It would appear that the parents' too-successful attempt to rear a perfect child has backfired. Cheryl's recent signs of releasing her hostility and aggression (note the aggressive tendency breaking forth in the smoking chimneys) in the home may have been brought to a head by the poor advice given to her parents by her previous teacher. That they accepted the advice and redoubled pressures which were already a burden bespeaks the nature of their own relationships with Cheryl.

A dramatic sidelight on Cheryl's H-T-P performance was revealed, by accident, when I entered the school for the purpose of testing her. Through a basement window, in a room used for art supplies, I saw that one of the easels held a large picture—really a somewhat disorganized set of "doodles" in black, red, and lavender— near the bottom of which the words "HELP ME" were printed in large red letters. Cheryl's name was signed to this production. This silent scream had apparently been released when Cheryl and some classmates had been sent to the supply room to mix water paints for an art lesson. It is interesting that her choice of colors included the same red and purple she featured in her chromatic male. The choice is odd for a child of Cheryl's conservatism and artistic flair, and would seem to reflect her unmanageable feelings and impulses. Upon inquiry by her teacher, Cheryl admitted to the signature, but denied having done the rest of the painting: another sign of the disrupting effect of her anxiety-state, as she is neither untruthful nor stupid, and must have been desperate to resort to such an unwieldy coping device. Cheryl was being badly burned by the fires smouldering beneath those out-pouring chimneys.

Cheryl's drawings portrayed not only her inner turmoil, but her global feelings of helplessness and self-doubt. The rootlessness of her Trees, the regressive placement of her drawings in the upper left-hand quadrant of the page, the miniature size of many of her drawings—particularly the achromatic Persons— all point toward deep feelings of inadequacy. The helpless posture of the Persons, with arms aimlessly waving—or perhaps reaching for a "magic" solution from above—the ages ascribed to her figures, and the infantile characteristics of the chromatic female all add to the picture of weakening ego controls and of a regressive pull toward an earlier stage of development. The need for buttons on this figure (a need which Cheryl as artist rejected for the sweater-like upper garment; she did not add the buttons) is another clear-cut sign of regression. But the most dramatic clues to a return to infantile dependency feelings were her whispered "Mother" when asked to whom her chromatic female was waving, and her defeated statement that the chromatic male, who had been caught in a grinder, would "stay that way, unless a miracle happens."

Cheryl's Person drawings show not only her acute feelings of dependence and inadequacy, but another problem: one of serious conflict and confusion about sex roles and sexual identification, plus guilt over masturbatory activity or sex play of some sort. That Cheryl may be deeply envious of male status and dissatisfied with her condition as a female is shown in her inability to draw a feminine-looking girl, her identical treatment of male and female above the waist and the choice of this area as best, and her preoccupation with and anxiety about legs. Her comment, "Girls don't have long, fat legs like boys," and her frantic obliteration of the chromatic male's leg, begun at the ankle, as soon as the crotch was reached, could well represent the resentment and inferiority feelings summed up in the phrase "penis envy." Her problem with hands, seen in her comment, "I don't like to draw hands," her distortion of one arm of the chromatic female, her choice of bright orange for its hands, and the closed hands of the chromatic male, curled up and away from the crotch, all point to the possibility of guilt about sex play.

Cheryl's mother said, in our conference, that her husband had expressed neither preference for a son nor disappointment at the birth of his first daughter. She went on to describe him, however, as introspective, an avid reader, a man who shies away from expressing his feelings and who is undemonstrative with everyone. He is strict with all the children—"When he speaks, they're expected to jump!"—and he treats them all alike. As long as two years ago, she added, he had expressed the fear that Cheryl was disturbed and had suggested taking her to a psychiatrist. The mother, however, had found it hard to believe that there was a serious problem until recently, when the symptoms had become acute.

Cheryl has apparently had little opportunity to enjoy being a girl, since her feminine appeal was ignored by her father (why?) and most of the advantages of being a girl in our culture were denied to her by her strict, achievement-oriented upbringing. Although he expressed no preference for a son, this father seems to have treated his little daughter not with the indulgent warmth which fathers often reserve for their girls, but with a firm and rather distant manner. At the same time, although an almost masculine strength and control were required of her by her father, this very pretty, shy child, beautifully dressed by her proud mother, may have been perceived by adults as "sweet" and "pretty" almost to the exclusion of any other identity. Often expected to be conforming, deferent, repressed—a "good little girl" to match the sugar-and-spice exterior—Cheryl may have found herself trapped into being "only a girl," with little of the freedom which is often granted to boys. A former Sunday School teacher said of her, "It's odd, and a little sad; when I try to think back on what Cheryl was like, all I can remember is all that beauty."

A sidelight on Cheryl's problems is the fact that her brother has learning problems, too. Billy (the "ugly boy"?) was tested not too long before I met Cheryl. Like his sister, he had been retained in first grade; unlike her, he was making no progress. Billy's personality seemed quite different from Cheryl's. He was certainly not free from anxiety, but he appeared able to avoid letting tension mount uncomfortably by simply refusing to become involved. He was a master at evading tasks he feared or found uncongenial, and he invested effort only in activities, such as block designs and puzzles, which he found intrinsically rewarding. Though he was over-dependent and lacked initiative, he seemed much less burdened than Cheryl was by self-doubt. I hazarded a guess, in his case, that he had been spoiled, or perhaps treated inconsistently, and had learned to evade his parents' demands without suffering serious consequences. One wonders whether the father's strict impartiality is as real as his wife considers it, and whether she herself has been, as mothers are frequently accused of being, more indulgent with her son than with her daughters.

Prognosis: essentially favorable. Cheryl is a strong child, still in her formative years, and she realizes that she needs and wants help. Her parents are conscientious – able, it would seem, to make effective use of the guidance clinic's help. It would be well if the clinic could involve the father more in the counseling process than is their usual procedure: his relationship with Cheryl may be more disturbed than the mother's, but his ability to recognize the problem has been greater than hers. It is fortunate that Cheryl, desperate in her need for help, has had this need recognized before anxiety could give way still further to despair. A pull toward giving up an unequal battle and withdrawing into a fantasy world is apparent. While there is tremendous strength in this child, it has been badly strained. At the time of evaluation, she was reaching a degree of exhaustion which might have led to a state of hopelessness in which she could not grasp effectively at any help offered.

Summary

Non-achievement is the primary symptom, in many elementary school children, of a variety of problems. In appraising these, the H-T-P has several advantages. A child's drawings often provide teachers with a more vivid glimpse of his inner world than can be obtained from his attempts to state his concerns in words, which are often hard to interpret because of his limited vocabulary or lack of fluency. This is particularly true of primary grade children, whose pictures make clear things at which their behavior, conversation, and limited responses on verbal projective techniques can only hint. This is also the case with anxious, inhibited children who have built strong defenses against communicating their real concerns. Even children who shy away from drawing and attack the task hesitantly or evasively often reveal much of themselves, if only in what they omit from their drawings.

The H-T-P proves as valuable with the verbalizer as with the silent, withdrawn child. Sometimes it is only in the drawings that the camouflage of verbiage can be cut through to find the roots of a youngster's difficulties. And for a tense, reserved child, an opportunity to draw offers a haven in which he can escape from the necessity for direct interaction, and can thus lower his anxiety to the point where he can begin to interact with relative ease. Cheryl, the stutterer, provides a dramatic example of the release provided for over-controlled children by an opportunity to express their feelings pictorially.

With the expansion of special programs for the retarded, the value of projective drawings in differentiating retarded children from those whose primary problem is one of emotional disturbance becomes more and more apparent. It is important to distinguish children whose disturbance masquerades as retardation from those who are really limited in mental capacity, though an overlay of emotional difficulties may compound their learning disabilities. The H-T-P productions often provide the clearest indications, in children suspected of retardation, of the nature and degree of their emotional disturbance.

References

Hammer, Emanual F. *The Clinical Application of Projective Drawings*. Charles C. Thomas, Springfield, Ill., 1958.

Rabin, Albert I., and Haworth, Mary R. *Projective Techniques with Children*. Grune and Stratton, New York, 1960.

After completing his internship and simultaneous with his obtaining his Ph.D. in Clinical Psychology in 1951 from New York University, Emanuel F. Hammer came to the Lynchburg State Colony, Virginia, to work with John N. Buck and the H-T-P. Shortly thereafter, Dr. Hammer was appointed Director of Intern Training.

He later returned to New York as Senior Research Scientist at the New York State Psychiatric Institute. At the National Psychological Association for Psychoanalysis he then undertook analytic practice, on the faculty and a training analyst at the Metropolitan Institute of Psychoanalytic Studies. He is head of the Psychiatric Clinic; Chief Psychological Consultant at the Lincoln Institute for Psychotherapy, and has recently been appointed to the faculty of the New York University Clinical Psychology doctoral program.

He has written approximately fifty papers and four books, among which are the well-known *The Clinical Application of Projective Drawings,* Springfield, Ill., Charles Thomas, 1958, and *Creativity,* New York. Random House, 1961. He is presently at work on a book, *Interpretation in Treatment: Its Place, Role, Scope, Depth, and Art,*

Honors and offices which he has held include: Fellow, American Psychological Association; Liaison Fellow, American Anthropological Association; Diplomate in Clinical Psychology, American Board of Examiners in Professional Psychology; Secretary, Society of Projective Techniques and Personality Assessment; President, New York Society of Clinical Psychologists.

Chapter 12

The Use of the H-T-P in a Criminal Court: Predicting Acting-Out [1]

Emanuel F. Hammer, Ph.D. [2]

Dr. Hammer explains that the real imperative in dealing with the projective data of subjects is the determination of aggressive potentials which may erupt and be expressed actively, either against others or against the self. It has been his experience, as it has been that of others, that it is the graphic materials which will best reveal clues to the underlying structure and dynamics in such cases.

The author presents a wealth of dramatic case material to illustrate ways in which H-T-P derived data have helped to establish a prognosis. From his experiences he had distilled a number of specific principles for predicting "acting-out" and he has presented them in some detail. Eds.

The prediction of imminent acting-out tendencies, of aggressive acts, of assaultiveness, homicidal potential, suicidal risk, or of sexual acting-out (like rape) is perhaps the most serious, most important, and most practical of all the challenges with which projective techniques are ever confronted. It is in this connection that the clinical psychologist comes closest to facing the issues of life-and-death.

To detect acting-out tendencies is the greatest and most complex problem facing the diagnostician who examines and writes recommendations concerning the people referred to him in a psychiatric clinic attached to a criminal court. It is also a vexed question of acute societal significance, one which is always infused with urgency and immediacy. The clinician who must determine whether or not the patient before him is likely to act out his paranoid delusion, or his

---

[1] Thankful appreciation is extended to Grune & Stratton, Inc., New York City, for permission to employ material from my chapter in Abt and Weissman (Eds.), *Acting-Out,* 1965 from which this presentation is expanded and revised.

[2] Head, Psychology Department, Criminal Courts, New York City.

passive-aggressive tendencies, or his impulse disorder, and harm or murder others or attempt to kill himself, well knows the enormity of the task confronting him. Here we must wrestle with the most awesome of the decisions which we in our field are ever called upon to make, one of depriving a man of his liberty or of risking a judgment that he will not seriously harm others or himself.

Bellak (Abt and Weissman, 1965) defines acting-out as the "non-verbal translation of an unconscious statement," and as such underscores its mechanism as one consisting of an externalization of internal conflicts. Can the likelihood of such acting-out, then, be predicted, and if so, how?

Projective Psychology has, by now, established the concept that every act, expression, or response of an individual – his gestures, perceptions, selections, verbalizations, or motor acts – in some way bears the stamp of his personality.[3] In projective drawings, the subject's psychomotor activities are caught on paper. The line employed may be firm or timid, uncertain, hesitant or bold, or it may even consist of a savage digging at the paper. The difficulties of capturing and recording the transient qualities of overt movement are thus met by the innovation of graphomotor techniques.

Wolff (1946) has made an interesting contribution to the area in his concept of the "rhythmic quotient," based upon careful measurements of drawings made by children, blind persons, epileptics, and even by a sample of African subjects. He has discovered that there are definite proportional ratios in the size of form elements which are characteristic of each individual, which do not vary much with his age, and which appear relatively early in life, thus demonstrating the reliability of expressive movement.

In assessing acting out potentials, the clinician may use any technique which taps personality via the psychomotor, as opposed to the verbal, modalities and has the distinct advantage of requiring less of an inferential leap in making predictions. Projective drawing, with its infinitely subtle language concerning body image and its motor tendencies, comes closer than do the Rorschach, TAT, and other verbal-expressive tools to sampling motility phenomena *directly*.[4]

Now, when a subject cooperates consciously and does not resist on a subconscious level, it is generally agreed by clinicians that the Rorschach usually provides a richer personality picture, but when the subject is evasive or guarded – as are those referred for assessment because of getting into acting out difficulties – projective drawings have been found to be the more revealing device. (Landisberg, 1953.)

---

[3] In fact, the pressing forward of facets of self-portraiture in art, the earliest form of "projective drawing," actually has been recognized for hundreds of years. Leonardo Da Vinci, the genius of so many spheres of activity, is credited with one of the early observations of this process of projection. The person who draws or paints, he recognized, "is inclined to lend to the figures he renders his own bodily experience, if he is not protected against this by long study. (Kris, 1952).

[4] Such motility phenomena include psychomotor tempo, flow of movements, smoothness, and integration versus jerkiness and irascible unpredicatability of action, speed of response, naturalness of motion, impulsiveness, rate and intensity of expressive movements, dimensions of constriction versus expansiveness, and dimensions of withdrawal versus charging forward into the environment.

A particular individual's Rorschach may not yield nearly so much dynamic or structural material as does his projective drawing, or vice versa. The former condition, the writer has found, is more likely to occur in concrete-oriented, more primitive personalities (of the sort more often referred for assessment of potential for anti-social impulse discharge), along with the occurrence of the Performance Scale I.Q. on the Wechsler-Bellevue exceeding the Verbal Scale I.Q. The latter condition, of the Rorschach (or TAT) protocol providing a richer yield than the projective drawings, occurs more frequently in verbal, "intellectual" subjects, with Wechsler-Bellevue Verbal Scale I.Q.'s exceeding Performance Scale I.Q.'s (Hammer, 1958).

The bulk of what the Rorschach yields of the subject's personality comes by way of a relatively indirect route. The subject's Rorschach percepts must, first, be translated into and, second, be communicated in, verbal language. In drawings, on the other hand, the subject expresses himself on a more primitive, concrete, motor level. In addition to the writer, Landisberg (1951) has found that patients exhibiting guardedness seem more likely to reveal their underlying traits and psychodynamics in the drawings. She states, "They are able to exercise more control over their verbal expression, seem to be more intellectually aware of what they might be exposing on the Rorschach. They tend to lose some of this control in their creative, motor expression (employed in drawings)."

An incident was related to the writer by a psychiatrist-colleague who had undergone a psychological examination in being screened for psychoanalytic training. Whereas he was able to withhold Rorschach responses and TAT themes, he felt might be damaging to his chances for admission to the psychoanalytic program, he was not able to manipulate his projective drawing production in a similar manner. While drawing the female Person, for example, he tried to place a smile on her face. But she turned out looking strict and forbidding. Attempting to present his relationships with females in as benign a light as possible, he proceeded to erase and redraw, but each new rendition only gave her face a more formidable and menacing expression than before. In spite of all his efforts, in the end she wore a stern expression. In his own words, "I just couldn't control the way she turned out."

Another case in point was that of an adolescent boy who was brought before a juvenile court on five charges of breaking, entering, and larceny and three charges of entering and larceny. Clinically, he appeared as a hostile, aggressive lad who, however, in his Rorschach and drawings attempted to give a benign impression. In the interview following the drawings, he offered the information that he had been "trying to draw a school boy, but the way it came out, it looks like a tough guy that hangs around the river."

These performances underscore the words of Machover (1953): "Stereotyped defenses are less easy to apply to graphomotor than to verbal projections." (p. 85.)

The present writer's (Hammer, 1954) experience with inmates at Sing Sing Prison further supports this view. Incarcerated subjects, for example, because of their basic mistrust and bitter resentment of authority figures in general, remain somewhat suspicious of all personnel employed at the institution, even after years of "public relations" effort on the part of the psychiatric and psychological staff. Loaded down with pervasive fear of revealing themselves to an authority figure even remotely associated with the prison setting, they manifest defensiveness, and the inmates dare not "see" anything off the beaten track. The number of their Rorschach responses, for example, tends to drop to a meager 10 to 12, with the most frequent record consisting of one noncommittal response given to, and thus dismissing, each card. Their TAT themes assume a barren quality, remaining for the most part on a relatively superficial and descriptive level. Expressions become stereotyped, and the inmate sticks to the "safe" response. Attempts at conformity and undeviating acceptability in voiced Rorschach and TAT percepts are the rule. Richness of imagination is stifled, and real feeling is hidden behind an obscuring curtain of constant control. The scanty record thus obtained loses the pith and the subtle nuances necessary for full or for accurate assessment of the individual type of personality reaction pattern.

In addition, inmates as a group are generally among those subjects who cling, for various reasons, to the concrete. They become anxious and threatened when confronted with the ambiguous stimuli of the Rorschach, and attempt to steer clear of real involvement with this type of projective situation, at least insofar as communicating and explaining verbally what it is that they may see.

To illustrate: sex offenders, for example, who are seen psychotherapeutically after psychological examination often confide to their therapist, once rapport has been cemented in a transference setting, that on the Rorschach they did not reveal everything they saw, e.g., "especially those dirty sex pictures that were there." In responding to the projective drawing task, on the other hand, these patients must reveal something of their sexual adaptation in one of two ways: either in their manner of handling the direct or symbolic sexual areas of the House, Tree, Person figures or else, all the more, by their omitting to draw areas that carry sexual implications, for example, the genital zone or secondary sex characteristics of the drawn Person, the chimney on the House, and the branches on the Tree. (Hammer, 1953, 1954.)

Fox, (1952) also reports, "drawings, relative to other projective techniques, are . . . difficult to falsify, and in its application there is no barrier to education or language." (p 249) Bellak's (1954) experience is in the same direction: "The verbal expression of aggression may be successfully controlled when its muscular expression is clearly seen . . . in tests probing the subsemantic area." (p 292)

But if the above demonstrates the *relatively* more appropriate utility of projective drawings to the problem of assessing acting out potentials, such cues on projective techniques, in general, remain a most elusive cluster of data to catch.

First, it should be emphasized that at this time a high degree of accuracy in our generalizations from projective drawings to life situations cannot be expected. It does appear, however, that we can achieve gross accuracy, particularly if we use a battery of tests, but we must always assume that the projective techniques have not revealed all major personality variables and their patterns of interaction. Also, "We must always make the limiting assumptions that fate often tips the scales of external circumstance one way or the other, regardless of the individual's character structure and intentions, and that to a significant extent the prominence of character features and pathological trends depend on external circumstance." (Schafer, 1954.)

Murray (1951) goes even further by pointing out that, "The patterns of the imagination (as revealed in projective tests) and the patterns of public conduct are more apt to be related by contrast than by conformity."

There are several examples in which the latent and the manifest levels of behavior are inversely related. Oral dependency needs may, for example, be conspicuously evident in the projective drawings. While such a finding may occur in an alcoholic subject who more or less acts out his oral dependency needs, it may also occur in the projective drawings of a striving business executive who is attempting to deny these needs in himself by proving quite the opposite in his behavior.

It is only by integrating the behavioral picture with the projective technique data that the full personality evaluation can de derived. When we view the frustrated oral needs evident in the drawings alongside of the driving, over-striving behavior in the business executive's overt behavior, it is the viewing of these two levels side-by-side which may allow for the speculative prediction of eventual ulcers, but we can not always predict from the presence of dependency needs on the projective drawings the overt form of these needs.

Homoerotic elements reflected in the drawings may be considered as another example. Whether the homosexual orientation, suggested by these draw-ings, results in inhibited heterosexuality, compensatory Don Juanism, or overt homosexual activities depends, in part, upon the interaction of the basic potential of the subject with the influences in his environment, the latter factors being generally outside the scope of those tapped by projective techniques.

To mention one more example, if the projective drawings suggest extreme aggressiveness, and the patient behaviorally assumes the role of a meek, docile, self-effacing and submissive individual, a *comparison* of the two levels of data may permit the valuable inference that this subject must suffer from the effects of suppression and/or repression of a significant amount of aggressive impulses. The mild exterior he presents, we may then deduce, is at the expense of creating considerable tensions within him.

Another handicap which interferes with clinicians' attempts to predict overt behavior exists in the fact that manifest behavior of any importance is invariably highly over-determined, the resultant of numerous interacting factors: identifi-cation figures, superego pressures, social and cultural settings, type and strength of defenses, traumatic experiences, and possibly constitutional predisposition would all have a great bearing on the ultimate overt pattern. (Schafer, 1954.) Often, we are able to infer the presence of a powerful trend, kneaded deeply into the personality, but cannot say which of several possible manifest forms it may assume. While it is true that at times the clinician can be impressively suc-cessful in predicting overt behavior, he cannot with confidence assume that he can consistently so interrelate the indicated factors as to predict, very specific-ally, the future behavior. The subject's resources and limitations with respect to adaptive, sublimatory activity, and achievement are often difficult to take into account. These factors tend to depend so much on situational support and threats, and on other external elements over which the subject frequently has little con-trol (and which themselves cannot be predicted).

The broadest common denominator, then, which interferes with prediction of future behavior and postdiction of genetic events is the operation of *multiple determinism,* both internal and external. Projective tests merely elicit feelings (and a small sample of behavior), and any conclusions derived from the projective test data are made predominantly by way of inference. Psychodynamic inference "is not something which is built into the tests, but enters the realm of general personality theory." (Korner, 1956.) Inferences from projective drawings, then, are not only bound by the extent of the clinician's knowledge of this clinical tool, but also by the limits of our present-day knowledge of psychodynamic principles.

Nevertheless, in spite of all of the above, in that which follows we will see that *clues* to acting out are at times available in projective drawings, to be picked up if one is sensitized to such subtleties.

To start, however, with the grosser and less subtle indications brought to eye-level in drawings, let us consider several instances of "acting out" *directly* on the drawing page itself.

Direct Acting out on Paper

An adolescent boy, referred to the writer because of excessive truancy, the flaunting of rules in school, and generally rebellious behavior, reflected his characteristic role in life in his drawing of a Person as presented in Figure 170. The drawn male is dressed in a soldier's outfit as a reflection of the subject's need for greater status and recognition as a male than he feels he possesses. The drawn Person turns his back on the world, much as the subject himself has done, and *introduces a regulation into the picture merely to break it.* His adding the sign, "No Spitting," just so that the drawn person may disobey it, clearly parallels the subject's seeking out rules and regulations merely to break them, to prove to himself and others that they do not apply to him, that he is outside the sphere that authority encompasses, that he is bigger and better than the rules and the people who make them.

For his drawing of a female, he offers us Figure 171, a female whose face is smeared and debased. He describes her as, "A young girl, flat as a board, trying out her new non-smear lipstick, and it smears." Here, again, we note that he directly acts out his anger on the drawn page, besmirching the figure's face in an aggressive laying on of the crayon. (We note, also, that he amputates one of her hands where it should attach to the arm.)

When we get to the Unpleasant-Concept-Test (the subject is asked to draw the most unpleasant thing he can think of) we note that he once again *acts out,* and this time all the more directly, his need to debase and vent his acute rage (see Fig. 172). Where subjects popularly offer the concept of war, disease, or death, this subject instead draws a man with a ludicrously elongated nose, a huge penis hanging out of his open pants, and then stabs him with a long sword running through his body. He then adds the tag, *Dad.*

In clinical practice, we may generally assume that a subject who acts out this violently on paper –and particularly when this acting out reaches such inappropriate extremes — would be prone also to act out the same needs to depreciate others, to search out rules and regulations to break, and to release

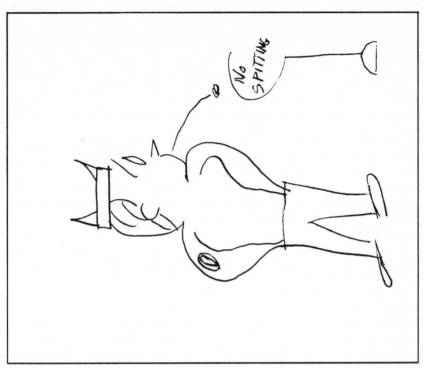

Fig. 170 (above)   Fig. 171 (below)

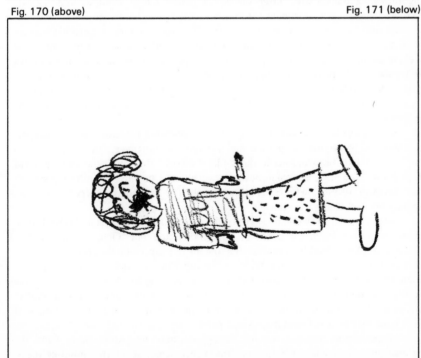

his accumulated anger at the immediate world around him.

Figure 173 represents another case of intense and multiple statements of a theme, mounting up to suggest the likelihood of this theme bubbling over into acting out. This figure was drawn by an adolescent boy who happened to be one of a group of subjects studied in an effort to get a normative population from a local high school.

The expansion of the shoulders into exaggerated, sharply-pointed, aggressive corners, the knife in the hand, the gun carried in the belt, the rough clothing and cap, the piercing eye, the sharp nose, and the mustache pulled down into a depiction of walrus tusks more than soft hair all add up to a reflection of an individual who is drastically motivated to prove himself aggressive, dangerous, and prone to violence. The fact that the feet are particularly out-sized and the shoes taken off suggests the primitiveness of his impulses, and that the subject appears to have shed considerations of social constraint and more sublimated behavior. When we add to this the fact that the entire figure seems to be pulled off balance by the aggressively pointed shoulder, we get a picture of an individual who suffers from a feeling of emotional instability which may quite easily be triggered into aggressive behavior.

After seeing so vocal a rendition of a compensatory and hostile theme, the writer consulted the school records and found that this youngster was indeed an actor-outer, having gotten into trouble for numerous fights in school, once having thrown a blackboard eraser through a closed school window, and recently having mugged a fellow student for money in the school bathroom.

To turn to an example provided in the drawing of a Tree, Figure 174 was offered by a 12-year-old boy who had been referred because he had been observed picking up baby pigs with the prongs of a pitchfork, throwing down baby chicks and crushing them under the heel of his shoe, and at one time setting fire to a bale of hay underneath a cow. On top of this, he had recently released a tractor to roll down a hill onto some children. (Fortunately, the children dodged the vehicle in time.)

His drawn Tree speaks as eloquently as does his behavior. It is a graphic communication, saying in distinct and unequivocal language: "Keep away from me!" Spear-like branches with thorn-like "leaves" decorate a sharply pointed Tree trunk. The branches reach out aggressively in a promise of inflicting significant harm to all those who come within reach. The drawing is steeped in sadism, aggression, and angry resentments.

Similarly, the drawing of a House in the House-Tree-Person (H-T-P) technique may also catch the clues to potential acting out. One 12-year-old boy (see Fig. 175) heralded his eventual running away from home by drawing a House in which a child was escaping through the top window, and a lower window as depicted slammed down on the mother's neck, pinning her there. In spite of the family's beginning to involve itself in therapy at that point, four months thereafter the youngster did actually run away from home, and it was not until a couple of days later that he was found asleep in a park.

At times the implications for acting out may be gotten more from the strained efforts at control than from the direct depiction of the impulses themselves. Figure 176 was offered by a 15-year-old youth who was brought to the

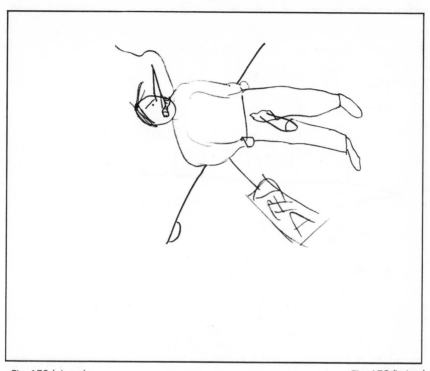

Fig. 172 (above)

Fig. 173 (below)

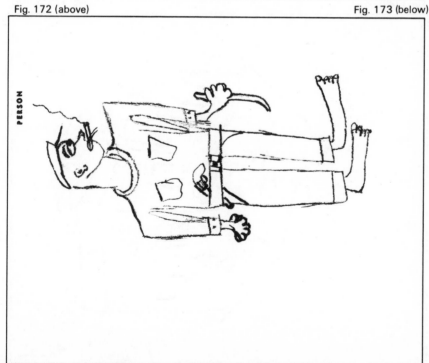

PERSON

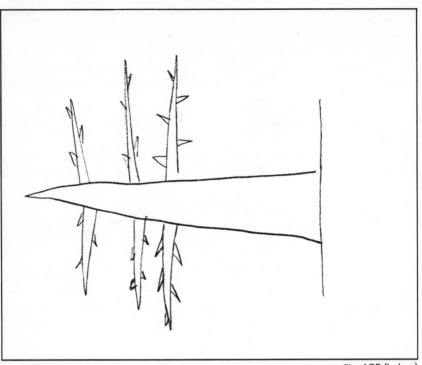

Fig. 174 (above)

Fig. 175 (below)

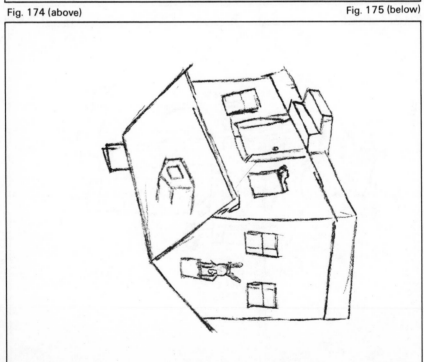

clinic because, according to his mother, he had threatened to kill her. The initial question which raised itself in our minds was of a differential diagnosis between vocalization on the part of an adolescent who merely wanted to get his mother off his back, and an actual homicidal potential.

The projective drawings administered at the time to the youngster provided rather vivid evidence on the side of the actual possibility of serious capacity for violence pressing forward in him. The strained facial expression, the exaggerated attempts to maintain control over bodily impulses, the head pulling tensely to the side with the eyes reflecting acute inner strain and efforts at control are all brought to focus by the hands presented almost as if to carry the suggestions of being manacled together to provide *external* controls against his lashing out in angry fury. To experience the actual kinesthetic feeling, the reader has only to reproduce the entire body position and twisted pull of the head on the neck along with the facial expression to feel in one's own musculature the struggle of control versus intense aggression within. Such a kinesthetic verification of the visual data may also convey a feeling of the almost vivid immediacy to this potential eruption.

The fact that his drawn Tree was presented as conspicuously off-balance adds all the more to the personality picture of a youngster whose felt equilibrium was very much in jeopardy and who was shaky in maintaining defenses against his volcanic violence within.

Following the emerging of this tension-flooded picture, the boy was referred to a mental hospital for more detailed observation. The impression of his therapist there later supported the implication that this was indeed a youngster who carried the active seeds of matricide.

The next case adds a second illustration of the principle that *over-emphasized control* in the drawings, provides the clues to potential acting out in overt behavior. Figure 177 was drawn by an exhibitionist. We see in the hand drawn as tucked-in under the belt which anchors it –and keeps it from moving to engage in forbidden acts (of exposing himself?) –the strong conflict of impulse versus control. When, however, external controls have to be resorted to (such as, in this instance, strapping the hand down), we may presume that internal controls are insufficient and the likelihood of acting out all the more probable. This is supported by the fact that while he draws the Person with hands pinned, at the same time the drawn Person does engage in the exhibitionism of the extremely long, phallic-shaped nose. The impulses circumvent the efforts at control.

At times, issues of life-and-death import themselves may be picked up by the projective drawings.[5] Figure 178 was drawn by a man suffering from an involutional depression. He drew the large figure first; then when he saw that he could not complete the entire figure on the page, he drew the smaller figure. He momentarily paused, looked at both figures, said that the larger figure lacked a collar, picked up the pencil he had laid down, and drew the "collar" by slashing the pencil across the throat of the drawn male. The writer got the eerie feeling that it was almost as if the patient were committing suicide on paper. Along with this, the patient offered a story to TAT Card 1 which consisted of the boy's

---

[5] As they were in the case of the youngster who suffered matricidal impulses.

picking up and smashing the violin. We recall Bellak's theory of the violin's representing the body image and here find consistency with the suicidal impulses acted out on the drawing page. The witnessing of this man slashing his drawn throat on paper was too vivid a demonstration to take lightly. Conferring with his psychiatrist resulted in the patient's being institutionalized. Some time later the patient actually made a suicidal attempt, but fortunately, owing to the protective surroundings of the institution, this was detected, and the bathrobe belt with which he attempted to hang himself was cut down in time.

In summary of this section, then, we may see in the cases presented that *the stronger, the more frank, the more raw and unsublimated the expression of impulses which break through in the projective drawings, the more the defensive and adaptive operations of the ego may be presumed to be insufficient in their assimilative function, and the more the likelihood of acting out may be taken to mount.*

Size

Of the variables employed by subjects to express their aggressive patterns, one of the most frequent ones is the handling of space on the paper. The drawing which is too large, which tends to press out against the page's edges, denotes a similar tendency to act out against the confines of the environment.

Figure 179 was drawn by a 28-year-old male. The most conspicuous aspect of the subject's drawing performance is the large size he gives the drawn male, causing it to crowd the drawing page at both top and bottom. Along with this, the firm line pressure, the overextended, broadened shoulders, and the stance (with the feet spread apart and the arms hanging away from the body, ready for action) all reinforce the impression one gets of someone who is trying "to prove himself." The subject cannot prove himself big enough in stature (that is, there is not room enough on the page to draw the person as large as he would wish it to be), nor generally impressive enough. The zoot-suit treatment, the stern, hard facial expression, and the almost ape-like, long arms that extend too far down the body length all emphasize the subject's attempt to prove himself on paper—to prove himself manly, active, deserving of status, and one not to be taken lightly. When we learn that the subject was examined because of a rape offense for which he had been convicted, we then see the close parallel of his trying to prove himself more manly than he actually feels, on paper as well as in real life.

Precker (1950), too, found that exaggerated size may be considered as evidence of aggressiveness or motor release. Zimmerman and Garfinkle (1942) as well found that lack of restraint in the size of drawings correlated with aggressiveness and a tendency toward the release of this aggressiveness into the environment.

Sequence

By analyzing drawing test data in terms of the sequential emergence of drive derivatives, defense, and adaptation, we may witness dynamic and economic shifts which at the same time lay bare structural features of the personality of the subject. By examining samples of ongoing drawing processes, we have an opportunity to study in slow motion, as it were, the structural features of conflict and defense.

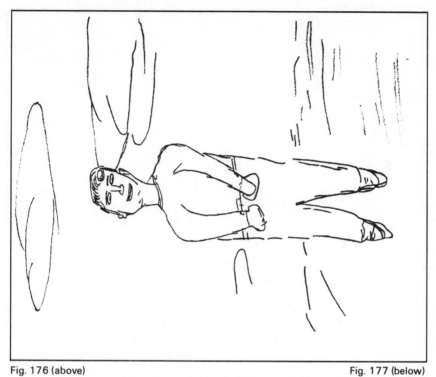

Fig. 176 (above)   Fig. 177 (below)

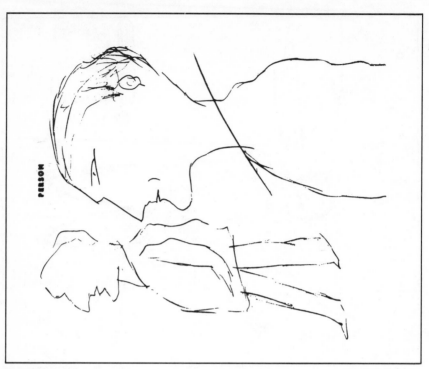

Fig. 178 (above)

Fig. 179 (below)

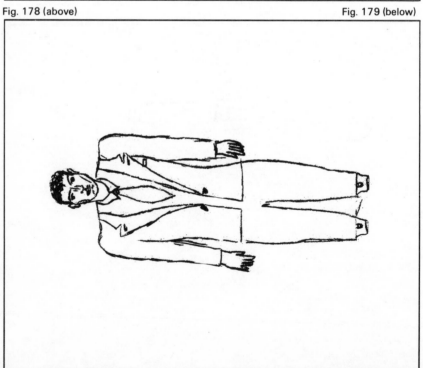

In the microcosm of the interaction between a subject and the drawing page we may, for example, see a subject give tiny shoulders to his drawn person, then erase them, and finally endow the drawn person with compensatory, overly-broad shoulders. Such a subject then looked at his drawing in a perplexing fashion as if some automatic phenomena had taken over, and he couldn't understand how this process got away from him. He commented, "I guess the shoulders expanded a little too much" as if *it* rather than he did it. From this we may postulate that the subject's first reaction to a new situation is one of inferiority feelings which he then quickly attempts to cover-up with a facade of capability and adequacy, which, however, he overdoes to the point of compensatory acting out which breaks away from him.

In a study of sex offenders sent to Sing-Sing prison, (Hammer, 1954) lack of ego-strength and inadequate control of impulses showed up as forming an important factor in the total picture. By this is meant the relative concept of a weak control mechanism for an approximately average amount of impulse strength, or else a control mechanism of about average strength, given the overwhelming task of keeping in check, pressures building up from excessive push. The majority of the sex offenders studied fell into the former category.

In fact, the vast majority of rapists and pedophiles studied had ego pictures of *rigid* control by weak control mechanisms, a control so inflexibly and tightly spread that it manifested a capacity for sporadic breakthrough of impulses. Only the incest group harbored a predominance of individuals in whom consistently *inadequate* control, as a result of a shattered ego, was the basic longstanding situation.

To illustrate the attempts at rigid control of the rapist and pedophile group, punctuated by short erupting interludes, the following excerpt from the psychological report on a rather representative case is cited:

> In reproducing the Bender-Gestalt figures, the subject started out by making them noticeably small, but ended with the last two figures growing excessively large; this would tend to reflect strong needs at constrictive control over emotional impulses which, however, cannot remain successful for a prolonged time without cracking and allowing an impulsive release of uncontrolled affect and/or behavior.

Conversely, defenses gaining dominance over impulses, and hence a contraindication to acting out are conveyed by the opposite sequence: for example, a male, 38 years of age, first drew a large, threatening female with feet placed in a broad stance and with face wearing a stern expression. She was clothed in a riding habit and carried a large whip in her hand. Following this depiction of a threatening, stern, and punitive female figure, the subject gazed at his drawing for a long time and then hesitantly reached for the next sheet of paper and drew a small, puny male who stood with shoulders dropped dejectedly, head bent, arms behind the back: all-in-all a most submissive, subjugated posture. The subject thus views females as menacing, and then attempts to placate them by assuming a passive, appeasing role.

Sequential analysis of the set of drawings may provide clues to the amount of drive or energy of the subject, and it may also provide data which allow an appraisal of the subject's control over this drive. Does the subject, for instance, break down under the emotionally-tinged associations that are presumably aroused by the different drawing concepts, or is he able to handle himself well in these spheres? Does energy maintain itself, peter out, or erupt? Progressive psychomotor decrease, as he proceeds from one drawing to the next in the set of projective drawings, suggests high fatiguability. Progressive psychomotor increase suggests excessive stimulability and potentials for acting out. A modulated, sustained energy level reflects more healthy personality integration.

Frequently subjects are somewhat disturbed initially, but soon become calm and work efficiently as they proceed from the first to the last drawing. This is presumably simply "situational anxiety," and is not indicative of anything more serious.

Pressure

Pressure of pencil on paper has been found, like size, to be an indication of the subject's energy level. (Hetherington, 1952; Kadis, 1950; Precker, 1950.) In regard to reliability, it was found by Hetherington that subjects are rather remarkably constant in their pressure.

Alschuler and Hattwick (1947) reported that children who drew with heavy strokes were usually more assertive and/or overtly aggressive than other children.

Consistent with this, Pfister, as reported in Anastasi and Foley, (1943) found that psychopaths, one of the most troublesome of the groups who act out, characteristically employ heavy pressure.

One youth, examined by the present writer at a reformatory, drew his House, Tree and Person with so fierce a digging at the paper that his pencil actually tore through the paper at various points along the line drawn. Several months later he stabbed a fellow inmate, in a dispute over a card game, with a "knife" he had fashioned from a spoon.

Stroke

Alschuler and Hattwick (1947) found that children who drew with long strokes stood out for their controlled behavior, whereas children who worked with short strokes showed more impulsive behavior.

Mira (1943) also writes, "In general, the length of movement of a stroke tends to increase in inhibited subjects and decrease in excitable ones."

Krout (1950) found that straight lines were associated with aggressive moods. Jagged lines (which incidentally appeared as the symbol of the most aggressive unit in Hitler's army) were associated with hostility, usually overt and acted out.

Detailing

Children or adults who have the feeling that the world around them is uncertain, unpredictable and/or dangerous tend to seek to defend themselves against inner or outer chaos by creating an excessively-detailed, rigidly ordered, highly structured world. The drawings of these subjects will be very exact. These people tend to create rigid, repetitious elements in their drawings. There is nothing flowing or relaxed in the lines, the drawings, or in their total presentation. Everything is put together by force, as though they feel that without this pressure everything would fall apart.

Too perfect a drawing performance, executed with unusual, exacting control and care, is offered by patients who range from obsessive-compulsive to incipient schizophrenics or early organics. But whatever the diagnosis, the "too-perfect" performance reflects the effort of these patients to hold themselves together against the threat of imminent disorganization. It is a direct manifestation of their hyper-vigilance, and implies the presence of a relatively weak ego, so afraid of acting out a breakthrough of forbidden impulses that it dares not relax its constant vigilance.

The most frequent emotional accompaniment of the excessive detailing of one's drawing is a feeling of rigidity. Stiffy drawn Trees or animals parallel the same quality in the drawn Person. In this regard, the latter may be presented as standing rigidly at attention, with body and head very erect, legs pressed closely together, and arms straight and held close to the body. The kinesthetic emphasis, in these projections, is on the erect posture and on the rigid tension with which the posture is held, keeping impulses in. These drawing performances often express a most unfree, and hence uncertain but rigidly-controlled defensive attitude. This is the characteristic drawing performance of people to whom spontaneous release of emotions is an acute threat. Impulses, when they are released, are not smoothly integrated, but tend toward the eruptive and uncontrolled.

Symmetry

Symmetry has long been regarded as one of the most elemental Gestalt principles. It is not surprising, therefore, that drawings which display an obvious lack of symmetry have been found to indicate equivalent feelings of personality imbalance, diminished integration, and hence increased chances of acting out.

Placement

In regard to placement on the horizontal axis of the page, Buck (1950) hypothesizes that the farther the mid-point of the drawing is to the right of the mid-point of the page, the more likely is the subject to exhibit stable, controlled behavior, to be willing to delay satisfaction of needs and drives, to prefer intellectual satisfactions to more emotional ones. Conversely, the further the mid-point of the drawing is to the left of the mid-point of the page, the greater is the likelihood that the subject tends to behave impulsively, to seek immediate, frank and emotional satisfaction of his needs and drives, and to act out. Koch (1952) independently, on the basis of his projective drawing work on the "Tree Test" in Switzerland, identifies the right side of the page with "inhibition," which is consistent with Buck's concept of emphasis on the right side of the page suggesting control. Wolff's finding that subjects who were attracted to the right side of the page in their drawings showed introversion, and those to the left side of the page extroversion, is also consistent with Buck's findings, in that introversion is associated with the capacity to delay satisfaction and extroversion the seeking of more immediate gratification.

Dissociation

Suggestions of dissociation, which are offered by incongruities between the graphic drawing and the verbal description of it (i.e., a clash between the two communication media) are perhaps the most pathognomonic of the clues to acting out tendencies.

This can best be conveyed by an example.

The patient, a 17-year-old white male, was referred to the clinic because he had been arrested for involvement in fights on the beach on several occasions and charged with felonious assault during racial riots. He had been transferred from high school to high school because of inability to relate to the Negro population in school, and hence was referred to the clinic with the idea of appraising his potential assaultiveness.

The essential problem for which we were asked to appraise this youth, namely his dangerousness, gains focus as we examine his performance as he moves through the projective drawing figures. He draws his first Person, a female, as an extremely puny figure, and then comments that it is "pretty skinny." He had left the top of the head out, and it now comes through that this was so that he could delay choosing whether to make it a male or a female. He decides to refer the question to the examiner and asks, "It doesn't matter, does it, whether I make it a male or a female, does it? . . . Which shall it be?" When this question was referred back to the patient, he elected to make it a female and added a curlicue of hair and earrings below. He then commented, "Holy Sweat, *it* looks like *it* went through the mill." Here, in addition to the feeling of debasement, we note that he chooses the neuter gender in which to refer to the figure.

The feelings of insufficiency, puniness, unimpressiveness, and confusion about psychosexual identification which come through in the first Person drawing are then handled in a passive-aggressive, compensatory maneuver in the following Person drawing (Fig. 180). He emphasizes the shoulder muscles and then opens the Person's mouth wide in a sort of savage roar, where facial muscles strain, the arms go out to intensify the energy he is expelling, and the teeth are bared. To add to the aggressive quality, he then makes the nose quite sharp. The demonstrative efforts to convey himself as angry, noteworthy, and certainly someone to be reckoned with are somewhat denied by the subtleties of the figure being empty, and thus without substance or the power he attempts to convey, and the fact that one arm appears as if grafted at the elbow. Thus we get an image which is essentially empty and attempts to play a role of aggressive savagery and anger.

In regard to the question concerning his potential aggressiveness, the important quality which comes through is not so much the aggressiveness of his character armor but rather the *dissociated* aspects of this aggression. This dissociated ingredient is discerned when he describes the drawn figure. When asked what the figure is doing, the subject commented, "just standing there." This comment cannot be dismissed as mere evasiveness, for the subject is frank, even vividly expressive, in his graphic communication. It is as if, rather, consciousness does not recognize the clearly angry quality which comes through around the edges of his awareness. When we then move on to a consideration of his drawn Tree, we find a sharp and somewhat unintegrated branch structure exists in among the foliage. This sharp, hostiley-pointed branch is not blended with the Tree but rather again appears to be a thing apart. Once more we get the feeling that aggressive qualities can be dissociated in him and surge outward,

Fig. 180 (above)

Fig. 181 (below)

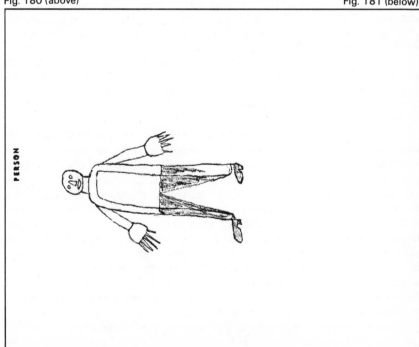

PERSON

away from his control. In summary, then, the uncertain quality conveyed in the first Person drawing gives way to the compensatory masculine posturing of the second. This posturing is re-enforced by anger to make it all the more impressive. But this rage is, in turn, handled by dissociation – unfortunately making it all the more dangerous and prone to be acted out.

Sometimes the clues to a state of dissociation of hostile impulses will come through within the drawing level alone, without involving a disharmony between the drawing and its verbal description. Figure 181, with its massive, highly-aggressive, and mechanical-like hands, attached as mere appendages at the end of the arms, illustrates this type of projection. The automation quality, particularly in the area of the aggressive urges, suggests that these impulses are acted-out automatically and without adequate integration with the personality proper.

Chromatic Drawings

Now for the last, and perhaps most dramatic, of the variables. The introduction of color to the projective drawing task, by asking for a new set of drawings, this time in crayon, adds an additional affective element. It has long been established that color symbolizes emotion. The many experiments establishing this are too numerous to mention singly. The most abbreviated sample will have to suffice. (Alschuler and Hattwick, 1947; Anastasi and Foley, 1943; Bieber and Herkimer, 1948; Buck, 1948; England, 1950;) Common parlance supports the experimental data. We speak of someone "red with rage," we associate "yellow" with cowardice and fear, "blue" as depression, "green" with envy, and refer to someone as "colorful" if he is in various ways freer in expressing unique personality ingredients and is generally at the opposite pole from the emotionally subdued or constricted personality.

Color stimulates people, as every fine arts painter or even advertising man well knows. Asking a patient to draw in crayon tends to supply an additional affective impact, and thus moves closer to sampling reactions to, and tolerance for, emotional situations – just those situations in which acting out, if it is to be released, is apt to be triggered.

Also, on the chromatic H-T-P the subject is in a somewhat more vulnerable state than he was when he produced his achromatic drawings. Even to the best adjusted subject, the achromatic H-T-P and the subsequent searching Post-Drawing-Interrogation are an emotional experience, for many memories, pleasant and unpleasant, are aroused, at the least. The chromatic series becomes a behavioral sample that is obtained with the subject at a level of frustration that is different from that which obtained when the achromatic series was sought. If the achromatic (as it frequently is for the well-adjusted subject) was a welcome catharsis, the subject may be far less tense than he was at the beginning. In the average clinical case seen for differential diagnosis, however, this will scarcely be the case. Such a subject will almost inevitably be emotionally aroused enough so that his chromatic series will reveal still more about his basic needs, mechanisms of defense, etc., than the achromatic.

In the achromatic series, the subject is afforded every opportunity to employ corrective measures: he may erase as much as he likes, and the pencil is a relatively refined drawing instrument. In the chromatic drawings, the only corrective

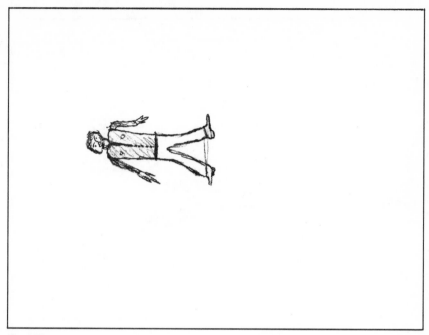

Fig. 182

measure available is concealment with heavy shading, and the drawing instrument, the crayon, is relatively crude.

Thus, at the beginning, with the subject in relatively fuller possession of his defensive mechanisms, he is given tools which permit expressive defensiveness; in the second phase, by which time the subject will be more likely to have lost at least part of his defensive control (if he is going to lose it all), he is provided with a grosser instrument, and with an opportunity to express symbolically (through his choice and use of color) the emotions, the controls, and lack of controls which have been aroused by the achromatic series and Post-Drawing Interrogation.

Thus, when aggression is *relatively* more mildly conveyed in the achromatic rendition, as in Figure 182, but is then presented by the subject in his chromatic expression (Figure 183)[6] in frank and unvarnished fashion, our experience has been that such subjects can more-or-less get by in ordinary relations but tend to erupt into violence in emotionally-charged situations.[7]

As we follow this particular subject from his achromatic to his chromatic Person drawing, we observe that the facial expression becomes more menacing,

---

[6] Illustrated in black and white.

[7] The patient had been charged with sexual assault, following a necking and petting session with a girl he had met at a dance and was now taking home. As he tried to advance to slipping his hand under her blouse, the girl objected; he, in an excited state, drew a knife and threatened her. The Probation Officer's report described the incident as follows: "He asked her to open her blouse, and she refused again. At this point the defendant ripped open her blouse with his hand. With the knife he cut her brassiere in the middle and fondled her breast. He made her bend down and he put his finger in her vagina. During the whole episode he made threats, and at one point banged the complainant's head against the side of the building. This knocked her down. He pulled her up, and wanted her to open his zipper." At this point the victim was able to break away and run to safety.

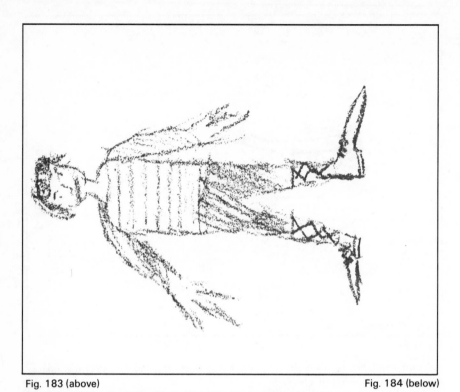

Fig. 183 (above)   Fig. 184 (below)

the hands now become so large that they are elongated, pointed, spear-like entities which fairly shriek "hostility." This time the shoes turn into a sort of Army boots affair which go up to almost the knees in conveying a feeling of brutality. All in all, the body-image gives way to the pressing forward of a chromatic depiction of a monster. His raw feelings of aggression and rage are similarly apt to come charging forward in emotional situations.

Before concluding, perhaps one more case should be added to those already shared with the reader. The clinician is, of course, just as interested in finding contra-indicating, as confirming, evidence for the question concerning whether a particular patient will act-out. This last case is that of a man who was referred for assessment concerning suicidal possibilities related to a depressive reaction he was clinically manifesting.

His bleak, stark, unadorned and barren achromatic Tree (Figure 184) is described as in a Winter setting, and the patient then calls the examiner's attention to a single snowflake he drew falling. The drawing mirrors the despondent, lonely and depressive condition the patient suffers.

When presented with crayons, however, he apparently reacts quite responsively to the affective stimuli, warms up and produces a flourishing, bountiful, well-nourished, alive and attractive Tree (Figure 185), colored in lively green and yellow, in amongst other trees, and youthful and well-sustained rather than at the end of its existence. Thus, on the deeper level tapped by the chromatic drawing, the throb of life is still quite full, and existence—both intra-psychically and in the world of others—attractive.

As we place the two Tree drawings side by side, we obtain the impression that the depressive feelings are not too pervasive or all inclusive. The fuller, more elaborated, and almost buoyant response on the chromatic rendition is a contraindication of that deep depression which harbors intense self-destructive, suicidal tendencies. The patient's subsequent movement in psychotherapy and his relatively rapid emergence from his depressive state provided eventual confirmation of this inference.

To step back from the empirical data for a broader view, we may note that the concept of the introduction of chromatic stimuli into the test battery, and the usefulness of this introduction in attempting to assess acting-out tendencies, have some precedence in theory and even some experimental support. Rorschach (1942), Schachtel (1943), and Rappaport, Gill & Schafer (1946) present the view that chromatic stimuli have different effects upon different groups of people. Shapiro's (1960) recent formulations provide a particularly noteworthy contribution to the theoretical framework for the understanding of the relationship between perception and color.

On the heels of these theoretical strides, experiments have followed. Colon (1965), in comparing different groups, found that impulsive subjects, in contrast to others, manifested the least capacity to delay responses when the stimuli were chromatic. Consistent with this, Siipola's study (1950) demonstrated that when color was added to the stimuli, it was the normal subjects who took more time to respond, reflecting their greater capacity for delay and appropriate choice of response. Stein (1949) found that the more direct responses to chromatic stimuli [color *(C)* and color-form *(CF)*] Rorschach responses were consistently as-

Fig. 185

sociated with shorter reaction times in comparison with the form-color *(FC)* responses. Thus, the less adaptive and less differentiated responses linked the more impulsive reaction to the chromatic impact.

Therefore, by introducing color into the H-T-P task, we may be more directly stimulating the very impulsive tendencies into expression—in those who are apt to be the more impulsive subjects—through which acting-out erupts.

A word of caution: the examples here were presented as illustrations only. In actual clinical practice, the dangers of basing interpretative deductions on isolated bits of data are obvious. In practice, confirmation of interpretative speculation on the basis of one drawing must be checked against not only the other drawings, but the entire projective battery, the case history, the clinical impression gleaned during the interview with the subject, and all other available information.

SUMMARY

Clues, but only *clues,* to the possibility of acting out may be reflected in projective drawings by strong, open, and unsublimated expression of impulses breaking through to flood the drawing page; by too large a size of the drawing so that it presses out against the page's edges as the subject himself will similarly tend to act out against the confines of the environment; by sequential movement from expression of controls to exaggerated expression of impulses (in contrast to the opposite sequence); by pressure and savage digging of the pencil at the paper; by stroke; by detailing, asymmetry, placement, evidence of dissociation, and by the triggering-off of the impulses in the chromatic expression.

As to the type of impulses apt to be released in the acted out behavior, this can be discerned in the content more than in the structure of the drawings, whether aggressive, exhibitionistic, suicidal, and so on.

The pencil or crayon stroke, at the moment of contact with the paper thus carries, in the words of the American artist Robert Henri, "the exact state of being of the subject at that time into the work, and there it is, to be seen and read, by those who can read such signs."

References

Abt, L., and Weissman, S (Eds.) *Acting Out*, N.Y., Grune & Stratton, 1965.

Alschuler, A., and Hattwick, W. *Painting and personality.* Chicago, Univ. Chicago Press, 1947.

Anastasi, A., and Foley, J. A survey of the literature on artistic behavior in the abnormal. *Psychol. Monographs*, 1940, *52*, 71.

_____, and Foley, J.P. An analysis of spontaneous artistic productions by the abnormal. *J. Gen. Psychol.,* 1943, *28*, 297-313.

Bellak, L. A study of limitations and "failures": Toward an ego psychology of projective techniques. *J. Proj. Tech.* 1954, *18*. 279-293.

Bieber, I., and Herkimer, J. Art in psychotherapy. *Amer. J. Psychiat.,* 1948, *104*, 627-631.

Brick, M. The mental hygiene value of children's art work. *Amer. J. Ortho.,* 1944, *14*, 136-146.

Buck, J. N. The H-T-P technique: A quantitative and qualitative scoring manual. *Clin, Psychol. Monogr.,* 1948, *5*, 1-120.

_____. House-Tree-Person (H-T-P) Manual Supplement. Beverly Hills, Calif., Western Psychological Services, 1950.

Colon, F., A Study of Response to Achromatic and Chromatic Stimuli, *J. Cons. Psychol.,* 1965, *29*, 571-576.

England, A. O. Color preference and employment in children's drawings. *J. Child Psychiat.,* 1952, *2*, 343-349.

Fox, R. Psychotherapeutics of alcoholism. In Bychowski, G. and Despert, J. L. (Eds.), *Specialized Techniques in Psychotherapy.* New York: Basic Books, 1952.

Hammer, E. F. The role of the H-T-P in the prognostic battery. *J. Clin. Psychol.,* 1953, *9*, 371-374.

_____. A comparison of H-T-P's of rapists and pedophiles. *J. Proj. Tech.,* 1954, *18*, 346-354.

_____. *The Clinical Application of Projective Drawings.* Springfield, Illinois: Charles C. Thomas, 1958.

Hetherington, R. The effects of E.C.T. on the drawings of depressed patients. *J. Ment. Sc.,* 1952, *98*, 450-453.

Kadis, A. Finger painting as a projective technique. In Abt, L. E., and Bellak, L. (Eds.). *Projective Psychology.* New York; Knopf, 1950.

Koch, C. *The Tree Test.* Berne: Hans Huber, 1952.

Korner, A. Limitations of projective techniques: Apparent and real. *J. Proj. Tech.,* 1956, *20,* 42-47.

Kris, E. *Psychoanalytic Explorations in Art.* New York: International Universities Press, 1952.

Krout, J. Symbol elaboration test. *Psychol. Mono. A.M.A.,* 1950, *4,* 404-405.

Landisberg, S. Personal Communication, March 1951.

——————— Relationship of Rorschach to the H-T-P. *J. Clin. Psychol.,* 1953, *9,* 179-183.

Lindberg, B. J. Experimental studies of colour and non-colour attitudes in school children and adults. *Acto. Psychiat. Neurol.,* 1938, *16.*

Machover, Karen. Human figure drawings of children. *J. Proj. Tech.,* 1953, *17,* 85-91.

Mira, E. *Psychiatry in War.* New York: Norton, 1943.

Murray, H. Uses of the Thematic Apperception Test. *Amer. J. Psychiatry,* 1951, *107,* 577-581.

Napoli, P. Fingerpainting and personality diagnosis. *Genet. Psychol. Monogr.,* 1946, *34,* 129-231.

Payne, J. J. Comments of the analysis of chromatic drawings. In Buck, J. N. The H-T-P techniques: A quantitative and qualitative scoring manual. *Clin. Psychol. Monogr.,* 1948, *5,* 1-120.

Precker, J. Painting and drawing in personality assessment: Summary. *J. Proj. Tech.,* 1950, *14,* 262-286.

Rapaport, D., Gill, J., & Schafer, R. *Diagnostic Psychological Testing.* Vol. 2, Chicago: Year Book, 1946.

Rorschach, H. *Psychodiagnostic: A diagnostic test based on perception.* Bern: Hans Huber, 1942.

Schachtel, E. G. On color and affect. *Psychiatry,* 1943, *6,* 393-409.

Schafer, R. *Psychoanalytic Interpretations in Rorschach Testing.* New York: Grune & Stratton, 1954.

Shapiro, D. A perceptual understanding of color response. In Maria A. Rickers-Ovsiankina (Ed.), *Rorschach Psychology.* New York: Wiley, 1960.

Siipola, Elsa M. The influence of color on reactions to inkblots. *Journal of Personality,* 1950, *18,* 358-382.

Stein, M. Personality factors involved in temporal development of Rorschach responses. *Journal of Projective Techniques,* 1949, *13,* 355-414.

Wolff, W. *The Personality of the Pre-school Child.* New York: Grune and Stratton, 1946.

Zimmerman, J., and Garfinkle, L. Preliminary study of the art productions of the adult psychotic. *Psychiat. Quart.,* 1942, *16,* 313-318.

The author received his B.S. from the City College of New York, 1945; his M.A. from the University of California, 1946; and his Ph.D. from New York University, 1960.

Dr. Jacks served as a clinical psychologist at the Attica State Prison from 1949 to 1952. From 1952 to 1955, he was associated with the New York Psychiatric Institute (as a Senior Research Scientist – Psychology) in a project dealing with a study of sex offenders at Sing Sing Prison. From 1955 to 1960, he was associated with the New York City Department of Correction (as Chief Psychologist during the first two years and Assistant Director of Rehabilitation for the next three). From 1960 to 1964, he was Assistant Professor of Psychology, at Temple University, Philadelphia, Pa. Currently he is Assistant Professor of Psychology and a Psychologist in the Division of Counseling at the Pennsylvania State University (Ogontz campus), Abington, Pennsylvania.

Chapter 13

The Clinical Application of the H-T-P in Criminological Settings

Irving Jacks, Ph.D.

Dr. Jacks deals at length in this scholarly, thoughtful and perceptive paper, with the ways in which the H-T-P can assist the psychologist in answering the three crucial questions inevitably asked him concerning the suspected or convicted criminal he has examined:

1. *Does this criminal's behavior represent an expression of psychopathology?*
2. *Is this behavior chronic or likely to become so?*
3. *Is it possible that this criminal will profit from rehabilitative or psychotherapeutic treatment?*

Dr. Jacks illustrates his discussion vividly by analyzing in depth the representative H-T-Ps of two specific cases of criminal behavior and also by searchingly comparing the H-T-P productions of various types of sex criminals. (Eds.)

Application of the House-Tree-Person test in the criminological context - in penal institutions and in court clinics - is by now a commonplace of clinical practice. The H-T-P (or some variant thereof, e.g. H-T-P-P) (Hammer, 1958) is widely accepted as part of the diagnostic battery used by clinicians in elucidating the personality and characterological dynamics of individuals involved in illegal behavior. On the one hand, it has been seen as enriching the insights derived from the traditional projective devices - which gain their advantage from a minimal degree of stimulus structuring - by requiring the subject to deal idiosyncratically with as unstructured a visual stimulus as you can get short of doodling - a blank sheet of paper and a mere concept, House, etc. Additionally, the H-T-P has been felt to possess a number of characteristics which make it especially valuable for use with offender populations. Among those which the present writer has found most attractive are: first, the uncomplicated administration – no awesome kit, no stop-watch, no long page of printed directions; second, the relative independence of cultural influences – the concepts involved are available to practically all patients, from the most impoverished backwater settlements to the most urbanized metropolis, throughout the range of human life past infancy, and at all levels of intellectual development. Not a single patient has been unable to produce *some* concept of a House, Tree, or Person during the fifteen years in which I have worked with this technique. (Which is not to say that in court and prison work, I have failed to encounter individuals who were reluctant, or who refused outright, to cooperate. Such instances, however, arose on other than conceptual grounds, in relation to the H-T-P *per se*).

Thirdly, I have been pleased with the economy of time expenditure in the actual administration of the technique. As most examiners working with delinquent populations will agree, the attention-span of this clientele is notoriously short. The fact that both the achromatic and chromatic forms can be administered to an individual in approximately forty-five minutes makes it suitable for use with this population. In institutional settings, where the unwieldy rule is large inmate populations and small treatment staffs, the time-saving may be further multiplied by administering the H-T-P in groups of up to twenty-five. To the purist, this may seem like a cavalier departure from prescribed technique. Certainly, I would feel happier if I could cite research either supporting the equivalence of group and individual administration, or at least supplying guides for interpreting in one or the other condition. Lacking such systematic support, I would submit the following: (a) The primary loss, from the standpoint of the clinician, is of the opportunity to observe his patient's informal approach to the task. This is a real loss, one I do my best to compensate for by a conscientious effort to observe and record the examinees' gestures and expressions while circulating through the group-testing room. With practice, an examiner-proctor will soon find that he can pick up a goodly number of the more obvious reactions of tension, irritation, concentration on task, etc. (b) It might be objected that group administration precludes a "post-drawing interrogation" (PDI). This objection is met in part by the use of a standard set of group-administered questions involving a minimum of verbal expression: 1) sex of each Person (M or F); 2) age of each Person; 3) age of Tree; 4) Tree dead or alive (D or A); and 5) season of year (W, Sp, S, F). Not only does this procedure give us some of the information of the longer "PDI", it conserves the desideratum of a *relatively* language-free testing situation.

Finally, it may be worthwhile to consider the utility of the H-T-P in comparison with the older, more traditional projective technique, the Rorschach. One of the key difficulties encountered in the administration of the latter in penological settings is the frequent brevity of protocols, stemming from the distrust of the inmate-client or defendant-client.[1] Thus, in reporting the

---

[1] In clinics attached to criminal courts, where examinees are undergoing adjudication, it is not unusual to find that they have been counseled by their attorneys to give minimal cooperation to the clinic examiners.

results of a large-scale study of sex-offenders incarcerated at Sing Sing Prison, the investigating team, of which the present writer was a member, felt constrained to comment, "Since the tests consist of unfamiliar, even esoteric-appearing material, the men tended to view them with distrust and suspicion. Some seemed to sense that by telling what they perceived in an ink-blot they might be revealing that which they preferred to keep hidden, from themselves as well as from the psychologist. Not being sophisticated in the psychological implications of the tests, and fearing that by responding too freely they might 'give themselves away', they tended to withhold responses, or restrict responses to the obvious, or to the essentially descriptive . . . Our records differ most notably from test records obtained with voluntary patients in their average length, as well as in a shift toward a barren quality of material. The modal record consisted of 10 to 14 Rorschach responses, with attempts at 'safe' or non-committal content predominating. (Glueck, 1956, p. 11.)[2] In the same study it may be noted, not a single subject failed to produce a productive set of H-T-P drawings.

Having noted some of the more general considerations favoring the utility of the H-T-P in the psychological evaluation of clientele encountered in legal settings, we turn our attention to the specific clinical parameters on which it may be expected to cast light. Hammer has published a concise report (1954a) covering the dimensions of personality elucidated by the technique. This will serve as a convenient framework around which we can develop the present discussion.

The clinical examination within the legal context tends to derive its focus from the stage of criminal processing at which it takes place. What this implies, in effect, is that the psychologist performing his examination in relation to the *trial process* – generally as the member of a court-affiliated clinic – will attend to elements in a defendant's response-pattern that will help elucidate the likelihood of his having committed the offense stated in the indictment. The question might be cast as follows: How high is the probability that the accused could have carried out the act of which he is charged? Let it be stated right here that any expectation that the figure-drawing will inform us of the actual *occurrence or non-occurrence* of an event is bound to lead to disappointment. Such an expectation is based on an incorrect understanding of criminal psychodynamics – one which neglects the fact that specific behavior is the resultant of forces which may be present in many individuals, of whom only a small number may become involved in antisocial behavior. Thus, it is not enough to know that some particular individual is powerfully motivated to aggress; more urgent, perhaps, is the manner in which his aggressive motivation is assimilated to both ego and super-ego functions, in attempting to assess the likelihood that he would commit the assault with which he is charged.[3]

[2] See also Landisberg, Selma, Relationship of the Rorschach to the H-T-P (1953).

[3] It will be well to recognize that the stage in the judicial process being considered at this point in our discussion – that is, prior to the legal determination of guilt or innocence – involves a rather significant legal implication. Thus, it behooves the ethical clinician to ascertain that the defendant is voluntarily submitting to psychological examination. If he is not, the clinician may be exposing himself to the charge that he collaborated in depriving the defendant of his constitutional safeguards against self-incrimination. Aside from any question of legal jeopardy, the psychologist who overlooks this consideration may find the validity of his report being vigorously challenged at the trial, thereby weak-

Can the H-T-P help us in evaluating the clinical contingencies in this overly simplified situation? Let us see. The hypothetical defendant is a seventeen-year-old boy charged with severely beating a middle-aged man, at about 2:00 A.M., and stealing the man's wallet. The boy and the man were unknown to each other, and each was unaccompanied at the time. Clearly our first question should be directed to the matter of aggressive potential: is the accused possessed of so much aggressive motivation as to make the charge plausible? Secondly, are his psychic controls such as to permit the direct acting-out of aggression in the circumstances described?

What elements shall we consider in gauging the level of aggressive potential? Let us summarize some of the signs which are widely recognized as pointing to externally-directed hostility and aggression in the H-T-P. They include: a) unrelieved enclosed areas of white space, (e.g., windows without panes, curtains, or shutters) "key-hole" Tree; b) two-dimensional branches resembling clubs, or sharply pointed branches or leaves; chimney excessively prominent, black smoke belching forth; c) mutilated or degraded House, Tree or Person; degrading details symbolizing aggressive hostility (e.g., an outhouse drawn beside a mansion, a garbage can on the front porch, a dog urinating against the Tree); d) the Person of the same sex as the subject depicted with sharply pointed appendages (e.g., fingers, toes, teeth); the Person of the same sex in explicitly aggressive posture or action (Hammer, 1954a, p. 50).

Prominent in the drawings of our hypothetical seventeen-year-old defendant is the fact that none of these signs was to be found in his achromatic figures. If anything his pencil drawings suggest a typically overcontrolled, fearful, and withdrawn individual—small in overall dimension, left of midpage, Tree trunk slender, male Person smaller than the female, neither Person involved in any identifiable activity, both Persons devoid of explicitly depicted hands and feet, and chimney barely visible over the roof of the House. The one element of his drawings contrasting with the overall effect of diminution is a surprisingly prominent sun with its rays practically touching the Treetop. The sun is the classical symbol of paternal authority: as Hammer puts it, "The drawing in of a large sun which dwarfs a House, Tree or Person indicates feelings of inadequacy in regard to authority figures and overconcern about the relationship with them. (Hammer, 1954a, p. 51). Interpretatively we may now form a preliminary hypothesis about our subject: He is probably a timid, passive, fearful boy who is not likely under normal circumstances to strike out aggressively against the environment. Paternal and, by extension, societal authority is perceived by him as intimidating, even almost overwhelming.

Can we safely conclude in our report to the court that the defendant most likely did not commit the assault with which he is charged? Fortunately, the H-T-P as it has evolved in practice affords us additional information at a somewhat deeper level than we have probed thus far. I refer here to the chromatic administration, e.g., having the subject produce a second set of House, Tree, and

---

ening his role as an expert. Most basic, however, in this writer's view, is the ethical obligation of the psychologist not to lend his expertise to any process which might be construed as abridging a defendant's right to a fair trial, including his right not to testify against himself either directly or indirectly.

Person drawings using crayons. There is reason to believe that the chromatic H-T-P succeeds in penetrating below the surface defenses of the subject's psychic structure, to reveal layers of motivation likely to gain overt expression only under conditions in which the ego defensive layers possess diminished strength, as, for example, in toxic states, under great fatigue, or under severe emotional stress. In *The Clinical Application of Projective Drawings,* Hammer (1958) states that the chromatic drawings "penetrate deeper beneath the patient's defenses and bring the more basic personality levels to view". He reports a series of illustrative cases, in which both achromatic and chromatic drawings are juxtaposed to demonstrate chromatic intensification of achromatic hints of underlying pathology, or of contrast between surface strength and underlying deficiencies.

Returning now to our hypothetical youth charged with assault, what possibilities present themselves as we scrutinize his chromatic H-T-P. Should they prove to be essentially duplicates of the achromatic set, we may feel greater confidence in our original hypothesis that this boy displays little propensity for the aggressive act with which he is charged. An alternative possibility was initially suggested by the symbolism of the sun which we noted in connection with his achromatic drawing of the Tree. Suppose that during the chromatic administration, he portrays the following: a) the Tree now practically fills the page, leaving room for just a bit of sun at the top, as if the sun were being forced out of the page by the now magnified Tree; b) the branches and/or trunk are pointed and outreaching; c) the red brick chimney extends beyond the roof of the house for a distance equal to the height of the House itself; and d) the male Person is an elderly man lying on the ground, weak and helpless. Can this be the same passive, timid boy described above? It is; but now he is telling us that the visible layer of passivity and timidity is the psychic cloak which he has developed to defend himself against the violent rage inspired in him by authority-figures, a rage to which he gives expression only when, after a few beers in a crowded taproom (where his being underage was ignored by the bartender) he again finds himself alone in the dark street. Now, however, the beer permits his anger at the original source of his fear and isolation – the older male – to well up, and he strikes at a plausible substitute, a middle-aged man on his way home. The taking of the wallet is almost incidental to the aggression, as if to make the aggressive act appear more rational in the boy's own eyes.

With our hypothetical, but not unrepresentative, case we have been able to illustrate an approach to employment of the achromatic and chromatic H-T-P in conjunction with one another, so that we are enabled to posit, and then test further, a preliminary clinical hunch regarding external behavior in an individual. Commonly, the role of the psychological examination, including the H-T-P, has tended to be most prominently involved at points, in the legal adjudication of defendants, subsequent to conviction. One of these points is the pre-sentencing phase. Having been found *guilty,* the defendant is referred by the judge for what has come to be known as "the pre-sentence investigation." One phase of this latter process involves a case study by the Probation Department. Thus the investigating probation officer may request a psychological evaluation, as a means of enlarging his understanding of the case material, in which case the psychological findings may be integrated into the overall case report. Alternatively, the Judge may refer the case directly to the court-affiliated psychologist, and obtain a clinical report to supplement the social work study submitted by the probation people.

What are some of the questions which the psychologist will be expected to answer at this stage?

1) Is the offense committed identifiable as an expression of underlying psychopathology? It does little good to respond here that all antisocial behavior represents pathology. As psychological examiners, we are being asked to assign relative weights to accidental factors, to sociologically-determined factors, and to individual psychological factors. More specifically, are the individual psychological factors of sufficient weight in themselves to have contributed significantly to the occurrence of the offense?

2) Accepting as valid the determination of guilt arising from the judicial procedure,[4] the court will desire information regarding the presumable chronicity of the behavior in question. Partly, of course, our answers will overlap with those given to the previous question, i.e., accidental factors, environmental influences. If individual psychological factors stand out prominently, our concern is likely to be with considerations such as type and strength of motivation, overall strength of controls, and specific areas of ego-defense lacunae, through which impulses might gain egress. The last is of major interest in determining chronicity and almost always refers to longstanding nuclear need-systems, and/or fixations. Examples would include: *sexuality* (e.g., nature of role identification and objects cathected); *hostility* (e.g., original sources and symbolic objects, as in the hypothetical example described above); *power* (related to participation in organized crime as well as social disturbance such as labor "goonism"); *dependency* (giving rise to legally defined "offenses" such as "habitual drunkard" or "narcotics addict"); *acquisitiveness* (important in the dynamics of habitual larceny patterns). It should be clear that the nuclear need-systems just referred to are by no means all possible ones, but are selected because of an impression of their relatively greater frequency. Moreover, they rarely exist in isolation; most often they conjoin to form configurations yielding particular behavior patterns. Thus, need-system "hostility" may be conjoined with need-system "sexuality" to yield sexual behavior in the form of rape. "Dependency" and "acquisitiveness" may be conjoined to yield burglary in the service of addiction; when hostility is prominent as well, we are quite likely to see robbery with violence (e.g., mugging) by the addicted individual.[5] "Sexuality" and "depen-

---

[4] Some clinicians may be inclined to question the necessary validity of the court's findings, as the writer has at times. Here, in our experience, the psychological evaluation can make a major contribution. While it should not be expected that a verdict of guilty will be overturned (assuming "due process"), the psychologist's findings regarding the potentiality for antisocial acting-out is likely to be given considerable weight by the sentencing Judge when it comes to final disposition — whether to incarcerate, length of sentence, type of institution, intensity and type of probation supervision, etc.

[5] It should be made explicit that we are not reiterating the popular myth of the "crazed dope fiend." Rather we are proposing that, since both hostility and dependency may exist side-by-side in the same individual — addiction serving the dependency need-system and violence the hostility need-system — they will at times join forces to produce behavior serving both systems simultaneously.

dency" may form a conjunction yielding pedophilia.

3) A third area on which the psychological examination is expected to shed light is that of the likelihood of recidivism. This problem may be posed in the following terms: Does this individual represent a continuing danger to society? From the psychological standpoint, we are asked to assess the individual's control over impulses, both in ego and superego terms. Having identified significant need-systems, our task now is to relate them to the strength and availability of psychic control mechanisms. It is a task which often enough is carried out with somewhat variable success. Perhaps one reason is that it depends on a rather broadly-based diagnostic approach, a distillation of information of varying depth and extent. Among other things, the psychologist must take into account the need-systems previously identified, the overall psychic compensation of the individual, the level of anxiety, the guilt mechanism present, the balance between superego (or socialization) forces and id energies, and the capacity of the ego to derive gratification from the environment.

4) Finally, the court will often wish to know whether the defendant shows a likelihood of benefitting from psychotherapy. The answer here largely depends on what the examination reveals of the individual's ego-strength, anxiety level, felt distress, and balance between id and superego forces.

Let us now see how the H-T-P can assist in answering the above four questions which we have specified as central to the court-related psychological evaluation. For each topic, in turn, we shall attempt to summarize relevant signs and, wherever possible, illustrate them by means of "guide-post definitions."[6]

A. Is the offense identifiable as an expression of underlying psychopathology? Our main task in this connection is to "rule out" psychotic (dis)organization. Among the more important clues to look for are evidences of disturbed reality contact, with the groundline a primary reality symbol, and the relation of the figures to the groundline symbolizing the quality of reality contact:

1) *House* lacking baseline; clear space between foundation line and groundline, so that the House appears to be hanging in air; roof only, walls absent.

2) *Tree,* with thin-line roots; roots resting some distance above the ground, or (a milder sign) upon the surface, rather than penetrating the ground.

3) *Person* drawn without feet – particularly where other appendages to the organism are depicted; milder indication includes space between feet and groundline (when not appropriate to the action as in running or jumping), and Person standing on tip-toe, or off-balance.

Other indices of decompensation, or diminished reality-contact include: distortions of perspective (transparency, double perspective), distortion of proportion (particularly outsized head in relation to figure's total size); inappropriate or inconsistent placement of details (windows at varying height from floor; arms coming out of head – except in young children; inconsistent move-

---

[6] The "guide-post definitions" are taken from a large body of psychological test data gathered at Sing Sing Prison, in examining over 200 inmates between June 1952 and June 1955. They are reported in fuller detail in Piotrowski, Hammer, and Jacks, *Psychological Worksheet* (in Glueck, 1956, pp. 329-401).

ment in opposite directions simultaneously).

Of particular importance in criminological diagnostics is the role of paranoid distortion, because of the readiness with which this condition may lead to assaultive acting-out. Paranoid individuals tend to reveal this class of reality distortion most frequently by means of presentation of the Person. Where the paranoid distortion encompasses a broad segment of the individual's apperception, he is likely to draw both Persons with their back turned to the viewer. Profile depictions and partial back-views are milder indices and should be checked against other details, such as view of the House and, particularly, overemphasis of sense organs. This last gains its significance from the fact that delusional individuals tend to stress, in their drawings, the sensory modalities through which their autisms are funnelled. Thus, the individual who is receiving auditory "messages" that his neighbor is sending deadly radioactive poisons via a hole secretly bored into the wall between their apartments, may feel thoroughly justified in attacking his neighbor in self-defense, and may reveal his special delusion by appending a large, carefully drawn, cocked ear to the head of his drawn Person.

Finally, as a mark of reality breakdown, we note what has been called the "schizophrenic Tree". This is a Tree, ". . . the trunk of which is actually two one-dimensional trunks because the side-lines of the Tree never meet at top or bottom . . . Such a drawing is as pathognomonic of schizophrenia as any single H-T-P sign can be said to be pathognomonic of anything. The drawing of such a split Tree is thought to symbolize the splitting of affect and intellect produced by the schizophrenic process." (Hammer, 1954a, p. 56) Here we are afforded insight into the strength of the subject's ego in holding in check primitive impulses rooted in the id. The absence of closure at either end of the Tree trunk – the trunk interpreted as a prime symbol of ego-strength – implies unsocialized and unmodulated access of such impulses to the environment, which is, of course, one essence of the schizophrenic process.

Thus far, we have dealt with indications of rather broad and pervasive personality disorganization. The wide-spread presence of the signs discussed above might, in many instances, be sufficient to warrant a recommendation to the court that the approach to the defendant might appropriately focus on the finding of mental illness and the treatment thereof, rather than – or at least, along with – the traditional penological disposition. Thus, where the H-T-P, in conjunction with other test and interview data, points to the existence of a clearcut psychosis, the psychologist would, on that basis alone, be justified in recommending commitment to a mental hospital, rather than to a prison. Where the findings point to somewhat less severe or less wide-spread disorganization, the report might include a recommendation for commitment to a penal institution having a treatment unit attached, where the defendant could be included in the therapy program.

As we narrow our consideration to more specific pathological patterns of which the offense may be expressive, we are confronted with the entire gamut of committable crime and, on the other hand, the full panoply of psychopathology. It would take us far beyond the compass of a single chapter to attempt such full-scope coverage. Instead, we have chosen to illustrate the application of the H-T-P by reference to a single class of criminal behavior, the sexual offenses.[7]

[7]In addition to the fact that the psychopathology of the sexual offense is *fairly*

The question involved is twofold: first, is the male sex-offender group differentiable from some control group of non-sex-offenders? Second, are there H-T-P signs which would help us to distinguish among the various types of male sex-offenders, e.g., between rapists and pedophiles? While the evidence on these questions is not yet definitive, findings to date are affirmative and suggest the following general rule-of-thumb. The further the sex *object* deviates from the culturally-prescribed one (i.e., an unrelated adult female), the greater is the likelihood of overall personality disorganization. A continuum of increasing deviation from socially-defined psychological normality exists roughly in the following order: non-sex-offender controls; rape and sexual assault; hebephilia[8] heterosexual; pedophilia heterosexual; hebephilia homosexual; pedophilia homosexual; incest with a prepubertal daughter.[9] Just how this works out in actual practice can be seen by the following table, based on the combined diagnostic impressions of the clinical psychologists working with the inmates in Sing Sing Prison.

TABLE XI

Personality Diagnosis [10,11]

	Total Sex Offenders	Non-Sex Offenders	Rape Sexual Assault	Hebe. Hetero.	Pedo. Hetero.	Hebe. Homo.	Pedo. Homo.	Incest
Normal (essentially)	– –	2	– –	– –	– –	– –	– –	– –
Character disorder	34	42	40	37	35	30	23	29
Neurotic	10	26	13	7	13	7	10	– –
Pseudoneurotic schizophrenia	24	32	20	43	28	43	33	47
Ambulatory or mild psychotic	29	28	33	33	35	37	37	35
Psychotic	8	2	10	7	10	10	3	6
Paranoid elements	32	14	37	30	33	27	30	29

clear-cut, and hence lends itself to didactic purposes, the writer has selected this group of offenses because of his active involvement for a number of years in a research project concerned with identifying the psychodynamic background of sex offenders committed to Sing Sing Prison in the State of New York (see footnote 6).

[8]Hebephilia is a classification used to define a sexual offense in which the sex object is post-pubertal, but under the age of sixteen. It was adopted by the staff of the Sing Sing sexual offender study in order to make explicit the conviction of the research team that there is a heuristic gain in differentiating between sexual concourse with a prepubertal child and a postpubertal adolescent.

[9]Obviously this is not an exhaustive catalog of sexual offenses. Rather it represents the categories available for the Sing Sing study. In a sense we are sacrificing exhaustiveness in favor of documentable generalization.

[10]Adapted from Piotrowski, Hammer and Jacks (1956, p. 400).

[11]All figures represent percentages of respective offense categories. Since many of the subjects fell into multiple diagnostic categories, the total for each column exceeds 100 percent.

The table offers support for the generalization that the total sex-offender group tends to be more severely disturbed than does the control group of non-sex-offenders. The overall trend across the subgroup of sex offenders, moreover, is consistent with the rule-of-thumb given above–with enough reversals, however, to warrant caution in regard to uncritical application of the rule.

Having sketched in the general background, let us see how the H-T-P can be employed in delineating specific psychodynamics among sexual offenders. In a series of research reports entitled "A Comparison of H-T-Ps of Rapists and Pedophiles," Hammer (1954b, 1955) found support for the following generalizations, resulting from the H-T-P Post-Drawing Interrogation:

1) Pedophiles attributed a significantly more immature age to their drawn Tree than did the rapists.

2) Both rapists and pedophiles tended to ascribe greater age to their female Persons than to their drawn male Persons; only for the pedophiles was the difference statistically significant.

3) The tendency to describe the Tree as "dead" in response to Post-Drawing Interrogation occurred on an ascending continuum from rapists through heterosexual pedophiles to homosexual pedophiles, with the difference between the first and third groups reaching statistical significance at the 5 percent level of confidence.

4) Homosexual pedophiles tended with somewhat greater frequency than either rapists or heterosexual pedophiles to draw the female Person before drawing the Male Person. In the relevant report, Hammer (1954c), responding to the failure to achieve a statistically significant difference among his groups– largely as a result of insufficient N's–underplays the observation that homosexual pedophiles had twice the incidence of females drawn first than either of the other two groups (25 percent, as against 12.9 percent and 12.1 percent, respectively).[12]

5) Sex-offenders, as a group, depict in their drawing an unusually high incidence of damage to various elongated appendages to their drawings: "Chimney, tree branches, arms, noses, legs, feet, hands and ties are portrayed as damaged, cut-through, broken or withered. Occasionally, and this is more frequent in the rapists, underlying feelings of phallic inadequacy are cloaked beneath compensatory elongation and emphasis of nose, feet, chimney, and so on, in the projective drawings." (Hammer & Glueck, 1955)[13]

A prime implication in this series of reports is the existence of a progressive increase in psychosexual deviation from normative identification levels, as one moves from the rapists through heterosexual pedophiles to the homosexual pedophiles. The findings are supportive of the continuum-concept suggested above, rather than of a clear-cut qualitative differentiation among the various types of sexual offenses committed by males.

Additional interpretative refinements suggested by Hammer's findings are

---

[12] See, in this connection, the study of Bieliauskas, V. J., "Sexual identification in children's drawings of the human figure" (1960).

[13] See also Hammer, E. F., "An investigation of sexual symbolism: a study of H-T-Ps of eugenically sterilized subjects" (1953).

the following: a) The age of the sexual object in the offense-pattern is largely a function of the psychosocial maturity level of the offender. b) The overall sense of inner weakness, even inner deadness, is in direct relation to the distance of the sexual object from social-acceptability, hence the greatest tendency of homosexual pedophiles to describe the Tree as "dead", followed – with diminishing frequency – by heterosexual pedophiles and rapists. c) The offender's sex-role identification, as reflected in the sex of his sex object, tends to be projected onto the H-T-P by means of the sex of the first figure drawn.[14]

B. Is the offending behavior of a chronic nature? Obviously this is a question likely to be asked primarily in instances where the conviction is the first one for the behavior in question. This is not so rare as it may seem. It happens not infrequently that an individual, once apprehended for illegal behavior, becomes subject to the suspicion that the behavior has been going on undetected for a long time before. Like it or not, such suspicion may make the difference between, say, a long term in prison or freedom under probation supervision. Let us consider the case of an individual convicted of petty larceny burglary, in a residential neighborhood where there has been a series of unsolved crimes of a similar nature. Can the H-T-P cast light on the probability that they have been committed by our subject? The answer is a qualified "yes," the essential qualification being that psychological plausibility does not imply positive identification.[15] The establishment of plausibility involves three steps: first, a behavioral description of *modus operandi;* second, translating the specific behaviors into broader hypotheses of psychological expression; and third, a knowledge of H-T-P symbolism related to the hypothesized psychological classification. Let us apply this approach to our convicted petty larceny burglar. His *modus operandi* has been described in the court record as an unaccompanied daytime entry through a backyard fire-escape window into the apartment of a middle-aged working widow living alone. His "take" consisted of cash kept by his victim in a closet shelf underneath her bed-linens; a jewel-box in a dresser drawer, whose contents were worth far more than the cash, was left untouched. With minor variations, this fitted the description of a series of burglaries in the same neighborhood over the past several years, particularly in regard to the victim and the proceeds. Psychologically, several hypotheses present themselves: a) the solitary nature of the offense suggests a socially isolated individual; b) the type of offense – burglary – might imply extractiveness within a passive or nonviolent personality configuration (as distinguished, for example, from the armed robber); c) the emphasis on the petty cash, rather than on more valuable loot easily obtainable, suggests an individual of somewhat diminished self-concept and limited aspiration-level (one who sees himself as only worthy of "petty" re-

---

[14] This is an area of some controversy, since the culture exerts an influence on individuals – whether heterosexual or homophilic – to depict the first drawn Person as of the same sex as oneself. Perhaps a safer statement would be that depiction by male subjects of the first Person as female is probably pathognomonic of homophilia, whereas the reverse situation contains a high incidence of false negatives.

[15] The situation is somewhat analogous to that which pertains to paternity tests based on blood-typing, where it is possible to rule out paternity where blood types of the adult male and the child are different, but where congruence of blood types is inconclusive of consanguinity.

wards); d) the selection of the middle-aged widow as a victim may be interpreted as a disguised expression of an oedipal nuclear need-system in conjunction with need-systems of dependency and hostility (see discussion above);
e) the fact that the crime was committed at all will lead us to search for superego lacunae. Before turning to a description of the specific H-T-P indications
which will assist in determining the tenability of our hypotheses, a word of
caution is in order; inasmuch as our interest is in possible chronicity of behavior,
we should not be satisfied by the presence of one or even several indications;
*temporal frequency of occurrence of behavior should be roughly paralleled by
frequency of occurrence of pertinent H-T-P symbolism across the sets of drawings.*

If our hypothesis of a socially-withdrawn individual is to be supported by
the H-T-P, what are some of the indicators to be sought in the drawings? The
first set of indicators which H-T-P workers are likely to consider has to do with
placement of the drawings in relation to the respective average midpoint on
the horizontal axis of the form page. In general, the interpretative rule states that
the farther to the left the figure, the greater the degree of social withdrawal. As a
corollary, the situational range of withdrawal is reflected in the number of figures tending to the left side of the page. Another group of signs fall under the
overall rubric of "accessibility." This is inferred on the basis of orificial and
boundary-line symbolism. Thus, the socially accessible individual will draw open
windows and wide access paths, will emphasize the branches of the Tree (often
outreaching), will draw the Person(s) in full-face and to the right-center of the
sheet, and will sketch the periphery of the figures with a light, relaxed hand.
The individual who is inclined to withdraw from social contact and make himself inaccessible to others is said to symbolize these trends in the following
ways: left-sided placement on the page; Persons facing to the left; omission or
diminution of environmental access symbols (doors, windows, steps, sense
organs, leaves, etc.); depiction of figures in middle or far distance.

The second leg of our "quintipedal" reconstruction of the convicted individual involves a hypothesis of nonviolent extractiveness. If our conjecture is to
gain in probability, what are the H-T-P indicators we are most likely to encounter? The House with a well or water-pump beside it; Person(s) with mouth(s)
open, or hand outstretched—these are prime symbols of extractiveness. The nonviolent aspect is derived by inference from the absence or relative insignificance
of aggressive projections.

The third element we posit involves diminished self-concept and limited
aspirations. Primarily, we depend here on the H-T-P indicators of the self-
concept of adequacy—size (the smaller the figures, the less adequate the self-
concept); treatment of phallic symbols (chimneys, branches, bodily appendages); intactness of ego-symbols (tree trunk; torso).[16]

Fourthly, we wish to test the hypothesis of passive-aggressive oedipal significance of the choice of victim—a middle-aged widow. Following the psychoanalytic model, the perception of self in relation to maternal figures is
frequently projected by means of oral depiction—oral dependency in the form
of open mouth and open windows, oral sadism with emphasis on teeth. Again,

---

[16] For a more detailed listing of examples of H-T-P signs of adequacy, see Piotrowski, Hammer, and Jacks (1956, pp. 363-366; 369, 371-373, 397).

a lack of oedipal resolution may at times be seen in the subject's confusion of sexual and maternal characteristics in the drawing of the female Person, as conveyed by the age attributed to the Person, in relation to the physical characteristics depicted (e.g., youthful, seductive female described as "50 years old"). Other signs include the Tree bearing fruit, and preoccupation with, or over-emphasis of, breasts on the female Person. Related to the latter in somewhat symbolic fashion is the drawing of the groundline as swelling up in breast-like fashion on either side of the House, Tree, or Person.

Lastly we turn to a consideration of superego development – this in order to gauge the probability that the subject is capable of repeated acts of an illegal nature. The H-T-P makes its contribution here largely by affording some insight into the subject's control resources. Thus, the individual with weak control of his impulses may have his figures leaning noticeably to the left, may enclose his figures within vague peripheral lines, may draw with quick impulsive lines, may show the Tree with open-ended branches, may draw his figures off balance, or may draw his Person(s) with the arms having reversed taper (that is, broader at the wrist than at the elbow). The individual with unusually rigid control is likely to be characterized by a meticulous and over-neat approach, may take a long time getting started on his drawing, may become irritatingly involved with minor drawing details, and is prone to depict Persons in rigid postures, arms stiffly at sides. Some subjects employ the symbolism of a large, low-hanging sun to reveal the intensity of superego forces having their origin in paternal authority.

The final hypothesis, the presence of superego lacunae, overlaps so extensively with our next topic – the likelihood of recidivism – that for the sake of brevity, we shall omit specific consideration of it here. Hopefully the reader will have little trouble in bridging the gap between the two sections.

C. The third area for which the court-requested psychological examination may be expected to supply guidance is that of the likelihood of recidivism. As was suggested earlier, this is a complex area and one handled with considerable variability of success. Unfortunately there have been few reports relating the H-T-P to subsequent repetition of illegal behavior. We shall, therefore, be drawing upon our clinical experience to build up hypothetical H-T-P patterns of probable recidivism. Obviously the recidivistic prediction will depend, to large measure, on the inference of chronicity drawn in accordance with the discussion just concluded. There is no better prediction of future behavior than that based on the individual's behavior in the past.

Perhaps the outstanding psychological consideration, following chronicity, is the presence of guilt-feelings, dependent, in turn, on superego, or socialization. Socialization is projected in the drawings along a continuum of conformity-deviation (relative to the cultural norm) of the content – as distinguished from the form-level. A House depicted in ultramodern or futuristic form, the Tree described as growing in the Antarctic or on another planet, Person(s) in unusual shapes or settings (e.g., Buck Rogers, seminude Miss America, A Martian) – all are examples of the type of drawings produced by convicted individuals of limited socialization (and with normal intelligence or better), typically sociopathic in orientation.

The use of projection as a major defense against anxiety will increase the likelihood of future acting-out. Along with the H-T-P indicators of paranoid distortion noted above — especially sense-organ emphasis — important clues are obtained by means of the Post-Drawing Interrogation. A striking example of this was obtained by the writer when he asked a chronic homosexual pedophile, shortly after commitment to Sing Sing Prison, what he considered to be the worst thing about his drawn male Person. The reply was: "Bad habits . . . filthy thoughts . . . meet a boy on the street, like to do some sex with him" (Piotrowski, Hammer, Jacks, 1956, p. 394).

In modern Western society, a significant ingredient in successful socialization is acquiring the ability to postpone gratification. The H-T-P provides the clinician with a number of signs which may assist him in gauging his subject's tolerance for such delay of, or on the other hand tendencies toward immediate gratification of, impulses. The impulse-control signs considered earlier are of obvious pertinence here. Additionally, we make the psychological inference that the individual who has acquired the capacity to delay overt gratification must have learned to obtain at least partial gratification in phantasy. Where socialization training has been overly-restrictive — leading to a perpetually-punishing superego function — we postulate that phantasy-gratification comes, in time, to supersede almost completely any active effort to derive pleasure from the environment. It follows from this that key H-T-P indicators of superego emphasis would be indicators of phantasy-gratification and introversion-extroversion. The H-T-P signs of phantasy-gratification tendencies are centered in depictions and symbolizations of head. Examples include: treatment of the House roof (relative size and emphasis); Treetop running over the top of the sheet; size of head, particularly forehead — all are directly related to the amount of gratification sought through phantasy (Piotrowski, Hammer, Jacks, p. 398). Conversely, underemphasis of roof, Treetop, and head suggest lesser capacity for phantasy-gratification, hence heightened probability of impulsive acting-out behavior.

The introversion-extroversion continuum is seen as correlative with the variable of phantasy-gratification. Hence, the H-T-P signs thereof serve either to strengthen or to diminish our clinical inferences regarding impulsivity. The introversive individual is likely to be the same as the one who gains gratification via his phantasy, rather than through interacting with the environment. The extreme extroversive type, on the other hand, expresses his gratification-needs in the form of "manicness" and/or impulsivity. H-T-P signs of introversion include the following: figures placed, or leaning, to the left; eyes closed; open-ended branches; use of subdued or dark colors in the chromatic set; double perspective; end of House truncated; emphasis on vertical planes; nude Person(s). Among the more frequent signs of extroversion are right-sided placement or leaning; Person(s) in attitudes of interaction (smiling, shaking hands, talking); light or lively colors; emphasized horizontal planes.

D. The fourth question which the court is likely to put to the psychological examiner has to do with the defendant's capacity to profit from some form of psychotherapeutic intervention. Again, the lack of adequate research will cause

us to lean heavily on our experience as H-T-P clinicians, and on our overall understanding of the dynamics of psychotherapy. Thus, we make the assumption
that therapeutic accessibility entails (among others) the following variables:
severity of symptoms; diagnosis; level of intelligence; motivation; and ego-
strength, including methods of handling stress, ability to gratify vital needs, and
level of social maturity. A number of these variables have been dealt with under
other headings at various points throughout this chapter. We shall, therefore,
address the burden of our remaining remarks to those elements of treatment
accessibility not hitherto considered.

1) *Severity of symptoms.* See sections on chronicity and recidivism.

2) *Diagnosis.* See section on "underlying psychopathology." In addition to
instances of psychosis, the prospects of successful therapeutic outcome are, of
course, dimmer in cases where signs of sociopathy (see earlier section on superego and socialization) or organic brain damage are prominent in the H-T-P.
Hammer has supplied a description of the more common H-T-P organicity indicators, which may be summarized in the following: preoccupation with symmetry and balance; blue-print drawing of the House; separation or segmentalization of parts; primitive, oversimplified, unidimensional figures; dangling Tree
roots; Person so rigid as to resemble an automaton; quality of the drawing of the
Person markedly inferior to the quality of the Tree; very primitive wholes, with
one or more essential detail omitted; perseveration of content; excessive pressure, along with poor union of lines; excessive amount of time required to complete the drawings; verbal expressions of impotency (Hammer, 1954a).

3) *Level of intelligence.* This entails an essentially global judgment by the
examiner giving particular attention to such elements as: correct placement of
parts; correct proportions; sophisticated (and nonautistic) elaborations and
adornments; and so forth. Buck has described the employment of the H-T-P in
the evaluation of intelligence in considerable detail, and the reader would be
well advised to consult the relevant sources (especially Buck, 1946, 1948, 1950).

4) *Motivation.* The H-T-P can be most helpful by revealing processes which
are directly or indirectly related to the motivation to change. The most significant of these is evidence of psychic pain – i.e., anxiety. Anxiety at the conscious
level is frequently expressed by the profuse drawing of shadows, as cast by the
House, Tree or Person(s). Here, the suggestion is of a situationally-related
response (possibly due to the fact of being "in the toils"), hence is less positively
associated with real motivation to change. More significant indicators of true
treatment motivation are: the introduction of clouds; faint hesitant lines; frequent erasures and corrections; excessive shading (the more dark and diffuse
the shading, the more intense the anxiety). The tendency to absence of anxiety is
seen in such things as: multicolor use; rapid reaction- and response-time; and,
especially, in uncritical satisfaction with inadequate drawings.

5) *Ego strength.* For many clinical workers, ego-strength is almost synony-
mous with cognitive processes; to them, our treating intelligence separately will
appear highly arbitrary. While we are quite prepared to concede the validity of
this position, we have chosen to follow our own clinical practice of treating
intellectual level apart from ego-strength.[17]

[17] We find warrant for this in Wolberg (1954).

Initial evaluation of the H-T-P picture of ego-strength is a global one from the overall impression of elaborateness as opposed to barrenness in the use of details. The quantity and diversity of drawn details reflect the breadth of inner resources available to the individual in coping with, and deriving gratification from the environment – the number of arrows in his quiver. Another relatively broad index with similar psychological significance is the balance between phantasy-gratification and active interaction with the environment. Lopsidedness in either direction implies weakness of ego-resources. A third broad index of ego-strength is derived from the diversity of mechanisms (as projected onto the drawings) available to defend against anxiety; in general, the wider the range, the stronger the ego's coping power.[18]

The specific H-T-P symbol, *par excellence,* of ego-strength, is the trunk of the Tree. Its diameter, height, and sweep are said to mirror the individual's subjective sense of his power to gain mastery over his environment. Somewhat the same significance attaches to the drawing of a Person's torso, although the treatment of the head – as the seat of cognition – must be considered as well, especially insofar as one recognizes the therapeutic interaction as dependent on both affective and intellective processes.

Finally, we note that the H-T-P can afford insight into a quality of ego function important to therapeutic success, one which has been termed "adaptability." To cite Hammer once again, "The degree of flexibility of branches, their number, size, and the extent of their interrelationship indicate the adaptability of the personality in general and of the gratification-seeking resources in particular. The integration of the branch structure is a reflection of the degree of integration of the ego with the environment . . . The Person drawn as walking along easily or playing and relaxed implies good adjustment and is found in the drawings of adaptive, spontaneous people. The position of the arms in a relaxed, flexible position, bespeaks good adjustment and adaptability." (Hammer, 1954a, p. 47)

The final component of ego-strength which we shall consider is that of psychosocial maturity. This is a component whose H-T-P manifestations have received direct research support, undoubtedly because subjects tend to project their maturity level fairly overtly into their drawings. Thus, we have seen previously that sex-offenders ascribe ages to the Tree and Person(s) which are correlative with the ages of their victims, and – reaching out to someone on their own developmental level – hence with their own age. (Hammer, 1954b).

As a rough guide to interpretation, the writer and his colleagues in the Sing Sing Prison classified individuals into psychosocial levels of "mature," "adolescent," "childish," and "infantile." (Piotrowski, Hammer, Jacks, 1956, p. 363). These were judged on the basis of age ascribed to the Tree and to the Person(s), as follows: 1) "Mature (adult) Persons and Trees"; 2) "Person or Tree 14-19 years old"; 3) "Child or Tree between 4 and 13"; 4) "Child or Tree below 4 years of age." Occasional uncertainty arises when there is a discrepancy between the physical attributes of the drawing and the numerical ascription of age. Having ruled out intellectual deficiency as the basis for the discrepancy, the safest

---

[18] See Piotrowski, Hammer, Jacks (1956, pp. 394-395) for a listing of H-T-P signs relating to various anxiety-defensive processes.

inference is that the drawing itself comes closer to the *felt* level of maturity, while the numerical ascription represents a conscious effort to satisfy social expectations. In analogous fashion, discrepancies between chromatic and achromatic projections of psychosocial maturity—whether graphic or numerical—may be interpreted in terms of depth: the chromatic depiction reflecting the underlying feelings, the achromatic the more superficial level of self-concept of maturity.

Additional corroboration of the inferred level of psychological maturity may be sought in the H-T-P signs of orality and sexual orientation to parental figures (see discussion above *re* oedipal involvement). (Piotrowski, Hammer, Jacks, p. 363).

SUMMARY

Drawing upon our own background of clinical experience and research with the H-T-P, as well as on the available research findings—particularly the work of Hammer; of Piotrowski, Hammer, and Jacks; and of Buck—we have attempted to show how the H-T-P can be utilized in the criminological setting. First, we considered in a general way the advantages of the H-T-P. Second, we noted several specific points in the criminal adjudication process at which the psychologist might employ the H-T-P. We reviewed the questions likely to be put to the psychological examiner in the criminological setting, and set out in detail the interpretative principles and signs whereby the H-T-P might be employed to obtain the answers to these questions.

Hopefully, when some other clinician comes to write a similar chapter some years hence, he will find it less necessary to depend predominantly upon his own empirical experience with the H-T-P, and will find that he can document his assertions with the abundance of research findings which the area of H-T-P application warrants.

References

Bieliauskas, V. J. Sexual identification in children's drawings of the human figure. *Journal of Clinical Psychology,* 1960, *16,* 42-44.

Buck, J. N. The H-T-P, a measure of adult intelligence and a projective device. *Virginia Mental Hygiene Survey,* 1946, *9,* 3-5.

_____. The H-T-P technique: a qualitative and quantitative manual. *Journal of Clinical Psychology,* Monograph Supplement No. 5, 1948.

_____. The use of the H-T-P in differential diagnosis in mental deficiency. Paper read at annual convention of American Psychological Association, September, 1950, State College, Pennsylvania.

Glueck, B. C. *Final report—research project for the study and treatment of persons convicted of crimes involving sexual aberrations.* Albany, State of New York Department of Mental Hygiene, 1956.

Hammer, E. F. An investigation of sexual symbolism: a study of H-T-P's of eugenically sterilized subjects. *Journal of Projective Techniques,* 1953, *17,* 401-413.

_____. Guide for qualitative research with the H-T-P. *Journal of Genetic Psychology,* 1954a, *51,* 41-60.

_____. A comparison of H-T-P's of rapists and pedophiles: I. Age ascribed to drawn Tree as an index of psychosexual maturity. II. Age ascribed to drawn Persons. *Journal of Projective Techniques,* 1954b, *18,* 346-354.

_____. Relationship between the diagnosis of psychosexual pathology and the sex of the first drawn person. *Journal of Clinical Psychology,* 1954c, *10,* 168-170.

_____. The "dead" Tree as an index of psychopathology. *Journal of Clinical Psychology,* 1955, *11,* 67-69.

_____. The projective drawing battery: a case illustration. In Hammer, E. F. *The Clinical Application of Projective Drawings.* Springfield, Illinois: C. C. Thomas, Publisher, 1958.

_____. & Glueck, B. C. Psychodynamic patterns in the sex offender. 1: Fear of the adult female sex object and feelings of genital inadequacy. *Psychiatry and the Law,* 1955, 157-168.

Jacks, I. Accessibility to group psychotherapy of incarcerated adolescent offenders. *Journal of Criminal Law, Criminology, and Police Science,* 1964, *55,* 100-106.

Landisberg, Selma. Relationship of the Rorschach to the H-T-P. *Journal of Clinical Psychology,* 1953, *9,* 179-183.

Piotrowski, Z. A., Hammer, E. F., & Jacks, I. Psychological worksheet. In Glueck, B. C. *Final report—research project for the study and treatment of persons convicted of crimes involving sexual aberrations.* Albany, State of New York Department of Mental Hygiene, 1956.

Wolberg, L. R. *The Technique of Psychotherapy.* New York: Greene and Stratton, 1954.

Dr. Wolk describes himself as "a rapidly aging 39-year-old" specialist in the field of gerontology. He received his Ph.D. from Yeshiva University in 1958. For many years Dr. Wolk has had a private practice and has engaged in what he refers to as "applied clinical psycho-gerontological" research. He is clinical research psychologist for the Office of the Consultant on Services for the Aged, New York State Department of Mental Hygiene, and is the author of a number of papers on the theory, diagnosis and treatment of the older person.

Chapter 14

Projective Drawings (H-T-P-P) of Aged People

Robert L. Wolk, Ph.D.

Dr. Wolk, in this chapter, shares with us his experience in the projective drawing assessment of the aging. In doing this he illustrates not only the special characteristics which are found in the H-T-Ps of geriatric cases, but also the sensitivity of the drawings to individual variation—variation which is found from case to case in spite of the muting effects of senility upon graphic expression and also the changes produced in the same case by psychotherapy even though the patient is in his 60's, 70's, or even 80's. Eds.

Drawings have been meaningfully utilized diagnostically for many subject groups ranging in age from young children to adults (Buck, 1948; Machover, 1949; Hulse, 1951, etc.). The projective possibilities inherent in figures drawn by aged people as projective tests, however, have been largely ignored as a diagnostic instrument by most clinicians. Ames (1954) evaluated the Rorschachs of aged people and attempted to establish norms for this older group. Other investigators have attempted to press child projective tests into service as a gerontological tool applicable to the older patient (Pelz, 1961). Special projective tests (Wolk, 1966) have been developed for the elderly, but drawings are frequently omitted from the psychological test batteries administered to older people.

Instrumentation in use for the psychological assessment of the aged focuses primarily upon *mental status* (Goldfarb, Kahn 1960), *the presence of chronic brain syndrome* (Goldfarb, 1959), *recall* (Ross, 1954), and *physical status* (VNS, Report 1966). For too long such focus has ignored the area of personality dynamics. It is as if the clinician loses interest in the older person as a person. It is as if the psychologist is interested only in the geriatric patient's social functioning level, rather than his inner life resources, affect, and potential for growth – the latter exists even amongst the aged, it must be remembered.

However, quite currently, a small, but increasing number of clinicians are in exploratory fashion, beginning to use drawings in their personality assessment of the aged. Because of the lack of a body of literature and empirical experiences with the H-T-Ps of the aged, most drawings by older people are analyzed essentially as one would analyze the drawings of other groups. This practice frequently leads to errors in evaluation because of the overlooked factors of limited psychomotor activity, failing eyesight, and even cultural constructs and mores which may differ, in many cases, from what the practitioner usually encounters.

The psychologist who handles drawings of older people adequately, however, would find such a device a most useful adjunct to the test battery. In more recent years, an additional dimension has been added to projective drawings – chromatic graphic representations. In this instance, the subject is requested to draw the House, Tree and Persons of both sexes in color, being given eight different colored crayons (the usual box of fifteen cent crayola crayons) for this purpose. Hammer (1958) points out:

". . . . The data . . . suggest the deduction is that the achromatic (pencil) and chromatic (crayon) drawing phases of the H-T-P actually tap somewhat different *levels* of personality. The chromatic H-T-P cuts through the defenses to lay bare a deeper layer of personality than does the achromatic set of drawings, and in this manner, a crude hierarchy of the subject's conflicts and his defenses is established, and a richer personality picture derived."

The value and sensitivity of drawings, both achromatic and chromatic, can be discussed best from experience within the context of pragmatic application. The current chapter will first describe a project undertaken in which drawings were utilized to measure various dimensions of the personality, both before and after aging people were exposed to a year of group psychotherapy. Specific drawings of patients engaged in the project will next be analyzed in this chapter in order to illuminate the use and yield of the H-T-P as a diagnostic tool for the aged.

The study reported here compares the effect of one year of group psychotherapy on two types of geriatric patients in a mental hospital – recently admitted patients and patients who aged while in the hospital – by comparing them with equivalent groups who received no group psychotherapy.

Fifty patients, 65 years of age or older, were chosen from one building in a New York State Hospital. Twenty four of the patients had been in residence at the hospital for a period of at least five years and had been admitted when under 65 years of age. The remaining twenty six patients had been admitted when over 65 years of age, but within the year prior to the beginning of the study. Names of patients over 65 years of age were chosen randomly from the hospital register. On the basis of length of institutionalization, the patients were placed into two groups. These two groups were then equated on the basis of hospital record information of age, intelligence, diagnostic classification, sex and physical condition, as well as for various sociological factors, but differentiated as to the length of their hospitalization. The two groups were further subdivided so as to provide one group of each type for treatment and one of each type to serve as a control. This division was made by the statistician who had no knowledge of any of the patients. He chose alternate patients from both the long term patients and recent admissions groups for assignment to the experimental and control sub-groups respectively.

The experimental subjects, both long-term and recent admissions, were randomly divided into two sections for the purpose of group psychotherapy. Each of the two groups contained approximately equal proportions of patients who were recent admissions and those who had been institutionalized for five years or longer. All the groups were fairly well equated with the exception of age at time of admission to the hospital, the control group of those patients who aged in the hospital being somewhat younger than the experimental group. (Control group, mean age 33.9 vs experimental group, mean age 42.8). However, the difference is not great and it was felt that the long duration of the patient's institutionalization would be more influential than the relatively slight difference in age upon admission.

Table XII presents the ages of the long-term patients and the recently admitted patients at the time of their admission to the hospital.

TABLE XII
Means: Patients' Ages At Time of Admission to the Hospital

	Males (N 23)		Females (N 27)	
	Experimental Group (N 11)	Control Group (N 12)	Experimental Group (N 13)	Control Group (N 14)
Mean: Age at time of Admittance to Hospital				
Aged in Hospital				
Mean	42.6	36.4	41.9	32.6
Range	34-50	18-46	35-50	16-46
First Admitted after 65				
Mean	74.5	71.0	75.5	70.0
Range	67-84	61-78	69-82	66-77

Table XIII shows the number of years the patient groups had been institutionalized.

TABLE XIII
Mean: Years Patient Groups Were Institutionalized

	Males (N 23)		Females (N 27)	
	Experimental Group (N 11)	Control Group (N 12)	Experimental Group (N 13)	Control Group (N 14)
Mean: Years Institutionalized				
Aged in Hospital				
Mean	31.2	37.4	30.7	38.0
Range	21-47	19-61	22-40	24-60
First Admitted after 65				
Mean	13 mos.	12 mos.	8 mos.	11 mos.
Range	8-18 mos.	10-14 mos.	3-13 mos.	3-18 mos.

Table XIV shows the patients' ages at the time of the study.

TABLE XIV

Mean: Patients' Ages At the Time of the Study

	Males (N 23)		Females (N 27)	
	Experimental	*Control*	*Experimental*	*Control*
	Group (N 11)	*Group (N 12)*	*Group (N 13)*	*Group (N 14)*
Mean: Age at time of Study				
Aged in Hospital				
Mean	73.8	73.8	72.6	70.7
Range	68-81	65-82	70-76	67-76
First Admitted after 65				
Mean	75.5	72.0	76.0	72.1
Range	68-85	62-79	70-82	67-78

The psychiatric diagnoses taken from the hospital records are given in Table XV.

TABLE XV

Psychiatric Diagnoses Taken From Hospital Records

	Aged in Hospital			First Admission after 65		
	Experimental	*Control*	*Total*	*Experimental*	*Control*	*Total*
Senile Psychosis & Psychosis with CAS	1	1	2	9	13	22
Psychosis with Convulsive Disorder	1	0	1	0	0	0
Schizophrenia	8	7	15	2	0	2
Cerebral Paresis	0	2	2	0	1	1
Mental Deficiency	1	0	1	0	0	0
Invol. Depression	0	1	1	0	0	0
Manic-Depressive	1	1	2	1	0	1
Total	12	12	24	12	14	26

This table demonstrates that the long-term patients, as a group, are largely schizophrenic and the new patients are essentially brain damaged.

The therapy groups met for one and one-half hours, once a week for a total of fifty sessions. The group psychotherapeutic technique employed was leader-oriented, focused upon interpersonal relationships and offered members only minimal interpretations (Wolk, 1960, Rustin and Wolk, 1963). On occasion, the therapist assisted patients in obtaining help from other hospital departments such as social service, medicine, physiotherapy and recreation.

House-Tree-Person Test

The H-T-P was administered in the usual way, with the exception that administration took place in groups of four patients each.

Two psychologists, the writer and a clinician with considerable experience[1] with aged persons, scored the H-T-Ps, both achromatic and chromatic, on four gross dimensions: depression, anxiety, interpersonal relations and the presence of chronic brain syndrome. Each of the dimensions was graded on a five-point scale indicating increasing severity or intensity.

All the protocols were evaluated blindly, that is, the psychologists did not know if the protocols were those of the experimental or the control subjects, if the drawings were done pre- or post-psychotherapy, or if the subjects were recent admissions to the hospital or were patients who had aged there.

Table XVI reflects the reliability of the H-T-P ratings between the two psychologists. Agreement in rating values is essential if the measures used are to be considered reliable. As seen in the table, scorer reliability is significant for all four measures – depression, anxiety, interpersonal relations and the presence and degree of chronic brain syndrome – for the pre-group psychotherapy testing. Reliability between the two psychologists' scores is also significant for the post-therapy factors, except for the H-T-P scores of anxiety.

TABLE XVI

H-T-P Reliability: The Degree of Agreement Between the Scores of Two Psychologists

	Pre-Therapy		Post-Therapy	
	Rho*	p	Rho*	p
Depression	.49	.01	.65	.01
Anxiety	.85	.01	.35	N.S.
Interpersonal Relations	.75	.01	.70	.01
C.B.S.	.90	.01	.85	.01

* *Spearman's Rank Order Correlation.*

The H-T-P scores for the patients were averaged to obtain a total score for each group of patients. The pre-group psychotherapy H-T-P scores are seen in Table XVII. There were no significant differences in pre-therapy scores between the control and experimental groups or between recent admissions to the hospital and long term patients. Since before group psychotherapy began the groups were well equated in regard to the four dimensions measured, and in all respects their environment and treatment during the year of psychotherapy was identical, any subsequent change might be attributable to the group psychotherapy process.

---

[1] The author wishes to acknowledge his indebtedness to Rochelle Seiden for her assistance in this phase of the research.

TABLE XVII
Means: Pre-Group Therapy H-T-P Scores

	Depression	Anxiety	Interpersonal Relationships	CBS
Means: Pre-Group Therapy				
Aged in Hospital				
Experimental	3.3	3.2	3.6	4.4
Control	3.2	3.2	3.8	4.2
First Admitted after 65				
Experimental	2.9	3.3	4.2	4.7
Control	3.2	3.2	4.0	4.4

No significant differences were found between the four treatment groups for H-T-P scores pre-therapy. The Krushal-Wallis one-way analysis of variance was used.

After the experimental patients had received one year of group psychotherapy, and the control group had grown one year older in the institution, the H-T-P was again administered in order to assess whether any measurable changes had occurred.

Table XVIII presents pre- and post-group psychotherapy scores for the experimental group and the controls group on the four H-T-P dimensions measured.

TABLE XVIII
Means: Pre- and Post-Group Psychotherapy Scores

	Depression		Anxiety		Interpersonal Relations		CBS	
	Pre-	Post-	Pre-	Post-	Pre-	Post-	Pre-	Post-
Aged in Hospital								
Experimental	3.3	2.1	3.2	2.9	3.6	2.9	4.4	3.5
Control	3.2	3.2	3.2	3.6	3.8	3.8	4.2	4.0
First Admitted after 65								
Experimental	2.9	2.4	3.3	3.2	4.2	3.2	4.7	4.4
Control	3.2	3.1	3.2	3.7	4.0	3.9	4.4	4.5

This table shows that the scores for levels of depression, interpersonal relationships and CBS severity improved noticeably, and for anxiety to some degree, for both short- and long-term patient experimental groups.

The control groups remained relatively static, but in the dimension of anxiety they grew worse.

As Table XIX indicates, the changes in pre- and post-therapy scores for both experimental groups receiving psychotherapy reached statistical significance ($p = .05$ or less) for depression, and for levels of interpersonal relations, and with the long-term patients, for chronic brain syndrome signs.

TABLE XIX

Changes After Group Psychotherapy As Measured By the H-T-P,
Administered Before and After Group Psychotherapy

	Depression p Value*	Anxiety p Value*	Interpersonal Relations p Value*	CBS p Value*
Aged in Hospital				
Experimental	.01	Not Sig.	.02	.01
Control	Not Sig.	Not Sig.	Not Sig.	Not Sig.
First Admitted after 65				
Experimental	.02	Not Sig.	.01	Not Sig.
Control	Not Sig.	Not Sig.	Not Sig.	Not Sig.

* *The Wilcoxon matched paired-signed ranks test was used to compute all p values.*

As measured by the H-T-P, therapy appeared to have been effective for both the patients who had aged in the hospital and those who had been admitted for the first time after age 65, but the therapy was more effective for the long-term patients than for the short-term group.

The greatest change took place in the areas of alleviation of depression and improvement of interpersonal relationships. No improvement was noticed along the dimension of anxiety for either group.

The long-term patients, however, demonstrated fewer signs of chronic brain syndrome on their post-therapy H-T-Ps than on their pre-therapy ones. We know that group psychotherapy can not reduce chronic brain syndrome, an organic process, but that frequently impaired mental functioning such as *signs* of CBS are actually masks of depression (Goldfarb, 1965). Where changes in CBS are noted after psychotherapy, and fewer H-T-P signs of the organic disorder were present, we may assume that the group process has lessened the patients' depression.

In contrast, there were no actual changes in CBS, pre- and post-therapy, among those patients whose first admission was after their 65th year. It can then be assumed that the recent admissions actually suffer from CBS (organic mental impairment that is not reversible) and/or "admissions shock" which makes them less accessible to group treatment and more in need of individual attention.

Although our data reflect only four features of the H-T-P profile – depression, anxiety, interpersonal relations, and the presence and degree of chronic brain syndrome – they serve to demonstrate the high degree of consistency between two psychologists on, as well as an experimental usage of, the H-T-P.

The results of additional qualitative analysis are consistent with these quantitative data, reflecting little or no change in the control group in contrast to the experimental group where drawing shifts were considerable.

H-T-Ps of Geriatric Patients: Some Systematized Observations

When the pre- and post-therapy H-T-P drawings were compared, we might expect some deterioration due to the patients' having aged another year.

Among the changes in the House drawings, we find that the Houses are drawn larger in size, but less well structured. The Tree drawings also deteriorated in that the second drawing of the Tree included a greater amount of foliage in most of them, but with the foliage less contained and spread all over the page with few ego boundaries holding the greater expressive content in check.

The shift to poorer form in both the House and Tree may be indicative of the advances of chronic brain syndrome, of a breaking down of ego control on an organic basis. In part, the deterioration may also be ascribed to the initial year of institutionalization. The recent admissions to the hospital demonstrated greater deterioration than those patients who had aged in the hospital.

In older persons, breakdown in form, when seen uniformly in all the drawings, is related in most instances to chronic brain syndrome rather than, as we would expect in younger people, to a psychotic state.

In evaluating institutionalized aging patients, our experience has been that greater emphasis must be placed upon the effects of the hospitalization itself than is the case with a younger group. The older person has greater difficulty in making new adjustments and reflects this feature of his personality in his drawings. Many older people exhibit signs of what appears to be withdrawal but actually turns out to be masked depression. The increase in the heavily shaded foliage in the Tree drawing reflects this factor, shading conveying anxiety and depression.

The drawings of the chromatic House frequently demonstrate breaks in ego control. The lessened frequency of the inclusion of a base line is indicative of loss of environmental contact. Less detail and lessened symmetry occurred during the second testing. The patients' choice of color also shifted from black to green indicative of one of several features of change in personality. The inappropriate use of the color can mean increased deterioration. However, we also see more positive signs in such color shifts, such as greater amounts of affect coming to the surface or the patients reaching out more actively into their own environment.

Color alone, when used by older people, can serve the diagnostic requirements of the clinician well. An example of the use of color by an older person might be found in Grandma Moses' paintings. Primitive but vivid, bright colors are utilized in the service of the painter's need to express her emotionality. Many who have painted most of their lives suddenly change their style in the sixth decade of life, frequently using more vivid color in an effort to "feel," to maintain some affective contact with the world. The exception to this, of course, is the artist who has become depressed later in life and at this point uses depressive blacks and browns or other somber hues. The critical factor is the maintenance of appropriateness in the use of color.

The control post-non-psychotherapy group's Houses contained fewer windows than their drawings did pre-therapy. This is suggestive of the patients' further withdrawal from the real world and their insulation of themselves. The patients exposed to group psychotherapy drew more windows after the course of treatment, indicative of a greater reaching out for real contact with their environment.

The form of the control group's chromatic Trees tended to break down during the second year's testing. Lines became lighter, indicating a general malaise and withdrawal. Less reinforcement of lines during the second set of drawings is consistent with their weakening of ego boundaries, resulting from further chronic brain syndrome deterioration.

Experience has taught us that the use of line in the diagnostic evaluation of older people should not be overemphasized, nor should interpretation necessarily be wholly similar to that utilized with the drawings of non-aged people. Psychomotor activity plays a role here. Many of these patients suffer from general body weakness and frequently also from arthritis and other conditions which affect line quality. However, the clinician should not be unaware of line quality. When the lines are consistently broken, for example, an interpretation of ego weakening or psychic distress should be entertained.

Both the pre- and post-psychotherapy achromatic drawings of the male figure by male subjects possessed poor form. In addition, lines became lighter and sex sequence was disturbed: i.e., the patients did not draw a Person of the same sex as their own for the first Person drawing. Consistent with this, we frequently see older males assuming, more and more, female roles in the matters of housework and shopping, and in their manner of expressing dependency.

There was a greater emphasis on the eyes and noses drawn on the faces of the male figure during the post-therapy testing. Old people are more sensitive to smell, and their emphasis upon noses can be equated with the emphasis upon eyes shown by younger subjects as an indication of a greater degree of suspiciousness of the outside environment.

When the nose is emphasized in a manner whereby the tip or top part is heavily shaded or darkened, frequently we can make the interpretation that the subject is plagued with feelings of loss of his male sexuality. However, we must be careful to differentiate the phallicizing of the nose from the "paranoid nose" [2] so frequently seen in older people.

A greater number of geriatric patients drew arms out of proportion, suggesting inappropriateness of expression due to beginning deterioration. The human body parts such as hands and parts ancillary to the drawing such as a stick or a pipe were present in fewer of the post-therapy drawings. Unlike younger people, aging individuals tend to try to make more compensatory adaptations. If they give up this defense, or if they no longer can manage to make compensatory adaptations, they tend to deteriorate more rapidly. The fewer body parts and ancillary parts of the drawings of the Persons in this study is suggestive of the deterioration that occurred in the year interval.

Enlarged arms drawn by older patients may reflect their frustration and/or rage. Frequently the too thin arms denote the frustrated patient who is unable to mobilize his affect into anger. At other times, they reflect generalized feelings of weakness or insufficiency. When the arm is drawn with a broad expanse between the arm's outer lines (like Popeye's forearm), we see the more overt expression of rage. When the arm is drawn shortened, we see the person

---

[2] As with the phallicized nose the paranoid nose is elongated, but the paranoid nose would be drawn with detail emphasis such as nostrils or with particular attention to the shape, which is rarely drawn straight.

with feelings of inadequacy. The arm, when drawn appropriately, suggests the maintenance of feelings of adequacy and self-confidence.

The chromatic drawings of the male control group substantiate the above picture. The color red is used less frequently during the second testing than it was a year earlier. The color yellow emerges more frequently now and may be indicative of less emotional responsiveness, heightened passivity or a greater degree of withdrawal. Again, as with the achromatic drawings, on retesting a year later, there was a more frequent over-emphasis on the eyes, reflecting the suspiciousness of a proportion of the institutionalized aging patients. Arms and legs were drawn out of proportion in greater numbers during the post-therapy testing. However, many of the legs which had been omitted during the first testing were now (a year later) drawn as stilts. It was as if the patients were having difficulty with the environment and felt the need to place reinforced distance between themselves and it.

When the patients of the control group drew the female figure achromatically, a great number of transparencies were found. When the same drawing was done chromatically, the transparencies lessened in number. The chromatic drawings also reflected the size of the figures, becoming smaller, indicating a lessening of felt adequacy in self image. Other dimensions related to self-concept also lessened: color became less distinct and was more poorly organized, and the mouth was much more emphasized suggesting the increasing oral-dependent needs of the patients. The number of arms on the female figure lessened from the first to the second year. In several instances, the body itself was no longer present, as if the patients were becoming disorganized and their concept of self was deteriorating. Breast emphasis also diminished consistent with the view of feelings of confusion about their sexual role.

The drawings of the experimental groups, after one year of treatment, were compared to their drawings prior to therapy. It was found that after the year of treatment the overall size of the House clustered around the median; there were fewer smaller Houses, but also fewer larger ones. The form of the House became better after therapy. Previous to treatment, many of the patients had drawn inappropriate forms for their Houses, such as triangles and circles, and even single straight lines.

The number of windows in the House increased during the post-therapy testing compared with both the control group and with the same group prior to treatment. This suggests that the patients developed greater contact with their outside environment through group psychotherapy. At the same time, as the number of windows increased, some were misplaced and not drawn appropriately. It was as if the affective needs, the seeking of contact with the outside world had been stirred into existence, but without a simultaneous ability to cope with this feeling.

Minor details on the House, such as the drawing of door knobs (also often indicative of a desire for more contact with the outer environment) appeared more frequently after psychotherapy.

In their achromatic drawing of a Tree, the experimental group, both prior and subsequent to therapy, drew more branches than were appropriate and also elaborated inappropriately elsewhere in the drawings. The control groups did likewise. Although the geriatric patients were striving for greater external facility, they felt unable to achieve their goals. The overelaboration of drawings by aged people may also indicate the fanciful, Pollyannish world which they tend to construct to surround themselves with in their withdrawn state.

The patients exposed to group psychotherapy drew greater amounts of foliage on the chromatic Tree and had fewer indistinguishable parts. There was a diminution during the post-therapy testing of stick-like, one-dimensional Trees. This would be indicative of the patients relating more satisfactorily to objects in their external environment after therapy.

The chromatic post-therapy drawings of the experimental groups' male figures became larger in size; form became better and reversed sexual sequence (i.e., a man drawing a woman first) diminished strikingly. The body became somewhat more rigid, the head of the figure was omitted far less frequently, and more usually was oversized. There was a greater frequency of mouths and teeth and, interestingly, among the male patient drawings, a cigar was seen more frequently during the post-therapy testing. These features would suggest a more adequate, if compensatory, approach toward the real world. Feelings of adequacy increased and the posture taken by the old person, even in his hospital community, improved.

The length of the neck diminished after psychotherapy, suggesting less need to separate feelings from thought, and an allowing of greater freedom of affect. These patients also drew a greater incidence of arms, and the fingers became more clearly articulated. Emphasis of these details increased on post-therapy testing. Legs were present more often and they were much larger. The hands were holding something more frequently and the body was generally better formed. The legs joined in the groin area more frequently in the post-therapy testing as well.

These findings of the experimental male group's chromatic drawings are suggestive of people who are reaching out, are less depressed, and are making an effort toward masculine striving (cigar present and hair emphasized). We also see greater mastery in the more articulated, even fingers, as if the patient were becoming more able to express anger outwardly, rather than to internalize or deny it – the latter state so frequently leading to depression. Also, the drawings, during the post-therapy testing were of figures holding on to things, as if contact with the external world was now more important to the patients.

With the chromatic male drawing, form improved after the group treatment, and brighter colors such as greens and reds were used with greater frequency than the browns or black. The sex sequence was self-sex figure first much more often, and the incidence of eyes, mouth, and neck in the figures was much higher.

The chromatic male figures thus suggest a livelier, more emotional group of people who were better able to identify sexually. There was also less dependency represented by an over-emphasis on buttons.

The chromatic female drawings of the group receiving therapy were drawn larger during the post-therapy testing, form improved, and the choice of bright colors such as green and red increased while the blacks and brown diminished in usage. The oversized head, more frequent presence of hands and fingers, and the

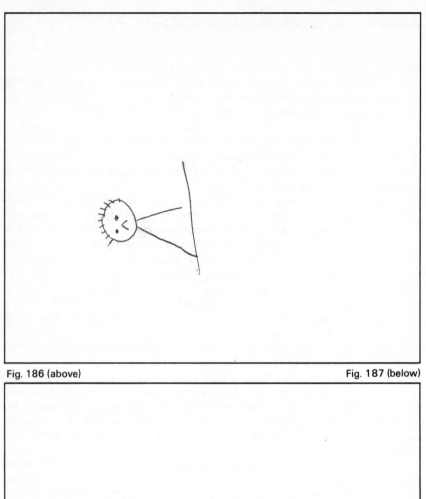

Fig. 186 (above)
Fig. 187 (below)

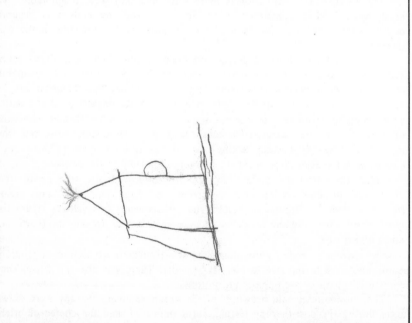

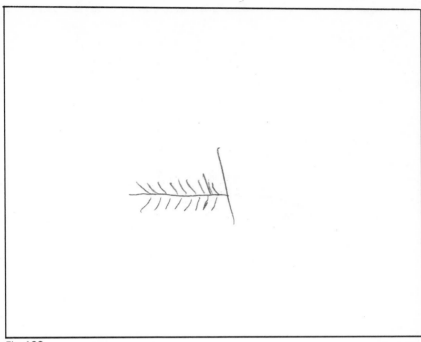

Fig. 188

legs in better proportion were also noteworthy during the post-therapy testing.

These drawings are suggestive of the changes that take place as a result of group psychotherapy. We see that the group receiving one year of group psychotherapy emerged somewhat differently from the control group. The experimental group, following the therapeutic experience, exhibited less depression, greater awareness and contact with their surroundings and greater awareness of self. More emotion emerges, there is less disorganization in perception, and there is more positive self-regard. The patients involved in group psychotherapy were better able to sustain their emotional well-being.

To illustrate geriatric H-T-Ps and their interpretations and, at the same time, the changes from pre- to post-therapy, the following two cases are presented.

The first patient, a 76-year-old male widower with no children, was a recent admission to the hospital. He had exposed himself while in a park near his home in a city housing project. He had been in the hospital for 8 months at the time of the initial testing. The patient had no memory of the exhibitionistic act leading to his institutionalization.

The pre-therapy H-T-P is that typically presented by a severely chronic brain syndromed person. Affect is inappropriate, as suggested by the poor choice of color. He drew the House in green, the Tree in yellow, the Person in blue. The patient lacked any integrated body image. On the achromatic Person, the legs are growing out of the head and both the achromatic and the chromatic male are fully open and empty, having really no enclosed body at all. It is as if his body, including the sexual organs, has lost all psychological significance. He feels withdrawn and shut off from the outside environment, as seen by the lack of windows and door on the achromatic House. The chromatic House possesses one window, but

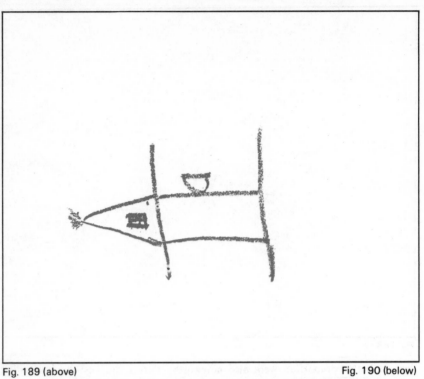

Fig. 189 (above)   Fig. 190 (below)

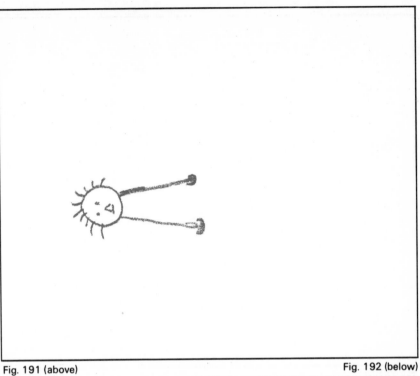

Fig. 191 (above)

Fig. 192 (below)

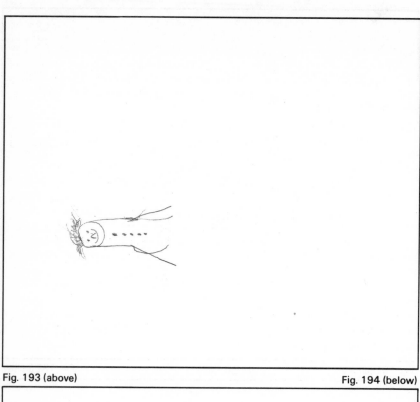

Fig. 193 (above)

Fig. 194 (below)

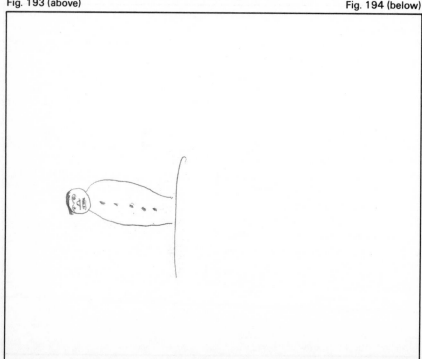

quite high off the ground. The chromatic drawings suggest a *potential* for better interpersonal relations and contact with others which, however, the patient cannot utilize at the present time. Another positive sign for future change may be found in the base line which allows the patient some contact with his reality. This can potentially be utilized in therapeutic work.

The achromatic House has smoke rising from it without benefit of a chimney. This would suggest a loss of sexual feeling; a demasculinization experience which the patient is attempting to deny. The smoke is his effort to extol his manhood; the lack of a chimney reflects his feelings of impotence.

The lack of foliage on the achromatic Tree drawing indicates the dessication of affect, the withdrawal of emotion from life experience. The same figure, when drawn chromatically, is in yellow, again reflecting the fading away of emotion. We must remember, however, that inappropriate use of color may at times reflect the presence of chronic brain syndrome. The malproportioned external door knobs in the House drawings also reflect the reality testing impairment present in chronic brain syndrome.

In the human figures, we see a noteworthy lack of sexual differentiation of the two people. The male figures, both chromatic and achromatic, do possess joining points between the legs which are attached to the head, which are closer together in the male than in the female.[3] This may be suggestive of a feeble attempt at tightness of impulse control in the patient, the need, when drawing a human figure of his own sex, to hold on, to contain his impulses. The drawings were obtained, we recall, shortly after the patient had gotten into trouble for having released impulses in his exhibitionistic acting-out. The short hair of all the Person drawn would suggest feelings of castration or diminished masculinity as does the cut off nose. The lack of mouth, in this case, describes the felt inability to communicate feeling or thinking processes.

The presence of chronic brain syndrome is raised as a consideration in this protocol by the following characteristics: the inappropriate choice of color and the patient's inability to use more than one color in a single drawing combine to suggest rigidity and an inability to shift direction or set. Form is also inappropriate, as conveyed in the external doorknob and the extensions of the roof line in the Houses. The Tree is rather typical of the CBS patient. The trunk and branches are of single line thickness and the branches are arranged in straight rows, one beneath the other, reflecting the organically impaired individual's need for order and his intolerance of ambiguity. Depression does not appear to be present to a significant degree.

The post-therapy H-T-Ps demonstrate significant changes. Affect becomes much more appropriate. The Tree (Figure 196) is drawn in green, the House (Figure 195) in red (instead of a green House and a yellow Tree as was previously done).

---

[3] The patient's drawing of the chromatic female Person, was misplaced subsequent to its analysis and the writing of this chapter and, consequently, cannot be shown. RLW.

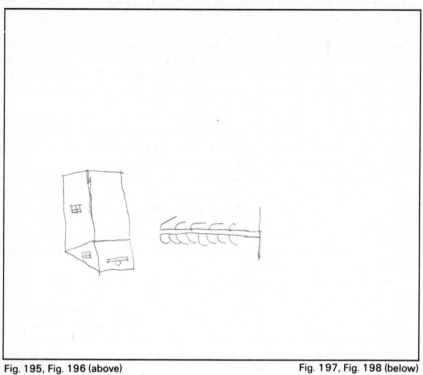

Fig. 195, Fig. 196 (above)   Fig. 197, Fig. 198 (below)

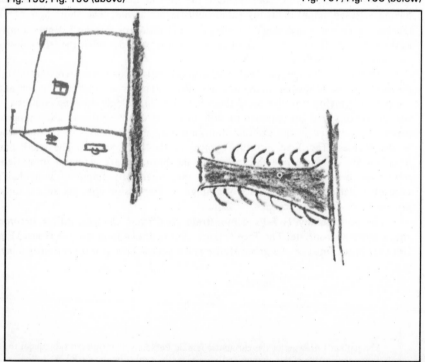

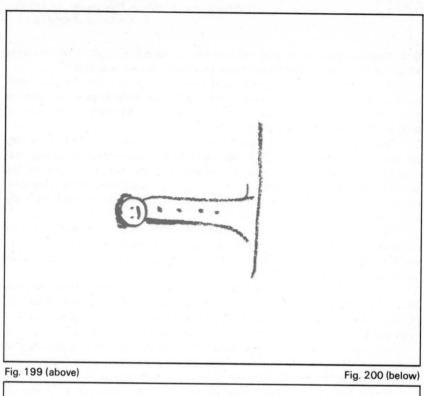

Fig. 199 (above)

Fig. 200 (below)

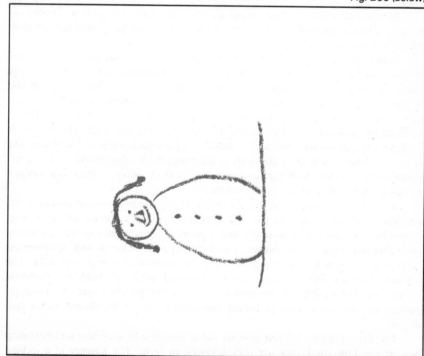

Body images is much better integrated, in spite of the chronic brain syndrome signs which are still present. The figures move into better contact with reality.

The House is much better structured, even to the point where the once external door knob is now more appropriately within the boundaries of the drawing itself. The patient demonstrates his increased desire for an interpersonal relationship: his House is more substantial and available.

Three of the four human figures are smiling, the patient reflecting his easier and better adjustment with himself and others. Dependency-indicating buttons are seen reflecting the patient coming to grips with and accepting the specific needs frequently appropriate to old age. To relax while being taken care of, if old and infirm, is to exhibit self-acceptance, to fight it inappropriately is vain defensive denial.

The achromatic male figure is presented with a base line and almost total encapsulation. Here we see that defenses have been marshalled – defenses which, although weak, are able to hold the patient together in better fashion than previously.

The chromatic drawings are more decisive and richer in affect than the pretherapy drawings. The human figures are reasonably well integrated. While the choice of color for the male and the female is still poor, and the figures lack real arms and legs, the use of the color green now is bright and cheerful.

The aged person's drawings frequently resemble the child's drawings in many ways. The principal difference may be the presence of more sophisticated aspects in the older person's drawings than would be present in the child's figures.

The second patient whose drawings serve as illustrations is a 72-year-old woman, a recent admission to the hospital, admitted upon petition of her daughter with whom she had lived.

Drawings numbered 201-208 are those of a woman whose pictorial representations suggest that she suffers from the effects of chronic brain syndrome. The choice of color is inappropriate; both Persons are drawn in yellow and the House in green. Color choice, restricted to one per drawing, is suggestive of an inability to shift set and of concretized thinking and judgment processes. Form is also inappropriate, as evidenced by the multiplicity of doorknobs (she labels them as such) on the achromatic House. The inability to integrate parts of the House (the steps, the extra line coming down from the roof, the misplacement of the supernumerary doorknobs) with the total structure, and the wavy, uneven lines suggest grossly disturbed perceptual-motor coordination.

Both the achromatic and the chromatic Houses indicate the still-present desire and need for closer interpersonal relationships and communication, as suggested by the presence of windows and a door. However, the chromatic drawing of the House reflects the deeper seated feelings of isolation and separateness suggested by the double walled House and the absence of a functional door. The patient obviously feels isolated and encapsulated, with her needs for closeness unsatisfied. The rigidity of structure also reflects the patient's needs to overcompensate for the recognition of failing functioning due to the chronic brain syndrome.

The Tree (Figures 202 and 204) are not affixed to a base or base line extending beyond the Tree trunk, nor are they accurate in form. The absence of a joining

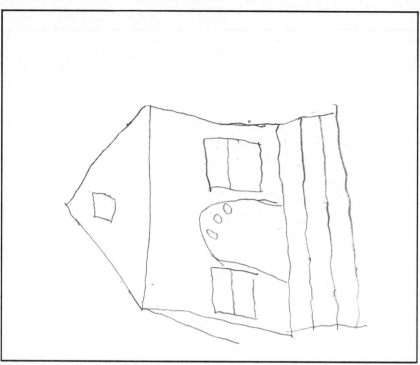

Fig. 201 (above)

Fig. 202 (below)

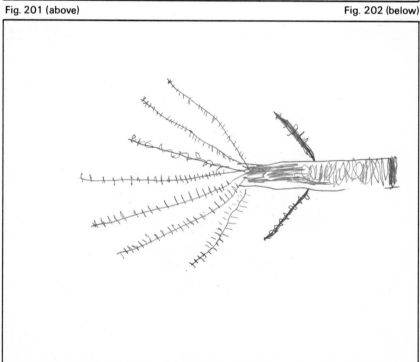

Fig. 203 (above)

Fig. 204 (below)

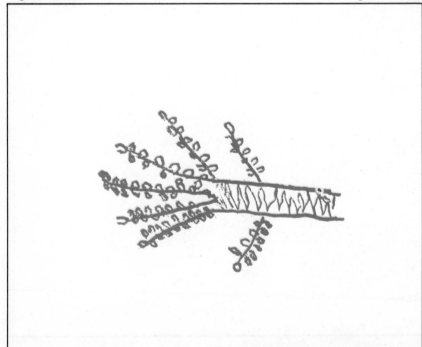

Fig. 205 (above)

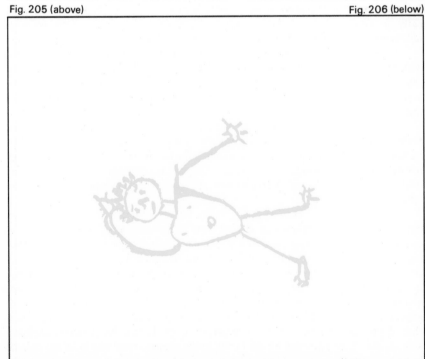

Fig. 206 (below)

of the chromatic Tree to a base (roots or ground) is indicative of the patient's feelings of retreat from reality. The poor form once again reflects the suggestions of chronic brain syndrome. The "sinking" branches (i.e. growing out of the midway point up the trunk) are seen frequently in geriatric drawings and suggest diminution of psychic energy usually accompanied by depletion in self-regard. The chromatic Tree, however, is drawn with a bit more foliage than the achromatic one and represents the patient's potential for growth and development which balances the drawing's more superficial depression and barrenness. The achromatic Tree is heavily shaded, reflecting anxiety, but we note the shading diminished with the intensification of boundaries in the chromatic Tree.

The emphasis upon the sexual organ of the achromatic Person drawings suggest a primitive regression accompanied by a decline in judgment, consistent with the view of chronic brain syndrome, but also suggestive of the possibility of a superimposed functional disturbance as well.

The figures are fragile, poorly integrated and lack firm boundaries at several points. The excessively long neck reflects the need for better impulse control, for the separation of intellectual and physical processes and the need to use intellectualization as a defense. The patient is trying to provide a firm contact with her environment by means of the emphasis on, and placement of, the foot, but, in essence, the figure is not grounded, indicative of the failure to maintain reality contact. The hands are overemphasized, as though the patient is expressing the need for manipulation and contact, but they are poorly executed. The placement of the puny fingers (petal-fashion and sometimes unattached) is pathognomonic for chronic brain syndrome. The single-dimensional arms reflect a self-concept of limited and inadequate capacity (Fig. 207)

The chromatic Persons are more firmly placed, but there is still no contact with the environment on which they stand. Sexual differentiation reflects some healthy signs. This, along with the presence of the additional foliage on the chromatic Tree, suggests the possibility that the patient can benefit from psychotherapy.

Thus, this 73-year-old woman, although apparently suffering from chronic brain syndrome, still possesses resources which may make exposure to psychotherapy feasible. She demonstrates strong motivation for reestablishing greater reality contact: she struggles to deny her loss of capacity: she still possesses relatively adequate intellectual functions and she recognizes her pain of isolation and loneliness.

The post-therapy drawings still reflect the presence of moderate chronic brain syndrome. Noteworthy of change from the pre-therapy drawings is the increase in the anxiety level possessed by the patient as reflected in the heavy shading of the achromatic House and both Trees. Anxiety was utilized for this patient's treatment as it represented a reshifting of her defense system. Anxiety, in this case, reflected greater awareness of self, dissatisfaction with what was and increased motivation for change. Both the achromatic and chromatic Houses are more accessible. Form has also improved somewhat. The isolated encapsulation of the patient reflected in her drawings of the House, has lessened considerably. Some of the openness we see is due to the changes resulting from the organic brain syndrome's having progressed for an additional year. However, the change

Fig. 207 (above)

Fig. 208 (below)

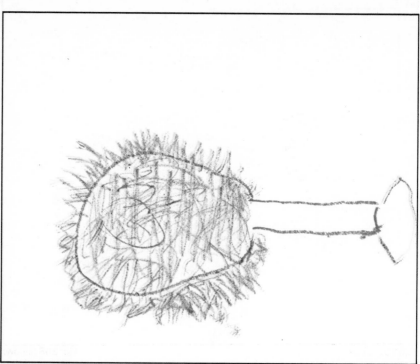

Fig. 209 (above)

Fig. 210 (below)

Fig. 211 (above)

Fig. 212 (below)

Fig. 213 (above)

Fig. 214 (below)

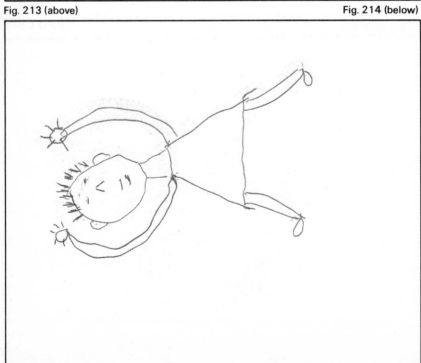

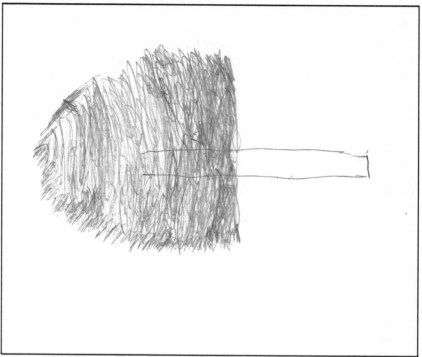

Fig. 215 (above)

Fig. 216 (below)

to a greater degree of openness was also due to therapy. The achromatic Tree is more appropriately drawn than the chromatic one, albeit, more expressive of anxiety, but for the most part serves as testimony to the patient's attempts at presenting a better integrated and healthy facade, despite her pathology. Internal controls have weakened but there are compensatory mechanisms at play and greater involvement in the outside world and conscious attempts to function in a more acceptable manner.

Sexual differentiation has been displaced from the genital and breast emphasis on the pre-therapy male and female drawings to a beard for the male and a skirt for the female in the later drawings. This is suggestive of a more conventional and better integrated approach to her feelings about herself and her identity as a woman.

The more vivid and active use of color in the chromatic drawings also reflects a greater recognition of affect on the part of the patient, a reaching out into the environment for a more solid life experience. While the colors are not, in all cases, appropriate, they do reflect a relatively greater feeling tone within the patient and as well, much less depression (greater use of more vivid colors).

The aggressive fingers are still present in the post-therapy drawings of the male and female. This aggressive feature of the patient's personality was capitalized upon in her treatment to liberate some of her vitality. No effort was made to reduce the aggressive impulses as they were directed into socially acceptable channels and did not interfere with her ultimate adjustment.

The post-therapy Persons appear less static than the pre-therapy ones, suggestive of better integration of the self with the environment and expressing a fuller affect in a meaningful, more healthy fashion.

SUMMARY

This chapter describes the value of achromatic and chromatic H-T-Ps in assessing personality change in aging people resulting from a course of group psychotherapy. The chapter also discusses and illustrates the analysis of older people's H-T'Ps in general, and points out differences in the interpretation of drawings obtained from the aging in contrast to that of drawings by other age groups.

References

Ames, L. B., Learned, J., Metreau, R. W., and Walker, R. W., *Rorschach Responses in Old Age.* New York: Paul B. Hoeber, Inc., 1954.

Buck, John N., The H-T-P Technique—a Qualitative and Quantitative Scoring Manual. *J. Clin. Psychol.* Monograph Supplement No. 5, 1948.

Goldfarb, A. I., Depression, Brain Damage, and Chronic Illness of the Aged: Psychiatric Diagnosis and Treatment. *J. Chronic Diseases, 9,* 1959, 220-233.

_____, Kahn, R. L., Pollack, M. and Peck, A., Brief Objective Measures for the Determination of Mental Status in the Aged. *Amer. J. Psychiatry, 117,* 1960, 326-328.

Hammer, Emanuel F., *The Clinical Application of Projective Drawings*. Springfield, Illinois: Charles C. Thomas, 1958.

Hulse, W. C., The Emotionally Disturbed Child Draws His Family. *Quarterly J. of Child Behavior, III,* 1951, 152-174.

Machover, K., *Personality Projection in the Drawing of the Human Figure.* Springfield, Ill.: Charles C. Thomas, 1949.

Pelz, K. S., Ames, L. B., Pike, F., Measurement of Psychologic Function in the Geriatric Patient. *J. Amer. Geriatric Soc., IX, 1961, 740-754.*

Ross, M., Some Psychiatric Aspects of Senescence: A Review of the Literature. *Psychiatric Quarterly, 28,* 1954.

Rustin, S. L. and Wolk, R. L., The Use of Specialized Group Psychotherapy Techniques in a Home for the Aged. *Group Psychotherapy, 16,* 1963, 25-29.

Visiting Nurse Service of N. Y. – Report Study of Psychological Needs of Aged Patients at Home. New York (Mimeo.), 1966.

Wolk, R. L. and Bruner, R. L., Group Psychotherapy with Geriatric Patients in an Out-Patient Psychiatric Clinic. Read at the meeting of the Amer. Society of Group Psychotherapy and Psychodrama, New York, 1960.

_____The Gerontological Apperception Test: A Unique Projective Technique for Aged People. *J. Long Island Consult. Ctr.,* 1966.

John N. Buck received his higher education at the University of North Carolina, Swarthmore College, and the University of Virginia.

His work in clinical psychology was at the Lynchburg State Colony, Colony, Virginia and its out-patient clinics, (1929-1951), except for the period 1944-45, at which time he was a Research Fellow in the Psychiatric Department of the University of Virginia Hospital.

He devised and developed the H-T-P Technique and is now internationally known as the "father" of this projective device. He is also author of the Philo-Phobe Technique (a formalized, but not rigidly structured, psychiatric interview) and the Time Appreciation Test (an emergency test of intelligence).

He has given Seminars and Workshops on the H-T-P at the University of Virginia, Emory University, Richmond Professional Institute and several Facilities of the Veterans Administration, as well as at the Colony.

He has published two books and thirteen papers on the H-T-P, and eight papers on other psychological topics. He was co-author of the Virginia law for the Certification of Clinical Psychologists.

He was an active member of a number of professional societies. He has been, at various times, National Vice-President for Psychology of the American Association on Mental Deficiency; Chairman of the Psychology Section and Member of the Council of the Virginia Academy of Sciences. He served two terms as Chairman of the Virginia Examining Board for the Certification of Clinical Psychologists.

The author holds the certificate in clinical psychology of the Examining Board for the Certification of Clinical Psychologists of the Commonwealth of Virginia.

Chapter 15

The Use of the H-T-P In the Investigation of the Dynamics of Intra-Familial Conflict

John N. Buck

This chapter offers the reader: (1) a perceptive rendering of the psychological anatomy of a marriage; (2) an illustration of personality changes which took place under therapy and their reflection in the H-T-P; (3) an example of the use of the H-T-P in marital counseling; and (4) a look over the shoulder of the author as with special clinical sensitivity he etches a set of personality portraits. (EFH).

    The writer has employed the H-T-P routinely in cases of intra-familial conflict (whether between husband and wife, child and sibling, or child and parents) to attempt to appraise in depth the personalities of the individuals involved; to check upon the probable accuracy of the disputants' views of the points at conflict; and to provide—through re-examination—a more objective measure of the progress of therapy than mere observation.

    The following case (a reasonably representative one) well illustrates what the clinician may expect from the H-T-P protocols.

    Mrs. Black[1] was visibly agitated as she entered the writer's office. She introduced herself rather brusquely, then sat down—poised on the edge of the chair

---

[1]All names of persons and places have been altered to preserve the anonymity of those discussed in this chapter. Ed.

like a bird about to take flight at the first threatening gesture. A relatively tiny woman with greying brown hair, she was dressed in a drab-colored, severely tailored suit, and since she wore no makeup to relieve the pallor of her sharply chiseled features, she might easily have been thought to be in her early 60's instead of her late 40's.

She smiled apologetically and announced that she had come to the writer not to seek professional assistance, but to get him to help her secure employment locally. She stated that she had become, as she put it, sick and tired of domestic drudgery and the restrictive and unstimulating environment of the small mountain town in which she and her husband lived, and she had decided to come to Lynchburg to work. She said that she had taught for a number of years, but did not wish to continue teaching. Instead, she would like to get a secretarial position.

It took the writer but a short time to establish that Mrs. Black was indeed well-qualified to function as a secretary. But when the writer asked Mrs. Black what her husband thought of her proposed move, she broke down and wept profusely for several minutes.

When she had regained control, Mrs. Black explained that she had quite literally run away from home. She had been told by a close friend that Mr. Black was frequently visiting another woman. When Mrs. Black had accused her husband of being unfaithful, not only had he not denied the charge, but he had shrugged it off as being of no consequence since, as he said, he certainly did not love the woman in question. Mrs. Black stated that it was intolerable that he had been so callously unfaithful to her.

Later (during the course of therapy, which we subsequently inaugurated), however, she confessed that what had really shattered her morale was not the act of infidelity itself ('though that was difficult enough to accept'), but rather the fact that he had taken a paramour who was of far lower social-standing than the Blacks, a woman who was, to boot, severely handicapped physically.

In a frenzy of rage and frustration, Mrs. Black had left home, taking only a few articles of clothing and very little money.

Fortunately the writer was able to get Mrs. Black satisfactory employment promptly. And Mrs. Black asked to be seen again —this time professionally.

HISTORIES
Mrs. William Black (nee Blanche White)
Blanche, an only child, was born in Vermont, 48 years ago, at full term and without untoward incident, to Mr. and Mrs. Thomas White. At the time of Blanche's birth, her mother was 36, her father 31.

Blanche's mother, a native of New York State, was a "sickly" child; never a robust adult. After graduating from high school, she went to New England to teach. There she met and married Thomas White.

Mr. White, a native New Englander, finished high school. His plans to obtain a medical education had been shattered by the death of his father (when Thomas was 17) which compelled Thomas to go to work at once to help support the family.

When Blanche was 4 years old, Mr. White moved his small family to the Middle West. They scarcely had settled in their new surroundings when Blanche's mother died of diabetes.

Mr. White maintained his home there for another year with the aid of a house-keeper (whom Blanche cordially disliked). He then felt it best to return East so that he could place Blanche in the home of her mother's older sister. From then on Mr. White (who was, so Blanche said, an ineffectual but lovable dreamer) did not figure prominently in Blanche's development: He did not live in her new home and Blanche saw him only on occasional weekends. Blanche always felt that he had deserted her.

Blanche's new household was far from ideal. The principal figure was the maternal aunt, far too occupied with looking after her totally incapacitated hus-band and two teen-age children to afford Blanche an adequate parent surrogate. Blanche soon learned that whenever she was frustrated in any way, she had only to burst into tears and cry piteously, "I want my mother," to get her way (actu-ally she scarcely could remember her mother). Needless to say Blanche was not a popular child. By the time Blanche was in her early 'teens, her father had begun to drink heavily. When she was 14, he was knocked down by a car and so severely injured that he died several days later.

Blanche was regarded as an outstanding student in the small high school she attended. During Blanche's senior year in high school, she developed what she called a "crush" on a Miss Jones, one of the younger female teachers (a graduate of X University). Miss Jones reciprocated strongly and finally persuaded Blanche to matriculate at X University, then arranged to return there herself for post-graduate work. Miss Jones and Blanche roomed together in a boarding-house near the University. Blanche had a "nervous breakdown" during her junior year and had to withdraw from school. Blanche flatly refused to discuss her relation-ship with Miss Jones or the "nervous breakdown" (the writer strongly suspects that guilt (1) over overt homosexual activities or (2) over an overwhelming desire for such activities precipitated the "breakdown").

After staying out of school for a year, Blanche returned to school (to another college) and graduated in due course without further difficulty.

Following her graduation from college, Blanche went South to teach.

William Black was born fifty years ago in a Western County of North Caro-lina, at full-term and without injury, to Belle and Major Caesar Black (at that time Belle was 30, Caesar was 57). William was the product of his father's fourth marriage and his mother's second (ultimately Belle and Caesar had four children of their union).

Caesar had had ten children by his first wife; one by his second; and two by his third. Belle had had four children by her previous marriage.

William was born on his father's birthday, a fact that was to have an aston-ishing influence on his life. The Major immediately decided that William was his favorite child—an opinion that the Major held unswervingly until his death. As a result, most of William's half-siblings (and later his full siblings as well) de-veloped a hostile attitude toward him that ranged from somewhat amused annoy-ance to frank dislike, and William, not unnaturally, identified wholeheartedly with his father.

Major Black was a rugged, heavily bearded, dominant male of the old school. He was the head of his family and he never let anyone question or forget it. He made all the decisions for the family (and never could understand why so many of his children left home at their first opportunity). The Major had little formal schooling; spent most of his life farming. When the Civil War began, as he was overly fond of telling it, he literally "left his horse in the field and the plow in the furrow" so that he might enlist in the Army.

All his life Major Black sought greener pastures. The family never lived in one place for more than a few years.

The Major always was quick to take offense: His inevitable reaction was to withdraw, usually psychologically, but occasionally physically as well. When he left home in a huff, he often took William with him.

William's mother was a stolid, reserved woman who had little influence upon him. She did not care for small children, so William received most of his childhood care and discipline from older half-siblings or from servants.

William was regarded as a "puny" child. He had a hyper-sensitive digestive system that periodically incapacitated him. He left the paternal home when he was 13 to live and work with the son of his oldest half-sister. He was willing and ambitious, and completed high school work in night school; later he graduated from business college.

In an effort to follow his father's example (and demonstrate his own masculinity) William promptly attempted to enlist after the United States declared war in World War I, but was turned down as underweight.

When William was only 20, he married Sara Smith who was some five years his elder. William was reserved, aloof, painfully meticulous in dress and habit, very fond of reading. Sarah was garrulous, gregarious, a careless housekeeper, fond of movies, dancing, etc..

Their essential incompatability is well illustrated by the following incident: One night William (after a lengthy debate) agreed to take Sarah to the movies, but only on condition that he might sit next to an aisle light so that he could continue to read the book in which he was then engrossed.

Early in their marriage they had a son. The child became a major source of contention between them. Finally Sarah took the child and went home to her mother. William took to drink and found sexual satisfaction away from home. Sarah sought and was granted a divorce. In lieu of alimony, William turned over to Sarah everything he owned except his car—he took that and left the state.

William had long been interested in accounting. He secured a part-time job and resumed his education.

Blanche White and William Black were married after they had known each other for about a year and a half. William continued in school; Blanche continued to teach.

In due course, William graduated and passed his C.P.A. examinations. He promptly secured employment with an accounting firm in the city in which they were living.

The first two years of their marriage apparently were happy ones. William, like his father before him, was dictatorial, but Blanche was delighted to have found the loving, firm, dominant male that she had always needed but never had. In turn, Blanche gave William the warmth and unquestioning adoration which he had been conditioned to regard as his just due.

In the fourth year of their marriage their son, Charles, was born after a prolonged, complicated, and very painful labor which was terminated by Caesarean section. Blanche was told that she must have no more children.

Both Blanche and William were delighted with Charles. Their views of the proper way to rear him, however, soon produced profound discord. Blanche was overly protective and over anxious, always pampering Charles. William felt that this was no way to prepare the boy for manhood.

Then came "The Depression." The Blacks lost the home which they were trying to buy and all their savings. But the stresses and strains of adversity brought them close together again. Blanche went back to teaching, and they economized with grim determination.

In the middle '30s William was offered a position in a small, Appalachian mountain town. Blanche begged him not to accept, for she thought that the town was "unspeakably ugly," devoid of all cultural advantages. William, however, thought otherwise and moved the family there.

Immediately after Pearl Harbor in World War II, William again tried to enlist. This time, after some weeks of pulling all possible strings, he was accepted. Four months later, however, he was honorably discharged – ostensibly because he was too old.

It was not long before Blanche and William began to quarrel frequently again. Blanche sought solace in a "flight into society;" William retreated into literature and the comforting arms of John Barleycorn. Blanche did her best to interest William in civic activities; he rebelled and drank more heavily. She was adjusting poorly to climacteric pressures and growing more and more shrewish. William began to look elsewhere for the emotional satisfaction denied him at home. Then Charles left home for college. Not long thereafter Blanche discovered William's infidelity and she, too, left – without leaving any word of her plans or probably future whereabouts.

We now move to a quantitative and qualitative analysis of Mrs. Black's achromatic and chromatic H-T-P, and a discussion of the Post-Drawing Interrogation. In the interest of economy of space, only pertinent highlights will be given.

TABLE XX

H-T-P Quantitative Scores

Achromatic		Chromatic	
	I.Q.		*I.Q.*
Per cent raw G	88	Per cent raw G	74
Net weighted	93	Net weighted	84
Good	93-94	Food	91
Flaw	94	Flaw	70

The degree to which Mrs. Black's present emotional disturbance is interfering with the efficiency of her intellectual function is strikingly apparent from these I.Q. scores. And the fact that in general the scores are sharply lower for the chromatic than for the achromatic is not a good prognostic sign.

Analysis of the raw scores for the achromatic drawings shows no D3s, one D2, and 10 Dls. The chromatic drawings, however, contain 4 D2s, and 15 Dls, and the Means Score scatter which encompassed only four adjacent levels on the achromatic rises to six on the chromatic—another pathological sign.

Her Detail scores for the Achromatic H-T-P are in the high Average range and only slightly lower for the Chromatic. This would suggest that Mrs. Black is not withdrawing from reality to any great degree and certainly would imply that her mood depression is neurotic-reactive rather than psychotic.

Her Proportion scores for the Achromatic are in the Moron to Borderline level; somewhat lower for the Chromatic. This implies that Mrs. Black's ability to appraise the immediate situation and to make sound judgments is well below her "normal."

Although the Good Perspective scores are in the Average range for both the Achromatic and the Chromatic series, the Flaw score for the first set is Dull Average and for the second is a striking Imbecile. These scores provide further support for the beliefs (1) that Mrs. Black is not fleeing from reality (Good scores) and (2) that her ability to appraise reality objectively and critically is seriously impaired (Flaw scores).

The House Good scores (both achromatic and chromatic) are Average. The Flaw score for the achromatic House is in the range Moron to Borderline; that for the chromatic House is radically depressed to Imbecile. It is certainly not surprising to find Mrs. Black unable to evaluate her domestic situation with objectivity and accuracy.

The Tree Good scores are superior; the Flaw score for the achromatic Tree is above average; that for the chromatic Tree is average. These would suggest that the emotional disturbance is not yet all-pervading and that it has not been of too long duration.

The Good and Flaw scores for the achromatic Person are Dull Average and for the chromatic Person borderline. Mrs. Black now finds it difficult indeed to function with her customary efficiency in psycho-social situations.

Achromatic House

Mrs. Black experienced great difficulty in producing the windows of her achromatic House; she erased frequently. She first drew the windows without any indication of panes, later attempted to conceal her latent hostility by dividing the large expanse of glass into relatively tiny panes producing, in turn, a definite bar-like effect which she fully recognized as she remarked, "These are not bars across the windows, they are panes (sic). I should know, I've cleaned them so much" (feelings of entrapment and rejection of the drudgery of housekeeping). The relatively tiny door expresses her reluctance to make unreserved contact with others (this reluctance was emphasized by her drawing—as her last item— a pathway leading from the door toward the viewer and then erasing it).

It is not surprising to find her having great difficulty with sexual symbols (she has never made a really satisfactory heterosexual adjustment; further, she is experiencing a stormy menopause and she had a hysterectomy some two years ago; in addition, she feels savagely rejected, betrayed, and a marital failure). The door and both chimneys were produced only with great difficulty—the full-

Fig. 217, Achromatic House No. 1 (above) Fig. 218, Achromatic Tree No. 1 (below)

length chimney was the 20th item drawn (note that it lacks strength, is without depth, is partially cut by both the roofline and the odd baseline – rejected, she rejects).

All lines are faint and indecisively presented (she has strong feelings of an imminent Ego collapse). She attempted to protect her House (but ineffectually) with overhanging eaves and a front porch without depth. She tied her House into the ground (reality) before providing any means of entrance.

Most striking in the drawing of one of her known basic intelligence level is her inability to present adequately the angular relationship of the main wall to the endwall (she draws her House as if it had a shed-type roof only). There are several transparencies (signs of a major critical failure). She drew the sun as a flattened, hollow, ellipse (her relationship to the authoritative figure in her immediate past – her husband – is now as deflated and distorted as was her relationship to those in her more distant past, her parents who, one after the other, died and thus deserted her).

Post-Drawing Interrogation

She quickly stated that this was her own House; that she would want her husband and child to live in it with her. When she was asked whether the House was near or far away, she replied (too emphatically, perhaps), "Oh! Close by!"

When she was asked if it were a happy House, she answered, "Exceedingly." And to the question as to what gave her that impression, she said, "Its size and large windows . . . Well as you open the front door, you see right through the House. It's all there waiting for you." (She feels equally "seen through" and the fact that she links "happiness with this feeling of paranoidal exposure suggests that among her defense mechanisms she includes emphasis upon a Pollyanish-like denial of whatever is painful.

It appears, too, that she has regretted profoundly her impulsive flight and entertains grave doubts that she will ever live in this House again. When the question, "What does that House need most?" was posed, she first queried, *"Mean* most to me?"

Chromatic House

The chromatic House is essentially a duplicate of her achromatic structure. The chromatic House is somewhat larger, but the major differences lie in the treatment of the bathroom window (immediately over the front door) which here becomes a frankly feminine sex symbol, and the door which is now even less accessible. When she began to draw, she picked up the black crayon (used it later as a pencil-substitute) and remarked, "Of course, you ought to draw in white." (Her oppositional tendencies are well-developed).

She used the four colors (black, green, red, and yellow) conventionally and minimally. Her failure to employ shading points up her defenceless position (and her great reluctance to submit herself to additional emotion-arousing stimuli).

The sun, which was in the upper left corner in the achromatic drawing, is now in the upper right (this may express her feeling that relations with her husband in the future will continue to be "abnormal").

It must be concluded that Mrs. Black is deeply disturbed about and by her domestic situation; disturbed to the point where she can no longer think clearly or objectively concerning it.

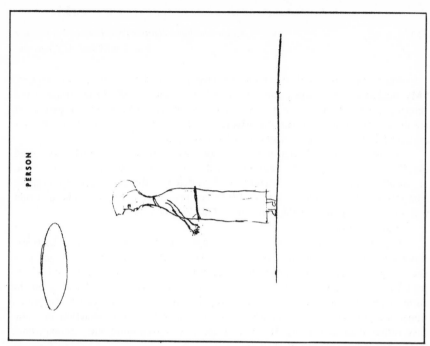

PERSON

Fig. 219, Achromatic Person No. 1

Achromatic Tree

This Tree would be a classical "keyhole" Tree, but for the groundline (drawn spontaneously). The branch structure is disproportionately small in comparison to the size of the trunk (pointing up her feelings of frustration at her inability to secure satisfaction in and from her environment).

The peripheral lines outlining the branch system (the existence of which is but barely implied) are faint and in some places actually broken. That fact, plus the absence of a branch system baseline and the presence of vine-like lines on the trunk, suggests strongly that she is finding it gravely difficult to control basic drives and to maintain Ego integrity.

The sun was drawn spontaneously —again as a hollow, flattened ellipse —in the upper left corner, but the peripheral line is so faint that the sun scarcely can be seen. The authoritative, warmth-giving (or withholding) figure in her recent life has been her husband, and she wishes to deny the presence of his influence, but cannot completely blot him out. This may express, also, her feeling that her parents "faded" out of her life.

Post-Drawing Interrogation

Mrs. Black stated that the Tree was a 150-year-old oak located at the rear of her own House. When she was asked whether the Tree looked more like a man or a woman to her, she replied, "A Tree to me is always male, Joyce Kilmer to the contrary notwithstanding." And when she was asked why, she continued, "Solidity of the trunk." To the follow-up question, "How does that typify masculinity?" she said, "Dependability, sturdiness." Quite aside from the obvious implication of the solid trunk, it is apparent that Mrs. Black wishes that her husband had the characteristics which she ascribes to her Tree, for she greatly needs a sturdy and dependable male.

When she was asked of whom the Tree reminded her, she quickly replied, "My husband!" And when she was asked why, she stated, "The strength and determination which I give to the Tree–backbone." (Note the "I give"). A major source of her present disturbance is the defeat which she feels she has sustained in her persistent efforts to reform William.

To the question, "If that were a Person instead of a Tree, which way would the Person be facing?" she countered with, "Do you mean north, east, south, or west?" (An interesting attempt at Ego-defense through misinterpretation: compass points are much easier to face than people or problems). The question was simply repeated, and she then said, "Oh! Facing you."

Chromatic Tree

The chromatic Tree is essentially a duplicate of the achromatic. There are, however, certain noteworthy differences: (1) the chromatic Tree is larger than the achromatic Tree (Mrs. Black becomes more expansive as she tires and is subjected to additional stimulation); (2) the chromatic Tree is placed higher on the form page and the branch structure's top barely is contained below the page's upper margin (she is developing a strong tendency to seek satisfaction in phantasy rather than in reality). Her use of color is conventional and minimal; once again there is no attempt at shading.

The Tree drawings provide evidence that Mrs. Black's emotional disturbance is not (as might have been hoped) largely restricted to the domestic situation. True, the signs of difficulty evidenced in the drawings of the Tree are not as severe as those seen in the drawings of the House, but there is good reason to fear that her reactive disorder is a progressive one.

Achromatic Person

This Person lacks an essential detail (the ear), always a pathological sign in a drawing produced by an individual of average or higher intelligence. The omission here was interpreted as indicating a paranoid reaction–a desire to avoid having to hear critical remarks (and perhaps the supplication of her husband that she return). Only later and during the course of Mrs. Black's psychotherapy was it learned that Mr. Black's paramour was totally deaf.

The hair is depicted as if it were a sort of constrictive cap (strongly suggesting obsessive thinking). The long neck stresses her divorcement of the physical from the intellectual and suggests that she has a puritanical view of sensuality. The transparent arm conveys rather strikingly the patient's feeling of relative helplessness in dealing with the problems of social intercourse, and the full profile stance indicates her reluctance to face others and communicate with them. The tiny ineffectual feet and ankles belie her proudly claimed feeling of independence and autonomy.

It would be difficult indeed to draw a less attractive female figure (rejected herself, Mrs. Black in turn rejects femininity).

Although she had drawn groundlines spontaneously for her achromatic House and Tree, it was necessary to request her to draw a groundline here (she has a distressingly depressive view of her competence as a female, feels it futile to attempt to tie into reality).

It was necessary, too, to ask her to draw the sun: and when she complied, she distorted the ellipse more than ever before.

Post-Drawing Interrogation

When she was asked who her Person was, she queried, "Did you see *The Barretts of Wimpole Street?* She's Elizabeth's maid; the one who went around on skates." The character to whom she was referring was a drab, mouse-like creature, who moved about unobtrusively and almost silently. There seems little doubt that Mrs. Black now views herself as little more than one who does the menial work about the home.

To, "What is she doing?" Mrs. Black replied, "She's just standing there. Being who she is, she's waiting for something to happen, I suppose. I haven't given her as much individuality as you're trying to bring out." (Mrs. Black, too, has spent much time wondering when her husband was coming home.)

To, "How does she feel?" after some tergiversation, Mrs. Black answered, "If I'm investing her with the individuality *I* have, she is waiting to be told what to do next." (Mrs. Black bitterly resents having to seek advice and thus reveal weakness.)

Fig. 220, Chromatic House No. 1

When she was asked to state how she might feel about such a Person, Mrs. Black said, with bitterness, "She has no chin, which means she has no character. She reminds me of a school teacher I had in High School . . . a negative person, she couldn't manage the class, couldn't teach, couldn't period." (It seems quite likely that Mrs. Black's attempts to manage Mr. Black have produced sharp conflict and mutual frustration.)

The Person needs most: "A chin, which as I said before is an indication of character." When she was requested to give her definition of character, Mrs. Black continued, "She makes no impression. In a room full of people, she's not there, if you get what I mean." [This is (1) a strange definition of *character* from a well-educated person and (2) a sad declaration of her feeling of inability to establish herself as an individual in her own right who could and would command the recognition of others.]

As a supplementary question Mrs. Black was asked what her Person was doing with her hands. She replied, as a further index of her identification with the drawn figure, "Two clasped. I find myself doing that all the time. Why do I do it?" She then demonstrated by placing her left hand, palm up, in the palm of the right hand.

Chromatic Person

Again the chromatic figure is larger than the achromatic. Otherwise it is essentially a duplication of the achromatic.

After the P-D-I[2] was begun, it soon became apparent that Mrs. Black's verbal concepts for the chromatic drawings were as much a duplication of the achromatic as the graphic productions had been. In the interest of saving time, therefore, as well as in broadening the investigation, it was decided to substitute the Philo-Phobe for the full chromatic P-D-I.

Philo-Phobe[3]

The theme of waiting, always waiting, pervaded many of Mrs. Black's responses to the Philo-Phobe (P-P) questions. She commented that she had spent many lonely, anxious hours waiting for her husband to come home at night; never sure when he would return or what his condition would be. Mrs. Black possesses and is possessed by a classical New England "conscience," with the classical exaggerated sense of "duty" and an uncompromising view of right and wrong.

She would rather *have* domestic happiness than anything else. But if she could not have that, she would want financial security and " . . . to be completely without ties of any kind and not care for anyone . . . because it would demand so little." She would rather be Houdini than any other famous person of whom she has ever heard, " . . . Because he could extricate himself from any situation."

For many years she has been plagued by the feeling that she may have committed the unpardonable sin when she married William (because he had been divorced). At times she says, she has become so deeply depressed that she has seriously thought of self-destruction (by overdose of drugs), but she doubts that

---

[2]At this time it was the custom to follow the chromatic as well as the achromatic drawings with the *full* P-D-I.

[3] For the Philo-Phobe as for the H-T-P, space restrictions permit presentation only of the most significant diagnostic and prognostic material.

she would have the right to do so unless she were hopelessly ill and an unbearable burden to others.

In reply to the question, "Do you think a person is *ever justified* in taking his pleasure wherever he may find it?" she replied, most emphatically, "No! Someone is *always* hurt. There aren't two unattached people."

When she was asked if she dreamed frequently, she first heard the word *dream* as *drink*. The excessive drinking first of her father and later of her husband has been a source of tremendous frustration to her.

Apparently her dream-life is rather rich, but by no means always rewarding. She often dreams of herself as a child with her father. She has dreamt of "adulterous acts,"[4] and this has upset her. She has a repetitive dream (always in color) in which she wanders through a valley (always alone) in which there is a small stream (it is always summer there)—she has no idea where she is going or why. She often phantasies dreams to conclusion if she is awakened before completion of the episode. In nightmares she is terrified: she feels herself menaced, but she does not know by what.

If one were compelled to place a diagnostic "tag" upon this case, the most reasonable one probably would be a somewhat atypical reactive depression superimposed upon a long-standing character neurosis.

The prognostic signs were not good but neither were they too bad. The quantitative scores for the chromatic series were well below those of the achromatic series—with both below the patient's norm—but not all wholes were equally depressed—such relative specificity would augur somewhat favorably for the future. From a qualitative standpoint all drawn wholes had pathological signs, but the drawings of the chromatic series were not significantly more pathological than the achromatic, which would suggest also that although the patient was seriously disturbed, the process was by no means irreversible.

Mrs. Black requested psychotherapy. Her request was granted, and she embarked promptly upon an intensive series.

Mrs. Black responded quickly and well to what were at first wholly supportive attempts. Soon she was able to write her husband where she was and what she was doing. Several weeks after therapy had begun, Mrs. Black announced with an admixture of pride, pleasure and surprise that Mr. Black was coming to visit her in a few days.

Mr. Black did come to see his wife, and to her obvious astonishment he readily agreed not only to talk with the writer, but to undergo a psychological examination as well.

---

[4]When she was asked, "What would you like most to feel?" she replied, "My husband's arms around me." (She seeks security and assurance, but no more demanding a sharing emotional relationship than that).

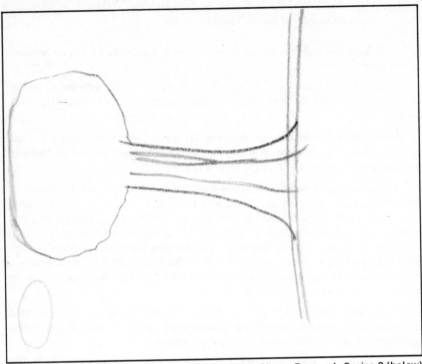

Fig. 221, Chrom.Tree 1 Series 2 (above)   Fig. 222, Chrom.Person 1 Series 2 (below)

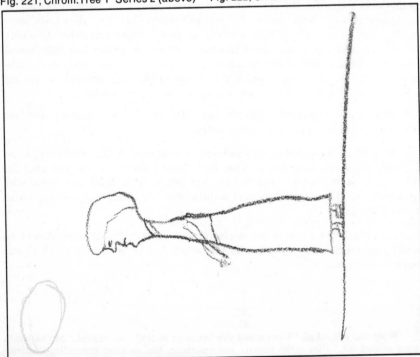

William Black

Mr. Black, a greying dark-haired, tall, 50-year-old man of rather slight physique, entered the examining room with an air of quiet, assured dignity. He was meticulously groomed and conservatively garbed.

Calm, poised, courteous, and cooperative throughout the interview, he volunteered little, but answered all questions without apparent reservation. He made it quite clear that he felt that his wife's reaction to his infidelity was little more than a "tempest in a teapot," that he believed that she would soon realize how foolishly she had acted by running away and would return to his home.

TABLE XXI

H-T-P Quantitative Scores

Achromatic		Chromatic	
	I.Q.		*I.Q.*
Per cent raw G	99	Per cent raw G	95
New Weighted	119	Net Weighted	114
Good	122	Good	119
Flaw	103	Flaw	94

It is immediately apparent that while there is greater scatter in the I.Q. scores than can be accounted for solely by advancing age (there is, it must be remembered, no correction for age in the H-T-P quantitative scoring system), Mr. Black's functional efficiency has not been radically affected by the marital rift. In general, the difference between scores for the chromatic series and those for the achromatic series is no greater than might be expected as a "normal" occurrence.

Investigation of the "factor" production on the achromatic drawings shows that Mr. Black has 9 D-scores, but they are Dls only, and to more than counterbalance them he has 11 S-scores. This almost by itself would rule out the presence of any serious emotional or organic disturbance and is in keeping with the high level of intelligence that the anamnesis indicates. On the chromatic series, he has 11 D-scores (one a D2), two more than on the achromatic, but he also has 14 S-scores, three more than on the achromatic. Again no evidence is seen of any major pathology, but one would suspect that the patient's efficiency level of function vacillates sharply at times and under different stress pressures.

The achromatic Detail scores are in the Above Average to Superior range (no withdrawal from, or denial of, reality is indicated). And even on the chromatic series only the Flaw Detail score is mildly depressed.

His Good Proportion score for both the achromatic and the chromatic drawings is in the Dull Average to Average range, which would suggest that he is becoming less flexible and is losing the ability to make quick and accurate judgments concerning immediate problems. This would not necessarily interfere with his work as an accountant, since in it he could function largely by drawing upon past experience.

The only quantitative score that is seriously depressed is the Flaw Perspective score, which is at the Moron level for both the achromatic and the chromatic drawings. This would suggest that Mr. Black is at times seriously lacking in

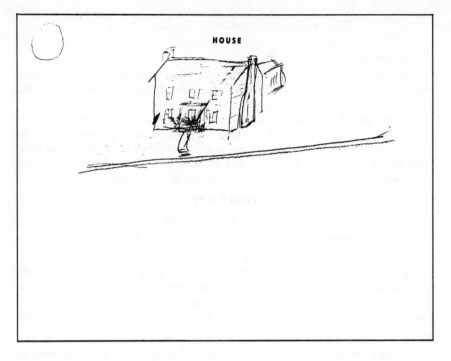

Fig. 223, Achromatic House No. 2

critical insight, particularly when he attempts to solve problems of a highly complex and abstract nature.

An examination of the quantitative scores, whole by whole, reveals that only the House Flaw score is seriously depressed (to Dull Average for the achromatic and Moron-Borderline for the chromatic). The obvious conclusions would be that Mr. Black lacks the ability to appraise his domestic situation objectively (a conclusion that is strongly supported by the history in this case).

The fact that his scores for the Person (again both achromatic and chromatic) are in the average range only—below his own norm—would imply that while Mr. Black presumably can make reasonably acceptable relationships with people in general, he is not overly concerned by, or particularly interested in, the psychosocial scene in general.

Qualitative Analysis
Achromatic House[*]

The task was accepted without protest, and the achromatic House was drawn quickly.

Mr. Black is a dextral: this House, therefore, is in reversed profile, which implies a strong conscious effort to maintain a conventional pose in the domestic situation.

The House is tiny (Mr. Black's extra-personal life is equally small); it is distant and seemingly both above and below the viewer (the subject doubts that

---

[*] A comparison of the drawings of the House by the respective disputants in cases of intra-familial conflict can be especially rewarding since the Houses are usually the shared home and represent in a sense the battlefield of combat.

he will ever attain a truly satisfying home situation and he is essentially icono-clastic in his view of domesticity). The placement of the House, this high upon the form page, implies that Mr. Black's satisfaction seeking is less concrete than abstract.

The peripheral lines are faint and indecisive throughout (the patient himself is more shaken than he cares to admit). The shading on the roof of the achro-matic House suggests that his phantasy life is tinged with anxiety. The shading indicative of wall material is that of a highly intelligent rather sensitive individual.

Mr. Black exhibited some difficulty when drawing his chimneys, and he left the full-length one transparent near the tip (sexual symbols disturb him).

His drawing sequence was atypical, but he was ultimately able to produce a whole that was well organized and in good perspective. Although his functional efficiency is somewhat interfered with by underlying emotional components, he still is able to organize acceptably.

Both the sun and the groundline were induced (the upward slope—to page right—of the latter suggests that his view of the future is certainly not optimistic). He added the pathway only after he had drawn the sun and the groundline (he is most reluctant to make himself easily accessible).

Post-Drawing Interrogation

This is his own home and he says that he sees it as close by (a view scarcely supported by the graphic evidence).

When he was asked what the House made him think of, he countered with, "You mean an abstraction? Oh! Security." But when this was followed with, "What does this House remind you of?" he returned to reality, so to speak, and continued with his previous answer, saying, "Now, I've drawn the wrong House for that."

When he was pressed to say what the House reminded him of, he commented that it reminded him of giving up his boy (the product of his first marriage) and he went on to say that this (his present) home was not a happy home. He spoke of the many times that he had moved when he was a child. He said that to him old houses are other people's houses and he added (with seeming surprise) that he'd never before realized that he had such an acute dislike for his present home.

To, "What does this House need most?" he snapped, "It needs a first class fire?" On further questioning he continued with, "Now what it needs most is a mistress (sic) to rake the leaves and redistribute the dust!" (This expresses with rather tragic and bitter succinctness what marriage means for him).

Chromatic House

The chromatic House is largely a duplicate of the achromatic, but there are several differences.

The rear wing of the achromatic House is no longer shown (color does not stimulate Mr. Black's productivity).

The House is now placed toward the upper left corner of the page (fatigue, additional stimulation, etc., promote expression of basically regressive and/or introversive tendencies).

The windows now have no panes and the door is very narrow and somewhat misplaced (fundamentally he is not an accessible, out-going sort of person). The

Fig. 224, Chromatic House No. 2 (above)   Fig. 225, Chromatic Tree No.2 (below)

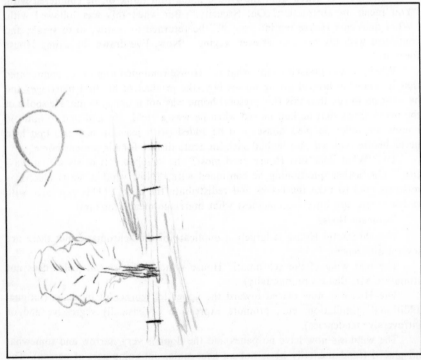

Fig. 226, Chromatic Person No.2 (above) Fig. 227, Chrom. House (Series 2) (below)

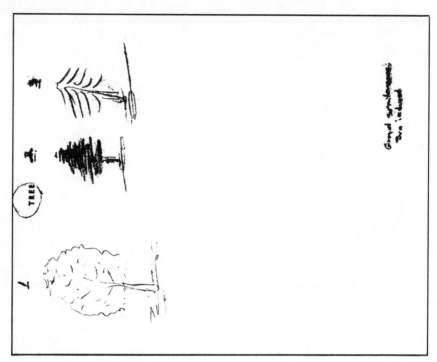

Fig. 228, Achromatic Tree No. 2

sharp, aggressive-like corners of the window frames symbolize his need to maintain a spiked wall of defense about his Ego.

Although an attempt is made to show the front porch, the porch now lacks the depth of the achromatic version (this, together with the fact that the line quality here is poorer than in the achromatic House, suggests feelings of frustration, impotence, and vulnerability).

Mr. Black used the black crayon conventionally as a pencil; only after the entire House had been completed in black (including the chimneys) was he able to use another color, red.

Again the sun and groundline were induced. He first drew the sun in black, then commented, "I could make the sun bright orange, couldn't I?" Orange at times has the connotation of ambivalence: certainly Mr. Black's view of his father is highly ambivalent (he has done his best much of the time to copy his father; yet he felt compelled to run away from home when he was only 13).

Mr. Black's use of shading on the chromatic House is definitely inferior to that on the achromatic (the shading here seems to reveal a basic Ego hypersensitivity). The chimneys are only partly shaded and there is a pathological transparency of the roof that permits a part of the chimney to the left to be seen through it (Mr. Black shows clearly once again that phallic symbols trouble him).

Achromatic Tree

When he was asked to draw as good a Tree as he could, Mr. Black countered with, "Any particular kind of Tree?" He then drew, a quite rapidly and to the writer's surprise, not *one* but *three* Trees – in the numbered order.

Tree No. 1 (which must be considered *the* achromatic Tree for the purposes of quantitative and qualitative analysis) is a relatively small figure. Mr. Black does not see himself as a powerful, vigorous and forceful figure; too, he is essentially introversive).

The placement of the Tree is definitely pathological (he'd apparently like nothing better than to be able to shuck off the trials and tribulations of adulthood and return to a dependent childhood state).

His high basic intelligence level is clearly demonstrated by his employment of a combination of actual presentation and presentation by implication for his Tree's branch system.

Feminine characteristics predominate in this Tree. Small wonder that the patient's attempts to emulate his father's dominant masculinity have been neither successful not satisfying. In many respects he is as aloof and refined as Major Black was overbearing and gross.

Mr. Black drew the groundline spontaneously here. He has a subconscious need to tie into reality and to seek stability. The sun (induced) is placed to the center in this drawing. If he could regress, he could have his father (the sun) as a source of warmth in the immediate future, yet the sun (father) surrounding the word Tree (self) would completely dominate him.

It is strongly suspected that Trees No. 2 and No. 3 represent subordinate factors (perhaps relatively well organized *alter egos*) within his personality. Tree No. 2 (definitely masculine in character) is rather deeply shaded (Mr. Black presumably has strong latent homosexual tendencies which he is able to suppress most of the time but which cause him anxiety). Tree No. 3 may well represent a wish that at some distant time he might assume a wholly mature masculine role (but the size of the Tree argues that he views such an attainment as highly unlikely).

Post-Drawing Interrogation

His Tree (No. 1) is a maple (definitely a feminine Tree) and he believes that it is alive because, "It (branch system) represents foliage rather than bare limbs."

After he had stated that Tree No. 1 looked more like a woman because of its roundness, he was asked whether Trees No. 2 and 3 looked more like a man or a woman and why. Of Tree No. 2 he said, "If I have to say, I'd say it looks more like a man . . . association of pine timber with strength." Of No. 3 he first commented, "I wish I hadn't drawn so damned many." When pressed, he continued with, 'though rather hesitantly, "I would say that resembles a man also . . . Christmas decorations are associated with Santa Claus – and I've always felt that the head of the house is usually the person who holds the purse strings." (About as wide an association swing as one sentence could well encompass).

He stated (with a display of emotion that he did his best to conceal) that Tree No. 3 reminded him of his mother (this after he had stated almost too vehemently that Trees No. 1 and 2 reminded him of no one).

When he was asked if Tree (No.1) was healthy, he responded with an emphatic, "Yes!" When he was requested to tell what there was about it that gave him that impression, he made no response at first and did not look at the drawing until he was specifically urged to do so. He then said, "That it's straight

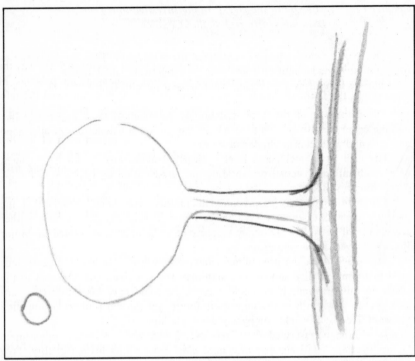

Fig. 229, Chrom.Tree 1 Series 2 (above)   Fig. 230, Chrom.Person 1 Series 2 (below)

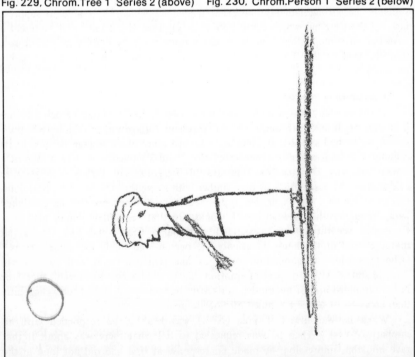

and that it's more or less symmetrical and that it's well developed." He was then asked if he liked precision and order and he replied, "*I* hang up my pajamas. My son thinks the floor was made to hang them on." He then volunteered the information that he would most certainly know it if anyone ever moved anything on his desk (a comment that speaks for itself).

In conclusion, he was asked to tell what sort of person each of his three Trees might be if each were a person and not a Tree. Of No. 1 he said, "I would like to be this Tree: it is more desirable from the standpoint of comfort and attractiveness with reference to the others." (Stilted language of a type often used by obsessives or paranoids). Of No. 2 he commented, "It is a good Tree in poor soil." (The environment, not he, is at fault). No. 3 would represent holiday festivities (he still longs for the happy childhood that he did not have).

Chromatic Tree

The chromatic Tree is, in essence, a duplicate of the achromatic, but there are certain differences.

The vine-like shading that Mr. Black uses on the trunk frequently is seen in the drawings of subjects who are having difficulty in controlling the expression of powerful basic drives.

Both the groundline and the sun had to be induced here.

The size of the sun in comparison with the Tree suggests that Mr. Black's father (though he has been dead for some years) still plays a major role in Mr. Black's life. In general, only children draw suns with rays.

After he had drawn the groundline, Mr. Black drew the fence (additional Ego protection and still another indication of his need to maintain himself relatively inaccessible).

When black is employed for the trunk of the Tree, it usually is used throughout the Tree (as a pencil, so to speak).

Achromatic Person

There was a noticeable pause after the instructions had been given and before Mr. Black began to draw. When he did begin, however, he worked rapidly and purposefully until the head—with features—was completed (there is little doubt that he has drawn this many times before—*Mrs.* Black later stated that it was almost a photographic reproduction of a portrait that they possessed of Major Black).

As he was producing the body, however, Mr. Black *sotto voce* muttered, "I think I never tried to draw a *complete* picture of a Person before."

Mr. Black's Person is very large indeed, compared to his House and Tree, and offers further proof, if any is needed, of the dominant role which his father has played (and still plays) in his life.

Here, in contrast to the House, we have the profile customarily drawn by a dextral subject. But the profile is absolute (Mr. Black shows once again that he will engage in psychosocial activities only on his own terms).

Again the whole is placed in the upper left corner (so far as Mr. Black is concerned, his Person's head is the Person). His deep desire to seek the security of the past (fragile as it was at times) and his equally deep reluctance to face the future are pointed up by the cliff-like slope upwards to the right of the groundline (induced).

Fig. 231, Achromatic Person No. 2

Mr. Black's feelings of masculine-role inadequacy are revealed by (1) his stress on the nose, the hair and the beard of his drawn Person in sharp contrast to (2) the inadequacy (and occasional transparency) of the remainder of the figure, below the head, and at the genital area, particularly.

In part, the patient's preference for intellectual activity over the more physical is shown by the relative size and precise delineation of the head.

Once again the sun (induced) is drawn in the future from a temporal standpoint in relation to the Person.

Post-Drawing Interrogation

Mr. Black quickly identified the Person as his father. He said that it was a copy of a picture that he had on the wall at home.

The drawn Person makes the patient think of "cordiality;" reminds him of "Mmmmm—Stability." (Major Black was gregarious and quite consistent.) Mr. Black stated that the Person was in good health; when he was asked what gave him that impression, he paused for a moment, then laughed and answered, "I don't know, except that my father was never sick, and it was intended as a representation of him." While he was saying this, he drew the picture toward him and reinforced the collar lines.

He was then requested to define his mother in two words. He said, "Gentle. You want *two* words? The other word would be *calmness*." (The present Mrs. Black does not possess these two traits.)

When he was asked if he felt that most people were happy, he answered forceful, "No, sir!" And when he was asked why he said that, he continued, "Well, it's a result of my observations. Most of my observation has been as an accountant." To, "Why did you take up accountancy?" he replied, "I got tired of selling the same sort of things to the same sort of people day in and day out. I thought accountancy would be mentally stimulating." (He has found figures more stimulating than people.)

When he was asked of whom his Person reminded him, he said, "I think of Robert E. Lee—the fact that he (father) was a Confederate soldier—and the profile." To, "Does that Person remind you of yourself?" he answered, "Not particularly." He then stated, in answer to a subsequent question, that he supposed that he would like to be like his father.

When he was queried as to what his drawn Person needed most, he said, after repeating the question thoughtfully, "I think he doesn't need anything; his wants were simple; he was a philosophical type of person; he was sufficiently resourceful to make do with what he had." (And there was a rather wistful note of envy in his voice.)

In reply to the question, "What has this Person got in his other hand (the one not visible)?" Mr. Black stated, "He's probably holding a tall cane—staff like." (He can present an impressive phallic symbol in phantasy only.)

Chromatic Person

As a general concept, the chromatic Person is similar to the achromatic: however, there are several differences that are somewhat favorable from a diagnostic and prognostic standpoint.

This Person is produced in more realistic proportion than the achromatic. The profile is no longer absolute and rigid. The staff was drawn with great difficulty and hesitantly, but it is visible.

And the drawn whole, for the first time since the achromatic House, is not placed as far up on the page and to the left as it can well go.

For Mr. Black the H-T-P seems to have provided a sort of beneficial catharsis (as it frequently does).

By the time he had completed his chromatic Person, Mr. Black was visibly tired and beginning to indicate a desire to bring the interview to a close. It was decided, therefore, to omit the chromatic P-D-I, since the drawings of the two series were so similar.

Mr. Black made it clear during this interview that he missed his wife and wanted her to return to his home; he was quite willing, however, not to press her and was apparently relieved when he learned that she was then in therapy. It can be stated with some assurance that Mr. Black loved his wife (unfortunately his concept of "love" bore only limited similarity to that of his wife).

After Mrs. Black had been under intensive therapy for three months, the clinical picture had improved markedly. All overt symptoms of the reactive depression had disappeared. Mrs. Black had made many friends in her new environment; she had become (so her employer said) a very efficient, in fact almost invaluable, secretary.

She was able to discuss her husband and their difficulties unemotionally and freely. But, as was probably to have been expected, she apparently understood William little better than before.

She spoke frequently of returning to William's home and of wanting to "pick up the pieces" and go on as if nothing had happened. But it was quite apparent that she intended to "forgive" him and then to embark again upon the hopeless task of reformation that she had undertaken so blithely and blindly years before.

It was decided to administer the H-T-P again to determine more objectively just how much improvement had actually been brought about and whether it had been more than merely superficial.

TABLE XXII

Quantitative Analysis, Mrs. Black, Series No. 2

Achromatic		Chromatic	
	I.Q.		*I.Q.*
Per cent raw G	96	Per cent Raw G	87
Net Weighted	100	Net Weighted	95
Good	102	Good	100
Flaw	94	Flaw	83

The I.Qs. for the achromatic drawings (series No. 2) are eight points higher than for series No. 1 except for the flaw I.Q. which is unchanged. For the chromatic series No. 2 (compared with series No. 1) the improvement is considerably greater.

Once again the chromatic I.Qs. are below the achromatic, but now none is of lower level than Dull Average.

Analysis of the Raw Scores shows a drop of 2 D-scores for achromatic series No. 2 when compared with series No. 1; and an increase of 3 S-scores over the first achromatic series. The chromatic series No. 2 has 6 less D-scores than series No. 1 and an increase of 2 S-scores over the first series. And the means score scatter for both the achromatic and the chromatic drawings for series No. 2 (well within "normal" limits) contrasts quite favorably with the relatively wide scatter of series No. 1.

For the achromatic drawings (Series No. 2) only the Good Proportion score and the Flaw Perspective score are below average (each is in the Dull Average range). For the chromatic series No. 2, however, both Proportion scores are Dull Average, and the Flaw Perspective score is still in the Moron area. From this one would assume that when she is not overly pressed Mrs. Black can now function at an efficiency level not too far below her true potential. She is still, however, in a rather vulnerable state, so to speak, and when she is faced with sudden and unexpected pressures, her intellectual functioning (particularly that involving objective, critical analysis of more abstract problems) can be expected to suffer a rather striking loss of efficiency.

On the achromatic drawings (Series No. 2) her scores for the House and Tree are of at least Average quality; for the Person, however, both the Good and the Flaw scores are Dull Average. For the chromatic series No. 2 the same scores pertain except that the Flaw score for the House is only Moron to Borderline. From these scores, we may presume that although Mrs. Black apparently has become able to develop a view of her domestic relationship that is more objective and less emotionally explosive, under pressure she probably would be unable to maintain an objective critical attitude. And she still is having difficulty in psycho-social situations in general because of her almost contemptuous view of herself as a failure as a person.

In sum, then, from a quantitative standpoint, there has been definite super-ficial improvement and even some change for the better that may be regarded as more basic.

Achromatic House

This House, which is qualitatively far better than achromatic House No. 1, seems to represent a corresponding improvement in Mrs. Black's reaction to her domestic difficulties.

She now is able to solve the angulation and other spatial relationship prob-lems which formerly proved insoluble.

The windows of the House no longer are barred. The sun (induced) now is not the deflated ellipse of the first H-T-P series.

She still cannot bring herself to correct all transparencies, however. The location of the transparency lends itself apparently to the following speculation: Mrs. Black feels that much of what she thinks is obvious (the roof area is trans-parent) and her Ego defenses are something less than adequate (the overhanging eaves lack substance). Mrs. Black, who has such contempt for failure, feels com-pelled to leave visible proof of her own inadequacy because of her deep-seated need for punishment.

Her line quality emphasis on the main (front) wall of this House seems to express her feeling that she must present an equally strong "face" to the world.

She still cannot give her chimneys (male sex symbol) depth, and her porch which protects, in a sense, her door (female sex symbol) had no depth either. She sighed deeply when drawing each chimney, incidentally.

Post-Drawing Interrogation

Once again this is her own home. She would want her husband and her son to occupy it with her. When she was asked why she would want those particular people, she said, "Why they – uh – they're the two people that belong there – ridiculous question."

The theme of "going home" pervaded many of her answers.

She declared that this was a happy House. To, "What gives you that im-pression?" she replied, "It's setting – with big trees around it; it's great archi-tectural plan." (This last shows a pathetic need for a status symbol and is sheer wishful thinking, for there are literally hundreds of houses in her State of iden-tical and equally unprepossessing design.)

Chromatic House

In most respects this is a duplication of achromatic House No. 2. As in series No. 1, Mrs. Black tends to produce larger figures when she is emotionally stimu-lated and fatigued.

Her continuing inability to deal adequately with sexual symbols (chimneys, porch and door) does not augur well for a satisfactory resumption of her marital state.

She makes no attempt to deal with color as such for the House itself, using the black crayon as a pencil substitute. Her use of green for the spontaneously drawn ground is, of course, quite conventional. The sun (also drawn spontaneously) is of conventional shape, but the orange color hints at an unfortunately ambivalent attitude toward the source of warmth in her domestic environment (her husband).

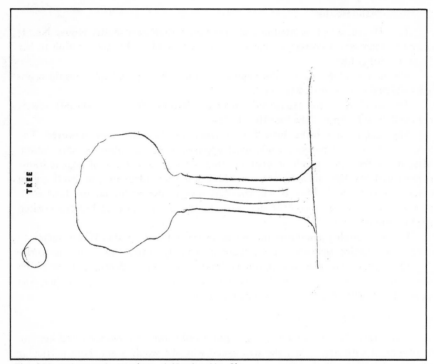

Fig. 232, Achromatic Tree No. 1 (Series No. 2)

Achromatic Tree

Mrs. Black drew her achromatic Tree (Figure 232) with considerably more assurance than she exhibited when she was drawing achromatic Tree (Figure 218).

This is still a "keyhole" Tree in effect (there is a great deal of latent hostility bottled up within Mrs. Black). The branch system still is small in comparison to the trunk (Mrs. Black feels sorely frustrated in her attempts to derive satisfaction from and in her environment).

There are fewer of the "vine-like" lines on the trunk: the patient is now better able to control her expression of basic impulses.

Post-Drawing Interrogation

She comments: "It's an oak Tree. It's very badly proportioned this time." To the question, "What's bad about it?" she replied, "Too much trunk for the foliage."

When she was asked how old the Tree was, she answered, "Of course if it's the *actual* Tree, it's very old." To the follow-up question, "How old is *this* Tree that you have just drawn?" she answered, *sotto voce,* "Oh! This one— I don't know." (It is Mrs. Black's *maturity* age, not her *chronological* age that is in question.)

In reply to, "Which does that Tree look more like to you: a man or a woman? she began, "I still say a Tree . . ." then stopped abruptly. When the original question was repeated, she said, "This might look more like a woman, since it has a head of hair, if you get what I mean." (She is beginning to be able to regard herself as a woman again.)

When she was asked which way the Tree might be facing if it were a Person instead of a Tree, she said, "Toward me, I guess. No—it's probably a profile; here's the head of the Person." With her finger she indicated that the Tree's "head" would be facing toward the left margin of the page. Such a comment indicates, almost invariably, that the subject "sees" the Tree as some specific person; this was the case here, as her answer to T23, "Whom does that Tree remind you of?" made clear. She said (after repeating the question) "The same! No! It couldn't possibly . . . " And when she was asked, "Why did you start to say *the same?*" she continued with, "Oh, the profile! The schiz. in me is coming out." Further questioning revealed that the Person in question was the teacher upon whom she once had had such a "crush," as she put it.

To, "What does that Tree need most?" she asked, "The Tree? The Tree seems to be fairly self-sufficient." (She, too, is now beginning to feel fairly self-sufficient.)

After the formal P-D-I had been completed, Mrs. Black was asked what the two vertical, vine-like lines on the Tree's trunk might be. She replied, "I don't know; it's just the trunk of the Tree. Bark doesn't run like that. It was put on to keep the Tree from looking like an ice cream cone." (This orally-fixated concept seems to express Mrs. Black's resentment at being treated by her husband as if she were—like the ice cream cone—a "sweet treat" of relatively little, and certainly fleeting, value. It seems also to reveal that for her, emotional warmth is as shattering of ego-defensive barriers as the rays of the sun are destructive of form for the symbol-concept). She continued with, "It gives solidity to the trunk to keep it looking like an empty container." (There seems no doubt that her hysterectomy was a severely traumatic experience for her; further, she feels emotionally depleted.)

Chromatic Tree

Once again the chromatic production is essentially a duplicate of the achromatic except for an increase in size and for the fact that in contrast to the achromatic Tree, the branch structure and the trunk are in reasonably satisfactory size relationship, which is a good prognostic sign.

Her inability to close completely the periphery of her branch system suggests that under pressure she may speedily lose control and behave impulsively and unwisely.

When she was drawing the vine-like lines on the trunk, she commented spontaneously, "I don't know what they mean, but I'm going to put them in, 'cause if you don't it looks so empty." (As was said before, there seems little doubt that her hysterectomy was a severely traumatic experience. It was difficult enough for her to regard herself as a woman even before the surgery.)

Her use of color for the Tree and the ground is quite conventional. The Tree was the only whole for which she was able to use color—other than black— (presumably because it is the least likely of the three wholes to arouse specific associations). Her failure to employ shading is in keeping with her compulsive need to approach everything bluntly, rigidly, and undiplomatically.

Fig. 233, Achromatic Person No. 1 (Series No. 2)

Achromatic Person

Mrs. Black still feels pathetically inadequate as a female and in general finds it necessary to devalue femininity.

All essential details now are present, however.

The only arm shown is inadequate, but it is reinforced (suggesting that she now is willing once again to attempt to manipulate her environment). The neck is still too long (one doubts that she will ever abandon her deeply ingrained Puritanical view of sensuality).

The figure would be in absolute profile, but for the fact that both feet are shown (she will always, one suspects, feel impelled to dictate the terms upon which she will deal with others). The feet ('though rather tiny and inadequate) are in considerably better proportional relationship to the whole figure than in achromatic Person (Figure 219).

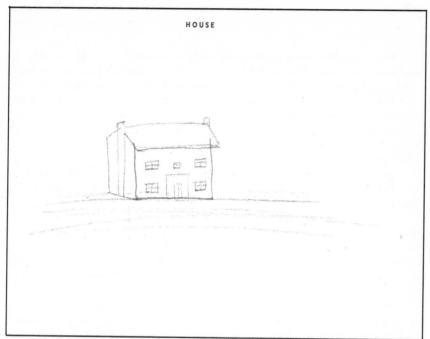

HOUSE

Fig. 234, Achromatic House No. 1 (Series No. 2)

The figure is completely lacking in grace and fluidity (it still reminds her of her husband's paramour and must, accordingly, be defeminized). The backline makes the Person look like a stooped-over old lady (certainly Mrs. Black feels decrepit and unappealing).

Despite all these factors achromatic Person (Figure 233) is qualitatively superior to achromatic Person (Figure 219)—a favorable prognostic sign.

Post-Drawing Interrogation

Mrs. Black first identified her Person as a "Woman–40-ish–nobody." But when she was asked about whom she was thinking while she was drawing, she replied quickly, "Me!"

To, "What is she doing?" she ejaculated, "Oh! God!" then sighed and continued with, "I don't know what she's doing. She's just standing -I insist she's just standing there." (At this time Mrs. Black was seriously thinking about going back to her husband and finding herself quite unable to make up her mind.)

When she was asked what her Person was thinking about, she first cleared her throat noisily, then said, "I don't know that either. She doesn't look very intelligent." And to the subsequent, "How does she feel?" she said, "All right– I suppose." To the follow up, "Why do you suppose she feels all right?" Mrs. Black continued with, "Why does she? I can't see that she has any feeling particularly–one way or the other." (Mrs. Black was then emotionally exhausted herself.)

To, "What does that Person make you think of?" Mrs. Black commented, "Phew!" Then, after a noticeable pause, she went on, "I don't know. I'm all mixed up about that Person." When she was asked, "What do you mean you're *all mixed up?*" she answered, "I think it's a dumb-looking drawing."

When she was asked of what the Person reminded her, she repeated the question, then said, "The same one I drew before." (referring to her husband's mistress). To the subsequent question, "Does it remind you as much of her now as it did before?" she replied, "Well this one has an ear." The writer than asked, "Was it so difficult to draw the ear?" to which Mrs. Black replied, "No. But I was conscious of it as I was drawing it." (To Mrs. Black this Person is alternately a rather vicious caricature of William's paramour and a savage travesty of herself; as a self-portrait it is disturbing to her.)

She said that the drawn Person was well, and when queried as to what gave her that impression, she stated, "Oh, she stands up there as though she was able to–go."

Mrs. Black says, shrugging her shoulders, that she reckons that the Person reminds her of " . . . that no 'count school teacher. She was a complete nonentity." This time it was *not* the school teacher with whom the patient had roomed at college. (Mrs. Black has a painful need to be able to control others, and Mrs. Black had nothing but contempt for this particular teacher's inability to control the class).

At the conclusion of the P-D-I, Mrs. Black was asked what the diagonal line at the Person's waist represented. She said, wryly, "That's the belt, so she doesn't look like a flour sack." (Mrs. Black herself is a very small person–in physique –and can in no sense be regarded as possessing an alluring figure.)

Chromatic Person

Once again the chromatic figure in essence is a duplication of its achromatic counterpart except that it is larger.

There was quite a bit of reinforcement of peripheral lines (fatigued and under additional emotional pressure, Mrs. Black feels threatened with an imminent loss of Ego control).

There is definite "reversed taper" of the arm here (it was barely suggested in the achromatic drawing)–it seems probable that here this expresses Mrs. Black's growing wish to extend the hand of amity and to seek reconciliation with her husband (with a concomitant fear, apparently, that in so doing she may lose control of the situation).

The chromatic Person is not rigidly "framed" (as was the achromatic Person). Another favorable prognostic sign–albeit a small one.

Mrs. Black employs bright color for the sun only, and again an ambivalent attitude toward the figure of warmth and power is expressed.

When she was asked to draw the groundline, Mrs. Black paused for a moment, then picked up the black crayon and began to draw, commenting, "The groundline mustn't be green here because she's inside."

To sum up: the drawings and the Post-drawing Interrogation of Series No. 2 show that Mrs. Black has made definite progress; the basic changes, however, are by no means as extensive as one would wish or as the clinical picture would suggest.

Several weeks later (against the writer's advice), Mrs. Black returned to her husband.

It was the writer's opinion that as things were then the chances for Mr. and Mrs. Black to enjoy a mutually satisfactory marital relationship were very poor. In the first place, neither had been well prepared for marriage. Both had failed to mature fully psychosexually. Both lacked the flexibility essential to a satisfactory sharing marriage.

True, Mrs. Black was no longer seriously disturbed, but otherwise she was relatively unchanged. Mr. Black had not changed at all. As for the marriage itself, only the precipitating point of conflict was altered: each of the principals still was seeking from the other what the other could not possibly provide.

The initial H-T-Ps provided the writer with what might be called three-dimensional personality portraits[6] of Blanche and William Black. Clearly revealed were the major elements of conflict and friction in the relationship to each other of these two unhappy people which had brought about their marital disruption.

Mrs. Black's second H-T-P, administered after she had been receiving intensive psychotherapy for three months, provided evidence which indicated that — as the clinical picture so strongly suggested — definite improvement had taken place, but that much of that improvement would have to be regarded still as tenuous.

Postscript

Mrs. Black left her husband again about a year later. During the subsequent decade there were three more reconciliations and three more separations. They are now living apart — apparently permanently.

---

[6] The reader must *not* assume that by "portrait" any photographic-like detailing is implied, or that by "three-dimensional" the portrait is believed to be all-revealing and conclusive. None the less, as this case demonstrates, valuable information in depth concerning the subjects' respective personalities was elicited.

Clifford E. Davis is the Church Occupations Counselor of the United Presbyterian Church of the United States of America. His undergraduate work was completed at the University of Pittsburgh and graduate work at Pennsylvania State University and University of Pittsburgh. He is a graduate of the Western Theological Seminary (Pittsburgh Theological Seminary). Dr. Davis is a member of the American Psychological Association.

He served nine years as a parish minister, then worked as a psychologist at the Western State Penitentiary in Pittsburgh, Pennsylvania. During this latter period he engaged in counseling at the Glenshaw Presbyterian Church.

During the early 1940's at the Western Theological Seminary, Dr. Davis pioneered in the church's use of newly emerging psychological tools for understanding human personality. This experimental program proved so helpful that in 1947 the Board of Christian Education of the United Presbyterian Church, U.S.A., asked Dr. Davis to attempt a similar program for the entire denomination. This program now includes testing of all applicants to the denomination's theological seminaries and all applicants for missionary service. This service also is used by the American Baptist Convention and several independent seminaries.

Chapter 16

Uses of the H-T-P Technique By and In the Church

Clifford E. Davis, Ph.D.

Clifford Davis offers an interesting account of the initially rigid resistance of Church personnel workers to the deeper psychodynamic theories and to the Rorschach. He describes vividly the suspicious vigilance of the Church's guardians who "watched with wary eye lest some personification of evil leap full-blown from the inkblots."

The author's account of the next step, one of acceptance of the H-T-P and its subsequent use in various phases of work in the Church, is both illuminating and heartening to those who have come in contact with the barriers which, at times, have separated theology and psychology.

Among the added dividends of his pointed and wry comments on the social scene, he offers us this poignant gem: " 'teen-age pregnancies often solved to the parents' satisfaction by a marriage service intoned over the heads of the reluctant principals." Eds.

Introduction

During recent decades the Church, with other social agencies, shared what formerly it had regarded as an exclusive area of concern: personality development. This involved attempts to control environment at two important points:

(1) control of stimuli reaching a person, and this included many forms of censorship and restriction, (2) attempt to interpret stimuli which reached an individual. A final and difficult goal was to adequately relate the impersonal world, as it entered through the sense organs, to ideals and values, which in ecclesiastical terminology often has been called "the inner world."

It always has been difficult to evaluate this "inner world." The appearance of personality tests, especially projective tests, offered a hope to some segments of the church, but was viewed with alarm by more conservative elements, as seen in the reaction against behaviorism and the concepts of Sigmund Freud, both encountering considerable resistance from the church, particularly noticeable in these two areas.

I. *Use of tests in reaching decisions.* Critics have noted that tests were not perfect instruments and should not be used as the sole basis for making decisions. Attention also was called that such use might limit attempts to encourage future growth. Counselors concerned with developing professional leadership were interested in helping individuals overcome personality immaturities and weaknesses and encourage maturity and wisdom in decision-making. Encouragement of such growth occurs during and after the seminary period and is related to many phases of future work in the Church, including counseling and making of administrative decisions. The desired growth was, of course, basic to the entire educational program of the Church.

II. *Fear of the unconscious.* Initial reaction of the Church to Sigmund Freud largely was negative. When the work of Horney and Sullivan became available, however, there was a sharp swing toward their philosophies. Serious discussion of Freudian concepts revealed a general attitude on the part of Church groups to ignore or deny rather than to study and attempt to achieve understanding. One projective technique accepted and in limited use in the United Presbyterian church is the House-Tree-Person Drawing Test. Its initial impact was favorable. Its administration presents minimal threat, since the drawing of pictures is a normal part of the educational process. The acceptance of this technique is in sharp contrast to attitudes shown toward the Rorschach where the stimulus and purpose are not fully understood and the uninformed watch with wary eye lest some personification of evil leaps fullblown from the inkblot.

Areas of H-T-P Use in the United Presbyterian Church

I. *Theological Students.* The H-T-P technique has been used as a group test for entering classes at several theological seminaries. The purpose was twofold:

    1. To aid in understanding group tendencies which might emerge. At times patterns appear as a high number of students with dependency needs or an unusually large number with low academic ability.

    2. To identify students in need of individual counseling.

II. *Young Ministers and Wives Mostly in their Third Year in the Ministry.* The test has been given to groups of young ministers and their wives, most of whom were in the third year of their vocational life. It has assisted in clarifying vocational goals and in identifying a variety of marital problems.

III. *Missionary Candidates.* Here the H-T-P was used to amplify further questions, about a candidate, previously raised by other tests or other sources of

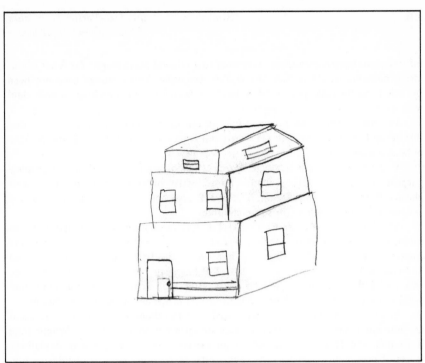

Fig. 235 (above)

Fig. 236 (below)

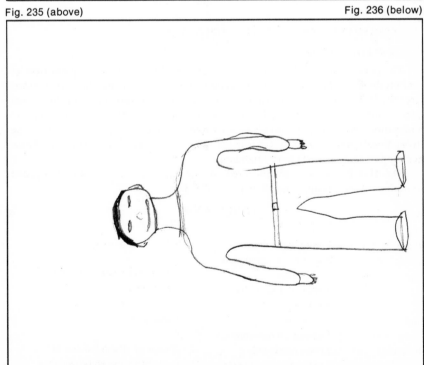

information. Such a candidate is referred to a clinical psychologist for fuller evaluation, and this would include the H-T-P technique. Test findings have not been the sole basis for making a decision, but have been useful in matching an individual with a job.

IV. *Adolescents and Young Adults in the Local Church.* Purposes of testing this group have been twofold: (1) vocational counseling and (2) counseling because of behavior problems.

V. *Primary Church School Children.* (School grades 1-3). Here the primary purpose was to note group tendencies to assist in determining points to emphasize in the teaching program. The H-T-P also has assisted in detecting active and/or potential problems in some children.

VI. *Missionary Children.* The H-T-P has been used on a modest scale to evaluate children of missionaries in India, largely for personal and scholastic counseling purposes while these children are in the first twelve grades of school in India. In addition, the use of the H-T-P has been incorporated into scholastic and vocational counseling for the years after high school when the individual usually leaves India for further education in Europe or in the United States.

In general the H-T-P has been used, not to "diagnose," but to understand an individual and clarify other sources of information about him. Where time is limited, the H-T-P has served as an excellent interview guide in explaining facets of personality suggested by other tests, or by other sources of information, i.e., references.

DETAILED EXPERIENCES WITH CHURCH GROUPS

Theological Students

The population tested consists of men approved by candidates' committees of local presbyteries and by admissions' committees of at least one theological seminary. Students have been interviewed; they have written statements of vocational purpose and have taken the following psychological tests: Minnesota Multiphasic Personality Inventory, Guilford-Zimmerman Temperament Survey, and the Strong Vocational Interest Test. Their college records have been examined. These men supposedly are satisfactory candidates.

The H-T-P test was administered to one entering class (- 45). Suggested limitations of this group, as noted on the H-T-P, were:

TABLE XXIII

	Achromatic	Chromatic
House	1 without chimney	3 without chimneys
	3 with weak, inadequate chimneys	2 with weak chimneys
		2 chimneys overemphasized
	5 without doorknobs	6 without paths
	9 without paths	
Tree	1 knothole	1 knothole
	1 sawed-off main branch	
Person (1)	3 drew heads only	3 showed strong feelings of
	2 with hands in pockets	inadequacy as symbolized by a
		badge, football uniform, and
		beard. (Some of these are listed under
		individual cases which follow.)

From the above group, and similar groups, two general problems can be identified from the H-T-P material.

I. *The Individual who holds a Conservative Theology.* This seems to be the type of person who leans heavily upon the authority of the Church both in its written creeds, as well as in its current hierarchy. This person tends to be inflexible in social contacts and intolerant of conflicting philosophies. This person tends to overemphasize his treatment of the chimney, seems to accept creeds and programs and passes them on without much modification. Such a person is a good "company man" but inadequate in dealing with people as unique individuals. His social inadequacies further are emphasized by inadequate or weak treatment of the door and path. More observations are needed to determine if limitations revealed in achromatic drawings can be resolved more easily than limitations revealed in chromatic drawings.

II. *Vocational Indecision.* This type of person is not sure whether to enter the work of the general pastorate or one of the specialized ministries of the Church. These specialized ministries often are seen as less threatening than the general pastorate which deals directly with a congregation. This type of personality tends to appear along with an inadequate treatment of the chimney, along with the inclusion of symbols as badges and uniforms. Symbols appear mostly in chromatic drawings.

Individual Case Studies from Groups I and II

A A is a single male, 24 years, I.Q. 113 as measured by the WAIS; he is completing his work in theological seminary. His social history, obtained from an autobiographical statement, reveals much mother domination and marked feelings of inadequacy. His original achromatic drawing of the woman was erased and a much larger one was drawn in her place. His chromatic drawing yielded a woman without feet and included a generous use of yellow. Among the theological students the use of yellow on the drawing of the female seems associated with female domination and underlying hostility toward the female drawn. His achromatic male drawing was enlarged after erasure.

A A has been greatly influenced by extremely dominant people in the Church. One is a militant evangelist who early captured his attention. The other is his minister, a similar personality.

A B is a single, male theological student. His I.Q. is 140 as measured by the California Capacity Questionnaire. His college grade point average is C+ showing a wide discrepancy between ability and performance.

A sharp contrast is seen in his two male drawings. The achromatic male (Figure 243) shows a vigorous, athletic type; the chromatic male (Figure 239) shows a weak, inadequate individual scarcely holding the two tools depicted which can be considered as male symbols.

The chromatic female drawing (Figure 240) at first glance suggests an attractive princess-like individual, but on closer scrutiny bears more resemblance to a witch.

His scholastic performance versus his I.Q. and H-T-P items reveals significant validation of the MMPI where the hypomania (Ma) score is at the 75th T

Fig. 237 (above)   Fig. 238 (below)

Fig. 239 (above)

Fig. 240 (below)

score and the schizophrenia (Sc) score is at the 70th T score. These scores suggest a person who is exerting great effort, at least on a superficial level, but is easily discouraged and retires into himself.

A C is a young man of Italian lineage who graduated from theological seminary and is serving in the first year of his pastorate. The H-T-P was given at the time of his seminary entrance.

His H-T-P indicates his lack of confidence in himself and his occupational ability. His Houses have no chimneys; the path sharply narrows as it nears the House. His achromatic Tree drawing is small, almost inconsequential and effeminate. The chromatic Tree shows a well developed trunk with a number of well developed but sharp-ended branches covered thinly with leaves. This Tree suggests a minimum conformity covering a defensive, hostile attitude. The achromatic drawing of the male figure (Figure 241) lacks facial details; the female (Figure 242) is a dominant Person. The chromatic male drawing (Figure 244) shows a priest in ecclesiastical garb before the altar, suggesting that the subject turns to the church to obtain the support and confidence he lacks in himself.

The MMPI general scales were satisfactory, the highest T Score (60) occurring on the hypomania (Ma) scale. Two of the auxiliary scales suggested a marked prejudice and the presence of pharisaic virtue as defined by the two scales bearing these names. Apparently he has considerable difficulty in assuming the role expected of him in being the pastor of the small town church he is serving.

A C consulted the writer about what he considered immaturity by his wife and her inability to make proper social adjustments. She is 21 years old, an attrac-

Fig. 241

Fig. 242

tive young woman teaching school who has been out of college only six months. She also is in the difficult position of serving as the minister's wife in a small church where most of the people are of French descent and maintain close social grouping within the community. This young man seems, in part, to project his feelings of social inadequacy on to his wife. Certainly the feature-less face of the male pencil drawing and the total back view of the crayon drawing are consistent with the inference that *he* is experiencing feelings of social inadequacy.

A E is a young man, 22 years old at the time of seminary entrance; he had a history of homosexual activity during high school, claiming this "habit" had been discontinued at time of college entrance. He had, however, a lonely existence with few social activities and no dates during his college life. After one year in the seminary, he served as summer pastorate where he had difficulty supervising the teaching activities of the Church, as well as in preaching. At the end of summer he shaved his entire body, which became known when he contracted a skin infection resulting from this act. His prolonged effort to assume a masculine role, which he had pictured for himself, apparently was too great. A year later he spent nine months in a hospital undergoing psychiatric treatment. Subsequently he graduated from the seminary, but his social activities are still limited. He never married and shows no real interest in the opposite sex.

A E is a slightly built, weak, effeminate man in sharp contrast to both his male drawings. The chromatic drawing (Figure 245) superficially is the more conventional of the two drawings. The presence of coat and tie suggest a minimum conformity to social standards, but indicate acute discomfort in such conformity. The strained desire for masculine dominance expected by our culture in general, as well as in his professional work, is suggested by the expanded shoulders. The achromatic male drawing (Figure 236) has only the stark symbols of masculinity. Erasures on this drawing weakened the arms. Both female drawings portray crude,

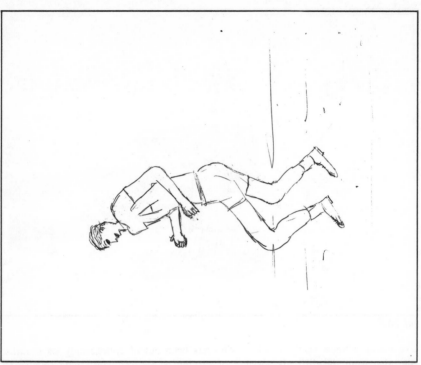

Fig. 243 (above)

Fig. 244 (below)

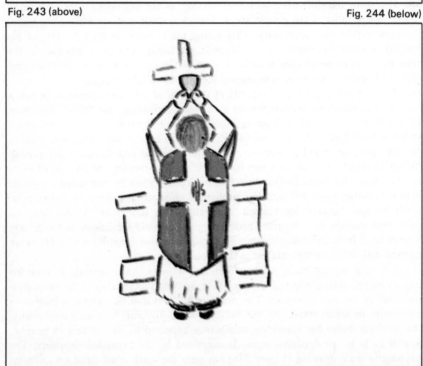

Fig. 245 (above)

Fig. 246 (below)

unattractive women. This may be connected with the cause of difficulty he reports in supervising female church school teachers on his first summer job.

Houses are drawn with no chimneys and no paths. The central way of getting out of the chromatic House (Figure 246), if one is to use a pathway, is through the garage which contains a car resembling a coffin. The window and roof and drawn in black. Both his phantasy life (roof) and social availability (pathway) are bleak and ineffective. Some effort toward social adjustment is seen in the enlargement (achromatic) of the door and the addition of the knob (Figure 235). "The achromatic House, with its progressively retreating stories, reveals dramatically the S's personality encapsulation. The very broad chromatic House with its numerous proportional and perspective flaws suggests a sort of last-ditch attempt at flight into reality. These drawings were made about nine months prior to his hospitalization. Perhaps it is in the chromatic drawing of the male as a ghoulish, lifeless automaton—reflecting feelings of depersonalization—and in the chromatic House drawing with the "coffin" in the garage—again reflecting impending feelings of devitalization and lifelessness—that the prophesying signs of his oncoming pathology most clearly can be read." [1]

Counseling Adolescents and Young Adults in the Local Church

The H-T-P technique has been used extensively in one large church in a suburban community where all types of behavior problems emerge and where a great deal of advice is sought from the professional staff regarding future vocational and educational plans. The H-T-P technique has served as an excellent "interview guide" and has been useful in understanding other sources of data. This test has assisted in identifying those with "normal" concerns about personal and social problems from those to be referred for diagnosis and counseling to psychiatrists or clinical psychologists. The former group of problems ordinarily can be dealt with by the pastor.

Material presented below deals with three case studies indicating some insights provided by the H-T-P technique. Notes and selected pictures are only suggestive and partially indicative of the assistance derived from the H-T-P technique.

B A is an attractive young woman, 20 years of age, whose parents were divorced when she was three. She lived with her mother until the ninth grade, at which time the father remarried. Then she lived with him ever since. She consulted the writer about difficulty making decisions and fear of men. She has occasional dates but usually breaks the association after two or three dates.

The achromatic Tree (Figure 247) shows a break in the trunk structure not far from the ground, as well as two knotholes, one low and one high. These may be associated, respectively, with the divorce of the parents and the disrupting change of residence when the subject shifted from the maternal to the paternal home.

Both Houses are without chimneys. The chromatic House (Figure 248) is drawn high and to the left. This placement of the House indicates strong regres-

---

[1] Thanks are extended to Mr. John N. Buck and Dr. Emanuel Hammer for their additional interpretation.

sive tendencies. The long path from the House is bordered with flowers on the right-hand side but has an austere left border, suggesting the past has been bleak but that she has good hopes for the future. Her phantasy life suggests a bright future but she does not quite know how to achieve it. The two Trees on the lawn, one masculine and one feminine, reveal her attempts to maintain a position between the two psychosexual identifications.

An interesting contrast is seen in the hand treatment of the two females. The chromatic drawing (Figure 249) shows one hand extended and accentuated by a yellow bracelet, while the achromatic figure (Figure 238) has this hand behind her back. Perhaps here is a commentary on an interest in social relationships but an inability to carry on meaningful or continued relationships.

BB is the case of a 17 year old girl who left high school in her junior year because of an illegitimate pregnancy. She is an adopted child. Parental discipline was sporadic and ineffective from early childhood. The parents lamented her social activity, while she was in high school, but showed no ability to guide her social development. She was promiscuous in dating activities, and some evidence suggests she is not certain of the paternity of her child. The achromatic drawing (Figure 237) shows a little girl with hair ribbon and hands behind her—the subject may be a girl who tries to get by by playing a coy, cute, "I-didn't-really-mean-any-harm,-I'm-only-a-little-girl" role in life.

Conflicting drives can be seen in the foot treatment where the primitive physical drives show a strong influence from the left, and the social and moral control a less adequate push from the right. The foot treatment suggests her primitive urges would overcome the controls and was confirmed by her subsequent conduct.

BC is a high school boy involved in several automobile accidents. Two of his accidents were severe and brought him into court. The third involved hitting and killing a pedestrian. The achromatic Tree shows three knotholes and three sawed-off branches which may be related to his traumatic automobile accidents. (See Figure 250.) The branches grow downward in a depressive-indicating direction. All other pictures were hazy and detached from reality, suggesting the possibility of the onset of schizophrenia, further emphasized by the extension of the Tree beyond the top of the page and by the treatment of the upper branches, hanging in space without support from the trunk. He was referred for psychiatric diagnosis and treatment.

Primary Church School Children (School grades 1-3)

Experiences described here were from a middle-class suburban community church of about 1800 members. The educational program of this institution included a nominal emphasis on traditional Protestant-American values. The lengthening interval between an affluent present and a past of economic depression has weakened emphasis upon:

1. Importance of individual effort.
2. Need for a sense of responsibility in planning education, marriage, etc.
3. Need to develop maturity in children, especially acute in boys from homes where fathers' jobs take them away much of the time.

This background reflects itself more specifically in:

1. Destructive vandalism.

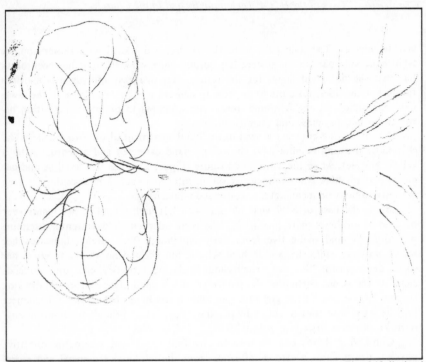

Fig. 247 (above)

Fig. 248 (below)

Fig. 249 (above)   Fig. 250 (below)

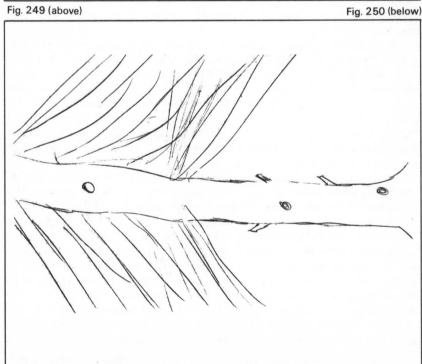

2. Need for scholastic motivation.

3. Teen-age pregnancies often solved to the parents' satisfaction by a marriage service intoned over the heads of the reluctant principals.

Testing in this church was carried out on two levels:

1. Group administration in grades one to three. The H-T-P was given to understand group conditions in the church school where parents cooperate with the Church in presenting an established and agreed upon set of social and religious values to their children.

2. Individual administration to older children, usually junior high and high school children with problems and where an understanding of personality structure is needed for adequate counseling.

Group Administration Grades 1 to 3

Grade 1: N = 8   Grade 2: N = 11   Grade 3: N = 11

HOUSES

H-T-Ps were administered in early fall shortly after the opening of the public school. First grade boys produced two paper-edged Houses; "edging" increased sharply to ten ($N = 11$) in the second grade and eight ($N = 11$) in the third grade. After their first year of contact with the world as individuals, apparently the second graders experience a feeling for a need of support and the majority express this need into the third grade.

In the chromatic drawings the boys of grades two and three drew sixteen paper-edged Houses. Six of these Houses also had inadequate and weak foundations. These findings support, in general, findings based on the achromatic drawings.

Even though a majority of these children attended nursery school and kindergarten, their outgoing social contacts were minimal. This may not reflect inadequate teaching as much as the failure of efforts to achieve desired social accomplishments before adequate maturation occurred. Each of the first and second grade series of drawings yielded two Houses without doors. However, by the third grade, all Houses had doors. Knobs usually are present. Paths are almost totally lacking. Obviously, paths cannot be added to paper-based Houses.[2] In psychological terms, the individual with a strongly felt need for security tends not to be outgoing in social contacts.

A striking pattern is seen in the chimney treatment. These children live in a community where many fathers are away from the family much of the time. Male symbolism of the chimney appears in achromatic drawings as follows:

At time of public school entrance most boys come from a female dominated environment and show inadequate male identification. This problem does not easily resolve itself in the church school environment where God, as a male image, is presented by a female teacher. Even in the third grade, nearly half the group were unable to produce an adequate male symbol in the drawing of the House. These comments apply to a specific denominational setting where, of course, gender does not apply to the deity. The child however is taught to think of God in terms of Jesus Christ where sex identification may be a factor. Only much later is he able to deal with such concepts as omniscience, omnipresence, etc.

---

[2] All chromatic Houses were paper-based. All but two achromatic Houses were paper-based.

TABLE XXIV

Chimney Treatment

	Grade 1 N = 8	Grade 2 N = 11	Grade 3 N = 11	Total N = 30
No chimney	5	2	2	9
Weak, inadequate chimney	2	3	3	8
Adequate chimney	1	6	6	13
Total	8	11	11	30

Chromatic drawings show an even greater lack of adequate male symbolism. Eleven of the Houses had no chimneys, four had weak or inadequate chimneys, and three showed exaggerated treatment of this symbol.

A low rate of anxiety is suggested by smoke coming from only a small number of chimneys. The writer is not certain whether this indicates a lack of anxiety or reflects the fact that in a community of gas or electrically heated homes many children never see smoke coming from a chimney.

TREES

The basic achromatic pattern in these subjects is an overly large trunk, in relationship to the size of the page and to the branch structure, suggesting a straining for a feeling of greater ego strength. Chromatic Trees are slightly less healthy. Five boys showed weak, inadequate trunk structures, reflecting the felt inadequacy beneath this compensatory straining; along with this, four showed trunks slanting slightly to the right suggesting a feeling of personality imbalance with an attempt to acquire more control over impulses.

Few achromatic Trees had adequate individual leaves. First graders showed two Trees with overly large, hand-like leaves, suggesting overemphasis on adjustment to the environment. (This does not appear in drawings of children of higher grades.) Four achromatic Tree drawings suggested dependency as noted by the presence of fruit. This same note of dependency was seen in chromatic drawings of these same children. The drawings served as a confirmation rather than a diagnosis of this condition, already noted by their teachers.

There were no knotholes on Trees drawn by boys of grades one and two; only three appeared on Trees drawn by third grade students. Knotholes, scars, or sawed-off limbs appear rarely on Trees drawn in this community, in sharp contrast to a slum community in the same city where 75% of the Tree drawings contained knotholes. This privileged community seems to spare its children many traumatic experiences occurring in the slum area.

PERSON

Achromatic Person drawings generally were adequate as to completeness, relative size, and line quality. Differences and inadequacies usually were in arm and hand detail, as indicated below.

Six boys drew female figures which suggested a female dominated environment. Only three males drawn were aggressive.

Arms usually were well depicted showing efforts to cope with the environment. However, an absence of striving and feelings of inadequacy were seen in two drawings. A slightly increased feeling of inadequacy was seen in the lack of

TABLE XXV

	First Grade		Second Grade		Third Grade		
	Without Arms	*Without Hands*	*Without Arms*	*Without Hands*	*Without Arms*	*Without Hands*	*Total*
Male drawings	1	2	1	1	0	4	9
Female drawings	1	3	0	3	1	4	12
Total	2	5	1	4	1	8	21

hands for both sexes, interpreted as symbolizing the difficulty of moving from a child-centered home to an environment where the child is treated as an independent individual and must make his own adjustments. This tendency was much more marked on chromatic drawings where eight males and eleven females were drawn without hands.

Several individual cases were noted for further attention. One shows a very young child playing with simple toys on a string. Two show very small individuals placed toward the top of the page. One shows a picture of fruit dropping into a basket. This boy came from a home dominated by a mother who will not allow him to grow up and has kept him in a dependent condition.

Females   Grade 1: N = 6   Grade 2: N = 14   Grade 3: N = 8   Total: N = 28

HOUSES

The same general need for support is seen among girls as among boys; low at the beginning of the first grade, a sharp rise occurs in the second grade, and continues into the third grade. Paper-basing occurred in the following instances in the achromatic Houses:

Grade 1: 2   Grade 2: 10   Grade 3: 6

The same general condition prevails in chromatic drawings where twelve Houses were paper-based and six showed weak foundations.

Grade three showed a sharp drop in adequate symbolism of the chimney. This may well be related to five knotholes which appeared in Tree drawings by these children, suggesting that a number of individuals in this grade have experienced traumatic episodes.

TABLE XXVI

Chimney Treatment

	Grade 1	Grade 2	Grade 3	Total
No chimney	4	1	1	6
Weak, inadequate chimney	1	6	5	12
Adequate chimney	1	7	2	10
Total	6	14	8	28

Girls appeared slightly more open to social contacts than boys. By the third grade all Houses have doors and knobs, but only one shows a path, seeming to indicate a development, though slow, of adequate contacts with the outside social environment.

In chromatic drawings all Houses had doors, though two were drawn without knobs. No paths were leading from the doors.

TREES

Girls show a greater tendency to slant Trees toward the right than do boys. Among drawings made by second grade girls, four Trees leaned to the right. In these same four sets of drawings, three drawings of Persons also leaned in that direction. Eight Trees slanted to the right in chromatic drawings of second and third graders. This may reflect society's demand that girls exercise self-control at an earlier age than boys.

PERSON

Girls generally indicated better contact with reality than boys. After the first grade all Persons were drawn with arms and hands. The female dominated environment is noted by the tendency to draw female figures slightly larger than male figures. In chromatic drawings, seven female figures definitely were aggressive.

Uses of the H-T-P with Missionary Children

The H-T-P technique was used by one missionary educator in India. His concern was with American missionaries' children who were of public school age and who would be leaving India for college educations in America or Europe. Two general tendencies appeared among these children.

1. *Female domination.* This seems inevitable in an environment where the demands of work take the father to other parts of the country for weeks at a time.

2. *A fear of growing up.* Since growing up means leaving the family and going half-way around the world for an education, this seems an understandable aspect of the personality of these children.

Three cases outlined below show some of the problems of these children.

C A is an 8-year-old girl who has been a school problem. Her concentration span is limited, although her intelligence is reported as "average." She is at the teacher's desk the first thing in the morning and the last thing in the evening always to "tell the teacher something." The number of her siblings is unknown, although all have been bed-wetters except the oldest. C.A still is a chronic bed-wetter.

The father tends to be alternately strict and permissive. The mother is less strict but shouts a great deal when disciplining her children. The mother becomes defensive when any criticism, real or implied, is made of her children.

Here the question is whether these missionary parents constantly are tempted or required to give an excessive amount of time to their occupational duties at the expense of their relationships to their families. An excessive amount of smoke coming from the chimneys of both Houses might imply anxiety in the relationships at home. There probably is self-identification as seen in the small animal placed outside the door and headed toward the left of the page, suggesting a reluctance to grow up.

The dependency needs are also seen in the appearance of fruit on both achromatic and chromatic Trees. Some traumatic experience apparently is indicated by the large knothole on the achromatic Tree. On the chromatic Tree, the knothole disappears, implying that the traumatic experiences may be connected with the more current responsibilities of growing up. As long as she can remain a small child and not face the normal responsibilities of her age, these traumatic feelings may be reduced.

It is interesting to note that her first Person drawing places him under the shelter of a Tree. This appears to represent a small, inadequate self-image as does the small animal in the House drawing.

C B is a boy, aged eight, the fifth child of missionary parents. His father is a physician and his mother a nurse. During the pre-school years his care was entrusted to an Indian female servant. He has been a consistent bed-wetter until recently. Their normal home is in the hills with periodic visits to the plains because of the demands of their work. When the mother spoke of returning to the plains, the bed-wetting started again. Both parents have been working in the hospital and have had little time for their children. The boy tells "tall tales" to the teacher so that she never is certain what is phantasy. These tales are about his activities and family achievements. His intelligence is better than average.

Two sets of H-T-P pictures were made by this boy. The first set suggested his strong need for security. He is reluctant to grow up and apparently is fearful of the experience of the growing up process. A threat to his personality is seen in his achromatic Tree drawing which slants sharply to the left and is marred by a hole in the trunk and by a nick in the trunk caused by a "man behind the tree chopping it." The chromatic Tree suggests dependency with rounded branches bearing fruit. Its sharp broken Tree limbs suggest aggression. Since the limbs are broken off, it suggests aggression directed at him from the outside. Most of his drawings of Persons are male images facing the right of the page, in all cases armed with guns or clubs. The weapons may symbolize his need for protection from outside aggression.

This boy was referred to a psychiatrist for further study. He may be helped by a stable environment, as much contact as possible with his father, and by his parents not comparing him with other children.

CC is an eight-and-a-half-year boy with an I.Q. of 122. He is a chronic bed-wetter, worries a great deal about disasters such as war, accidents, plane crashes, etc. He plays alone because he says no one will play with him. His mother was formerly a Roman Catholic, but recently has had few formal contacts with her religion. The boy asked permission to join the Catholic Church and this was granted about three or four months before he was tested.

The mother is meticulous in her housework and often suggests the boy go and remain outside. Then he secretly slips back into the house and goes to his room to play. The father always is "tired" and does not talk much when at home.

After a conference with his school counselor, C C stopped his bed-wetting for eleven nights. He resumed it, however, on the day his parents received a letter of praise concerning his younger brother away at boarding school.

The boy has a great need for security. On his achromatic House, he labels each room with a name so its function will not be misunderstood. It is interesting to note that access to his House is directly from the outside to his dressing room which he thus can enter in privacy. In the kitchen two people are shown eating. The third and fourth members of the family do not appear. Figures are so small it is impossible to tell their identity. There is inadequate male symbolism. The priest undoubtedly plays a much needed substitute father role during this boy's attendance at boarding school.

The achromatic Tree drawing presents a leaning figure suggesting a weak and uncertain personality development. Two knotholes raise the question of traumatic experiences, one may have been the birth of his younger brother. The self-image of this boy is inadequate. He seeks shelter which apparently he is finding in the Catholic church.

His self-image is clearly shown by his chromatic drawing of the male figure, a ludicrous, harmless clown, who ordinarily is not expected to meet the usual social demands. The female Person is a witch, probably his image of a mother figure as mean, threatening, and forbidding, which explains his avoidance of her.

Conclusion

The Church is interested in cultural factors which furnish the raw materials for personality development as well as in the processes by which these materials are fashioned into unique personalities. This interest is expressed by trying to understand, control, and guide personality development in ways which will match moral and spiritual development with technological advances. The Church moves eagerly to understand symbolic meaning when a child of ten years retreats from the everyday world of television and second-hand cars toward a world in which genii can be summoned to fill his desires; or when a Negro boy of nine years draws brown rabbits which lay larger eggs than white rabbits as he faces the inequalities of a life which must be lived within his brown skin.

Perhaps a young Indian man best illustrated the mirror of art which reflects the deep places of the human spirit as he stood in his native desert, showing his failures as an adult by the cut branches of his Tree drawing. On the "thumbs" of the eroded buttes of his home environment he revealed his dependence on the past and his personal inadequacy in facing the future. Even the fragile symbol of the yucca plant drooped as it reflected his inadequate manhood. Time ploughed deep furrows into his native land which divided, defined, and limited his life. Hope, manifested by a weak but colorful wing, lifted him above his reality for a brief exhilarating period before plunging him back to his unchanging eternal present.

Perhaps as the Church learns to delve deeper into the remote abysses of the human spirit, weakness will be strengthened, phantasy become reality, and hopes translated into accomplishments. The inner world of men as seen in their drawings of Houses, Trees, and Persons proliferates into a social order dominated by the computer and machine. But these too, hopefully, man can control and use with honor, dignity, and compassion.[3]

---

[3] The H-T-P technique was *used* in all cases except those mentioned under "Conclusion." Drawings mentioned here were obtained from a variety of situations.

Naohiko Fukada received his B.A. degree in 1950 from Doshisha University of Kyoto, Japan. From 1950 to 1961 he was a member of the psychological staff of the Kyoto Prefecture Child Guidance Clinic. In this capacity he examined many children and also worked with them in psychotherapy.

Since 1961 he has been Assistant Professor of Psychology at Dosisha Women's College of Liberal Arts in Kyoto.

Mr. Fukada long has been interested in projective drawings (H-T-P, Draw-a-Human-Figure, Draw-a-Family, Draw-a-Group, etc.) and has accumulated hundreds of drawings of children (both Japanese[1] and Tongan).

Mr. Fukada has published some ten papers, most of them relating to projective drawings.

---

[1] Mr. Fukada's illustrations (q.v.) show well the progressive quantitative and qualitative maturation of the concept of the Tree with the developing age of the subject. Ed.

Chapter 17

Japanese Children's Tree Drawings

Naohiko Fukada, B.A.

Mr. Fukada discusses the maturation of Japanese children's concept of a Tree, appraising maturation on the basis of their employment of six fundamental details in their achromatic Tree drawings. He illustrates with tables and graphs, and with drawings picked from his collection of more than 1,800.

The author also presents the results of his studies of the placement of the drawings of House, Tree, and Person on the form page by Japanese children of different ages and school grade levels. Of particular interest is his comparison of his findings with those of Jolles and Beck in their studies of American children.

Introduction

Historical investigation of the psychological studies of drawing behavior reveals three major approaches.[2] These are arranged successively below.

1. The first was a period when many psychologists concentrated on the developmental stages in children's drawings. Leading researchers were Kerschensteiner, Luguet, Eng and others. This period was organized around researches dating from the 1880's.

[2]*Acknowledgement:* The author expresses his deep thanks to Mr. John N. Buck, formerly Chief Psychologist, Lynchburg State Colony, Lynchburg, Virginia, for his suggestions in regard to the investigation and organization of this paper, and to Dr. Emanuel F. Hammer for his help with his paper's organization and English. Thanks are also due to Mrs. June Yoshikawa, Professor of English, Doshisha Women's College, Kyoto, Japan, for help in correcting the author's use of the English language.

2. The second period was opened by Goodenough, who utilized data from the first period, and standardized an Intelligence Test based upon the procedure of asking a child to draw a man. After this, investigations were made dealing with such variables as age, sex, and race. Goodenough's Draw-a-Man Test was widely used throughout the world.

3. Finally, the third and current period arrived. Buck, in 1948, published a new *projective* drawing technique. *The H-T-P Test.* In 1949, Machover published her book, *Personality Projection in the Human Figure.* These two major contributions inaugurated the new period. This phase might be called the "Projective Drawing Period." Goodenough had used her Test to assess intelligence, but by now Buck and Machover, as is well known, used drawings as a vehicle for personality projection. These developments are described clearly in Goodenough's (1928), and Goodenough & Harris's (1950) historical overview.

Drawings are of much interest to psychologists, but their use as a projective device still presents many problems. What are the various relationships to be found between drawings and personality? Many clinicians with considerable interest in projective techniques recognize the value of projective techniques, but others still question the validity of such tools for personality analysis.

Problem

Before a projective test is used, it must be examined for its validity.

The H-T-P Test provides many useful ideas, especially the drawing of a Tree; this is a new and charming approach. The Human Figure drawing as an idea is not as new. The House drawing presents some problems in cross-cultural use. Japanese houses are very different from American houses, as are houses in other countries different from each other. Buck's most significant contribution for cross-cultural research is the Tree drawing.

Individual projective drawings of the Tree differ very much from one another. Many complex factors appear in such productions: some are the product of age, some of sex, some of intellectual factors, and some of other individual personality factors. The simplest factors are those of development and sex. Hence, the writer has attempted to find developmental trends in the Tree drawings of male and female children.

Research, 1

In Kyoto, 917 Day Nursery children in day nursery classrooms were asked to draw a Tree. There was no time limit. Twelve color crayons (Green, Red, Blue, Yellow, Black, White, Pink ("skin color"), Yellow-Green, Brown, Orange, Gray and Gentian Blue) were supplied. The drawing paper's size was 25cm x 18cm. The writer examined the drawings for the presence or absence of the six fundamental parts of a tree: Trunk, Branch, Leaves, Fruit, Roots, and Blossoms. The results are presented in Table XXVII. (Fukada, 1957)

Research, 2

The next higher age range now was sampled. Similar to Research 1, in Kyoto, each of 919 Elementary School pupils was asked to draw a Tree. The conditions were: No time limit, use of a pencil, and freedom to erase. The writer examined these drawings for the presence or absence of the aforementioned six basic parts of the Tree. The results are shown in Table XXVIII. (Fukada, 1959)

TABLE XXVII

Frequency, by Age and Sex, of Children's Drawings: the Various Basic Parts of a Tree

N—917
Boys—502
Girls—415

Age	3:0-3:11		4:0-4:11		5:0-5:11		6:0-6:11	
Sex	Boy	Girl	Boy	Girl	Boy	Girl	Boy	Girl
Trunk	6 (46)*	11 (85)	58 (98.3)	46 (100.0)	128 (95.5)	108 (96.4)	279 (94.5)	241 (98.8)
Branch	2 (15)	5 (38)	32 (53.3)	21 (45.7)	80 (59.7)	78 (69.6)	203 (68.8)	164 (67.2)
Leaves	2 (15)	2 (15)	23 (38.3)	18 (39.2)	73 (54.5)	54 (48.2)	123 (41.7)	151 (61.9)
Fruits	0	3 (23)	8 (13.3)	6 (13.1)	44 (32.8)	30 (26.8)	106 (35.9)	72 (29.5)
Root	0	0	3 (5.0)	0	31 (23.1)	21 (18.8)	107 (36.2)	81 (33.2)
Blossoms	0	2 (15)	6 (10.0)	9 (19.6)	15 (11.2)	30 (26.8)	65 (22.0)	76 (31.2)
Number of Children	13	13	60	46	134	112	295	244
	26		106		246		539	

*The number in the parentheses shows the percentage of children who draw the part of the tree in each age level.

Tables XXVII and XXVIII show the number of children in each group, according to sex, age, and grade. The respective percentages are included, Graph I expresses in percentage form the combined data from Tables XXVII and XXVIII.

Table XXIX (and Graph 2) show the average number of drawn parts of a Tree by age, school grade, and sex. As may be seen, the average number increases to the first grade, then dips mildly, and thereafter more or less maintains itself.

Goodenough found an increase in score on her Human Drawing Test up to ten years of age. But, according to Graph 2, Tree drawings reach their highest score at the age of about seven years.[3] Perhaps the easier any object is to draw (if it is not absolutely too simple), the more it serves to elicit projective material. Hopefully this paper will stimulate further research in this area.

Discussion, 1

Buck (1948, P. 52) says regarding the order of elements appearing in drawing a Tree, that it is first the trunk, then the branch, and then the leaves. In my study in another culture (Tonga Island, Fukada, 1961), I, too, found the order of sequential presentation to be trunk, then branch, and then leaves. This supports Buck's theoretical underpinning of the H-T-P, and of cross-cultural research with the H-T-P. The relatively basic and culturally-uncontaminated aspect

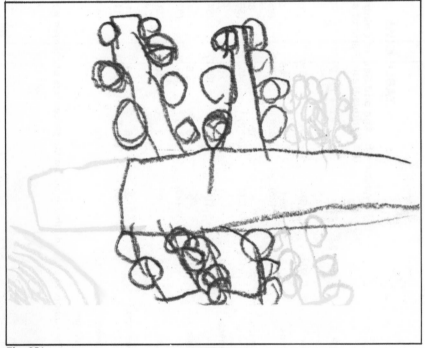

Fig. 251

---

[3] This is by the author's simple item count method and *not* by that of the H-T-P quantitative scoring system which includes details, their method of presentation, and their size and spatial relationships. (Ed.)

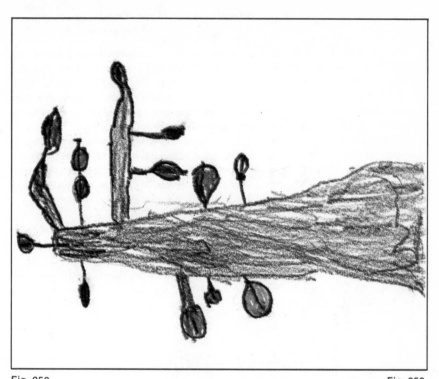

Fig. 252

Fig. 253

TABLE XXVIII

Frequency, by School Grade and Sex of Older Children's Drawings: Various Essential Parts of the Tree

Grade	1st		2nd		3rd		4th		5th		6th	
Sex	Boy	Girl	Boy	Girl	Boy	Girl	Boy	Girl	Boy	Girl	Boy	Girl
Trunk	73 (100.0)*	68 (100.0)	82 (100.0)	72 (100.0)	81 (100.0)	72 (100.0)	82 (100.0)	76 (100.0)	79 (100.0)	80 (100.0)	82 (100.0)	72 (100.0)
Branch	64 (87.6)	59 (86.7)	72 (90.3)	62 (86.1)	70 (86.4)	52 (72.2)	69 (84.2)	69 (90.8)	65 (82.4)	76 (95.0)	67 (81.7)	63 (87.5)
Leaves	69 (94.5)	58 (85.3)	64 (78.0)	50 (69.4)	72 (88.9)	62 (86.1)	68 (82.9)	54 (71.0)	73 (92.4)	68 (85.0)	64 (78.0)	64 (88.9)
Fruits	38 (52.0)	32 (47.1)	29 (35.4)	27 (37.5)	34 (42.0)	27 (37.5)	35 (42.5)	31 (40.8)	28 (35.4)	26 (32.5)	28 (34.2)	29 (40.3)
Root	6 (8.1)	1 (1.5)	2 (2.4)	3 (4.2)	2 (2.5)	1 (1.4)	0	1 (1.3)	1 (1.3)	6 (3.7)	3 (3.7)	0
Blossoms	3 (4.1)	7 (10.3)	13 (15.8)	15 (20.8)	2 (2.5)	3 (4.2)	0	0	1 (1.3)	5 (6.3)	2 (2.4)	0
Number of Children	73	68	82	72	81	72	82	76	79	80	82	72
	141		154		153		158		159		154	

*The numbers in parentheses show the percentage of children drawing the various parts of the Tree.

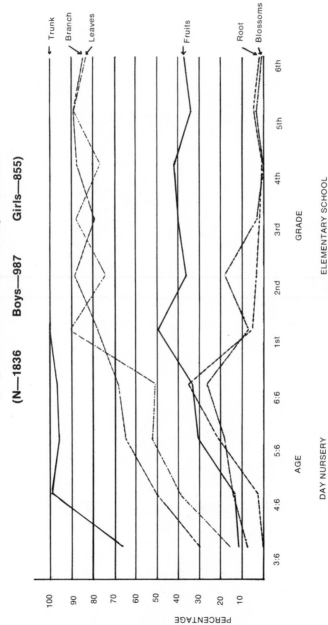

GRAPH I

Developmental Trends of Drawings of Basic Tree Parts by Age and School Grade of Boys and Girls

(N—1836   Boys—987   Girls—855)

Fig. 254

Fig. 255

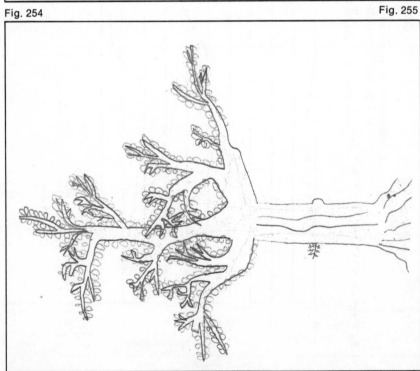

provided by the drawing of a Tree makes its use suitable for the developmental assessment of subjects in different cultures.

It is interesting to note the developmental curves of the fruit and blossom elements in Tree drawings. Both curves rise up to six years of age, but after that they drop. Why should this happen? To speculate: Younger children draw what they know, not what they see. Children in their earlier years imagine, in an idealized manner, that all Trees possess everything: that is, trunk branch, leaves, root, fruit and blossoms. However, later they become more realistic and find many Trees in their daily life which have neither blossoms nor fruit. After this, both of these parts disappear from their Tree drawings.

The drawing of blossoms or fruit by older children then may be a symptom of regression or fixation. Surely there are few older children who draw fruit or blossoms, and developmentally these items belong to the years below seven. Generally, boys and girls show similar developmental trends. See Table XXVII and XXVIII, and Graph II.

Research, 3, and, Discussion, 2

The writer collected 870 H-T-Ps from three different public elementary schools in Kyoto City. School grade and sex distributions appear in Table XXX. The investigation process was similar to that of Jolles and Beck (1953a, 1953b) who divided each drawing sheet into half-inch strips, then for the horizontal placement study quantitative values were assigned to each strip from left to right, as -8, -7 to +7, +8 for the House drawing, and -7, -6 to +6 for the Tree and the Person drawings. Similarly for the vertical placement study, from top to bottom +6 to -7 were assigned to the House drawing, and +8 to -8 were assigned

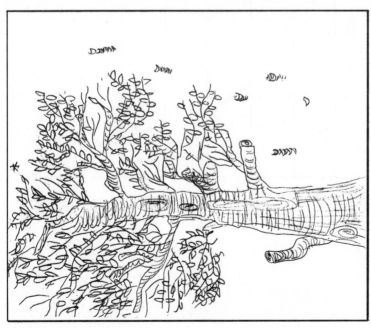

Fig. 256

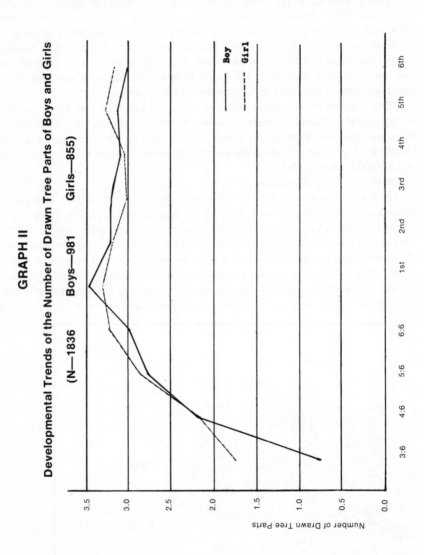

GRAPH II

Developmental Trends of the Number of Drawn Tree Parts of Boys and Girls

(N—1836   Boys—981   Girls—855)

for the Tree and the Person drawings. Using these assigned numbers, the horizontal and vertical placement results are shown in Tables XXXI and XXXII.

In horizontal placement, the writer identifies a few trends, as follows:

1. Generally, the average midpoint of the drawings was to the left of the geometric center of the sheet.

2. The midpoints of the Person, the Tree and the House were, respectively, from left to right across the sheet.

Similar trends appeared in Jolles' and Beck's data. But no clear trend was present of the drawing's center's moving to the right side of the sheet as the children became older.

In vertical placement, Japanese children show a general trend: As they grow older, their drawings rise in vertical placement.

Though Jolles and Beck found that the midpoint of the House drawing tended to be the highest, followed by the Tree, and last by the Person, Japanese children show a different order: Their order of placement, from highest to lowest, was the Person, the House, and the Tree. This differs from the order which Buck found: In American samples the Tree was placed higher than the House or the Person. Further investigations concerning this point will be made.

In school grade development, neither boys nor girls have shown clear differences either in their horizontal or their vertical placements.

TABLE XXIX

Average Number of Each Child's Drawing Parts

Age or Grade	Sex	Total No. of Drawn Parts	Number of Children	Average Number of Drawn Parts by Individual
3:0-3:11	Boy	10	13	0.77
	Girl	23	13	1.77
Total		33	26	1.27
4:0-4:11	Boy	131	60	2.18
	Girl	100	46	2.17
Total		231	106	2.18
5:0-5:11	Boy	371	134	2.77
	Girl	321	112	2.87
Total		692	246	2.81
6:0-6:11	Boy	883	295	2.99
	Girl	785	244	3.22
Total		1668	539	3.09
1st	Boy	253	73	3.17
	Girl	225	68	3.31
Total		478	141	3.39
2nd	Boy	264	82	3.22
	Girl	229	72	3.18
Total		493	154	3.20
3rd	Boy	261	81	3.22
	Girl	217	72	3.01
Total		478	153	3.12
4th	Boy	254	82	3.10
	Girl	231	76	3.04
Total		485	158	3.07
5th	Boy	247	79	3.13
	Girl	261	80	3.26
Total		508	159	3.19
6th	Boy	246	82	3.00
	Girl	228	72	3.17
Total		474	154	3.08

TABLE XXX
Distribution of Subjects

Grade		1	3	5	8	Total
Sex	M	110	107	92	121	430
	F	123	101	107	109	440
Total		233	208	199	230	870

TABLE XXXI
Means and Sigmas for Horizontal Placement of Each Whole: According to Sex and Grade

Drawing	Sex	GRADE				
		1	3	5	8	Means
House	M	-0.15	0.06	0.03	0.15	0.00
		(1.45)	(1.13)	(1.27)	(1.16)	(1.26)
	F	-0.33	-0.02	0.00	-0.04	-0.10
		(1.53)	(0.96)	(1.24)	(1.33)	(1.30)
Tree	M	-0.88	-0.83	-0.59	-0.67	-0.75
		(1.13)	(0.95)	(0.66)	(0.75)	(0.91)
	F	-0.80	-0.63	-0.59	-0.52	-0.64
		(0.92)	(0.72)	(0.74)	(0.78)	(0.81)
Person	M	-0.92	-0.91	-1.13	-0.64	-0.89
		(1.05)	(0.95)	(1.00)	(1.15)	(1.00)
	F	-0.85	-0.74	-0.82	-0.65	-0.77
		(0.97)	(0.99)	(0.73)	(1.04)	(0.93)

Numbers show Means, *and numbers in parentheses show* Sigmas.

TABLE XXXII
Means and Sigmas for Vertical Placement of Each Whole: According to Sex and Grade

Drawing	Sex	GRADE				
		1	3	5	8	Means
House	M	-0.32	-0.01	-0.01	-0.01	-0.10
		(1.91)	(1.33)	(1.22)	(1.27)	(1.47)
	F	-0.51	0.01	0.00	0.27	-0.01
		(1.69)	(1.19)	(1.28)	(1.22)	(1.41)
Tree	M	-0.45	-0.32	-0.32	0.00	-0.26
		(0.95)	(0.90)	(1.09)	(0.86)	(0.96)
	F	-0.24	-0.18	-0.11	0.03	-0.13
		(1.08)	(0.83)	(0.93)	(0.80)	(0.93)
Person	M	0.00	0.14	0.14	0.15	0.03
		(1.67)	(1.37)	(1.26)	(1 14)	(1.38)
	F	0.08	0.09	1.11	0.11	0.09
		(1.53)	(1.21)	(1.13)	(0.96)	(1.21)

Numbers show Means, *and numbers in parentheses show* Sigmas.

Summary

Fully 1800 children in Japan were asked to draw a Tree. Their drawings were examined for the presence or absence of six fundamental parts of the Tree. In addition, 900 Japanese children were asked to draw a House, a Person and a Tree. On the basis of the results from these studies, the author tentatively draws the following conclusions:

1. The Tree drawing, as a simpler concept than the Person drawing for children to produce and as a drawing concept in which maturational or intellectual factors drop out sooner, may serve at an early age as a device through which personality factors may be projected relatively less muted by the intellectual-maturational dimension. Therefore, the younger the subject, the greater may be the projective usefulness of the Tree drawing in comparison with the drawing of the House and the Person.

2. The drawing of fruit or blossoms in the Tree drawings, as the developmental trend suggests, may be a regressive sign and all the more so as the subject moves past the seven-year mark.

3. The midpoint of the H-T-P drawings of Japanese children is to the left of the geometric center of the drawing sheet. The Person is drawn farthest to the left; next comes the Tree, and the House is drawn comparatively nearer to the right side of the sheet.

4. The vertical placement of Japanese children's drawings rises as the children become older.

References

Buck, J. N. The H-T-P Technique, *J. Clin. Psychol.*, 1948.

Goodenough, F. L. Studies in the psychology of children's drawings. *Psychol. Bull.*, 1928.

—————————— and Dale B. Harris. Studies in the psychology of children's drawings, 1928-1949, *Psychol. Bull.*, 1950.

Fukada, N. YŌJI NO JYUMOKU BYŌGA NO HATTATSUTEKI KEN-KYŪ. (The development study of children's tree drawings.) SHINRIGAKU-KENKYŪ *(Jap. J. Psychol.)*, 1957.

—————————— GAKUDŌ NO JYUMOKU BYŌGA HATTATSU-TEKI KENKYŪ. (The development study of children's tree drawings.) *SHINRIGAKU — KENKYŪ (Jap. J. Psychol.), 1959.*

—————————— TONGATŌ JIDŌ NO BYŌGA. (Tongan children's drawings.) *Twenty-fifth Japanese Psychological Association Annual Meeting Report*, 1961.

Jolles, I., and H. S. Beck. A study of the validity of some hypotheses for the qualitative interpretation of the H-T-P for children of elementary school age: 3 Horizontal placement. J. Clin. Psychol. 1953a.

—————————— A study of the validity of some hypotheses for the qualitative interpretation of the H-T-P for children of elementary school age: 4. Vertical placement. *J. Clin. Psychol.*, 1953b.

Dr. Victor Barnouw received his A.B. degree from Columbia College and his Ph.D. degree in Anthropology (1948) from Columbia University, where he studied with Ruth Benedict, Ralph Linton, and Abram Kardiner. He was trained in Rorschach test administration by Florence Miale and attended Workshops on the Rorschach (Klopfer), the Thematic Apperception Test (Tomkins), and Drawing Analysis (Hammer and Landisberg).

In the summers of 1944 and 1946, he did field work in culture-and-personality at the Court Oreilles and Lac du Flambeau Chippewa reservations in Wisconsin, collecting life history material, ethnographic data, and projective test data. In the Fall of 1952 and from August to December, 1963, he made a study of a Sindhi refugee community in Poona District, India.

He taught Anthropology at Brooklyn College, University of Buffalo, University of Illinois, Washington University, and at present is full Professor of Anthropology at the University of Wisconsin-Milwaukee.

His publications include: "The Phantasy World of a Chippewa Woman," *Psychiatry*, XII, Feb., 1949, pp. 67-76; "Ruth Benedict: Appolonian and Dionysian," *University of Toronto Quarterly*, XVIII, April, 1949, pp. 241-253; "Acculturation and Personality Among the Wisconsin Chippewa," *Memoir No. 72 of the American Anthropological Association 1950;* "The Social Structure of a Sindhi Refugee Community," *Social Forces*, XXXIII, Dec., 1954, pp. 142-152; "A Psychological Interpretation of a Chippewa Origin Legend," *Journal of American Folklore*, LXVIII (Part I, No. 267), Jan.-March, 1955, pp. 73-86, (Part II, No. 268), April-June, 1955, pp. 211-223, (Part III, No. 269), July-Sept., 1955, pp. 341-355; "Rorschachs of 13 Nepalese Men and Children," *Primary Records in Culture and Personality*, Microcard Publications, I, No. 2, The Microcard Foundation, 1956; "Rorschachs of Eighteen Chippewa (Ojibwa) Men and Women," *Primary Records in Culture and Personality*, Microcard Publications, II, No. 6, Madison, Wis., 1957; and the well received book, *Culture and Personality*, The Dorsey Press, Homewood, Ill., 1963.

Chapter 18

Cross-Cultural Research With the House-Tree-Person Test

Victor Barnouw, Ph.D.

Victor Barnouw, in his chapter on cross-cultural research with the H-T-P, provides an excellent example of the rich investigative possibilities in this complex area. He very ably switches perspective, first looking at the various cultures through the spectrum of projective techniques and then looking at the projective data from the frame of reference of the different cultures. Toward the end of the chapter, he combines the material to distill some rather interesting, specific conclusions. (Eds.)

My experience has been that the House-Tree-Person Test provides a highly promising technique for studies in the field of culture-and-personality. I have used a modified form of the H-T-P in two projects. One was a comparison of H-T-Ps from college students in three countries: Japan, India, and the United States. The second was an experiment with the H-T-P and Rorschach protocols of 100 married Maharashtrian men from a rural district near Poona, India, of whom fifty had undergone voluntary sterilization and fifty had not.

The chapter is in three parts. Part One, an introductory section, draws briefly from a previously published chapter on drawing analysis (Barnouw, 1963); it deals with advantages and limitations of cross-cultural work with projective drawings. Part Two is concerned with the comparative study of the H-T-Ps of Japanese, Indian, and American college students. Part Three describes an experiment using the H-T-P and Rorschach protocols of 100 rural Maharashtrains. Data in Parts Two and Three are presented herein for the first time.

Part One: Introduction

Analysis of Drawings from Non-Western Cultures

Anthropologists working in the field of culture-and-personality often have collected drawings in the field but often have not published analyses of such material. There are exceptions, notably Trude Schmidl-Waehner's interpretation of Alorese children's drawings collected by Cora du Bois (Du Bois, 1944) and Jane Belo's discussion of Balinese children's drawings (Belo, 1955). There also is an excellent unpublished master's thesis by Michal S. Lowenfels on the interpretation of Chippewa children's drawings (Lowenfels, 1950). In each of these studies drawings were unstructured, with no specific directions as to what to draw.

Drawings are easily collected in the field. They require little equipment — mainly paper, pencils, and crayons. Such drawings, once acquired, provide permanent records of expression of personality.

Some writers have argued against the use of drawing analysis in cross-cultural studies on the grounds that a subject's drawings reflect cultural traditions, local art styles, and mannerisms. It is easy, for example to recognize the influence of Balinese art in Belo's drawings by Balinese children, or the influence of Northwest Coast art styles on the drawings of local Indian children (Anastasi and Foley, 1938). Wayne Dennis writes that when Bedouins draw a person, they make drawings averaging only two inches in height and consisting of little more than straight lines with darkened surfaces. Dennis says this occurs because Bedouin art mainly involves small geometric decorations. He therefore is skeptical about the validity of the Machover test. (Dennis, 1960.) Perhaps the character of Bedouin art in some ways reflects Bedouin personality. One expects there would be mutual interplay between cultural traditions and the modal personality of a society.

Schmidl-Waehner's blind analysis of Alorese children's drawings had much in common with Emil Oberholzer's blind analysis of Alorese Rorschachs and with Abram Kardiner's interpretation of Alorese life history material. Similarly, Michal S. Lowenfels' blind analysis of Chippewa children's drawings yielded results which agreed strikingly with a Rorschach study of Chippewa children made by Blanche G. Watrous, and with William Caudill's interpretations of Chippewa children's TATs.[1] These apparently successful experiments in the interpretation of drawings drawn by members of non-Western societies give us reason to think that efforts in this field are worth making.

In connection with the H-T-P, some allowances must be made for cultural differences. Some societies have flat-roofed houses. Buck's interpretations about the symbolism of the roof may not apply in such a culture. Kinds of trees known to subjects also must be considered. When asked to draw a Tree, 42 Indian college students in my sample of 111 drew coconut trees. There may be psychological reasons for this selection, but one obvious reason would be the widespread presence of coconut trees in India. Degree of familiarity with paper and pencil and representational art must also be taken into account. Uneducated Maharash-

---

[1] For this material, see Barnouw, 1963, pp. 278-283; also pp. 250-252 and 268-269.

trian Indian peasants drew crude, primitive-looking pictures when compared with Indian college students in Poona.

Instructions must be given in the native language with difficulties in translation possibly ensuing. For example, in looking through my Indian H-T-Ps, I was surprised to find many subjects instead of drawing a Tree, had drawn a plant in a pot. This often was a tulsi plant, considered sacred. The reason for this response is the Marathi word for tree also may mean plant. A question as "What is the best part of the Person?" already ambiguous in English, may receive further twists in meaning through translation. These are not crucial difficulties, and certainly less than with verbal projective techniques like the Rorschach and TAT. The best way to gauge the usefulness of the H-T-P in other cultures is to observe its use in a specific cultural milieu. Therefore, let us consider the H-T-Ps of Japanese, Indian, and American college students.

Part Two

Comparisons of H-T-Ps of Japanese, Indian and American College Students

A modified form of the H-T-P was administered by the writer to undergraduates in Tokyo, Poona, and Milwaukee. The H-T-Ps were administered on a group basis to introductory psychology classes in Japan and India in the Spring and Fall of 1963, and to introductory anthropology classes in the United States in the Fall and Winter of 1964-65.

Colleges were Sir Parashurambhau (referred to as S.P. College), Poona, India; Seijio University, Tokyo, Japan; and the University of Wisconsin-Milwaukee, U.S.A.[2] In all three of the colleges, the student body may be characterized as middle-class, although this term may have somewhat different connotations in the three countries. Most of the students were freshmen, 18-19 years of age (see Table XXXIII).

Administrative Procedures

In each test administration students were given recently sharpened No. 2 pencils and two 4-page sheets (7 x 8½ inches), one for drawings, the other for the written part of the test. Students were instructed not to write their names but to state age and sex. After the third drawing[3] in which students were asked to draw as good a Person as they could, they were instructed: "If you drew a male Person in the last drawing, now draw a female. If you drew a female Person, now draw a male." Students were allowed about ten minutes for each drawing.

When drawings were completed, they were asked the following questions:

1. How old is the House? How old is the Tree? How old are each of the two Persons?

2. What is the best part of the House? What is the best part of the Tree? What is the best part of each of the two Persons?

---

[2] I express my thanks to those persons who made it possible to administer the H-T-P, particularly Principal Malegaonkar and Professor K. N. Pillay of S. P. College, Professor V. K. Kothurkar of the University of Poona, and Professor Hajime Nakamura of the University of Tokyo, Professor Yoshihisa Tanaka of the University of Tokyo and of Sejiio University and Professor Takao Sofue of Meiji University, Tokyo.

[3] House and Tree being first and second drawings.

TABLE XXXIII [4]

Ages and Sex of Subjects

College	17	18	19	20	21	22	23	24	25	26	27	Totals
					AGE							
Tokyo												
Females	0	65	19	0	0	0	0	0	0	0	0	84
Males*	0	4	13	3	7	0	0	0	0	0	0	28
Total	0	69	32	3	7	0	0	0	0	0	0	112
Poona												
Females**	7	30	34	8	3	0	0	0	0	0	0	84
Males***	0	7	5	3	3	5	3	0	0	0	1	28
Total	7	37	39	11	6	5	3	0	0	0	1	112
Milwaukee												
Females	6	62	6	5	5	0	0	0	0	0	0	84
Males	0	19	5	1	2	0	0	0	1	0	0	28
Total	6	81	11	6	7	0	0	0	1	0	0	112
TOTAL	13	187	82	20	20	5	3	0	1	0	1	336

*One male did not give his age.
**Two females did not give their ages.
***One male did not give his age.

The total number of H-T-P records was 336: 252 by women, 84 by men.

3. What is the worst part of the House? What is the worst part of the Tree? What is the worst part of each of the two Persons?

4. What does the House need most? What does the Tree need most? What does each of the two Persons need most?

5. Is the Tree alive or dead?

6. Write a description of each of the two Persons.

Indian students also were asked to write a description of the House.

The foregoing questions, suggested by Dr. Emanuel F. Hammer, were designed as an abbreviated substitute for Mr. Buck's post-drawing interrogation, which I felt was too long and time-consuming.[5]

Instructions and questions were given by class instructors in English and Marathi in Poona, and in Japanese in Tokyo. Students generally wrote answers in

[4] I made use of some H-T-Ps collected by Dr. Takao Sofue from students in a course on Cultural Anthropology at Meiji University. Dr. Sofue gave the same instructions and followed the same procedures as I did. From his collection of 20 H-T-Ps I selected the records of nine younger students ranging from 19 to 21 years. Selection of records also was made on the basis of completeness of the test, weeding out those whose answers were very brief or who omitted answering questions.

My presence in India was made possible by a Faculty Research Grant from the American Institute of Indian Studies, although my project there had no relation to the H-T-P studies discussed here.

[5] As an alternative, the new chromatic (22 question) P-D-I seems well suited for group administration. See the House-Tree-Person Technique: 1966, by John N. Buck.

their native language, although many Indian and a few Japanese students wrote in English. Records later were translated into English by Mr. H. V. Phadke (Marathi) and Mrs. Joy Tsuzuki (Japanese).

My impression was that in each H-T-P administration students enjoyed taking this test. They welcomed it as a break from the usual college routine; it was something different. In each instance I said a few words about the test after drawings were turned in.

This was an exploratory study. No hypotheses were established beforehand. The purpose was to determine if there were characteristic differences in H-T-P drawings made by three groups of students. If such differences were found, did they reflect differences in cultural traditions, personality patterns, or combinations of the two.

The following analysis emphasizes uses of the H-T-P Projective Technique in the formation of hypotheses rather than in testing of hypotheses.

THE PERSON DRAWINGS

Rear Views and Profiles. Here there were characteristic differences in the three collections of drawings. A striking example was that nine Indian girls drew a woman as seen from behind: three Japanese girls drew rear-view female figures, while no American girls did so. Two of the nine Indian girls drew a girl as sitting before them. These partial figures showed only the top half of the Person. The other seven rear-view drawings were full figures. One was described as going shopping, another as going to school, and a third going to worship. (See Figure 257.) The others were not described as doing anything specifically.

A possible contributing factor to the Indian rear-view drawings is a greater emphasis on hair by Indian girls. The girls in all three countries tended to emphasize hair. In eight of the nine Indian rear-view drawings the girl was dressed in Indian style with sari, and with the hair rolled up at the back of the head or hanging down in a pigtail. An Indian girl's hair is best seen from a rear-view perspective, although nine other Indian girls drew front-view female figures with the pigtail coming down in front. According to Buck (1948), profile and back views indicate a reluctance of the subject to face his environment, a desire to withdraw and hide his inner self.[e]

TABLE XXIV

Incidence of Profiles

Profile Type	Tokyo	Poona	Milwaukee	Total
Absolute profile, full figure	22	25	23	70
Absolute profile, partial figure	0	16	15	31
Body front, face in profile	12	33	5	50
Totals	34	74	43	151

---

[e] Mr. Buck, in a personal communication commented: "In view of the statement concerning the hair, the rear-view drawings of the Indian girls' Female Persons would be interpreted primarily as showing strong but subtle exhibitionistic tendencies (subtle because the figure has its back decorously turned). This would not rule out the presence of a reluctance to face environmental threat, of course."

Do Indian students also draw more profiles than do American and Japanese students? Indians drew more absolute profiles than did the Japanese, but not many more than did American students. One type of drawing, however, was much more common in the Indian H-T-Ps: a representation in which the body is facing the front, while the face is in profile. (See Table XXXIV.)

Fig. 257

Profiles and back views are more common among Indian students than in the other two groups.

Partial Figures. Partial figures, showing only head and shoulders, were rare among the Japanese drawings, more common among the Indian drawings and very frequent in the American H-T-Ps. See Table XXXV. One difference between the Indian and American partial figures is in drawing size. Nine American students drew large heads, using most of the drawing page. This was not done by any Indian or Japanese students. Partial figures of less than three inches in height were drawn by 7 Indian and 10 American students, but by no Japanese.

Ages of Persons Drawn. Returning to a consideration of the Indian girls' drawings, it is noteworthy that 20 Indian girls drew girls below the age of 12 years; only 11 Japanese girls and 8 American girls did this. Eighteen Indian students drew children playing; only 6 Japanese and 5 Americans did so. Five Indian girls drew a girl skipping rope; only one Japanese and no Americans did so. An impression

TABLE XXXV

Partial Figures: Head and Shoulders

Partial Figure Type	Tokyo	Poona	Milwaukee	Total
Female drawing of female	3	8	28	39
Female drawing of male	1	11	27	39
Male drawing of male	1	9	5	15
Male drawing of female	2	5	3	10
Total	7	33	63	103

is formed that among the Indian girls there is a clinging to childhood, a nostalgia for it. Indian girls did not draw Persons their own age as often as did Japanese and American girls. See Table XXXVI.

TABLE XXXVI

Ages of Persons Drawn by Girls

Person	Poona	Tokyo	Milwaukee	Total
Girl below 12 years	20	11	8	39
Girl over 27	9	3	8	20
Girl 17-20	26	34	39	99
Boy 17-20	18	28	29	75
Total	73	76	84	233

Both Japanese (21) and American girls (30) drew more "glamorous" pretty-girl drawings than did Indian girls (15). Of course, there is a cult of the pretty girl in the United States. Glamorous girls are ubiquitous in advertisements, movies, TV, and magazines. Tokyo is sufficiently westernized for this cult to be in evidence there, but it probably has not yet affected India to the same degree.

The focus on the pretty girl is related to concepts of romantic love. Dating and courtship occur in the United States and in Japan. In India, however, the situation is different. Although S. P. College is co-educational, there probably is not much dating in Poona, and marriages generally are arranged by parents. (S. P. College is situated in a conservative part of Poona; I have been told that most of these students are Brahmans.)

References to Conservatism and Religion. Some of the Indian girls' descriptions of the drawn female Person strike a note of conservatism:

> "This picture is of a woman in which attempt has been made to depict Hindu culture. This is a symbol of Indian womanhood standing on the threshhold of the ancient and modern culture."
>
> "She is not an ultra-modern fashionable girl, but rather conservative to some extent. She is in a pose to play an Indian game, *fugadi;* her hair-tail is rolling on the front part of her body."
>
> "This is a girl who does all things with conscience. She thinks about all. She is anxious about all things."

References to religion were much more common in the Indian H-T-Ps (16) than in the Japanese (4) or American H-T-Ps (1). One Indian girl drew the god Krishna for the male figure; another drew Buddha. One boy drew a *sadhu,* or holy man. who had renounced the world.

Some written references to religion by Indian students were:

"This is a 22- or 23-year-old man, and he is looking like a gentle-man. He is praying to God."

"This is a peon in the primary school. He looks very rough. We consider children like the flowers sent by God. This peon loves the children very much. The children also get together around him during the recess. The name of this peon is Rama. The children tell him not to ring the bell just after the recess is over, but he never gets angry at them. He also treats them as if they were his own children. He also considers them God-sent."

"This picture is of Gautama Buddha, who is sitting under a tree in complete meditation after having renounced the world and become a recluse."

"This woman is going to worship by taking the necessary material like flowers, etc."

"This woman is standing with folded hands. She wears a sari in a round way, and she is praying to God."

References to religion also appear in some Indian students' descriptions of even the House. Here is one:

"The House is in a lonely place. The rocks are behind it. There are so many trees around it. The man in the House likes to see the beauty of nature. Every day he comes out of the House and composes a poem. Then he prays to God. The House is very small, and no one lives with him. He likes to live in that situation. He has a great wish to know something of God. That is why he built such a House in such a situa-tion. The swastika is a symbol of peace. So he drew it on his House. The door is closed. There is a bird on the tree which is behind the House. It is singing for him."

Nothing similar to this emphasis on religion appears in Japanese or American records. In one case, anti-Muslim feeling was expressed by a Hindu girl who drew an 18-year-old Muslim boy. When asked what his "worst part" was, she wrote his religion. Another Hindu girl, who drew a Muslim woman, said that purdah was the worst part. (Purdah is rare in Poona and refers to the seclusion of women and the veiling of the face in public. Her drawn figure was partially veiled.)

Female "Disparagement" of the Drawn Male Person. It is interesting to note that 15 Indian girls, in drawing the male Person, drew a Person of low caste or class, like the school peon referred to in one quotation. Among other lower-class figures were a Muslim boy, a "backward" fish-seller, a lame beggar, a poor hawker, a flower-seller, and a poor paper-seller. Here is one description:

"This is a man who looks like a beggar. He is thin and his stomach is thin. He is a rather short man, about 25 years old. He wears only a *lahenga,* and otherwise he has a bare body. He is perhaps begging with his hand forward. His hair is thick, and his face seems pale."

Such responses might be interpreted as a device for keeping male figures at a distance or also might represent rebellion by the modern well-educated Indian woman against the traditionally dominant role of the male. Five Indian girls de-scribed their male figures as weak or unhealthy. Three described males as dirty or untidy. Here, again, some rejection or down-grading of the male seems central in the responses.

Comparable reactions taking place among Japanese or American girls take a different form. Specific references to economic class are rare in both groups. The male Person, however, may be described as immature, weak-willed, undependable, or delinquent. Eleven Japanese girls characterized their male figures in such terms. Three American girls wrote that their male figures were immature; two described their males as a hoodlum or hood. One described the male Person as obnoxious and conceited; another said he was a "depressed braggart". One American girl described her male Person as "a rough sailor looking for trouble." Another wrote that her male Person had a complex. Another said the man was a psychopath with "shiftless" *(sic)* eyes. Still another wrote that the male Person was crazy and needed psychiatric help.

There seems to be some cultural patterning in the forms taken by female disparagement of the male in different countries.

Sizes of Figures Drawn. Japanese students tended to draw larger figures than do the Indian or American students; and they drew fewer small figures (See Table XXXVII.)

TABLE XXXVII [7]

Size of Persons Drawn

	Tokyo		Poona		Milwaukee		Total	
	No.	%	No.	%	No.	%	No.	%
Male person 6" and over	93	46.3	50	31.3	53	31.7	196	37.1
Male person 1" to 4"	13	6.5	36	22.5	35	20.9	84	15.9
Female person 6" and over	87	43.3	48	30.0	51	30.6	186	35.2
Female person 2" to 4"	8	4.0	26	16.2	28	16.9	62	11.8
Total	201	100.0	160	100.0	167	100.0	528	100.0

An impression of relative self-confidence is given by Japanese drawings, from size and completeness, and skill in execution. The draughtsmanship of the Japanese students was by far the best of the three groups. This was my impression, but I felt it best to check it. Therefore I submitted all drawings from the three groups to two anthropologists giving a course on Primitive Art, Dr. Robert Ritzenthaler and Dr. Lee Parsons, both of the Milwaukee Public Museum. Since both had a strong interest in the arts of different cultures, their esthetic judgments would be broader and more sophisticated than that of the average person. Ritzenthaler and Parsons rated the drawings in five categories: Very Poor, Poor, Fair, Good and Excellent. Results in Table XXXVIII show the Japanese had by far the highest ratings in categories of Good and Excellent, and by far the lowest in the Poor categories.

Presence or Absence of Motion. As noted, the Japanese more often drew complete figures than did the Indian or American students. Of the three groups, the Indian students had the highest incidence of figures in action (see Table XXXIX).

Although the Japanese figures generally are standing, often they are so well drawn there is an appearance of liveliness or motion in the figure. Conversely,

---

[7] If the drawing was 4½" tall, it was rated as 5"; 6½ was rated as 7", etc. If it was less than 4½", it was rated as 4", etc.

although the Indian figures often are depicted in motion, or so described, the stiffness of the drawing often creates a static impression.

TABLE XXXVIII

Ratings of Drawing Ability

	Very Poor	Poor	Fair	Good	Excellent	Total
Tokyo	0	2	45	52	13	112
Poona	5	23	60	19	5	112
Milwaukee	3	17	67	20	5	112
Total	8	42	172	91	23	336

TABLE XXXIX

Complete Figures Standing, Sitting and Moving

	Tokyo	Poona	Milwaukee	Total
Male standing	95	51	61	207
Female standing	85	47	68	200
Male sitting	2	1	3	6
Female sitting	8	5	6	19
Male moving	12	31	13	56
Female moving	9	32	7	48
Total	211	167	158	536

Indications of Compulsiveness and Repression. It often has been stated that rigid bilateral symmetry in a Person drawing is an indication of compulsiveness. The same has been said of exacting detailing, as in the depiction of buttons and pockets. Rigid bilateral symmetry is very common in all three groups, being found in the Person drawings of 76 Japanese, 73 Indian, and 64 American subjects. Forty-four Japanese drew three or more buttons in a Person drawing. Fifty-two Indians and 29 Americans did so. Twenty-four Japanese, 22 Indians, and 14 Americans drew pockets. According to these criteria, then, all three groups seem to have some compulsive tendencies. Perhaps the common denominator is the student one.

One might have expected a higher incidence of buttons and pockets in the United States, since these are usual aspects of Western clothing. If one is to draw a fairly complete picture of a Person, particularly a male, it would seem such attributes would be included. However, their relatively low incidence in the American H-T-Ps, as compared with the other two groups, in part may be accounted for by the high number of partial figures, showing only head and shoulders.

Among the Indian students, 49 female and 8 male students drew women wearing Indian dress. No buttons or pockets thus would appear in these drawings. Six female and 4 male students drew men in Indian style clothing. These also would lack buttons and pockets. Sixteen female students and one male drew women in Western dress. Twenty-five female and 16 male students drew men in

Western clothing. Since more figures were drawn in Indian than in Western dress, the relatively high number of drawn buttons and pockets is surprising.

A common type of detailing in the drawings of women wearing Indian dress was the drawing of necklace beads, bangles, and earrings. Perhaps these correspond to the detailing of buttons in figures wearing clothing of Western type, although the jewelry has greater symbolic meaning for Indians. The detailing of beads, bangles, and ear-rings was found in drawings of 58 Indian students. These features, along with the forehead cosmetic mark, also commonly drawn, are symbols of womanhood in India.

Although 13 Japanese students drew women wearing kimonos, which lack buttons and pockets, the majority drew Western type clothing. Japanese students also, in general, drew complete figures. Since these figures generally were frontal views of standing persons, with bilateral symmetry, it is not surprising that buttons and pockets often were depicted in Tokyo.

A common type of drawing by Japanese girls is a girl, often clothed in a bouffant Western type skirt, with hands hidden behind the back. (See Figure 258).

Fig. 258

Only 2 Indian and 10 American girls drew figures with hands hidden this way, as against 27 Japanese girls.

An emphasis on belts, or depiction of a narrow, pinched waist supposedly suggests repression. Narrow, pinched waists have about similar incidence

(Tokyo: 9, Poona: 8; Milwaukee: 10), but 25 Japanese emphasized the belt, as against 8 Indian and 14 American students. However, this may be of little significance.

The relative absence of belt emphasis and waist construction in drawings of Indian and American students again is influenced by their comparatively high percentages of head-and-shoulders drawings. Moreover, the Indian sari does not emphasize the waist, and 56 of the Indian students drew women wearing saris. The relatively high incidence of head-and-shoulders drawings in the Poona and Milwaukee samples also affects the lower incidence of figures with hands behind the back.

Opposite Sex Drawn First. To draw a person of the opposite sex in the first Person drawing may indicate confusion of sexual identification. Numbers of male students drawing female figures first was about the same in each group - 7 for Tokyo, 7 for Milwaukee, and 5 for Poona. More American girls – 24 – drew male figures first, as against 17 for Poona and 11 for Tokyo.

Masculine Self-Assertion. Efforts toward masculine self-assertion are seen in some American and Japanese male students' drawings of the male Person. Seven Americans, two Indians, and one Japanese emphasized the beard or chest hair. Five Americans, three Indians, and ten Japanese emphasized broad shoulders. Two American students equipped the male Person with a knife; one Japanese gave him a pistol. The Indian students did not emphasize their masculinity in this way.

Hair and Headgear. As mentioned, there is much emphasis on hair in all three groups: 54 for Tokyo, 60 for Poona; 76 for Milwaukee. Indian students depicted more headgear (29). as against 18 Japanese and 16 American students. Nine Indian students drew Persons carrying jars or baskets on their heads. No Japanese or American students did so. This may be a reflection of cultural differences. Also it is possible, however, that there is a psychological aspect to the Indian emphasis on hair and headgear. G. Morris Carstairs discusses the importance of the head or head-gear in a chapter on the Hindu body-image in his book *The Twice-Born.* As the feet are considered the lowliest body part, so the head is held to be the most sacred. Semen is widely believed to be stored in the head (Carstairs, 1958: 77-84). The Brahmans, associated with the priesthood and highest of the four *varna,* traditionally were said to have issued from the head of God, the Kshatriya, or warriors, from his arms, the Vaishya, or merchants, from his thighs, and the Sudra, or workers, from his feet.

The concept that height is associated with sacredness also may be found in Japan and the United States, but in India there seems to be a particular emphasis on the symbolic significance of the high and the low. Some evidence to that effect is presented in the following section on the Tree drawing.

THE TREE DRAWING

Height and Age of the Tree. The Tree drawing is held to be an unconscious self-portrait of the Individual at a deeper level than the Person drawing. Is there some correspondence between size of Person drawing and size of Tree drawing in the three groups? And is there some correspondence between age of Person and age of Tree?

TABLE XL

Height of the Tree

	Tokyo		Poona		Milwaukee		Total	
	No.	*%*	*No.*	*%*	*No.*	*%*	*No.*	*%*
Tree 2" to 4"	2	2.0	12	12.1	2	2.0	16	5.3
Tree below 6"	11	10.9	27	27.6	6	5.9	44	14.7
Tree 7" and over	88	86.1	59	59.3	93	92.1	240	80.0
Total	101	100.0	98	100.0	101	100.0	300	100.0

As Table XL shows both Japanese and Americans drew many large Trees and few small Trees. Indian students drew fewer large and more small Trees. If Tables XXXVI and XL are compared it will be seen that Japanese students were consistent in drawing smaller figures for Trees and Persons. Americans drew larger Trees than Persons. Perhaps this suggests a basic self-confidence in American students. However, Tree drawings of all three groups generally give a healthy impression, with some exceptions noted below.

Not all students complied with the request to give an age for the Tree. Table XLI gives the results of those who did.

TABLE XLI

Age of the Tree in Years

	1-10	*11-15*	*16-20*	*21-30*	*31-50*	*51-80*	*80-100*	*100+*	*Total*
Tokyo	15	6	19	13	18	8	7	19	105
Poona	29	11	15	16	20	3	8	2	104
Milwaukee	15	8	17	13	28	14	5	7	107
Total	59	25	51	42	66	25	20	28	316

 The Indian students tend to give lower ages for the Tree than do the Japanese or American students. Forty Indians gave an age below 16, as against 21 Japanese and 23 Americans. This is consistent with the pattern in Table XXXVI, which shows a tendency for Indian students to give lower ages for the Person drawings too.

Dead and Dying Trees. Depiction of a dead Tree is believed to be a pathoformic, if not pathological sign. It may indicate, among other things, apathy or despair. More American students drew dead or dying Trees than did Japanese or Indian students. The Indian students had the fewest such responses (see Table XLII).

TABLE XLII

Dead or Dying Trees

	Tokyo	*Poona*	*Milwaukee*	*Total*
Dead Trees	6	2	11	19
Dying Trees	5	1	6	12
Totals	11	3	17	31

To the question "Is the Tree alive or dead?", eleven Indian students wrote, "The Tree is, of course, alive," or "The Tree is certainly alive." This degree of emphasis was not noted in the Japanese or American answers.

Some of the dead or dying Trees drawn by American students gave a marked picture of despondency. One 18-year-old girl, for example, drew a "diseased" Tree with a heavy X-mark across the trunk. Beside the Tree was a sign "For Sale with House." The girl wrote "The Tree will die this year." In answer to the question "What is the best part of the Tree?" she wrote, "The X marking it for up-rooting."

Tree Holes and Broken Branches. Tree-holes or scars are believed to symbolize traumatic experiences; broken branches are sometimes held to express feelings of castration. American students drew by far the greatest number of Tree holes—25; as against 7 for the Japanese and 7 for the Indian students. The Japanese drew more broken branches—8; as against 2 for the Indian students and 4 for the Americans.

The rarity of broken branches in the Indian drawings may be influenced by the fact that many Indian students drew coconut Trees where branches do not so frankly figure.

Best and Worst Parts of the Tree. Since the three groups of students live in different geographical regions, it is understandable that they drew different kinds of Trees. Forty-two of the Indian students drew coconut Trees and seven drew fruit Trees. In answer to the question, "What is the best part of the Tree?" 26 Indians answered, "The coconuts" or "The fruits." Few coconut or fruit trees were drawn by the Japanese and American students.

In answer to the question, "What is the best part of the Tree?" 24 Indian students wrote, "The top of the Tree is best." This might be interpreted as a reference to the fruits, coconuts, or leaves. (Nineteen students wrote leaves were the best part.) However, the preference for the top of the Tree may reflect the symbolism of high and low referred to earlier. An indication that this is the case is found in some answers to the question, "What is the worst part of the Tree?" Ten Indian students wrote the bottom or base was the worst part. Otherwise, such responses were not found in Japanese or American records.

Forty-one American students wrote the trunk was the best part of the Tree; only 10 Indians and two Japanese gave this response. However, 12 Japanese students wrote that the best part of the Tree was its sturdiness. The Japanese tended to interpret "best" or "worst" part as "aspect" or "characteristic" of the drawn Tree, *per se,* and often gave answers which involved self-criticism of the drawing. Thirty-four American students said the branches were the best part of the Tree; only 8 Indian and 7 Japanese said this.

American responses perhaps could be interpreted as expressing the values of ego-strength (trunk) and social contacts with others (branches).

THE HOUSE DRAWING

Small Japanese House Drawings. Although the Japanese tended to draw larger Persons than the Indian and American students, they drew more small

Houses. A House was labeled "large" if it was 6 inches long and about 4 inches high. (If it was 6 inches tall and 4 inches long, it also would qualify as large, but such cases were rare). A House was labeled "small" if it was about 2 inches long, or less, and about 1½ inches high. Table XLIII shows incidence of large and small Houses, as defined.

TABLE XLIII

Incidence of Large and Small Houses

	Tokyo	Poona	Milwaukee	Total
Large House	21	24	28	73
Small House	15	1	3	19
Total	36	25	31	92

All but one small Japanese House were drawn in the upper left hand corner of the page; the one exception was drawn in the upper right hand corner. The smallest House was less than three quarters of an inch in length; another was only a fraction longer.

According to Buck (1948), upper left placement is found among markedly anxious or regressed subjects. In the 15 Japanese records in which small Houses appear there were some indications of maladjustment to support this generalization. Three of the 15 subjects said their Trees were dead; one said it was starting to die. Since only five Japanese students drew dead Trees and only one drew a dying Tree, the correlation of a small House with a dead or dying Tree is rather striking.

It might be argued the Tokyo students drew more small Houses because they live in smaller homes than do Indian and American students. Probably this is true but Table XLIV shows the Japanese also drew more two-story houses than did Indian students.

TABLE XLIV

House: Number of Storeys

	Tokyo	Poona	Milwaukee	Total
1-storey house	59	71	46	176
2-storey house	51	37	57	145
More than 2 storeys	2	4	10	16
Total	112	112	113	337

The Japanese generally did not introduce trees, bushes, fences, or other content in their House drawings. Only 25 Japanese students introduced scenery, as against 64 Americans and 77 Indian students. One explanation may be that most of the Tokyo students are apartment-dwellers. It is likely that both in Poona and Milwaukee there are more students living in private homes. However, this is a matter of speculation.

Another interpretation of the small Houses and the relative lack of introduced content is to relate the House drawings to the confused post-war conditions in Japan. It is likely that many Japanese students came from homes in which the father or close relative was killed during World War II. The composition of the family and the traditions concerning family life have been greatly affected by post-war developments as the occupation, rapid introduction of Western culture patterns, and the economic boom of recent years. During this period the family or home may not have offered as much security as in former times.

Indian House Drawings. Perhaps one should account for scenery in the House drawing rather than its absence. It has been noted that 77 Indian students introduced scenery, as against 25 Japanese students. Buck considers such content to be a deviation from the average, representing a basic need to structure a situation more completely, and implying the presence of feelings of insecurity. He believes trees and shrubs by the House often represent persons, usually members of the subject's family (Buck, 1948; 367).

Of the three student groups, the Indians made the most elaborate House drawings, with the House often surrounded by trees. Ten Indian students introduced the sun (often held to be a parental symbol) in their House drawings, as against three American students and one Japanese student. Fourteen Indian students drew birds in their House drawings.

Twenty-four Indian students drew open doors in their Houses, as against one Japanese and two Americans. This constitutes a striking difference. It has not been determined if this reflects for the Indians greater hospitality, a warmer climate, or a need for emotional contact with others. Hammer has stated the drawing of a door as "open" . . . conveys an intense thirst to receive emotional warmth from without (if Post-Drawing Interrogation reveals the House as occupied). If the House is said to be vacant, the open door connotes a feeling of extreme vulnerability, a lack of adequacy of ego defenses." (Hammer, 1958: 176)

None of the Indian students who drew open doors described tne House as vacant. In 18 cases there was evidence of occupation, in persons introduced, smoke from chimney, etc. In five cases there was no evidence of occupation but no evidence of vacancy either. The data thus lean toward the hypothesis of a need for emotional warmth, if the climatic variable is not considered.

Descriptions of the House by Indian Students. In their descriptions of the House, those who drew open doors did not make statements of loneliness. On the contrary, as in many House descriptions by Indian students, they wrote in a euphoric vein.

Some Indian students described the houses they were occupying. Others described a dream house, often a simple retreat in the country, far from the disturbances of city life. Frequent references were made to good ventilation and cool summer breezes.

Examples of House descriptions by Indian students, all by students who drew open doors, follows:

> "This is a small but sweet House; in other words, it's a simple but great House. All happiness and purity, or virtues like that, are com-. bined together in this simple House." (girl, 19)
> "House. It is really a word of two letters only (i.e. in Marathi). But everybody's whole world is contained in it. Everybody feels proud of his House and he becomes gay by the very idea of it. Indeed, my House is small and beautiful in a beautiful setting. The coconut tree has been standing nearby for a number of years." (girl, 19)

"The House is in a village. It is an early morning, and the birds are chirping, and the sun is just rising. The hostess comes out with a view to decorate the ground in front of the House with white powder. One may be able to appreciate this sight. This is a simple House having tiles on the roof. There are small trees in front of the House. Behind the House there are mountains and dense trees." (girl, 21)(See Figure 259).

"This is my home, which is very dear to me. It is simple but massive and small but sufficient to us. There are two blocks with the two

Fig. 259

doors, and one window between the doors. In front of our House there is a yard, and we used to sit together and play cards on full-moon nights.

"The roof of the House is made of thin bricks. That is why the House remains cool in the summer days and does not get so cold in winter. We are quite happy in our House." (girl, no age given)

"Away, away from all the miseries of life, outside the city, I wish to live in my small home outside on a hill. The House will be as follows: It will have a ground floor and first floor made of tiles, having a gallery, with three windows on each floor. A coconut tree stands beside the House, inside the compound. The House will have a gallery from which I could see the isolated world. There will be flower pots in front of the House." (male, 22)

Descriptions like the above were written also by students who did not draw open doors. One example by a 19-year-old girl follows:

"I feel that my House is like a palace. In my House there is always a good atmosphere; and, therefore, I am always cheerful, and my family members and myself get the same kind of delight as one might get in a palace. My House is surrounded by a garden. One forgets all one's pains when one enters the garden and feels happy when the water from the fountain sprinkles over his person. There is also a big swing hanging in the garden."

The euphoric nature of these descriptions and the elaboration of the House drawings with their introduced content testify, it seems to me, to the strength of the joint family household, strong in the conservative section of Poona, from which many Indian students come.

In answer to the question, "What is the best part of the House?" 18 Indian students wrote "The front of the House." In answer to the question, "What is the worst part of the House?" 19 wrote, "The back of the House." This seems to correspond to the rating of the top of the Tree as best and the bottom of the Tree as the worst part. Two students combined these four responses, while five students combined three of them. Four students wrote that the top of the House or the upper room, was best; one wrote that the bottom of the House was worst, and two wrote that the front of the Tree was best.

Perhaps the designation of the front part of the House as the best means that the "facade" or impression given to the outer world is the best aspect of the House. Responses of this sort were not found among the Japanese students, although two Americans said that the back of the House was the worst part.

American Houses. Like Houses drawn by Indian students, the Americans' Houses tended to be large and often to have introduced scenery. Following the logic of the foregoing analysis of Indian House drawings, it would seem that the family also looms large in the life of the American student.[a] The American family is a much smaller one than the Indian family, and it allows more autonomy and freedom of choice to young people. No American descriptions of the House were collected to compare with those from India but it seems doubtful that American students would write in as ecstatic a way about the House as did the Indian students. (I have been told this is consistent with Buck's and Hammer's experiences.)

To the question, "What does the House need most?" 20 American students wrote it needed people, or a family. This suggests the House was seen by them to be empty. On the other hand, 35 Americans drew smoke issuing from the chimney, thus indicating that someone was home.

The Americans, like the Japanese, tended to draw large windows, but in both cases this may reflect the existing culture. Wide picture-windows often were depicted by American students, especially in ranch-type houses.

Treatment of the Roof. The roof has been held to symbolize the fantasy area of life. Overly large roofs are believed to indicate strong introversive trends, immersion in fantasy.

A roof was rated "high" if it was between one-third to one-half the height of the House. Japanese students drew the largest number of high roofs (73) as

---

[a] John N. Buck has commented on this point: "There is, I feel, the strong possibility that large homes equal high social standing for the American college students." (personal communication)

against only 25 Indian and 46 American students. This may not tell much, since high roofs are more prominent in Japanese and American than in Indian architecture. Indian students often detailed the tiles on their roofs—57, as against 45 Japanese and 19 Americans. In this case Indian over-concern with the roof apparently was manifested by detailing rather than by proportion. In descriptions of the House 19 Indian students mentioned it had a tiled roof. Five Indian students detailed bricks in the wall of the House. Interest in detail therefore, was focused more on the roof.

Pressure. The degree of line pressure in the drawings was gauged subjectively. Each H-T-P record was classified as exhibiting Faint, Medium, or Heavy pressure. Most students in each group were rated as using medium pressure. There seemed about the same amount of heavy pressure for the three groups: 6 for Tokyo, 8 for Poona, and 9 for Milwaukee. More Indian students (20) were rated as using faint pressure, as against 1 in Tokyo and 7 in Milwaukee.

Some General Conclusions

Having considered separately the three H-T-P drawings in three different samples of students, certain generalizations about the three groups of students can now be made.

The Students at Poona. Judging from the rarity of dead or dying Trees, Tree holes, and broken branches in the Indian H-T-Ps, it may be concluded tentatively that the Indian students have a stronger basic sense of security than do the other two groups of students. Their security may stem, in large part, from the joint family household, eulogized in many of the House descriptions. But the joint family system also demands compliance and obedience; it may inhibit self-assertive tendencies. William Stephens Taylor, G. Morris Carstairs, and others have discussed the Indian family's stress on conformity and submission in family life, which results in a passive, dependent personality (Taylor, 1948: 123; Carstairs, 1958: 67; Shils, 1961: 62-3; Smith, 1962: 180).[9] This stress on compliance may account for the relatively light pressure used by many Indian subjects and for the greater percentage of young children drawn by them than by the other two groups. The development of a strong ego does not seem to be encouraged.[10]

There was a higher incidence of profiles in the Indian sample than in the other two groups, as well as more rear-view drawings of female Persons by Indian girls. Such representations can be seen as expressions of negativism or withdrawal. Margaret Cormack has written: " . . . in general it seems that frustration, with Indian girls, leads not to aggression but to autistic regression, repression, and resignation." (Cormack, 1953: 83) The H-T-P data and Cormack's conclusions, based on interviews with Indian girls, provide mutual confirma-

---

[9] Mr. Buck has commented: "The open door may imply a feeling by the Indian students (taking the House as a self-portrait) that they cannot develop significant personalities of their own, but must remain subject to parental values." (personal communication)

[10] The Indian writer, Dhirendra Narain, has observed that strong masterful heroes like Clark Gable and Gregory Peck, do not appear in Indian films. Narain points to the Indians' stress on themes of suicide and aggression toward the self. He believes Hindu asceticism is of a masochistic and punitive variety (1957).

tion and some elaboration. Sublimation in religiosity also is suggested by the H-T-P protocols.

One form of security provided by the Hindu social order, at least in the higher ranks, is the caste system. Brahmans have the satisfaction of knowing they belong to the highest and purest caste. Consciousness of relative status is suggested by the girls' drawings of Persons of lower caste or class. High-low symbolism may express caste consciousness and tendencies toward sublimation. Thus there was emphasis on the head and rejection of the lower parts. Many Indian students drew only the head and shoulders. Hair and headgear tended to be emphasized. The top of the Tree was regarded as the best part, the bottom as the worst.

The Students at Tokyo

The Students at Tokyo. The training of Japanese girls has much in common with that in India. Girls are taught to be polite, modest, reserved, and submissive. This is brought out in the following quotations from girls' descriptions of the female Person drawn:

(Of a girl described as age 5): "A doll-like character, not at all dynamic; a typical Japanese child. She's on her way to a shrine, dressed in a kimono."

(Of a ten-year-old girl): "I like to stay at home reading or playing with dolls. I don't like to go out and be with many friends whom I don't know very well."

(Of a girl drawn in polite, formal, kneeling position): "The girl is waiting for a cup of hot tea. She's a very modest, refined girl."

"She's feminine, modest, and gentle-looking, but there's something lonely about her facial expression. Besides, she's thin, and that makes her look nervous (high-strung)."

"Cute, obedient, and has been taught very good manners. I think she'll grow up to be a fine person."

Stress on obedience and modesty may foster compulsive tendencies, as evidenced by the noticeable detailing of buttons and pockets and by the often rigid bilateral symmetry of Person drawings. More Japanese students emphasized belts than did Indian or American students—possibly as indicator of repression or the need to maintain control. Japanese students more often hid the hands behind the back, despite having the best drawing ability of the three groups.

Although the training of girls in India and Japan has some similarities there probably is more autonomy and freedom of choice in Tokyo. Marriage by individual choice is a steadily increasing practice. Opportunities for all kinds of work are abundant.

The Japanese girl gets a good start in life. From all accounts, Japanese maternal care is indulgent and affectionate. It is not difficult, therefore, for girls to identify with their mothers. Of the three groups, the Japanese girls drew the smallest number of opposite-sex drawings first, less than half the number of those drawn by American girls.

The Japanese girl seems able to retain her femininity, despite the competitive atmosphere of present-day Japan. Many students, in their descriptions of the Person drawn, referred to the strains of study, work, and achievement, but this generally was mentioned in connection with the male drawn Person. Examples by girls were:

"He's on his way home from school and exhausted from his studies and playing. His stomach is empty."

"Striving not to be defeated in the struggle for existence caused by Western culture."

"He is a college student from the country. The bustle of the city has appalled him, and he's become a little neurotic."

"A serious boy; he's standing and waiting to be told to do something."

"Sonny, how did you damage your eyes? Perhaps he studied too much. With a school system that makes a little boy his age study so that he damages his eyes, the future youth are all going to be so overly studious that their lives may end without truly developing to the fullest. I wish that the present school system would be revised in a hurry."

"He's living with hopes for the future."

"He's a school teacher. His arms are outstretched as he is blocking the hallway and just about to catch and reprimand the grade school children who are running in the hallway."

Several girls, in commenting on the male drawn Person, expressed a wish he were stronger, more masculine, or engaged in sports.

"He'd improve with more masculinity."

"He works in an office, but I wish he were healthier and could engage in sports on Sundays. If so, he'd probably do better at work and could lead a happy life."

"He seems to be a warm man with common sense, but I wish he was portrayed as a strong, forcibly masculine, sturdy and positive kind of person."

"Don't you think he ought to engage in some sports?"

"He has leadership qualities. However, this is demonstrated only within an intellectual group. He ought to engage in sports more. Then perhaps he'd grow taller."

The descriptions of male Persons by male students also reflect the stresses of contemporary life. Some express high aspiration levels.

"He looks most serious and gives the impression of being dauntless."

"He is good in any sports, but especially judo, in which he's a third degree expert. In studies he's best in math. He'll probably lead Japan in the future."

"He conquers the strong and aids the weak; he's our constant ally."

"At first glance he looks like an ordinary student, but musically he's practically a genius. He sings beautifully, can play any instrument, except for one drawback which is that he's not particularly good on the drums. He also does excellent school work and is sociable, but his one other fault is that he's a philanderer."

"Burning sense of justice; zealot in his fight against evil. A bit stubborn, but this trait is very attractive to women."

"He has a very sharp mind and does excellent work at school. At the moment he's looking for a job, so he can earn money for a trip to Hokkaido."

In other descriptions by male students, a fear of failure is expressed:

"An obedient student, but not very promising."

"Not very intelligent; yet he wants to be drinking. He's convinced that he's masculine, handsome."

"Being a fifteen-year-old boy, he's in his second rebellious stage, and has a rebellious spirit about everything. Thus, he disobeys his parents and naturally tends to depend on his friends, and at the same time he desires to have girl friends. Such is his present state."

"The man got into a bad group from a minor incident. He's addicted to nicotine and is losing faith in everything. However, he himself wants to wash himself of this kind of living. He's a pitiful man."

The possibility of failure and inadequacy appears in some girls' descriptions of the male Person:

"A weak-willed student. Doesn't care to do anything; is just being idle."

"A modern youth type. A sort of dandy. Doesn't study much and doesn't know how to think deeply."

In a minority of the Japanese H-T-Ps there are indications of anxiety or regression, suggested by the small Houses drawn in the upper left hand corner of the page. The usual Japanese student does not appear overwhelmed by the stresses of modern life. An impression of self-confidence is given by the size and completeness of the figures drawn.

The Students at Milwaukee. Needless to say, the competitive atmosphere characteristic of Tokyo is evident in the United States. Here efforts for success in academic and economic spheres and on popularity and being well-liked by others were emphasized. In descriptions of the female drawn Person, American girls often alluded to her as being well-liked or fun to be with. She often was described as intelligent, friendly, warm and lovable. As the following quotations suggest, the well-balanced, warm, and popular girl is a wish-image, an ideal type.

"The girl is delicate and petite. She is graceful and feminine. She's a kind person as well as intelligent, and she dresses beautifully. She's a career girl, but will marry the right man."

"She is cheerful, lovable, and a good personality. She acts her age and listens to her parents. She has a happy home life and many friends."

"The girl is intelligent and rather quiet, fun to talk to, with worthwhile opinions."

"The girl is a young housewife who is waving goodbye to her husband, who is on his way to work. She is a sweet, hard-working and lovable girl—a truly perfect mother and wife."

"Person is a 'teenager going on date to a ball. She's in a lot of activities and chairman of the prom committee. She likes nice clothes and nice fellows."

"Female young 'teen-ager thinking about prospective plans of marriage. She is an intelligent girl with high ideals. She is fun to be with and has a captivating personality."

"The girl is about 16 and in high school. She is pretty, dresses well, gets good grades, and is friendly."

"The female is a college girl of 20. She is standing on a stage giving a speech. She is very poised and also very intelligent."

"The female is a career girl who enjoys being on her own. She likes people and is a warm personality."

"She is slight to the point of being delicate. She's also warm and friendly, and loves children. She's intelligent and sensible."

The girls sometimes describe the man in similar positive terms, that he has a great personality, is warm, fun to be with, etc. But several American girls, like some Japanese girls, characterized the male as immature or delinquent, as was done by some American male students.

As in Japan, there is a polarity of success and failure. The stakes are high. American students who see themselves as not able to make the grade are apt to be self-disparaging and depressed, perhaps accounting for the high incidence of dead and dying Trees in the American H-T-Ps.

Large heads, filling most of the page, were drawn by several American students, perhaps expressing their intellectual ambitions, among other things. High aspirations are reflected in descriptions of the drawn Persons. However, these are not so extreme as in some male Japanese descriptions. Rather than achieving a specific goal, effort seems to be exerted to become a particular kind of person. American girls want to be warm, intelligent, attractive, and popular. American male students want to be masculine and successful, and like some Japanese students sometimes emphasize masculinity by drawing broad-shouldered males.

In general, Japanese and American students have much in common, as in their ambition to succeed and responsiveness to glamor, while the Indian students appear more passive, more dependent, and more religious.

The above constitute *hypotheses* derived from H-T-P samples. Now cross validation studies from the respective cultures involved seem indicated.

Part Three: The Sterilization Project

A second experiment was made concerning the psychological effects of voluntary sterilization upon married men in rural Maharashtra, India. The H-T-P was used in this study.

In recent years thousands of men have been vasectomized, or sterilized, in the state of Maharashtra. Essentially it is an irreversible operation. The purpose is to prevent insemination and thereby reduce the birth rate. Similar programs are under way in other parts of India. Officials of the Office of Family Planning and members of the Gokhale Institute of Politics and Economics in Poona have interviewed some vasectomized men to determine reactions toward this operation, its affects on their sex life, etc. In general, they found that there appear to be no harmful effects (Dandekar, 1963). However, no "depth" techniques were used to explore the possibility of harmful psychological consequences. That was the purpose of this research which had the cooperation of the Office of Family Planning in Poona.[11]

[11] I thank Dr. K. T. Chitre, Mr. R. N. Saxena, Mr. K. H. Tergaonkar, and Mr. D. R. Maheshkar for assistance in this project. Thanks also are given to Mrs. Kunudini Dandekar and Mr. N. V. Sovani of the Gokhale Institute for their interest and help with this project.

In November of 1963 the author administered the Rorschach Test and tne House-Tree-Person Test to one hundred men from three rural villages near Poona. Fifty men had been sterilized; fifty had not. Subjects were selected by officials of the Office of Family Planning. The researcher did not know which men had or had not been sterilized. Members of both groups were presumed to be from the same social groups – caste, religion, income level, etc. All one hundred subjects were married, generally having two or more children. Most were Hindus, but there were some Muslims, Buddhists, and Jains in the groups. Most were poor farmers; many had never been to school. Data collected from each subject related to age, number of children, occupation, approximate income, caste, religion and years of school attendance. An excellent interpreter translated the men's Rorschach responses and interview replies from Marathi into English. Tests and interviews took place in the villages where the men lived.

In the modified H-T-P subjects were asked in the usual manner to draw a House, a Tree, and the two Persons. Drawings were made while waiting to take the Rorschach Test. After a subject completed the H-T-P, the interpreter and the author went over the drawings with the man, asking for clarification of ambiguous features, nature of introduced content, sex and ages of Persons drawn, age of Tree, type of Tree, what the Persons were doing, etc. Best and worst parts of House, Tree, and Persons, or what they needed most, were not asked. Nor whether the Tree was alive or dead unless it gave an impression of being dead, was asked. Descriptions of the two Persons were not requested.

Many subjects were rather frightened, probably not knowing clearly what the testing was about. Some perspired freely, leaving wet patches on the table where their hands had been. These were not ideal conditions for administering projective tests. However, not all the men were so affected and reasonably adequate H-T-P and Rorschach protocols were obtained.

Sorting Experiments. Sorting experiments were made with materials collected.

The first experiment was to determine to what extent the author and two of his colleagues could determine from projective data which men had or had not been sterilized. The list of sterilized men was on file at the Office of Family Planning in Poona. Our determinations were sent in to the Office of Family Planning. Then the correct list was sent to us.

A second experiment involved making a list of the men judged to be the better-adjusted fifty and a list of those judged to be the less well adjusted fifty. On receiving the list of sterilized men, studies could be made between the sterilized and unsterilized, as well as the experience of sterilization, degree of adjustment as measured by the tests, etc.

Dr. Emanuel F. Hammer, working with the H-T-P Tests and Dr. Blanche G. Watrous working with the Rorschachs were my colleagues. Dr. Hammer drew up a list of the fifty men, based on their H-T-P's judged to have been sterilized, and a list of those judged to be the fifty best adjusted.

Dr. Watrous, working only with the Rorschachs, made the same sortings. The author also made these sortings, working with the Rorschach and H-T-P protocols.

Dr. Hammer has set criteria for determining the presence of castration anxiety in H-T-P drawings. These include broken branches, toppling chimneys, and approximately a dozen other indicators (Hammer, 1953). These signs were used by him in his sortings for the sterilized list. In working with the drawings, the author made use of the same criteria, but with less success, as will be noted.

In working with the Rorschachs, the author was influenced by sexual and anatomical responses and references to broken or mutilated objects. Dr. Watrous set her Rorschach criteria for the sorting of the sterilized list as follows: "1) Associations related to 'broken', 'bent', 'death', bodily mutilation; 2) use of Beck's Y (in associations to 'black' as a determinant; 3) massing of sexual, anal, midline associations – the first two with frequent disregard for form of blot detail."

When the three independent lists were brought together, there was triple agreement on 17 cases designated as sterilized. Dr. Watrous and the author were in agreement on 33 cases; Dr. Watrous and Dr. Hammer were in agreement on 28 cases; and Dr. Hammer and the author were in agreement on 23 cases.

All three agreed on 17 cases on the better-adjusted list. There were 38 cases in which Dr. Watrous and the author were in agreement; Dr. Watrous and Dr. Hammer were in agreement on 23 cases; and Dr. Hammer and the author were in agreement on 25 cases.

The next step was to draw up master lists on which all three could agree, if possible. The author met Dr. Watrous and showed her the H-T-P drawings and ratings by Dr. Hammer and the author. As a result, we made some changes in our ratings. This still left a number of unresolved cases: 41 in the sterilized-unsterilized lists, and 45 in the better-adjusted less-well-adjusted lists; Dr. Hammer was sent ratings by Dr. Watrous and the author, together with the Rorschach records. He made second sortings based on the Rorschach and H-T-P records. When his second set of lists was returned, there remained two ambiguous cases. The author made the final assignments of these two cases.

Both Dr. Hammer and Dr. Watrous expressed skepticism about our ability to determine correctly which men had been sterilized. Dr. Hammer's reservations were expressed in a letter:

"Now that I'm done, I find I feel very little confidence in the results approaching any level of statistical significance. So many of the total 100 subjects seem to show castration anxiety. Could it be that many of those who weren't sterilized were considering sooner or later making the same move, and thus the difference between the two groups – on a psychological level – becomes contaminated? One thing which does obscure the difference between the sterilized and unsterilized groups is the middle age of almost 90% of the subjects. The *Involutional Period* produces feelings of diminished masculinity, doubts about an approaching sapping of virility, drive, and energy, and a general feeling of greater uncertainty regarding masculine prowess in a good proportion of all males. As such, the heavy preponderance of subjects in this *Involutional* age range, from 40 to 55, masks the similar feeling of castration due to sterilization. Beyond this, subjects of this age range, particularly in a more primitive culture where aging begins earlier, tend to give H-T-Ps which are barren and organically flavored with the signs of senility which crowd out the richer personality clues and emotional subtleties, which, in turn are necessary to reflect the underlying nuances of castration feelings, psychosexual uncertainty, or a shift toward more feminine identification . . . If you find yourself repeating such a study, it might be advisable to restrict the population to those below age 40 . . . ''

In analyzing the results, it turned out that our determinations were poorer than chance: There were 22 correct identifications. Twenty-five correct guesses would have been made by chance. This does not mean the experiment was a failure, for an interesting association was found between our list of better adjusted men and the sterilized list.[12] This Association is shown in Table XLV.

It is seen that 33 of the men rated as better-adjusted were in the sterilized group, exceeding chance expectations and significant at the one percent level of confidence. One problem is whether the men rated as better adjusted *actually*

TABLE XLV

Association Between Sterilization and Adjustment Ratings

	Sterilized Men	Unsterilized Men	Total
Better Adjusted	33	17	50
Less Well Adjusted	17	33	50
Total	50	50	100

are better adjusted. Also the definition of adjustment is problematical. Nevertheless, the fact remains that a better than chance association appeared between sterilized men and those who appeared better adjusted according to the projective techniques.

Two interpretations suggest themselves. One, that only the better-adjusted men decided and went through the sterilization. Two, perhaps the men with *less* castration anxiety elected to be sterilized. This explanation has the virtue of accounting for the inability to determine correctly which men had been sterilized. Perhaps the investigators were looking for castration anxiety in the wrong group of men. If this is the case, it is comprehensible that the master list was less

TABLE XLVI

Anatomical and Sexual Responses in the Rorschach Test

	Sterilized Men	Unsterilized Men	Total
Anatomical	18	34	52
Sexual	8	20	28
Total	26	54	80

successful than the original uncorrected lists of Dr. Watrous and Dr. Hammer.

In support of the interpretation of data to the effect that those with less basic castration anxiety were the ones who availed themselves of the sterilization procedure, Table XLVI shows that the unsterilized seemed to show body-preoccupation by giving more anatomical and sexual responses than did the sterilized. Some

---

[12] In reviewing our first sets of determinations, before drawing up our master lists, Dr. Hammer's assessments were the best, having 29 correct identifications. Dr. Watrous came second, with 24; and the author trailed with 16. One might have expected the master list (all three agreeing) to surpass the original separate lists. Instead, Dr. Hammer and Dr. Watrous did better the first time around. One also might have expected, on most of the 17 cases agreed on by the three experts sterilized in our first uncorrected lists there would have been a high incidence of correct identification but only 8 of these men were sterilized.

unsterilized men gave classic castration responses. One man, responding to Card X, said "Sterilization. Something is cut there." (A Whole response.) Another saw a broken penis in Cards I and VI; the one seen in Card VI (upper central Detail) was "broken from an operation." Another man saw a "penis which may be cut in two" in the bottom central Detail of Card V. These men were assumed to have been sterilized, but they were not.

Internal organs and genitalia were drawn by the sterilized and unsterilized in the Person drawings in the H-T-P. More internal organs were depicted by sterilized (9) than by unsterilized men (7). (See Figure 260.) A penis or vagina was drawn by 7 sterilized and 5 unsterilized men.

Fig. 260

Body preoccupation seems a widespread characteristic among Maharashtrian peasants. According to Carstairs, anxiety about loss of semen is the "commonest expression of anxiety neurosis among the Hindu communities of Rajasthan, and perhaps elsewhere as well." (Carstairs, 1958: 87) This kind of anxiety therefore may be common among the sterilized and unsterilized men in the experimental sample.

A second interpretation of the association between better adjustment and sterilization (see Table XLV) is that sterilization removes the fear of further pregnancies. Such men might have less fear of economic disaster and thus have a more relaxed view of life. It might be erroneous to make such assumptions, for Morris E. Opler has argued that rural Indian villages regard a large family as an economic advantage. (Opler, 1964: 214-15.) In the experimental group in this study, however, the men presumably saw an advantage in sterilization.

Saxena, Chitre, and Lobo in an unpublished study (1963) on interviews with 180 sterilized Maharashtrian men and their wives (in the same area as this study was made) stated that 14.4% of men interviewed reported an improvement in their health after the operation, while 7.2% reported a worsening. Of their wives, 64.4% saw no physical change in their husbands; 20% reported an improvement, and 15% a worsening. An increase in weight[13] after vasectomy was reported by 13.3%; none said they had lost weight. These figures suggest a slight general increase in well-being after the operation, at least among some subjects. It seems significant that 92.2% of the sterilized men had advised other men to be vasectomized.

Both interpretations for the association noted in Table XLV may have validity. They are not in conflict.

Following the first line of reasoning, other hypotheses were suggested: If those requesting to be vasectomized have more ego-strength and intelligence than the others, perhaps they will draw larger Trees and Persons than the men in the unsterilized group. And, perhaps they will give more responses in the Rorschach.

These hypotheses were rejected as there were no significant differences in points raised. Thirty-six sterilized and 33 unsterilized men drew Trees four inches or taller. Fourteen sterilized and 17 unsterilized men drew Trees under four inches in height.

Subjects were divided into those who gave ten or fewer Rorschach responses, and those who gave more than ten responses. Thirty-one sterilized men gave ten responses or less; 19 gave more than ten. Thirty-two unsterilized men gave ten responses or less; 18 gave more than ten.

Other Factors. Sterilized and unsterilized men differ in a number of ways, such as age, number of children, and amount of education. These differences appear in Tables XLVII, XLVIII, and XLIX. Sterilized men are older, have more children, and have had less education than the unsterilized.

TABLE XLVII
Ages of Subjects

	Sterilized	Unsterilized	Total
Below 36	8	24	32
36-40	9	13	22
41-45	9	7	16
46-50	18	2	20
Over 50	6	4	10
Total	50	50	100

Age and family size seem the most crucial factors which determine whether or not a man is to be vasectomized. In this area, a Hindu farmer, over 40 years of age, with four or more children and with two or more sons will have a good chance of being vasectomized. Of course, not all men in these categories will volunteer for the operation. Many factors determine this decision and personality variables are among them. Table XLV suggests that better-adjusted men are more apt to be sterilized.

---

[13] These men are mostly thin, and by our standards, undernourished.

TABLE XLVIII

Number of Children

	Sterilized	Unsterilized	Total
Less than 2 sons	7	20	27
2 or 3 sons	25	20	45
4 or more sons	18	7	25
4 or more children	44	18	62
Total	94	65	159

TABLE XLIX

Amount of Education

	Sterilized	Unsterilized	Total
No schooling	21	14	35
Grades 1 to 3	12	5	17
Grades 4 to 7	14	21	35
Above 7th grade	2	9	11
Total	49	49	98

As shown in Table L, there was no great difference in reported income.[14]

TABLE L

Reported Income Per Month

	Sterilized	Unsterilized	Total
50 Rupees or less (about $12.50)	30	23	53
50-100 Rupees	12	15	27
More than 100 Rupees	18	12	30
Total	60	50	110

If further work with projective devices is done in exploring the psychological consequences of sterilization, it is suggested the men be tested before and after the operation. Ideally, three testings should be made: 1) shortly before the operation, 2) shortly after the operation, 3) after the lapse of several months.

To conclude, the H-T-P is an illuminating research technique in the field of culture-and-personality. It is easy to employ, requires little equipment, can be administered with only a rudimentary knowledge of the local language, and the drawings provide a permanent record of a subjects expression of personality. Allowances must be made for cultural factors – differences in House types, Trees

---

[14] More sterilized men were farmers (31) than unsterilized men, (21). In the latter group there were 4 teachers, 4 men in business, 3 peons, 2 drivers, 2 clerks, etc. Among the sterilized men there were 5 tailors, 2 barbers, 2 merchants, etc. Most men in both groups were Hindus (44 for sterilized and 37 for unsterilized). There were 6 Muslims in the unsterilized and none in the sterilized group. The unsterilized group was more heterogeneous in occupation and religion. About an equal number of men of untouchable caste (Mahar, Mochi, etc.) was in each group – 6 or 7.

known, local art styles and traditions, etc. There also may be difficulties in translation of instructions and answers to questions. Nevertheless, rich material can be derived from the H-T-P especially when used with interviews and other projective techniques.

References

Anastasi, A., and Foley, J.P. Jr., "A Study of Animal Drawings by Indian Children of the North Pacific Coast," *Journal of Social Psychology,* Vol. 9, 1938, pp. 363-374.

Barnouw, V., "Drawing Analysis," in Barnouw V., *Culture and Personality,* Homewood, Illinois; the Dorsey Press, 1963, pp. 276-300.

Belo, J., "Balinese Children's Drawings," in Mead, M. and Wolfenstein, M., eds., *Childhood in Contemporary Cultures,* Chicago: University of Chicago Press, 1955, pp. 52-69.

Buck, J. N., "The H-T-P Technique. A Qualitative and Quantitative Scoring manual," *Journal of Clinical Psychology,* 4, 1948 (published as a whole as Monograph Supplement 5, 1948).

Carstairs, G. M., *The Twice-Born. A Study of a Community of High-Caste Hindus,* Bloomington, Indiana: The Indiana Press, 1958.

Cormack, M. *The Hindu Woman,* Bureau of Publications, Teachers College, Columbia University, New York, 1953.

Dandekar, K., "After-Effects of Vasectomy," *Artha Vijnana, Journal of the Gokhale Institute of Politics and Economics, Poona, (India),* Vol. 5, No. 3, Sept., 1963, pp. 212-224.

Dennis, W., "The Human Figure Drawings of Bedouins," *Journal of Social Psychology,* Vol. 52, 1960, pp. 209-219.

Du Bois, C., *The People of Alor. A Social-Psychological Study of an East Indian Island.* With Analyses by Abram Kardiner and Emil Oberholzer, Minneapolis: University of Minneapolis Press, 1944.

Hammer, E. F., "An Investigation of Sexual Symbolism: A Study of H-T-P's of Eugenically Sterilized Subjects," *Journal of Projective Techniques,* 1953, Vol. 17, pp. 401-413.

_____ "The House-Tree-Person Projective Drawing Technique: Content Interpretation" in Hammer, E. F., ed., *The Clinical Application of Projective Drawings,* Springfield, Illinois: Charles C. Thomas, 1958, pp. 165-207.

Lowenfels, M. S., Free Drawings as a Projective Test in Cross-Cultural Investigations, University of Pennsylvania, 1950, unpublished ms.

Narain, D., *Hindu Character (A Few Glimpses).* University of Bombay Publications, Sociology Series, No. 8, 1957.

Opler, M. E., "Cultural Context and Population Control Programs in Village India," in Count, E. W. and Bowles, G. T., eds. *Fact and Theory in Social Science,* Syracuse: Syracuse University Press, 1964, pp. 201-221.

Saxena, R.N., Chitre, K. T., and Lobo, J. A., Follow-up of Vasectomy, Typescript, 1963.

Shils, E., *The Intellectural Between Tradition and Modernity: The Indian Situation,* Comparative Studies in Society and History, Supplement 1, The Hague, Netherlands: Mouton & Co., 1961.

Smith, B., *Portrait of India,* Philadelphia: J. B. Lippincott Co., 1962.

Taylor, W. S., "Basic Personality in Orthodox Hindu Culture Patterns," *Journal of Abnormal and Social Psychology,* Vol. 43, 1948. pp. 3-12.

Francis W. King received his B.S. from Bowdoin College in 1940, his A.M. from Boston University in 1941, and his Ph.D. from Harvard University in 1952.

He is a Fellow of the Society of Projective Techniques and Personality Evaluation and a member of many other professional organizations.

Dr. King has been associated with Dartmouth College since 1949. The greatest part of his time is spent as Clinical Psychologist in the Dartmouth College Health Service, Department of Psychiatry. He is also a Professor of Medical Psychology in the Department of Psychiatry of the Dartmouth Medical School as well as Professor of Psychology in the Department of Psychology in Dartmouth College.

Chapter 19

The H-T-P As An Adjunct
In Psychotherapy

Francis W. King, Ph.D.

Dr. King discusses ably and succinctly÷albeit briefly÷what has been found to be one of the most rewarding of the applications of the H-T-P but about which little has appeared previously in the literature. As the author points out, the H-T-P-derived material lends itself readily to employment directly in the treatment process by any clinician regardless of that clinician's theoretical orientation or preferred system of therapy. (Eds.)

Over a decade ago, this author wrote: "Despite the growing literature on the evaluative and predictive roles of projective techniques in relation to various kinds of treatment, few references exist on the direct use of projective techniques within the therapeutic situation" (King, 1954, p. 65). The use of play, art, and drama were specifically excepted, since such techniques may be considered, according to their use, as diagnostic techniques or therapeutic techniques. The twelve-year-old quotation needs little emendation today. It is primarily the Thematic Apperception Test (and its variants) that has been employed directly by clinicians in the therapeutic process (e.g., Deabler, 1947; Hartwell, Hutt, Andrew, & Walton, 1951; Murray, 1951; Pepinsky, 1947).

In the vast literature on projective techniques and on treatment, the deliberate psychotherapeutic utilization of drawings, such as the H-T-P, DAP, and the like, has been reported most infrequently. It should be noted, however, that in an H-T-P workshop as early as 1950, Buck advocated psychotherapeutic application as the second major use of his then recently expanded projective technique. The role of the H-T-P in psychotherapy is set forth and elaborated in what is familiarly known as *The Richmond Proceedings* (Buck, 1950). Yet even in Hammer's

(1958a) comprehensive volume on the clinical applications of projective drawings, there is little emphasis on their direct use in therapy. In that inclusive collection of papers, the section on projective drawings in a psychotherapeutic setting
includes a general statement by Naumberg (1958a) on the nature of art therapy;
spontaneous art productions are viewed as symbolic communications and the
patient is encouraged by psychoanalytic and other uncovering techniques to dis-
cover the latent meaning. Another chapter by Naumberg (1958b) demonstrates
the process with a case illustration. Hammer (1958b) has utilized informal
doodles in the therapy session in a variety of ways. He sees the doodle as comparable to dream material and believes that as such it may lead to productive
associations and/or guide the therapist in his understanding and in his planning
of the therapeutic process. In the final chapter in this section of the book, Bender
and Schilder (1958) discuss the use of art productions as a vehicle of expression
for the patient and of enhancement of the therapist's understanding. Hauser
(1956) has described, from an Adlerian point of view, the employment of drawings in child psychotherapy. Her aims in using drawings are to (a) evoke blocked
capacities, (b) aid in explaining to the child his style of life, and (c) provide the
patient with encouragement as he develops, since encouragement is considered to
be real psychotherapy in Individual Psychology. Grold (1961) has employed a
structured interview session in which the patient first draws his parents on a
sheet of paper and then adds a drawing of himself on the same page; while accomplishing the drawings, he is asked to say whatever comes into his mind. Although
this technique was designed as an aid in psychiatric evaluation, in numerous
instances the drawing technique and subsequent discussion of the productions
have had beneficial therapeutic effects. Drawings are one of a large number of
expressive media found to be effective by Murphy & Fitzsimons (1960) in the
treatment of stutterers.

It is only in the "projective counseling" of Molly Harrower (1956a; 1956b;
Harrower, Vorhaus, Roman, & Bauman, 1960) that one finds within the psychotherapeutic process a systematic and focal use of a variety of projective techniques,
including drawings. Projective counseling, in essence, "amounts to confronting
the person, or persons, with his own productions – with the raw material from the
projective tests at those times in the re-educational process when this material
can best be used with insight" (Harrower *et al.,* 1960, pp. 3-4). Thus, she makes
direct use of the projective material within a therapeutic session by "the sharing
of responses with the patient to allow further reactions to them, or to use them as
a basis for interpretation of attitudes and feelings . . . Some of the projective
tests may be repeated at each session more easily than others and a 'House,'
drawn and described has proved a useful one" (Harrower *et al.,* 1960, p. 33).

The major purpose of this chapter is to illustrate the usefulness of directly
employing the H-T-P as an adjunct in the course of psychotherapy; the similarity
to Harrower's projective counseling will be self-evident. Despite the therapeutic
intent here, the writer has frequently been struck by the sophisticated interpretations of patients who were essentially or completely naive with respect to the
psychodynamic principles usually employed in the diagnostic use of such drawings. Although the "hard-nosed" scientist would understandably scoff at such
evidence as the basis of validity claims, such interpretations do, at the very least,

shed some light on why clinicians continue to employ projective drawing techniques despite Swensen's (1957) highly critical review.

The case illustrations here are all drawn from a male, college undergraduate population. The patients are all bright, reasonably articulate, nonpsychotic, and of middle class status (or aspirations). They are the kind of people that middle class psychotherapists seem to find it easy, or at any rate, comfortable, to attempt to treat.

HOUSE

The H-T-P was introduced in the tenth interview with Mr. Blocque, a young man in his early twenties who had described himself in his initial interview as closed up, blocked, tensed up, unable to move, and unable to communicate with people. Part of his immobilization stemmed directly from his difficulties in asserting himself.

The very simple drawings were executed with such rapidity that the therapist could not write a note while the patient was accomplishing them. In the subsequent discussion of the H-T-P drawings, the patient admitted that the request to draw made him anxious lest he be exposed by revealing more than he would in a regular interview. He repeatedly commented upon the absence of a door and windows in the House (see Figure 261).

After some preliminary and mildly defensive and evasive remarks, he said, "It's a rotten House; it's closed off—a lot like my letters when you come right

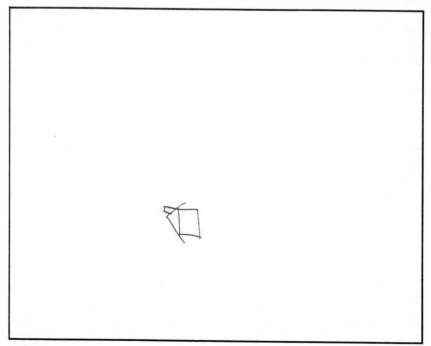

Fig. 261

down to it . . . (He had said he had) not much visceral conception of a House. I resist drawing on past experience for a House. I have an idea of a House and what should go on between people. (An interpretative question focused on the conflict between the visceral and the idea.) You get into trouble when the two collide. (The therapist asked if he was saying the drawing was himself.) In a way, yes. I have a feeling it is an important drawing–seems to express a lot–of what I am and what I think of myself: simple and limited. As I keep sitting here, I get to hate that drawing–interesting! A way of saying I keep sitting here, and get to hate myself. (What do you hate?) It sits there like a blank; out of proportion. The relative size compared with the 8½ x 11 paper. Small, slightly off center, mathematically off center. (In reply to a request for elaboration, he folded the sheet of paper vertically and horizontally so that the crossing of the midlines indicated the center of the paper.) Almost precisely off center!"

He was asked what the drawing said to him. "Something about incompleteness–insecurity, attitude toward the world. Its positioning; general execution of the thing. Two-dimensional. No in or out. No smoke. No doors or windows; no way to get to it or from it. General relation to page is a mess–very inhibited and held back. If that's a human being's relationship with his environment, that 8½ x 11 sheet–that occupies one ninety-first of the sheet."

The implication of cautiousness in his meager drawing led to his wondering how cautious he was when sitting across the room in his usual place during the interviews. This, then, provided an opportunity for looking at his behavior in the interview and at his relationship with the therapist and two interviews later led to an exploration of his relationship with his mother which previously he had cautiously and conscientiously avoided. His next drawing was a sparse, unprotected pine Tree. He could not bring himself to draw "a maple, with a round ball and leaves." To Mr. Blocque that would have been like putting flowers in the window of the House with the sun shining in the background. Following this, with minimal therapist activity, he related the House and Tree as both showing "a need to reject–to reject warmth, softness, childishness, home–to present a stark, hard exterior." In such cases, which are not uncommon, when the patient develops similar or identical themes in two or more drawings, the effectiveness of the therapeutic use of the H-T-P is greatly enhanced. The probabilities of repetitive themes are, of course, greater with the H-T-P than is the case in simply having the patient draw two human figures. Furthermore, the impact is greater since the themes are developed from such disparate content as a House, a Tree, and a Person.

TREE

The presenting symptoms of a second patient, Mr. Young, also in his early twenties, were that he was smoking an excessive number of cigarettes and that he was masturbating several times daily; he said he had a "guilt complex" about his studies and about a girl friend with whom he had just terminated a relationship. At the end of the sixth interview the patient noticed a book on the clinical use of drawings on the desk in the office and expressed an interest in the subject. The writer, who had the use of projective drawings in mind for this patient, took advantage of the expressed positive attitude and scheduled an extra appointment for the H-T-P. In this instance his discussion of the House and his associations to it were not very productive. However, his description of the Tree (see Figure 262) and his interpretations of it provided a focus on the very central problem of his denied, but dominating, dependence. This drawing was immediately described as a dying Tree. When asked what the Tree might be dying from, he said, "I don't know what a Tree would die from, a disease of some kind, I suppose—a lack of nourishment." Somewhat later on in this session, the therapist asked whether anything came to mind as Mr. Young looked at the Tree. After a rather lengthy period of silence, marked by the absence of his usual friendly and ingratiating smile, he replied, "Symbolically, yes. It more or less represents an· undernourished person." Mr. Young went on to say that he had not intentionally drawn a self-representation, but saw that this could very well be the case nonetheless. When such an important theme as this "lack of nourishment" one is produced in a patient's talking about the Tree, it is hardly surprising that related material either occurs spontaneously, or is easily evoked, in associations to the drawing of a Person. Thus in Mr. Young's verbal elaborations of his drawing of a female, he described her breasts as "full" in the sense of being large and also as "ample for feeding a child." This associative material was the more pertinent and useful

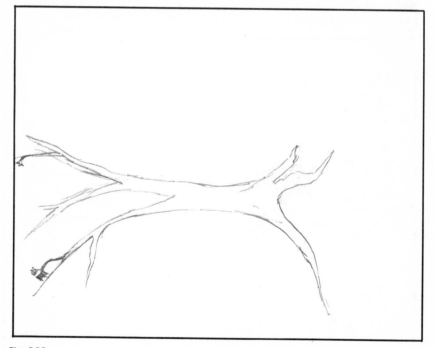

Fig. 262

since he could see that another individual might perceive the figure as "flat-chested." It was immediately after his attribution of high nutritional quality to the breasts of the figure that he laughed and commented: "I just caught a passing glimpse of the mother image." He continued by saying that he cared for his mother a great deal, that an unqualified relationship existed between them, that he was fed on her love, and did not have to do anything to obtain her love. At this point, appropriately enough, he asked permission to light a cigarette even though he had previously smoked in interviews prior to briefly giving up smoking. The development of a thematic sequence such as the foregoing, although not inevitably productive of flashes of insight, does produce, and nearly inevitably, an unavoidable set of data which the patient must work through or with which in some other way he must come to terms.

PERSON [1]

Mr. Logos, a twenty-year-old student, began an extended series of interviews in the middle of his junior year in college. There were none of the frequent academic complications for he was a brilliant and efficient student who was elected to Phi Beta Kappa during this same year. If diagnostic labels were to be employed, the term obsessive-compulsive could not possibly be omitted, for this highly effective young man scheduled his activities on college vacations as rigorously as he planned his college course work—and he abided by his schedules! "Rational," "logical," and "intellectual," were his favorite words—and defenses. Additionally, it should be mentioned that his history was marked by a number of homosexual relationships.

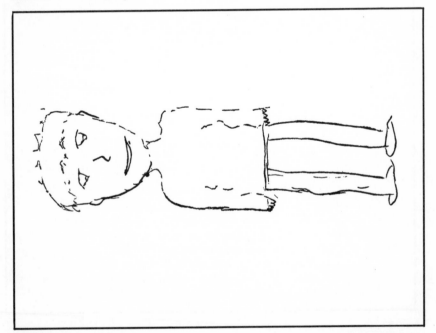

Fig. 263

---

[1] This *section* of the present chapter is reproduced, with revisions, from an earlier article (King, 1954). The editors wish to express their appreciation to the Journal of Clinical Psychology for permission to reprint parts of the article in this volume.

A series of nearly thirty interviews throughout a semester was interrupted for sixteen weeks by the college summer vacation. Until this lengthy interruption occurred, therapy had been progressing in a painfully slow manner, but nonetheless progressing. Dynamic material of some depth had occupied a considerable portion of the therapeutic hours and some significant, if small, changes had

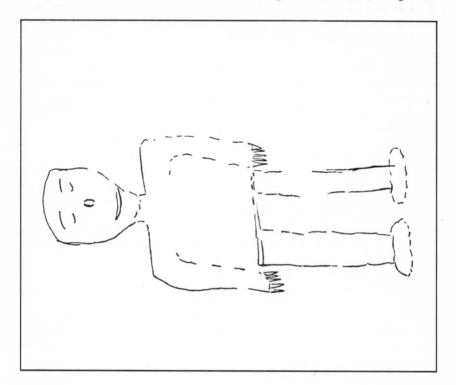

Fig. 264

taken place in attitude and behavior. Homosexual activity had ceased and there was some loosening up here and there of his many rigidities.

However, when the interviews were resumed in the fall, weeks passed without any apparent therapeutic progress. Detailed accounts of the vicissitudes of a continuing friendship made during the summer occupied seemingly endless hours of interviews. Finally, in the hope of redirecting the patient's attention to less externalized matters, the therapist introduced projective drawings into the latter part of one of the interviews. Figures 263 and 264 reproduce the Persons drawn during this session.[2]

The following verbatim transcription presents the patient's comments while executing the drawings and his most revealing subsequent interpretations and associations.

---

[2]The original drawings, only faintly sketched for the most part, have been slightly darkened for better reproduction.

Therapist. Would you draw a picture of a human being?

Patient; (Laughs) Well, in elementary school and in high school, there were two subjects with which I used to come home with E's on my report card— penmanship and drawing. That was something I could never do.

T.   I'll not ask you to write, just to draw a picture.

P.   I haven't done this since . . . my niece could do a better job *(erases) (laughs).* I hope no one ever sees this. Let's see, this is supposed to be a profile. I think it would be easier if I drew a *(erases)* . . .

T.   Turn the sheet over if you like.

P.   *(Turns paper over and starts new drawing.)* In elementary school or in high school—I guess it was in elementary school—the fellow who sat next to me used to do my drawing and I used to do his math. I think this is the most difficult thing . . . *(erases)* . . . fingers, modern art. *(Last phrase unclear.)*

T.   Pardon?

P.   I said, modern art, and that is supposed to be a human being.

T.   Fine. Now I want you to draw a picture of the opposite sex.

P.   Is that supposed to have a sex? *(Points to Figure 264)* I guess that would be a man. *(He starts to draw a profile again with much erasure)* I'm trying to do a profile again *(turns sheet over)* . . . *(laughs)* . . . *(erases)* A little out of proportion. Looks the same. This is, as I said a little while ago, not my field. I . . . find that this was something I could never do—was drawing anything that looked like anything; it was something I always wanted to do. My father, on the other hand, draws very well—not very well—at least he's able to do it. And drawing seemed to be a . . . skill of some sort which was similar to athletics possibly in some ways.

T.   What sort of a Person is that one? *(pointing to Figure 264)*

P.   That looks like something out of Buck Rodgers—or a robot. Certainly it looks well built, broad shouldered, muscular, I guess. It looks like something a two-year-old drew. It always seemed to me that something you could do with your hands, a skill, was more worthwhile than something you thought about or came to through thinking. When I was young, I guess, oh five or six or so, I used to be a wonderful mechanic and very handy with tools. My mother tells me that my father was quite sure I was going to be an engineer, and very soon that interest and skill disappeared, although some of the interest was still there. Nevertheless, I . . . in elementary school, we had shop and I wasn't any great carpenter or anything. I had difficulty in getting something straight, or planing an edge properly or something.

T.   Can you tell me more about what kind of a Person that is?

P.   The Person doesn't look very smart, he looks sleepy, I guess. I . . . think that what comment I could make about both of these people—they both seem sexless. The only thing that differentiates these two—this one's *(Figure 263)* smaller than that one *(Figure 264!)* which would possibly make me think of this as a woman *(Figure 264),* and this one's a man—has broad shoulders. That's supposed to be curly hair on that one *(points to Figure 263)* but it doesn't look like it. Looks like she needs a shave. But certainly you couldn't tell that it was a woman, looks more like a little boy. I think that if I could draw, I would possibly have done something else. In drawing a woman, I think if I could draw, I would have attempted to draw a profile which would make it more obvious that what I was drawing was a woman – than something like this.

T.   It is hard to tell which is a man and which is a woman because you have a defect in drawing.

P.   That would seem like an awfully stupid reason. It . . . I could say that sometimes I find it very difficult to tell whether I was a man or a woman, and that difficulty remains until today. When I find that in certain situations, the role I should be playing I could play more accurately as a woman than as a man. One of those situations occurred to me the other day – I remember wanting to remember to mention it. I guess it slipped my mind.

T.   Both of these characters look to you to be sexless.

P.   Yeh . . . Sometimes I've thought that if people were actually sexless, that would possibly be the easiest way to *(record unclear)* but on the other hand I sometimes thought that if I could act the same way toward people of both sexes, that would make things much easier . . . As I've said it has always been very hard for me to understand why it wasn't possible or permissible to have feelings of affection toward a male as it was to have those same feelings toward a female but . . . although it is *(word unclear)* I certainly would say it was possible to have those feelings but it isn't possible to express them the same way toward both people.

T.   There is a complete denial of sexuality in these drawings.

P.   Ummm – the only way in the drawings I attempted to indicate the figure's sex was the curly hair and I was going to try to give her better-formed legs . . . but I couldn't do it. I still would possibly be inclined to say that it might be a defect in my drawing ability. I said if I were able to draw better, I might have drawn something else.

T.   You feel that if you could draw better it might have been possible to, if you had more skill or talent in drawing, it might have been possible to sketch in more definitely indications of sex.

P.   . . . Yeh – I think that, as I said a second ago, I would have drawn the female in profile, if I was able to draw . . . but . . .

T.   You can't act out your feelings.

P.   . . . Well, again I've always thought of drawing as a skill or something that would have about as much connection with my feelings as the ability to sew or to knit or to do something of that sort.

T.   I think that perhaps in looking at these drawings some of your comments have perhaps gone to the core of the problem here. Possibly the repressing of sexuality completely on the one hand versus acting the same toward men and women and perhaps even more, the most basic of all, is not knowing that you yourself are a man or a woman.

P.   . . . That . . . second problem which you mentioned has been one which I guess I've spoken about in the past, and one which has troubled me particularly on many, many occasions. I think that . . .

T.   It is not one that we've worked on much this year. We've managed to skirt around it pretty effectively. Pressing minor issues have prevented us from getting at that perhaps.

P.   I think that one of the reasons that the Army is . . . could possibly be appealing is that it would show quite clearly whether I was a man or a woman.

Perhaps the most immediately arresting characteristic of these drawings is
that, in the words of the patient, "they both seem sexless." The patient's subsequent admissions offer strong evidence for the diagnostic meaning of the drawing
of figures in which there is essentially no sexual differentiation.

However, for purposes of the present chapter, the writer wishes to stress the
effect upon the therapeutic process of employing this simple projective technique. After an essentially unproductive series of interviews, the therapeutic
activity was once more directed toward a very fundamental problem in the patient; in fact, it might almost be said simply that therapeutic activity was rein-
stated. In his own consideration of his drawings, he had brought clearly into the
focus of therapy his basic confusion of sex identity. Although this confusion had
been alluded to previously, he had now raised this problem in a different context
with new and unavoidable implications. He had now made a start toward grasping the widespread ramifications that this confusion was producing in his interpersonal relations. Thus, there had been established, and by the patient himself,
a basis with a concrete point of reference for the subsequent interviews.

The development of material derived from projective techniques is always of
interest to the therapist; it may provide him with new clues about the dynamics
of the patient's functioning or it may confirm hypotheses already formulated by
the therapist. These are essentially diagnostic functions. More importantly in
terms of facilitating the therapeutic process, such material may lead directly to
the development of insight in the patient. Perhaps more frequently it uncovers
and brings into the therapeutic transaction attitudes, feelings, and relationships
that have been by-passed, regardless of the patient's level of awareness of these
unspoken matters. Even when the drawings and the associative interview's contents are less than richly rewarding the H-T-P may still be put to effective therapeutic use. To cite a brief example, another patient made extremely simple and
primitive drawings, but unlike Mr. Blocque, his verbalizations matched his
drawings. The therapist suggested that these drawings expressed compliance
marked by minimal cooperation. This led directly to the patient's expression of
annoyance at being requested to perform such a task, to a brief discussion of the
similarity of the therapist's manner to that of the patient's father, and finally, to
a profitable discussion of the patient-therapist relationship.

The foregoing examples of the utilization of the H-T-P as an adjunct in
psychotherapy have been kept relatively brief and are intended as illustrations
of one therapist's use of the techniques. This writer shares in the common experience of hindsight and dismay that occurs when interviewers hear recordings
of their sessions or, even worse, read toneless transcripts; this is particularly the
case in the instance of Mr. Logos and that interview of long ago. However, the
H-T-P is recommended here not as a system of psychotherapy, but as an adjunct
to whatever relatively systematic approach is employed. Furthermore, regardless of the formal system and orientation, the individual therapist will inevitably
tailor the technique and pursue the potential leads in his own fashion. The writer
feels that there is ample evidence in these illustrations to suggest, at the very
least, consideration of using the H-T-P within the therapeutic framework. In

contrast to some of the other projective techniques, notably the TAT, the H-T-P has certain specific advantages—for example, it is less time-consuming in administration, and since it obviates the necessity of preparing a transcription for the patient, its use is more flexible within the interview.

References

Bender, Lauretta & Schilder, P. Simplification of the word and its problems in the art of asocial delinquent boys. In E. F. Hammer (Ed.) *The Clinical Application of Projective Drawings.* Springfield, Ill.: Charles C. Thomas, 1958. Pp. 584-595.

Buck, J. N. *House-Tree-Person (H-T-P) Manual Supplement.* Beverly Hills, California: Western Psychological Service, 1950.

Deabler, H. L. The psychotherapeutic use of the Thematic Apperception Test. *J. Clin. Psychol.,* 1947, *3,* 246-252.

Grold, L. J., Jr. Drawing the family triangle: an adjunct to the psychiatric evaluation. *Bull. Menninger Clin.,* 1961, *25,* 69-77.

Hammer, E. F. (Ed.) *The Clinical Application of Projective Drawings.* Springfield, Ill.: Charles C. Thomas, 1958.(a)

_____ Doodles: an informal projective technique. In E. F. Hammer (Ed.) *The Clinical Application of Projective Drawings.* Springfield, Ill.: Charles C. Thomas, 1958. Pp. 562-583.(b)

Harrower, Molly. Projective counseling. A psychotherapeutic technique. *Amer. J. Psychother.,* 1956, *10,* 74-86.(a)

_____ Projective tests and psychotherapy. In W. Wolff. *Contemporary Psychotherapists Examine Themselves.* Springfield, Ill.: Charles C. Thomas, 1956. Pp. 184-191.(b)

Harrower, Molly, Vorhaus, Pauline, Romas M., & Bauman, G. *Creative Variations in the Projective Techniques.* Springfield, Ill.: Charles C. Thomas, 1960.

Hartwell, S. W., Hutt, M., Andrew, G., & Walton, R. E. The Michigan Picture Test: diagnostic and therapeutic possibilities of a new projective test in child guidance. *Amer. J. Orthopsychiat.,* 1951, *21,* 124-137.

Hauser, Andree. The drawing as a help in child-psychotherapy. *Amer. J. Ind. Psychol.,* 1956, *12,* 53-58.

King, F. W. The use of drawings of the human figure as an adjunct in psychotherapy. *J. Clin. Psychol.,* 1954, *10,* 65-69.

Murphy, A. T. & Fitzsimons, Ruth M. *Stuttering and Personality Dynamics.* New York. Ronald, 1960.

Murray, H. A. Uses of the thematic apperception test. *Amer. J. Psychiat.,* 1951, *107,* 577-581.

Naumberg, Margaret. Art therapy: its scope and function. In E. F. Hammer (Ed.) *The Clinical Application of Projective Drawings.* Springfield, Ill.: Charles C. Thomas, 1958. Pp. 511-517.(a)

_____ Case illustration: art therapy with a seventeen year old schizophrenic girl. In E. F. Hammer (Ed.) *The Clinical Application of Projective Drawings.* Springfield, Ill.: Charles C. Thomas, 1958. Pp. 518-561.(b)

Pepinsky, H. B. Application of informal projective methods in the counseling interview. *Educ. Psychol. Measmt.*, 1947, *7*, 135-140.

Swensen, C. H., Jr. Empirical evaluations of human figure drawings. *Psychol. Bull.*, 1957, *54*, 431-466.

Index

raph 9, (which begins with, "...Yeh--I think that, as I
nd ago..."), insert the following question and answer:

been able to draw a profile it would have looked more
ely like a woman.

that it would have looked more like a woman...I think
my mind I can see what I would like to draw. I can see
fferences in different pictures, but when it comes to
it on paper, it's not possible.

rences, the first title should be: "...Simplification of
.."

List of Major Errata in

Advances in the House-Tree-Person Technique: Variations and Applications

edited by John N. Buck and Emanuel F. Hammer

PAGE XIV: Paragraph 2, Line 2, change to read: "...he then undertook analytic
               practice, and is now on the faculty..."

               Line 5, change to read: "He is head of the Psychology Department,
               Psychiatric Clinic, New York City Criminal Courts; Chief Psycholog-
               ical Consultant at..."

PAGE 34   Last Paragraph, Line 6, change to read: "A start is offered in the
               yield of the experimental follow-up..."

CHAPTER 2
PAGE 47:   Last Paragraph, Line 3, should be changed to read: "...be a with-
               drawn,..."

PAGE 57:   Paragraph 2, Line 6, should be changed to read: "...watercolor Tree
               is not unusually well..."

PAGE 91:   After Table VIII, insert:

               Null hypotheses rejected (by chi^2 tests of four-fold tables, without
               correction for continuity, because the observed data are not
               restricted to integral amounts):

               That male and female subjects are equally likely to use the Complaint
               theme (.001).
               That male and female subjects are equally likely to use the Destruc-
               tion theme (.05).
               That male and female subjects are equally likely to use the Loneli-
               ness theme (.001).
               That Men do not differ from other subjects in use of the Inspiration
               theme (.01).
               That adults do not differ from children in use of the Escape theme
               (.02).
               That Wm and Wf' do not differ with respect to the combined use of
               the "masculine categories," Complaint, Destruction, and Inspiration
               (.05).
               That Wm and Wf' do not differ with respect to the combined use of
               the affinitive categories, Harmony, Friendship, and Maternal (.05).
               That Gm and Gf do not differ with respect to the combined use of
               these same categories (.01).

PAGE 96:   Paragraph 3, (of text) Line 1, should be changed to read: "Table X."

PAGE 96:   Paragraph 3, (of text) Line 9, beginning with the last word in that
               Line, Houses, change to read:

               "Houses, in stories by men, bear more resemblance to Trees, in
               stories by either sex, than to Houses in stories by women. Houses
               in stories by women seem to be unlike Trees by either men or women,
               but there is a suggestion that they are more like Trees by women
               than like Trees by men."

               Next to last Paragraph. The first sentence should be changed to
               read: "These relationships may also be seen in Table XI..."

PAGE 97:   The Table at the top of the page should be headed: "Table XI."

PAGE 144:   Paragraph 1, Line 2, on this page should be retarded; not related.

PAGE 189:   Paragraph 1, Line 1, after <u>Person</u>, insert the letter <u>E</u>.

PAGE 197:   Paragraph 2, Line 3, change to read: "...saying instead, 'Draw a man or a woman, <u>or</u> a boy or a girl...'"

PAGE 199:   Next to last Paragraph, Line 2, change to read: "...verbal I.Q. of 47, and a full-scale I.Q. of 57."

Last Paragraph, last Line, change to read: "...(8-6) with an I.Q. of 57..."

PAGE 208:   Line 5 of this page, the Peabody Picture I.Q. should be <u>68</u>, not <u>64</u>.

CHAPTER 10
PAGE 222:   Paragraph 2, last sentence, should read: "From 1963 to 1968, he was School Psychologist for the Thornton Township Special Education Association of Harvey, Illinois. Since July, 1968, he has been a School Psychologist with the Fairfax County, Virginia, public school system.

PAGE 235:   Paragraph 1, Line 4, should be changed to read: "...lines of the walls of the House. Her rigidity..."

PAGE 237:   Question H4b should read: "Whom would you like to have live in that House with you?"

PAGE 253:   Next to last Line on this page should read: "...Cheryl's reading skill was more than one year retarded; the I. Q. ..."

PAGE 259:   Paragraph 1, Line 6, should read: "...was a noticeably excited..."

PAGE 262:   Paragraph 2, Line 1, should read: "As can be expected of..."

PAGE 266:   Paragraph 2, Line 2, change to read: "...he then undertook analytic practice, and is now on the faculty..."

Line 5, change to read: "He is head of the Psychology Department, Psychiatric Clinic, New York City Criminal Courts; Chief Psychological Consultant at..."

PAGE 278:   Paragraph 4, Line 3, change to read: "...at both top and bottom (in the original drawing the page's top seemed to be pressing down on the drawn Person's head, and the bottom of the page pressed up against the Person's shoes). Along with this..."

PAGE 287:   Paragraph 2, Line 4, change to read: "...at least part of his defensive control (if he is going to lose it at all), he..."

CHAPTER 13
PAGE 294:   Paragraph 2, last sentences should read: "He was an Assistant Professor of Psychology and a Psychologist in the Division of Counseling at the Pennsylvania State University (Ogontz campus), Abington, Pa., from 1964 to 1966. He was then Counselor and Associate Professor of Psychology at Parsons College, Iowa, for a year. He is now Associate Professor of Psychology at Illinois State University, Normal, Illinois.

Dr. Jacks is an active member of the American Psychological Association, the American Association for the Advancement of Science, the National Council on Crime and Delinquency, the Pennsylvania Psychological Association, and the Philadelphia Society of Clinical Psychologists. He has been licensed as a psychologist by the State of New York and by the Pennsylvania Psychological Association.

Dr. Jacks has been the author or co-author of a number of articles which have been published in psychological, psychiatric, medical, sociological, or criminological journals.

PAGE 319:   All p value fi

PAGE 321:   Table XIX: al be preceded by

PAGE 331:   Last Paragraph is drawn in gre

PAGE 338:   Last Paragraph, drawings (Figur

PAGE 351:   In Table XX und

PAGE 352:   The subheading " "Achromatic Hous 234 in this chap tion will be foun q.v. JNB.

PAGE 375:   Paragraph 5, next continued with, " looking..."

PAGE 384:   Paragraph 7, Line

PAGE 396:   Under Group Admini relationship to Gr relationship on Pa

PAGE 400:   Paragraph 2, Line places her first d

PAGE 428:   Paragraph 2, Line 1

PAGE 429:   Paragraph 1, Line 3 and XL are compared consistently drew b the Indian students and Persons."

PAGE 442:   Paragraph 4, 2nd and first is that only t through with the ste tion anxiety."

Footnote 12, last se also have expected a the 17 determinations all three experts, bu

PAGE 443:   Paragraph 4, Line 5:

PAGE 456:   Paragraph 12, (which Buck Rodgers..."). I

"I used to take everyt put it together again.

Last Paragraph, Line 5 woman (Figure 263)..."

PAGE 457:   After Para said a seco

T. Had you definit

P. I think that i the di puttin

PAGE 459:   Under Refe the world.

PAGE 462:   In column and the re American

In column ate points

PAGE 463:   Column 2, ately fol

PAGE 464:   Column 1, TAT, See 74, 75-8

Column 1, dimension

Column 2,

Column 2

GUIDE TO ILLUSTRATIVE PLATES IN ADVANCES IN THE HOUSE-TREE-PERSON TECHNIQUE: VARIATIONS AND APPLICATIONS